Constructing Rajpootana-Rajasthan

Constructing Rajpootana-Rajasthan

Collected Narratives in Remembrance of Bhupendra Hooja

Edited by

Rakesh Hooja
Rima Hooja
Rakshat Hooja

RAWAT PUBLICATIONS
Jaipur • New Delhi • Bangalore • Hyderabad • Guwahati

ISBN 81-316-0328-8

Published by
Prem Rawat for **Rawat Publications**
Satyam Apts, Sector 3, Jawahar Nagar, Jaipur 302 004 (India)
Phone: 0141 265 1748 / 7006 Fax: 0141 265 1748
E-mail: info@rawatbooks.com
Website: www.rawatbooks.com

New Delhi Office
4858/24, Ansari Road, Daryaganj, New Delhi 110 002
Phone: 011 2326 3290

Also at Bangalore, Hyderabad and Guwahati

Typeset by Rawat Computers, Jaipur
Printed at Chaman Enterprises, New Delhi

Dedicated to the memory of

Bhupendra Hooja (1922–2006)

He consistently attempted to analyse and understand the past and the present, and actively joined in the endeavour to improve the future.
He also served as a generous mentor to many in their various quests.

Indian Book Chronicle, *Shodhak: A Journal of Historical Research* and Institute of Rajasthan Studies associate themselves with the editors in this dedication.

Contents

Acknowledgements

Bhupendra, or Bhupi, or B. Hooja (1922–2006) had in turn been a student leader in Lahore, radio broadcaster at various places for All India Radio (at about the time of partition) and for BBC at London (1949–54), a government information and public relations officer (Delhi Administration during the mid and late 1950s), a journalist and author, a senior civil servant (serving in the Indian Administrative Service from 1958 to 1980 mostly in Rajasthan and also in Himachal Pradesh), writer, editor, publisher, activist, mentor to many, a lover of books and a perennial seeker of knowledge.

History, including that of Rajasthan, as well as the contemporary transformation of Rajasthan in which he had actively contributed since settling in Jaipur in 1958–59 fascinated him.

Thus, his passing away in April 2006 led us in his family and many well wishers to feel that one of the ways to remember him would be to put together some of his writings, some other articles by members of his family (whose drafts and contents he had been ever ready to comment upon or to discuss), and by some other Rajasthan scholars who had come in contact with him in one way or the other, into a volume. They offered us both freshly written articles and older previously published papers for this book.

It was felt that this miscellany, or potpourri, should contain writings on Rajpootana (the area that was eventually to become the present-day Indian state of Rajasthan) and its history and evolution from prehistoric-days to India's achieving independence and the merger that created the modern-day province of Rajasthan, as also on post-merger Rajasthan. In addition, since Bhupendra Hooja was intimately involved in the life and activities in Jaipur for the last 48 years of his life and had edited a special issue of the magazine *Indian*

Book Chronicle on Sawai Jai Singh II, who had founded Jaipur in 1727 (which he had been planning just before his death to get reprinted in a book along with some other material on Jaipur and Rajpootana), it was felt that Amber and the foundation of Jaipur should also feature significantly in the book.

The book had been planned as a quickie to be brought out by what would have been Bhupendra Hooja's birthday in December 2007, but somehow it took longer.

Bhupi Hooja carried out systematic (and at times random) reading and study on many themes including those related to Rajasthan's history. But, more often than not, he could be found reading about and writing upon four or five different topics at the same time. His inquisitive mind led him to speculate, question, read up and analyse on many diverse matters. Even on Rajasthan history, he did not limit himself to any period, region, or aspect but he cast his net wide and touched varied features as his questioning nature led him in one direction and then another. Accordingly, we decided not to limit the authors as to what they would like to contribute upon so long as it was some aspect of Rajasthan's history. The resulting potpourri of a volume would, we hope, interest many readers because of its variety.

The book starts with an article on "Rajasthan: Present and Past" based upon Rakesh Hooja's inaugural address delivered on December 29, 2005 at the Fifth Annual Conference on Rajasthan organized by the Institute of Rajasthan Studies at Jaipur.

"Some Notes and Questions on Rajasthan History" by Bhupendra Hooja was originally published in *Shodhak* Vol. 20, Part B, No. 59, 1991 and had been prepared so as to set the stage for deliberations in a seminar organized by *Shodhak* on 30–31 March, 1991. The seminar publication *Rajasthan History – Miscellanea, Shodhak*, Jaipur, October 1991 also contained this piece.

Susanne and Lloyd Rudolph offered a number of papers to select from for this volume and eventually we mutually agreed upon including the paper "Rajputana Under British Paramountcy". This had earlier been published in *Essays on Rajputana* by Susanne Hoeber Rudolph and Lloyd I. Rudolph (Concept Publishing Company, New Delhi, 1984), and still earlier in *Journal of Modern History*, Vol. 38, No. 2, 1966.

"Dynamics of Change in Rajasthan Before and After 1947" by Bhupendra Hooja was earlier published under a different title in P.C.

Mathur edited *Social and Economic Dynamics of Rajasthan Politics* (Aalekh Publishers, Jaipur, 1996). It had been written as a comment on a thematic note circulated at a national seminar, whose theme was the same as the title of P.C. Mathur's book, which was held at the Department of Political Science, University of Rajasthan, Jaipur on November 4–5, 1995.

Dilip K. Chakrabarti of Cambridge University was kind enough to write "The Aravallis as an Early Centre of Agriculture and Metallurgy" specially for this volume and his was among the first contributions received.

The next paper "Archeology in Present Time: Four Desert Temples of Rajasthan" by Michael Meister, Lawrence Babb and John Cort was originally presented at the 19th International Conference on South Asia Archeology at the European Association of South Asian Archeologists in Ravenna, Italy, in July 2007, by the first author.

G.S.L. Devra and K.K. Maheshwari respectively obliged with specially written articles at short notice during the latter part of 2008.

Rakesh Hooja's "A Non-Historian's Personal Discovery of Tod and His Impacts" has been developed from the second half of his inaugural address at the Fifth International Conference on Rajasthan organized by Institute of Rajasthan Studies, Jaipur from 29 to 31 December 2005.

"Origin and Evolution of Tribals in Rajasthan: Ancient Days to Modern Era" by Bhupendra Hooja was originally published under the title "The Tribal Scene in Rajasthan" in *Shodhak,* Vol. 13, Pt. B, No. 38, 1984.

The next paper "Remaking a State Policy: Ganga Singh to Sadul to Karni Singh and the Accession and Merger of Bikaner" by Rima Hooja and Bhupendra Hooja is a revised version of a paper with a slightly shorter sub-title originally presented at a national seminar on Democratization in Rajasthan, organized by Department of Political Science, Maharshi Dayanand Saraswati University, Ajmer and ICSSR, Northern Regional Centre, New Delhi on 25–26 March 2000 at Ajmer.

The next paper by Bhupendra Hooja "Between Old and New: Modernization of the Princely State of Tonk, 1765–1947" was originally published in P.C. Mathur (Ed.), *Social and Economic Dynamics of Rajasthan Politics*, Aalekh Publishers, Jaipur, 1996.

Ranbir Sinh specially wrote "Theatre in Rajpootana" for this volume.

Ram Pande's "People's Movements in Rajputana and their Role in India's Struggle for Freedom" has borrowed from a number of his own articles and a book published by *Shodhak*.

We would have liked to have included an article by Bhupendra Hooja and Rakesh Hooja originally published in the now defunct *The Illustrated Weekly of India* (Vol. XLVI, 45, November 9, 1975) on lesser known places of Rajasthan entitled "The Rajasthan You Do Not Know", but could not trace out a copy of the article.

The two papers in Section II "Amber: Erstwhile Capital of Dhundhar's Kachchwaha Rajputs" by Rakesh Hooja and Rima Hooja, and "Kachchwahas of Amber from Dhula Rai to the Founding of Jaipur: Dynastic Succession, Military Campaigns, Architecture, Literature and the Arts" by Rima Hooja and Rakesh Hooja had both been circulated at the Fifth Annual Conference on Rajasthan, organized by the Institute of Rajasthan Studies, Jaipur from 29 to 31 December, 2005. Shorter, majorly revised and edited versions of both the papers were also published in Shikha Jain (ed.), *Princely Terrain: Amber, Jaipur, Shekhawati* by Surabhi Publishers, Gurgaon in 2005.

Section III (Articles 17 to 32) is the text of the special number issued to mark the 300th birth anniversary of Maharaja Sawai Jai Singh II by *Indian Book Chronicle* (Vol. XIII, No. 11, November 1988). Bhupendra Hooja, then Chief Editor of *Indian Book Chronicle*, was the guiding spirit and principal worker behind the preparation of the special number. P.C. Mathur, Rakesh Hooja, I.K. Sharma, Rima Hooja and Subodh Bhushan Gupta were the other members of the editorial team of *Indian Book Chronicle* at that time. Mulk Raj Anand, Ashim Kumar Roy, Ashok Das, R.N. Chowdhury and V.S. Bhatnagar had specially agreed to act as advisors for the particular special number.

Bhupendra Hooja has introduced the various articles in the section in Humble Tribute to Maharaja Sawai Jai Singh. While some of the articles had been specially written for the special number of *Indian Book Chronicle*, Mulk Raj Anand's two pieces "An Epistle of Dedication" and the poem "The City of Jai (Victory) and Joy" had both been extracted and reproduced from *MARG: A Magazine of Arts*, Vol. XXX, No. 4, September 1977. Satish Chandra's "A Statesman of the 18th Century" was originally published in the Indian History Congress Proceedings 1948, V.S. Bhatnagar's "...and Many Flowers Bloomed!" was extracted by the author from his own book *Life and Times of Sawai Jai Singh* and there are relevant extracts from James Tod's *Annals and*

Antiquities of Rajasthan and from Ashim Kumar Roy's *History of the Jaipur City*. It had been Bhupendra Hooja's dream that the contents of the special number of *Indian Book Chronicle* on Sawai Jai Singh be republished, which is being realized through this volume.

We have also included an appendix "Constructing Rajasthan" by Lloyd I. Rodolph and Susanne Hoeber Rudolph, which was circulated on January 23, 2008, at the Jaipur Literary Festival, 2008 during a session of the two Rudolphs in conversation with Rima Hooja about the contemporary construction of the idea of Rajasthan which according to the Rudolphs was a result of the pursuit of Rajasthan Studies, whose history is briefly set forth by them in the appendix.

We thank all the contributors to the volume, as also *Indian Book Chronicle* (where the three editors of the present volume are currently Associate Editors), *Shodhak* and Institute of Rajasthan Studies for associating themselves with the editors in bringing out this book in memory of Bhupendra Hooja and permitting use of some material originally used at their forums. Also to be thanked is the publisher Kailash Rawat of Rawat Publications, who readily agreed to bring out the book at short notice.

Rakesh Hooja
Rima Hooja
Rakshat Hooja

I

A Rajpootana-Rajasthan Potpouri

1

Rajasthan Present and Past

Princely States to Modern-Day Province

RAKESH HOOJA

Rajasthan – possessing 10.4 per cent of India's total land area, 5.4 per cent of India's vast human population, 16.7 per cent of national food production, but having only slightly more than 1 per cent of the country's water resources (both surface and groundwater). Rajasthan – divided by the Aravalli hill range, which acts as the 20-inch rainfall line with lands to the east of the Aravallis receiving more than 20 inches a year and those on the other side less than 20 inches. Rajasthan – containing within its fold what is perhaps the most populated of the world's deserts. Rajasthan – a land rich in history going back to much before the Ahar culture as excavations at Kalibanga and Bagor, Jodhpura and Ganeshwar have shown, and which took new shape with the rise of the Rajputs from about the 8th century AD; yet ironically perhaps not thought of as a common entity or region till Colonel James Tod came along and wrote his *Annals and Antiquities...* in the early 19th century. Rajasthan – a state of the Indian Union that took shape in six stages between 1948 and 1950 when 19 princely states and two chieftainships gave way to the new state of Rajasthan with Ajmer-Merwara (earlier directly ruled by the British) and Abu etc., being subsequently joined to it through the states reorganization of 1956. Rajasthan – having built, in the form of the massive Indira Gandhi Canal (formerly Rajasthan Canal) project, what one well-travelled and experienced foreign developmental consultant once referred to as an achievement comparable to the Great Wall of China, and also having witnessed the construction of numerous historical forts and fortifications, palaces, havelis, baodis and hunting lodges that dot the Rajasthan landscape.

This is the first half of the inaugural address delivered by the author at the Fifth Annual Conference on Rajasthan organized by the Institute of Rajasthan Studies at Jaipur from December 29 to 31, 2005.

Rajasthan – located on the trade routes between the heartland of the Indian subcontinent and the land to the west of Rajasthan and having bourne the brunt over the centuries of more than one invading force. Rajasthan – a territory that throughout history, and particularly in the medieval period, both benefited from and suffered due to its proximity to Delhi. Rajasthan – a major destination of both foreign and domestic tourists due to its various and varied attractions. Rajasthan – an area now emerging onto the map of the contemporary boom in industrialization. Rajasthan (the state that that I feel privileged to live in) – is an area well worth the attention of scholars from various disciplines and others from various walks of life.

Accordingly, the endeavours of the Institute of Rajasthan Studies in the last decade or two at facilitating scholars and others from far and near who are interested in Rajasthan to collect and share observations, experiences and research work in periodic conferences on Rajasthan are to be appreciated.

As I have already indicated, Rajasthan did not have a tradition of Provincial Government before independence. Despite the formation of the Rajputana Agency in 1832, the internal affairs of the princely states were primarily managed by the rulers and their advisors. The ruler may have locally deferred to the British Resident, but he was spared from looking up all the time to a provincial or state capital for decisions of administration and government (though he did have to ensure that the Governor General and Government of India did not find anything amiss in his princely domain).

Thus (even though some princely states contained smaller imitations in the form of Nizamats) of the district administration of the provinces of the British Raj which were directly ruled by the British, the District Collectors in the districts of Rajasthan, which got newly created after independence and merger or integration, did not have a tradition like in the British ruled areas of deferring to state government officials or to the Provincial Boards of Revenue – and evolved their own traditions of by and large managing on their own. The poor communications of those times also encouraged this tradition.

I recall a former Chief Secretary of the state the late Mohan Mukherji, saying years ago that Rajasthan had a tradition of posting young officers as District Collectors and trying to send them to the districts full of self-confidence, even verging on arrogance, so that they would sort out issues locally as also undertake initiatives on their own without waiting for the state government to send directions or detailed guidelines. It had almost sounded to me as if the earlier lot of Collectors were being expected to show independence of decision making like the Maharajas' or Raja's who had been there before.

The people also used to, till recently, refer to Collectors as *Annadata* (provider of food), a term of address earlier used for the princely rulers. Perhaps in the minds of many the Collector had replaced the Raja/Maharaja as the local focus of, and dispenser of, governance.

In fact on the one hand the districts functioned semi autonomously, and on the other hand the proximity of the new State capital to the national capital and the earlier history of some of the princely rulers deferring to the Moghuls or the British authority at Delhi or Calcutta, meant that the new state government developed the tendency to look up to New Delhi. Thus processes of coordination, monitoring and control from the state level took quite some time to get institutionalized in Rajasthan, and Collectors started functioning, and are still expected to function, independently to a large extant.

Local princely state loyalties still survive in the minds of the people, and many a person often jokes that the Rajasthan Administrative Service (RAS) actually comprises in practice of the Udaipur or Mewar Administrative Service, Jodhpur Administrative Service. Bikaner Administrative Service, Ajmer Administrative Service, etc. since officers of the RAS (and in fact of all government State Services) prefer to get posted, and to keep their families located, within the areas of the erstwhile princely states or of their extended sphere of influence, rather that to accept with equanimity a transfer across the state of Rajasthan. I believe many Jodhpur residents still fell that they cannot sleep peacefully if they cannot see Jodhpur's Mehrangarh fort every day and thus are reluctant to leave Jodhpur and settle elsewhere for professional reasons.

One other result of the different princely state history of Rajasthan, as compared to that of the British Raj, is evident in the sphere of Panchayati Raj (or village councils and related local self-government units about which a booklet containing two of my co-authored articles with my wife Meenakshi and entitled *Continuity and Change in Rajasthan's Panchayati Raj* is being circulated at this Conference). Bombay Presidency had a long tradition of district

Collectors and District Councils during the British Raj – so when Panchayat Raj was launched in the late 1950s they went in for a district panchayat or Zila Parishad based model of Panchayati Raj. However in Rajasthan the districts were set up only in the early 1950s – thus when Rajasthan became the first state in the country to adopt Panchayati Raj in 1959, with the system of districts not being as institutionalized in Rajasthan as it was in areas that had been directly ruled by the British, the state went in for a Panchayat Samiti or Community Development Block based model of Panchayati Raj rather than a district based one.

The fact that Rajasthan has been built up from erstwhile princely states, rather than having been a British-ruled province, has also affected the administrative culture here. Unlike the successors of the ICS in the erstwhile British governed provinces with their formalized norms of interaction, the civil services in Rajasthan have picked up traditions from the administrators employed in the princely states who were subsequently absorbed into the state or district administration after independence and mergers.

Inter personal relations within the state bureaucracy are thus relatively relaxed and informal – a point brought home to me when I exchanged notes with my IAS batchmates working in States that were earlier directly ruled by the British. For example in Uttar Pradesh even in the 1970s and early 80s the Collector going to his office (that is the Collectorate) was an event. He normally functioned from his small office in the residence where few from the general public, let alone district level officers or his officers and staff from the Collectorate, could meet him without a prior appointment. He normally toured the district only during a month long district tour – and the hierarchical distance between officials (even if there was little difference between them in seniority) was scrupulously maintained. In Rajasthan the District Collector, and other officers, have traditionally been available in office and regularly accessible and responsive on a daily basis, accustomed to frequent touring throughout the year, where they naturally made themselves accessible to the villagers, and the interaction between persons of different seniority and different hierarchical positions is much smoother. This helps in better administrative coordination and responsiveness to the needs of the people.

Ever since my college days it has intermittently struck me during casual conversations, or even during more serious discussions, that my home state of Rajasthan (we have lived here since I was 9 years old) or say a state like Orissa (substantial portions of whose area had earlier formed parts of princely states) have a different ethos and react to problems in a different way than states like Uttar Pradesh, Bihar, Maharashtra, etc. which had a history of direct British rule. Even within Rajasthan, those regions around Ajmer which had been directly ruled by the British had a different feel from areas that had been ruled by various rulers, which despite having been ruled by different dynasties and having had different princely traditions, appeared to have many things in common-say for example the extreme respect for authority witnessed in Rajasthan villages till even the late 1970s.

Similarly it has often appeared to me that, perhaps due to traditions of the movements that had formed part of the freedom struggle, the tendency for populations in the erstwhile directly British-ruled areas to resort to agitations, strikes etc. has been much greater than in the areas of former princely states, like present day Rajasthan, where Praja Mandal movements, though having links with the freedom struggle and the pre-independence Congress, had been different from the mainstream nationalist movement in British India.

I am conscious that the directly ruled British provinces in India, 1947 had seen the administrative system continue intact, though the proportion of British officers in the districts as well as provincial capitals reduced, and similarly, the political system built on the system of elected ministers who were already dealing with transferred subjects as a part of limited provincial autonomy had been enlarged to enable them to deal with all subjects assigned to the states in independent India. The princely states, on the other hand, had to deal not only with mergers of small princely states into the larger post-independence states, but also with the traditional personalized systems of princely rule being converted to what was a totally new system for the region – one of administration through a system of newly created districts, divisions and the state, with the creation of new legislative, executive and judicial institutions. This went hand in hand with the co-option of personnel who had been serving the princely states into positions in various wings of the government of the newly created state.

It appears to me that this led to a different administrative culture evolving in the states that had been part of princely India from that which existed and evolved further in what had been British India. It perhaps even impacted on the type and magnitude of corruption, which differed between the two areas.

As I have already hinted, to my mind both the administrators and the political ministers were, after independence, more accessible and responsive (comparatively) in the former princely states, than the successors to the British rulers including the District Collectors in the former British provinces.

The reverence with which the former Maharajas, Rajas etc. and their families continued to be held especially during the two or three decades immediately after independence, and their social and political position in their erstwhile princely states, does not seems to have any parallel in the British provinces.

The impact of purdah system also perhaps lingered longer in the former princely states. (One even hears stories of how, in pre-independence days, certain ladies who observed purdah while in the territory of a princely state, used to dispense with purdah when they travelled to territory directory governed by the British.) This naturally impacted on the position of women in the two types of territories and perhaps even influences how women are treated and how they themselves behave today.

My impression is that, despite a few very good English medium schools and colleges having been set up in the princely states, by and large the literacy (including female literacy), and even education levels, were much lower in the princely states than in British-ruled India. While this is subject to being checked out and verified as to whether it applied to each and every princely state territory, such a difference has naturally impacted on how the two types of areas developed economically and socially after independence.

The erstwhile British provinces had by and large been more industrialized than the princely states and this naturally gave them an advantage after independence. However, correspondingly the British provinces also had traditions of trade union movements in their centres of industry, while the princely states had by and large been free of trade unionism. This has also affected how the two types of territories developed after 1947.

I believe that not only contemporary Rajasthan's relatively peaceful industrial relations, but also the good law and order situation, owes a lot to the fact that it was a part of princely India rather than of the British Raj.

These factors along with the fact that Rajasthan today possesses a good pool of English educated youth, the electric power position in

Rajasthan is better than that of many other neighbouring states, our proximity to Delhi (which has improved due to the excellent National Highway 8), and the fact that many Haryana industrialists have professed to their finding Rajasthan's bureaucracy at district and lower levels easier to deal with, has meant that despite a very attractive Central Government package for industrialists setting up industries in Uttranchal, Himachal Pradesh, Jammu & Kashmir etc., entrepreneurs not only from Delhi and Haryana, but also at the national and international levels, are coming to the state, means that Rajasthan is not all about the past (which, of course, fuels Rajasthan's tourism industry where Rajasthan leads the country in heritage tourism) and about how we have been influenced by its history.

Now Rajasthan is building upon our traditional strengths in handicrafts, tourism, mining and stones, dairy and livestock. The mood in Rajasthan, as those who come from outside must be noting, is one of optimism, buoyancy and belief that we appear to be well set on the path of development and growth.

2

Some Notes and Questions on Rajasthan History

BHUPENDRA HOOJA

Perhaps I would not be misunderstood if I were to suggest that history is seldom 'objective' or 'impartial', as we have been brought up to understand it. There is always some 'angle' to the understanding and appreciation of history, even in the compilation of historical facts or the narration of events and social, cultural or political movements as such. Perhaps my point will be duly appreciated if we can address ourselves to some of the following obvious questions: Why history? Who needs it? To what use can history be put? etc. etc. One can add more questions in a similar vein of enquiry.

I can perhaps try and make myself clear yet another way. For hundred of years, we have lived with legends, mythology, *Pauranic kathas* of *Ramayana* and *Mahabharata*, which have become integral parts of our cultural beliefs and arts etc. But suddenly, a time has come when we need to look back into that hoary historical past to unravel new facts or secrets of history, so as to give fresh meaning to our present-day life.

There is an obvious linkage between our present and the past, as it is, or vice versa. Perhaps we can add yet another dimension. May I suggest that there is also a linkage between our past and the future.

We cannot have a proper sense of history of respect for it, unless we have some clear vision about the future and our society, of the world at large and humankind.

When we talk of the 'angle' or the 'vantage point' from which we look back at our past, naturally, we have to draw upon our immediate and day-to-day experiences, both in material terms and in the sphere of ideas or beliefs, hopes and dreams. Howsoever, one may try to be 'detached' from the current environment of experiences and ideas, one cannot be free from their deep-rooted impressions or influences.

***

Unfortunately, as it is generally believed, we Indians (especially ancient Indians) did not have a due 'regard' for history. We had our mythological epics, our *vanshavalis*, chronologies and narratives; but we did not have history or historical records. Or, whatever there was, seems to have been lost, except for the ruins of monuments and the memories of our ancient texts.

It is said that record-keeping or chronicles etc. came with the visits of foreign travellers and more so, with the advent of Arab, Turkish or Afghan invaders, especially those who stayed back to rule over the sub-continent. If we go through these accounts, we can easily notice the slant with which they have been recorded. Even Al Beruni or before him the Chinese travellers had their own angles of review points, through they tried to faithfully record what they saw or experienced and appreciated of Indian society, culture and polity.

Then came the Europeans from different countries of Europe along with merchants and missionaries and their historians, who had their own 'views' and 'interests' or concerns to serve. Among these, the British tried to delve into our past and reconstruct our history for us. Can we call them to be 'objective'? What was their "history of India", and its interpretation, was put together from their own trade-promotion and empire-building concerns or points of view. For example, it is worth asking: What made them divide the history of India into its ancient/Hindu, medieval/Muslim and modern/British periods? Why was not the last period of modern history called 'Christian', if the earlier periods were clubbed together and dubbed as 'Hindu' and 'Muslim' respectively? In the case of the so-called Muslim period, in particular, we have to be very careful and identify the Arab, the Afghan, the Turk, Mongol and the Persian invasions and inroads into north-west India.

In fact, from the Indian point of view, the time has come when we ought to be find out how north-west India stood up to resist or assimilate these foreign inroads and influences not only militarily or politically, but also socially, culturally, economically and, if you like, in terms of religious urges and aspirations. We also need to go back to long before the Muslim period, to the dawn of Indian history, and take account of all the sixty and odd invasions. Have we cared to ask why there were so many invasions? Or, what happened before and after each inroad? And, who came first, or why?

We all know that various mythological epics and legends have references to the geographical tracts or parts of what now constitutes the new state of Rajasthan. There have been some excavations, archaeological finds and other discoveries. These do not help us to compile a continuous and consistent narrative of our past. I suggest that the time has come, when, well-planned, continuous and concerted efforts should be made to put together all the historical materials, and interpret them in a suitable manner, so that the history of Rajasthan, as we know it today, or its component parts in the remote past, should begin to make some sense.

What happened in these parts at the dawn of history? There is a wide and big gap between the culture of the Satluj valley/Kalibanga and Bagore/Ahar civilizations, which needs to be correlated to the culture of the ancient Matsya and Charamavati areas. But perhaps, the more significant and challenging task would be to explore and identify the past of the Pushkar valley. How, for example, Pushkar came to occupy an important place in our religious and socio-cultural tradition? Many pieces of the historical, political, socio-cultural, religious and philosophic jigsaw puzzle have come to our hands. We have to put them together and identify what pieces are missing and how they can be discovered or put together. We must revive the project of "Rajasthan through the Ages" and attempt "A Cultural History of the People of Rajasthan" as parts of our contributions to the history of the Indian sub-continent. Also, there is need to look again and afresh at the various District/State Gazetteers and revise, update and rewrite them.

***

There is yet another problem. While the history of the rest of north India from about the end of so-called Classical Age offers us many known and obvious features, how is it that there is a curtain of doubt and darkness over the desert land of Rajasthan during that period, say from about the 5th–6th century AD to almost the rise of the Rajputs and inroads of the Arab neo-Muslims from the West? How can these gaps be filled up? How can we find out whether or not the numerous hordes of Shakas or Hoonas and others swept through Rajasthan region? And what impress or impact did they leave behind?

Here I would also like to pose a speculative question about the origin of the Rajputs, especially those who were "fire-born". Were they not some foreign or alien elements or out-castes or representatives of the so-called lower and backward castes from amongst the Hindus who had to purify themselves through the ordeal of fire or *yajna* at Mount Abu? In the legends of *Mahabharata* too, we have references to *Agniputras* or characters born out of a fire-sacrifice or *yajna*. Perhaps they signify the assimilation of civilization of the rulers/communities of the Himalayan ranges into the Hindu-fold. May be, something of that sort actually happened centuries later in north-west India, after the early forays of the Arab soldiers and may be as an after-effect of the knocks given by the hordes of Shakas or Hoonas and other warring tribes sweeping down upon north-west India.

A similar question would also need to be asked and answered about the spread and migration of other important communities like the Jats and Gurjars, among many others. In fact, a time has come when the history of Rajasthan, especially the chronicles of early middle ages, need to be reviewed from multi-polar viewpoints, and studied as interplay of numerous communities, not only the Rajputs, on the stage of our history. We have plenty of information about the Rajputs, but hardly any about the other communities.

In particular, we seem to know very little about the tribal communities of Rajasthan, especially the Bhils and the Minas, Sahariyas and Garasias, but they still constitute a substantial part of the population. There were/are other tribals, perhaps aborigines (or *Adivasis*) who seem to have gradually vanished, except in some remote areas. But, the Bhils and the Minas did have considerable sway and spread over vast tracts of the land, except perhaps the desert areas, where the Janglis might have survived until quite late in historical times (if we were to go by the references to the Jangal Pradesh in our ancient texts.) In the north-east, there were the Meos of the Mewat region, an altogether different story of a socio-cultural halfway halt between Hindu and Islamic influences.

What was the tribal society or state power like? How were these communities organized in their small, local areas of presence or domination? How did they relate each to the other, and with the outside world? These are some of the questions, which need to be probed and answered.

Also, how did they manage to survive so long, even upto the modern times? Did the tribals of Rajasthan follow (or fall under the spell of) the Hindu religion in its wider sense? Were their gods, the same as the Hindu gods, so to say? Or, was it the other way round? When did the process of Hinduization start (if at all there was any such process)? Was Sanskrit of the Vedic age or the Prakrits of the Boudhas and Jains the language from which the Bhil or the Dhundari languages have emerged? There are a host of questions, which seem to crop up in these areas of study; and I wonder why the historians of Rajasthan have not turned their attention to these and other possible questions.

***

Perhaps it is not right to start (or emphasize) the history of Rajasthan with the arrival/emergence of the Rajput warriors and dynasties. In any case, the origin and the early history of the Rajputs remains debatable to some extent. However, this is not to deny the dynamism and the vigour or the enterprise of the Rajputs, who managed to carve off for themselves, not one but dozens of principalities, chiefships and kingdoms during the medieval ages, from about 9th century until about the close of the 19th century. On the one hand, they had to snatch power from the tribal Minas and the Bhils and other indigenous communities as the case may be; and on the other hand, they had to withstand various invasions from the north-east and north-west and conquests from the new Afghan or Mughal rulers of Delhi and Agra, and later on, the Maratha and the British in the guise of the East India Company, before the British crown entered into a new relationship with the Rajput rulers.

What gave the Rajputs their will and tenacity to fight for survival? What was there in these inhospitable and poor soils which they sought to defend? And what was it, what treasure, that the intruders and adventures were after? Surely not the hands a few pretty Rajput maidens? Another intriguing question is why did not the Rajput braves come together and coordinate their efforts in a confederation of resistance each time a new adventurer or invading army descended upon them? Why did they choose to do their *Shakas* and *Johars* singly and one by one?

Their mutual relations and those with the rulers of Hindustan have also remained enigmatic. How much sovereign, free and equal were they? Or, were the Rajput rulers always subordinate?

Even after we were to call this an age of feudalism or *samantvad*, we need to define the contours and parameters of the system as it grew and developed in various parts of Rajasthan, and as it prevailed towards the final stages of its development, some aspects of which are parts of our living memory. Neither the state nor the society, the technologies or modes of production, the organization of Rajput warriors into well-organized armed forces were 'static', or remained the same throughout the 1,000 years or so of their domination of these parts.

There are various chapters of honour and glory, struggle and sacrifice, which have inspired the imagination of successive generations, not only within Rajasthan, but even in the distant parts of sub-continent. Yet, there have also been some chapters of defeat and despair, of intrigues and inglorious acts, of betrayal compromise and adjustments. Unfortunately, we seem to have been brought up on a romantic tradition that the Rajput rulers or the warriors were all 'defenders' or 'saviours' of Hindu *dharma* or the ancient Indian heritage. May I submit that without reducing the significance of their role in the repeated struggles for self-preservation and preservation of their traditional culture and heritage, we need to look at the whole matter with less romantic and more unbiased minds. May I suggest that it was not 'Hinduism' as such that the successive Rajput warriors stood and fought for, though their struggles and sacrifices did contribute to the preservation of a kind of Hindu culture and Hindu *dharma*. Let us concede that each Rajput kingdom or faction also stood for its own defence and its own identity, even when one local prince or ruler fought another, and there were many such fights for whatever reason. Did they fight only for the Rajput *aan* and *shaan*, the clan and a code of honour?

Or was there some other motivating and driving force? Yet another interesting aspect is the co-existence of the Rajput state and social structures with the tribal communities like the Minas and the Meos or Meos Bhils and Garasias.

***

In their valour, the Rajput princes also gave shelter to many refugees or fugitives. There are some very interesting episodes from various princely states on such themes. There are also indications of the Sufis and other Muslims saints and thousands of non-Hindus who had come to settle down in various princely states, there to ply their trades and skills in comparatively more secure or settled conditions. The Rajput rulers and their subjects had developed a more or less secular, tolerant and accommodative philosophy or attitude towards such fugitives and migrants. In spite of the wars, there was harmony amongst the various sections of society, which has survived up to our present times. One can say that a sort of composite culture grew and developed at the grass-roots, rural and urban levels, under the Rajputs.

Apart from the literary, cultural or artistic developments and patronage of arts and crafts by courts, the Rajput era, if we may call it that, also witnessed the emergence and the spread of a number of religious and social reform movements. Among the leaders are the names of Meera and Dadu, as also the Sufi *sant* of Chisti tradition and many other lesser known *sants*.

There is need to explore the socio-cultural, economic and political, even religious, background of all these various *sants* and their sects. Why did these movements grow? And how? With or without princely patronage? Was Meera, for example, a 'rebel'? And, if so, was she the only one? What were others trying to do – the Dadus or the Bishnois and many before them – those who rejected the existing state system and the society with their set codes and laws, and these was sought to reform and restructure the various social institutions? How much did the fundamental core of 'Hinduism' change under their impact? For them, and for the generations, that followed them? Was their faith or *dharma* and *Neeti*? Or, was it as preached, prescribed and practised by the various leaders of social and religious reform? Today, when we speak of Hinduism, should we or can we ignore these saintly incorporations and interpretations, and give a call to go back to the *Vedas*? Or to the teachings of the Buddha or the Jain Tirthankars?

There is another intriguing and fascinating aspect of these movements or developments, which is reflected in the mixed Hindu-Muslim culture of the Meos; or in what happened in the so-called Shekhawati area – in that long period of Hindu-Muslim or the Pathan-Mughal and Rajput encounters, or what has come to us now in the shape of the so-called Qaimkhani communities? Then, what about the caste groups or communities which remained outside the pale of these developments, not only the tribals, but also the various types of pastoral nomads or the *ghumantu* tribes, the Banjaras etc., and those who were condemned as criminal or ex-criminal tribes at a much later, and our near contemporary stage of British domination.

***

This also brings me to the need for histories of arts and crafts, trade and commerce, dialects (folk stories) and literatures of the social reform or religious movement – above all, the interfacing, interaction and accommodation of cultures. Ignoring any aspect of the life and culture of the people is denying its existence, but denial is not the business and purpose of history. History should prepare us to question and then accept our past. It is a process of critical and rational appraisal, both in the study or research and writing or teaching of history.

One more question, and I would be done. (I resist the temptation of raising questions about the more recent past). My question or a plea is about the status of the Rajasthan rulers, or the nature and texture of their 'sovereignty', in the context of their relations with the changing rulers of Hindostan – from the Slave Kings to the Mughals and later the Marathas and the British – and amongst each other. Were they 'co-qual' or 'subordinate' to the Pathans, Mughals/Marathas and more particularly the British/East India Company? I raise the point because we have/had nourished a sort of romantic notion that the Hindu/Rajput rulers/states were islands of *Swarajya* and *Swabhiman*. Both Dayanand Saraswati and M.K. Gandhi (among other scores of reformers and chronicles) suffered from this illusion. This partly explains why, for example, the Congress resisted the requests or advances of the leaders of the Bijolia and similar peasant or urban local struggles for support, until quite late in the day.

We must also give a fresh look at what these isolated recent movements aim at? Why did the braves of Bijolia only want relief from feudal taxes, and not end of feudalism? Why did they want panchayats and no change in the state administration? And, why not land to the cultivators?

The nagging question is when did the process of 'modernisation' start? What was it? What modernizations did/do the natives want? And where have we landed/ended up? My point is, how do we look back at the contemporary history of Rajasthan? And privileged of that experience and knowledge, how do we look back at the past? And towards the future?

What are/should be our angles 'or viewpoints' for the study of Rajasthan history? These questions have been posed for consideration as one approaches a study of the history of the area.

3

Rajputana under British Paramountcy

The Failure of Indirect Rule

SUSANNE H. RUDOLPH AND LLOYD I. RUDOLPH

When India became independent in 1947, nineteen princely states and three chiefships of Rajputana were amalgamated into a single political unit – Rajasthan – that became a state within the Indian Union. The special form of indirect rule – paramountcy – which Britain exercised in the princely states had not prepared Rajputana for independence. Princely rule and legitimacy, based on birth, was abruptly replaced by parliamentary government and the authority of democracy. Institutional changes, which had taken place in British India over more than one hundred years, were brought into being in Rajasthan in less than five. This work was accomplished not by those who stood at the head of the old regime but by those who had opposed it from within and by the new men of the central government in Delhi.

Rajasthan succeeded states which, after the making of treaties with Britain in 1818, had lived under that ambiguous conception of sovereignty which deprived the princes of their foreign powers and left their domestic powers subject to certain supervision. The gentle breezes of change and British political influence modified Rajput monarchial and feudal institutions but did not replace or even fundamentally transform them. The princes and their administrators learned what makes a respectable modern state and began, often with British guidance to construct new institutions. Sometimes these were effective and meaningful; more often they had the insubstantiality of stage setting. The political community expanded very little, but newly aware groups did take shape and hover near its boundaries waiting to assert their claims. The gradual extension of the rule of law and a growing appreciation for modern administration began but did not complete the separation of the state and its public offices and finances from the private estate, retainers, and income of the prince. These changes contributed to a consciousness of political rights and liberties but failed to make them constitutional. Until the crises and traumas of 1947 revealed their hollowness and fragility, the traditional ideas and practices of legitimacy and rulership, which paramountcy was designed to protect from external and internal dangers, continued intact.

Vagueness concerning the limits of power is likely to be helpful to those who exercise it. The British government studiously avoided precision in defining paramountcy, the exercise of power over princely states.[1] Its meaning derived from a wide variety of treaties concluded with different princes and a system of case law and precedent whose interpretation lay with the paramount power. The Butler Commission concisely summarized the deliberate ambiguity of paramountcy in 1928 when, in response to a request from the princes to define the concept, it merely stated: "Paramountcy must remain paramount".[2] Paramountcy implied that the Governor-General of India would exercise power in the field of foreign affairs, defence, communications, and coinage on behalf of the princely states.[3] It left the states internally autonomous while guaranteeing the rulers protection against enemies foreign and domestic. The guarantee against domestic enemies – brought with it unsystematic intervention in domestic affairs to insure that there would not be too many of them. An agent or a resident drawn from the special administrative cadre, known as the political service, represented the Governor-General in the state and exercised these powers.

The influence of the British on the states depended on the overall policy espoused by the Governor-General and the respective qualities of the political agents and the princes.[4] A hands-off policy toward the princely states followed the rebellion of 1857, which frightened the British government away from strong interventionism. This policy ended at the turn of the twentieth century when Lord Curzon began to impress the princes with their responsibilities. The example of Maharaja Ganga Singh of Bikaner, who in 1899 sharply protested against the political agent's desire to review the dismissal of two petty state officials, was not exceptional in the Curzon era. "Nothing is further from my mind [the agent wrote] than interference with your orders, and I trust there will never be any greater need than there is now for contemplating such interference. It is, however, the duty of every political agent to satisfy himself that the state with which he is, is well and justly governed, or how it is governed, and he can only do this by occasionally asking for reports on selected petitions".[5] Lord Minto's easy-going policy eased the pressures for reform and intervention that Curzon had applied, but Lord Linlithgow's viceroyalty in the 1930's once again brought an emphasis on administrative modernization and reform, and hence greater intervention.[6]

The British exercised influence through numerous channels even in areas beyond the ordinary concerns of paramountcy. The Crown drew to itself the right to recognize the successor to the *gaddi* (throne) of any state, and thus became involved in settling succession disputes. Since legitimate successors were often minors, and since during succession disputes unprotected minors sometimes expired prematurely, the Crown took some responsibility for the minority administration. It appointed the regent, often making its selection within the state, sometimes sending in a member of the political service to conduct the administration. Minority rule provided the occasion for strong, often creative, intervention and laid the basis for subsequent influence.[7] At the end of a twenty-year minority administration exercised on behalf of Maharaja Umed Singh of Kotah by the political agent to that state, he offered the following 'advice' to the newly invested ruler: "Your Highness will in all important matters consult the political agent, be guided by his advice, and obtain his concurrence before introducing any important change in the measures carried out during your minority".[8] Similar 'advice' was given at Bikaner at the same time, although in later years, the maharaja of that state became notoriously independent.[9]

The channels of British influence were both direct and indirect. The political agent advised in the matter of the prince's education. In the twentieth century especially, English tutors were often employed, unless the prince attended one of the princes' and nobles' schools established with Government of India blessings to transmit the more superficial trappings of English public school education.[10] Less superficial traits, like the dutiful asceticism of ruling classes trained at Eton, Harrow and Winchester were more difficult to transmit to heirs who arrived with retinues of ten servants.[11] In the twenty years before independence, the larger states often appointed Englishmen from the political department as *dewans* (chief ministers) and ministers.[12] In the latter years of the British Raj, when Indian members of the Indian Civil Service began to control provincial administration under the direction of Indian ministers in British India, a senior member of the political service observed: "The administration in so-called Indian India was sometimes more under the control of British officers than it was in British India".[13]

The emergence of nationalism in British India had a curious effect on both the British attitude toward the princes and on the princes themselves. To the extent that the princes were a bulwark of British power, particularly when it began to be challenged in British India, the Government of India was inclined to treat them generously. To the princes, generosity meant being left alone. Yet, the need for internal improvements became more apparent as nationalism and reformist sentiment grew. Improvement meant interference.

The chamber of princes was established on a permanent basis in 1921,[14] the year after Gandhi turned the nationalist movement in British India in a popular direction. The chamber provided a forum in which princes could protest against efforts by the government to intervene and hurry them along and a context in which they became more conscious of one another and of the requirements that accompanied being a 'modern ruler'. The chancellor of the chamber of princes in 1927 circulated a memorandum summing up some of the most significant reforms on which he hoped they might all agree; suggested reforms included limitation of the privy purse to 10 per cent of state revenues, an independent judiciary, security of tenure for state civil servants, a promulgated code of law, and the maintenance of an efficient and honest police force.[15] The chamber began to create an environment in which good government became more fashionable. Princes vied with one another to secure the services of one of the four or five men who had built all-India reputations as able chief ministers in princely states.[16] Paramountcy did, then, affect the structure and quality of government in the princely states. But, the channels of British influence were too irregular and undefined to exploit consistently the available opportunities. Imperial policy, which varied with the outlook of the viceroy, his agents, and the developments in British India, never achieved the direction or firmness necessary to make it otherwise.

Caste, clan, land and chivalric reputation had legitimized rulership in the old princely states ruled by Rajputs, members of the warrior-ruler caste (Kshatriyas). After conclusion of the subsidiary alliances in 1818,[17] British recognition and support were required as well. The addition did little, however, to change explicitly the way most Rajasthanis understood the legitimacy of their maharajas or nobles; ascriptive factors justified the exercise of power in 1947 as they had done in 1818.

Yet the old ideas about what made government legitimate were subtly undermined during the period of paramountcy by a tentative new concern with effectiveness and consent. The example of events in British India and British pressures suggested that a prince justify his rule by performance. As Lord Curzon, who was wont to lecture the princes on this subject, put it: A ruler's "*gaddi* (throne) is not intended to be a divan of indulgence, but the stern seat of duty", and "by this test will he, in the long run, as a political institution, perish or survive".[18] Princes were pressed to convert their courts into more 'public' institutions and to orient their rule toward public rather than personal and familial benefits. The differentiation of the princes' privy purse from the public revenue, incomplete as it was in many states, and reports on administration that provided a rudimentary accounting of how government had discharged its task were the chief manifestations of this shift. The same influences affected the bureaucracy, which was urged to consider itself a public and professional service, not a body of private retainers.

The idea that greater public service would not only add luster to the name of the maharaja – that idea had already existed in pre-British days – but also become a condition of legitimate rule was by no means universally understood. Only a few, some of the new-style court bureaucrats and members of a tiny educated class, saw its relevance and import. But a good many maharajas, affected by their English tutors or schools, pressure from the political department, the communications spill-over from British India or far-seeing ministers, began to believe that they should serve as well as rule. Their consciousness of themselves as public men was affected by this idea even though they failed often to act on it. At the time of independence, the maharajas' feeble resistance to the challenge of democratic authority and leadership arose in part from an awareness of their failure to meet the new standards.

Traditional ideas of legitimacy were modified in another and more subtle respect. Ordinarily, the maharaja sought not to offend and listened to the grievances and advice of the limited political community of the twice-born castes – the Brahmans, Kshatriyas and Vaishyas – who could help or hinder him spiritually, militarily and financially. Most Rajasthanis were politically irrelevant and thought that they should be. Before 1935, only a tiny circle of intellectuals and modern nationalists without status and power thought otherwise. After 1935, the potential political community, those seeking to share power in the state and to influence government, expanded. A handful of school-masters, lawyers and journalists began to awaken the urban and rural common people by telling them that their interests and aspirations were relevant for government and that its authority should rest on their will. They made little progress; only after independence during the first general election of 1952 did Rajasthanis begin to perceive a connection between popular sovereignty and legitimacy.

If some maharajas accepted the notion that their right to rule depended in a measure upon performance and service, none conceded that it depended upon the support of organized public opinion. Some used means to consult public opinion, such as great annual *durbars* (royal public audiences), to inform themselves and their governments of public grievances and aspirations, but none entertained the notion of reigning rather than ruling by transforming the state into a democratic constitutional monarchy. Only towards the end of World War II, when the signs of the times pointed to the loss of British support and a more democratic future, did some princely states introduce elections based on limited franchise for legislatures to be dominated by an official or appointive majority.

The presence of the idea of democratic authority, though it lacked a large social base and effectively organized political support, weakened older beliefs and paved the way for its own ultimate realization. The strongest safeguard for any concept of legitimacy is for it to appear as natural; without rivals, its self-evidence stands unquestioned. The innocence of alternatives, which was traditional legitimacy's most powerful safeguard, was shattered by knowledge of the growing influence of organized public opinion in British India and its nascent expression within Rajasthan.

Prior to the British arrival, power in the Rajput states was shared by a territorial nobility and a maharaja, who was often their clan chief. The initial effect of British paramountcy in the nineteenth century not only sustained this diffusion of power but also undermined the attempts of some rulers to centralize power at the expense of their nobility.[19] Sir Alfred Lyall, in the late nineteenth century, saw the nobles as a countervailing power of the kind that had created feudal liberties in the West.[20] This belief persisted into the twentieth century when it was challenged but not replaced by a British policy of centralization designed to create financial viability and orderly and efficient administration. In the small states, the new policy was resisted by the maharajas since it involved partial if not total surrender of sovereignty, but in the larger states modest advances were achieved.

The pattern of decentralization in the nineteenth century had not been uniform. In Kotah, Dewan Zalim Singh virtually replaced the maharaja and reduced the independent territorial power of the nobility by making them dependent on the Crown.[21] In Dholpur and Bharatpur, two eastern states of Rajasthan ruled by Jats rather than Rajputs, territorial nobility on the Rajput pattern never existed.[22] Formally classified as a peasant caste, the Jats had a recent history of military prowess and local rulership. Their states were centralized in the negative sense that they lacked strongly articulated local power, but not in the positive one that they possessed a vigorous central government. The Rajput states confronted a dual task: to reduce the power of the nobility and to strengthen state government.

Maharaja Sawai Man Singh's efforts in Jaipur throughout the 1930's to strengthen his hand against his feudality illustrates one of the more successful attempts to reduce feudal power. It did not produce striking results. His effort to diminish the extensive financial, civil, police and judicial powers of the state's great nobles in Shekhawati began in 1932 with the appointment of C.V. Wills, a British Indian official, to investigate the historical and legal relations between the maharaja and his nobles. The proceeding itself, utilizing western legal concepts, departed from traditional methods. Wills' findings, perhaps not surprisingly, established that the nobles' claims to a separate and quasi-autonomous status had no legal or historical justification.[23] Not until 1939, seven years after Wills began his labours, did the Jaipur *durbar* venture to assert the powers which his investigations had persuaded it that it could claim: to vary the assessments of the *thikanas* (nobles' estates) which, by remaining fixed, had rendered the state revenue inelastic; to treat the state as a single economic and commercial unit by extending its customs cordon to include the *thikanas*; to abolish residuary civil and criminal powers reserved by some *thikanedars*. Only in 1939, then, did Jaipur clearly claim the minimum fiscal and legal powers characteristic of a modern state.[24] Having done so, the *durbar* announced that in practice it would insist on only some of them. The *durbar* was "graciously pleased", it announced, for example "to order that the *muamla* [assessments] be declared to be permanently fixed at the existing figure in all cases",[25] foregoing, thereby, that enhancement of revenues so vital for substantial expansion of state functions.

The paramount power's responsibility for external security rendered the military forces of the states less significant, but they too reflected the diffusion of power. State forces were maintained to keep law and order and for ceremonial purposes and, from the 1890's, as imperial service troops to aid the Government of India in foreign wars.[26] The *thikanas* kept armed retainers to satisfy their obligations to the maharaja and for their own purposes. Only in 1925 was the end of feudal military relations in Jaipur formally recognized. At that time the *thikanedar's* obligation to provide mounted and foot soldiers to the Jaipur *durbar* was commuted to cash.[27] After this change, some, nevertheless, continued to maintain military units. In 1937, the Jaipur *durbar* confronted the last gasp of feudal military power when its forces faced ten thousand armed retainers in Sikar, the state's largest *thikana*.[28] Bikaner, more forward in this respect, faced its last significant challenge in 1905.[29]

It is possible that, but for British intervention, effective centralization might have gone further in such vigorous and forward-looking states as Bikaner and Jaipur. The political department tried, on the one hand, to encourage modernization and, on the other, to prevent an efficient autocrat such as Bikaner or a gentler one such as Jaipur from running roughshod over his nobility. The two aims were incompatible. Effective centralization could not proceed without reducing or transforming the civil and judicial power of the nobles, as well as the immense economic power they exercised over their estates, which covered over half the territory of most Rajput states. Crucial to control of the *jagir* (nobles' grants) areas were settlement operations that would establish occupancy rights and revenue payments, and state intervention to enforce these and other relationships between peasants and nobles. But vigorous efforts to restrict and control the landed nobility, such as in Bikaner in the first decade of the century, Jaipur in the 1930's, and Jodhpur in the 1940's, invariably generated resistance and raised the possibility of the paramount power having to fulfil its pledge to protect rulers from internal rebellion.

The political department considered risking such difficulties. In 1942 it prepared to press for fair rent, occupancy rights, and records of rights in Rajasthan, especially in Jaipur. But, the advice of officers familiar with the area persuaded the department that the proposal was too risky.[30] The political department's desire to avoid the difficulties that economic or social or administrative changes entailed, especially when the Congress in British India was prepared to use such difficulties for its own purposes, was buttressed by a solicitude for the property rights of the nobility. The result was a policy of marginal and limited changes in land relations. On the other hand, without British supervision, most Rajput princes would not have pressed for radical change. Efforts to amalgamate police, judicial, and certain administrative functions of some of the smaller Rajasthan principalities, for example, ran into resolute opposition from princes concerned to preserve their dynastic and territorial sovereignty and individuality.[31] The political department considered centralization and greater administrative efficiency desirable but was not prepared to risk much on their behalf by forcing the princes or coercing the nobles.

Most states sought to rationalize government in such a way that central power could reach further as it became stronger. The establishment of specialized government departments with defined responsibilities and jurisdictions strengthened executive control. A letter by the twenty-one-year-old Maharaja Ganga Singh of Bikaner illustrates the early efforts of an able Rajput ruler:

> There is nothing laid down as to the limits of power which each Member [of Council] *or* the Dewan [chief minister] can exercise over the departments under their control. The result is that sometimes important things are decided and settled by officers above mentioned, whereas some trifling things are sometimes referred to the full Council or to me. In fact, owing to there being no rules everything is done in a haphazard way. There is also a general tendency to shirk responsibility as much as possible, and for everybody to try to have a finger in the pie whenever they have a good opportunity. The result is unsatisfactory and injurious to the interests of the state while much extra work is thrown on my shoulders.[32]

Ganga Singh eventually became the ablest Rajput ruler in the twentieth century, but he too opposed the development of regular procedures where they interfered with his personal rule. He saw that bureaucratization itself, even without responsible government, involves a restraint on power. For years he resisted appointing a permanent and responsible chief minister to direct the government even though he was often out of the country. Ganga Singh also resisted the establishment of competitive civil service recruitment. On the other hand, Bikaner state was divided into districts and sub-districts for purposes of revenue administration as early as 1872, strengthening crown control.[33] Not until 1945, and then only for the crown lands, did Jaipur establish district officers responsible for revenue, law, and order and give them powers approximating those of British Indian officers.[34]

The competence of the bureaucracy in many states increased during the era of paramountcy. Academic qualifications, reflecting the growth of educational opportunities in the twentieth century, were added to those of caste and heredity, but since they were no guarantee of competence, the state administrative cadres remained something less than merit based services. The qualifications, however, did represent a concession to recruitment by achievement rather than by ascription. The increasing emphasis on educational qualifications can be seen from a comparison of princely state officials recruited in the 1920's, 1930's and in 1940–47. Among 143 *tahsildars*, chief administrative officers for *tahsils* (sub-divisions of a district), selected from princely state services for positions in the administration of post-independence Rajasthan, 10 per cent of those recruited in the 1920's, 56 per cent of those recruited in the 1930's, and 94 per cent of those recruited in the 1940's had B.A. degrees.[35]

Apparently no state recruited through competitive examinations before 1940, and none established security of tenure.[36] In 1941 Udaipur established a formal civil service, recruited competitively; Jodhpur began competitive recruitment in 1942, Jaipur in 1943 (judicial) and 1944 (civil), but Bikaner never did.[37] Thus, while professional competence was more highly valued, the states did not, until World War II, give bureaucrats the job security nor insist on the merit which might have strengthened them against accepting irregular subventions from below or currying favour above. Taken as a whole, the princely state civil servants selected for the post-independence services of Rajasthan showed the marks of patrimonial service and court relations in their manners and style.

These years also saw the growth of new ideas of financial and administrative accountability. Their realization, however limited, played a significant part in the conversion of princely rule from private and familial estate management to rule directed toward public concerns and benefits. The demand that princes give some public account of their administration first came from the paramount power toward the end of the nineteenth century. In response, the states began to issue annual reports on public administration which gave abbreviated statements of the fiscal situation of the state and of programmes and policies. They provided even less enlightenment than the dullest British Indian provincial reports. But, the need to publish a rudimentary budget encouraged the modern-minded maharajas to differentiate their privy purses from public funds. This in turn led to a sense that purses should have a known and regular relationship to state revenue. In time, 10 per cent came to be considered the correct proportion. This limit was not always observed. Thus, Kotah, in 1935–36, allocated 16 per cent of state revenues to palace expenses, and Bikaner allocated about 17 per cent in 1935–36.[38] States often conveyed the impression in annual reports that they observed the 10 per cent limit when they did not, hiding major palace construction in the figures for the public works department. In 1937–38 Jaipur reported a Rs 1,428,255 palace expenditure but did not choose to report how much of the Rs 1,586,649 public works department figure had gone to the splendid Jaipur House then being built in Delhi, or the George V Solarium, also under construction.[39] (One wonders to what extent princes protected themselves against criticism from the political agent by naming some extravaganza "Prince of Wales Hall".) The reports did not circulate widely but did provide the basis for some public scrutiny. Spokesmen for the sporadic democratic movements in the states liked to point out that the maharaja of a million people ought not, perhaps (as in Bikaner), receive a privy purse of approximately $450,000 when his state spent only about $50,000 for education.[40]

Princes gave such accountings as they did because they were anxious to win approval of the political department. A 'red tick' put opposite their names by the political agent was thought to be most undesirable. The remarks by the viceroy, Lord Irwin, addressed to the Maharaja of Jaipur at the maharaja's formal assumption of office in 1932 indicate the steps taken by the Government of India to insure a ruler's concern with administrative performance, and also illustrate the benignly paternal atmosphere from which that concern took its meaning.

> For the last six months you have been receiving administrative training in your own State under the personal supervision of Mr Glancy. In that time, short though it is, you have had an opportunity of studying the working of all principal State departments, have regularly attended the meetings of the Council and have made several tours of inspection in

> more distant portions of the State. It is a great pleasure to have received from Mr Glancy such favourable reports of quick understanding displayed by Your Highness of State affairs and of your appreciation of duties of your high position.[41]

The more educated princes were also eager to win respect in the world of modern-minded maharajas. Enough of the twentieth century rulers had been abroad or had received a cosmopolitan education to know what was expected of a modern state and to develop some aspirations to build one. Democratic movements, made up of individuals whom the princes considered inferior or *déclassé,* were probably least influential among those to whom the maharajas felt accountable.

All of these reforms, from the known and limited privy purse to departmental reorganization, while they did introduce elements of rationalization and reduce the scope of personal government, were more formal than substantive. If an annual report bore witness that the appurtenances of contemporary administrative practice had been achieved, they also contained more aspirations than accomplishments. The larger states did more than the smaller, and of the larger, Bikaner, Jaipur, and possibly Jodhpur progressed farther than traditional-minded Udaipur. The quaint accounts of visiting political agents and the quainter language of the administrative reports sometimes give a more reliable impression than the administrative reports' facts. In Udaipur, for example, according to Sir Arthur Lothian who had occasion to know it well as resident, the attempt to maintain personal rule in the literal sense continued to recent times. His account of the Maharana of Udaipur, who died in 1930, illustrates how thin a veneer reforms could be:

> I have never seen a finer or more dignified countenance than that of the old Maharana. Kindliness and nobility were written all over it. He was the quintessence of courtesy, and an excellent Ruler, according to his lights. He, old-fashioned however, attempted to control the administration of his big state in every detail himself, which under modern conditions was beyond the capacity of any human being. Although, therefore, he wore himself out with his constant labours, the arrears became so great that the administration got hopelessly clogged... One instance of the arrears into which things had fallen came to my personal knowledge. The return of prisoners in the State Jail happened to be shown to me one day, and I noticed that two men had been confined in jail under sentence of death for twelve years. On enquiry into what had

> happened, it transpired that the death sentences, which required the Ruler's confirmation, had been sent to the late Maharaja twelve years before for this purpose, but had got mislaid somewhere amid the masses of papers awaiting his attention, and the prisoners were, therefore, kept on indefinitely as if they had been under trial. In the outcome this redounded to their advantage as they were sentenced to twenty years rigorous imprisonment in lieu of the death penalty and the years they had already served in jail were deducted from this.[42]

Changes in the relationships between princes and noblemen, the degree of public accountability, and administrative and financial reforms were parallelled by movements to expand the political community, to make government popularly accountable, and to secure the rights of subjects through settled legal and administrative procedures. The Rajputana states had insulated themselves with remarkable success from the social and intellectual ferment that affected British India in the mid-nineteenth century. What is sometimes (and curiously) referred to as the Indian 'renaissance', that mixture of English liberal and Indian nationalist ideas which captured the consciousness of the burgeoning professional and business middle classes, affected Rajasthan hardly at all. Nor did changes in the economy, communications and education touch it substantially. Control of the press and bad communications conspired to prevent the excellent British Indian papers from circulating regularly in Rajasthan. Jai Narayan Vyas, later Chief Minister in post-independence Rajasthan, had to print nationalist literature in Ajmer, a British Indian enclave set in the midst of the Rajasthan states, and to smuggle it out.[43] Some of the princely states insisted that not merely presses but even typewriters be registered. Education lagged, and so did the emergence of a modern economy and modern middle classes. Urbanization was insignificant. Political associations were few and usually ephemeral and severely restricted.

The feebleness of modern associational life until the mid-1930s was in part due to the lack of interest or the timidity of subjects. Also responsible was the Indian National Congress decision, taken in 1920 when it laid plans for the mass organization of nationalism,[44] not to include the princely states. In its Nagpur Constitution of 1920, Congress assigned responsibility for particular princely states to established provincial Congress committees.[45] Political activists from the princely states could belong to the nearby provincial committees, but Congress failed to take the same interest in their activities as it did in those of British India. Both practical and ideological considerations shaped this policy of self-restraint. Many members feared, Pattabhi Sitaramayya wrote, "Congress [would] be embroiling itself with the local vagaries and idiosyncracies of a variety of states, 562 in number, a task obviously beyond the pale of the practical politics Congress".[46] Gandhi went further: "That part of India which is described as British has no more power to shape the policy of the states than it has (say) that of Afghanistan or Ceylon".[47] His views were representative of the conservative wing of Congress.[48] To its adherents foreign autocracy was more reprehensible, apparently, than was indigenous autocracy. The Congress Left, including Nehru, opposed "this hush-hush policy [of non-interference]... adhered to by [Gandhi] in spite of the most extraordinary and painful occurrences in the States".[49] Nehru pictured Gandhi's views as most welcome to the rulers.[50]

Gandhi's attitude towards Indian princes, under whom his father and grandfather had served as chief ministers, was indeed positive. Their benign autocracy did not disturb him, although specific abuses might. If (for certain purposes and in certain contexts) he supported democracy, he never fully committed himself to the principles of popular or representative government over those of responsive autocracy. In line with important aspects of Indian traditional thought, which looks to inner virtue rather than institutional restraints as the guarantor of public morality, Gandhi was more concerned in the 1920's with the personal debauchery of princes, where it existed, than with their failure to grant political liberty:

> My ideal of Indian states is that of *Rama Rajya* [the rule of the epic hero Rama]... By abandoning his kingdom and living in the forest for the sake of truth. Rama gave to all kings of the world an object lesson in noble conduct. By his strict monogamy he showed that life of perfect self-restraint could be led by a royal householder. He lent splendour to his throne by his popular administration and proved that *Rama Rajya* was the acme of *swaraj* [self-rule]. Rama did not need the very imperfect modern instrument of ascertaining public opinion by counting votes. He had captivated the hearts of the people. He knew public opinion by intuition, as it were... Such *Rama Rajya* is possible even today.[51]

Although the All-India States Peoples Conference was formed by prominent Congressmen in 1927, and thereafter acted as a kind of sister organization to Congress, it was hardly militant in its early years. Some of its leaders, moderates in Indian politics like C.Y. Chintamani and Ram Chandra Rao, former Chief Minister of Mysore, were not involved with the more radical nationalist movement and steered the Conference conservatively. Only in the later 1930's under the leadership of Pattabhi Sitaramayya and eventually Nehru, did the States Peoples Conference take a more militant turn. At the same time, both Gandhi and Congress shifted to a more active interventionism. They did so partly because pressure by popular movements in some non-Rajput princely states, notably Mysore, forced them to. As Sardar Patel, the Congress's great organizing talent, put it: "The policy of non-intervention by the Congress was, in my opinion, a perfect piece of statesmanship when the people of the States were not awakened. That policy would be cowardice when there is all-round awakening among the people of the States".[52] Congress also changed its policy following the passage of the Government of India Act of 1935 because the prospect of a federal government under it, including representatives from the princely states, spurred Congress on. So long as government in the princely states was autocratic, the princely states' delegations could be counted upon to be nominees of the princes, who in turn could be expected to support conservative and anti-nationalist policies in the federal legislature. Faced with a coalition of princely state representatives and other non-Congress elements, Congress could expect to be a minority. By devoting more attention to the movement for freedom in the princely states, Congress hoped to soften or neutralize if not capture their representatives. In the event, the princely states could not make up their minds to join the federation, and a federal legislature never met. Before this result became apparent, however, the prospect of it so doing affected associational life and political consciousness in the princely states.

The policy of the Congress began to shift in 1936, and the Haripura session in 1938 sanctioned the organization of Congress committees in princely states provided they undertook neither parliamentary activity nor direct action in Congress's name.[53] By 1939, Gandhi personally backed the States Peoples Freedom Movement, as it became known, to the extent of reviewing and guiding all the activities of the Jaipur Praja Mandal (Jaipur People's Society), the popular movement's organization in that state. He was drawn into its activities by his close friend and disciple, a wealthy Rajasthani businessman, long-time Congressman, and treasurer of the Indian National

Congress, Jamnalal Bajaj. Bajaj, as president of the Jaipur Praja Mandal, was refused entry to the state, and the Mandal was forbidden to hold public meetings and proceedings. Bajaj and his followers offered civil resistance and were sent to jail.[54] One brief letter exchange illustrates Gandhi's close but conservative interest in Jaipur affairs. Bajaj wrote to Gandhi on January 29, 1940: "I showed you the letter I received from the Home Minister of Jaipur. I enclose a draft of the reply I propose to send him. You will kindly return it to me with the necessary corrections." Gandhi replied: "Your draft is not properly worded. Your complaint is directed against the Maharaja. I don't consider it advisable to bring him in".[55]

Most of the larger princely states had active movements towards the end of the 1930's, though some had them much earlier.[56] The movements were led mostly, though not exclusively, by Brahman and Kayasth (caste of scribes) schoolmasters, such as Hiralal Shastri in Jaipur, Haribhau Upadhyaya in Ajmer, Bhogilal Pandya in Dungarpur, Manikyalal Verma in Udaipur, and Master Bhola Nath in Alwar, and by the new profession of lawyers, generally also Brahman or Kayasth,[57] and were supported by some members of the merchant castes.[58] That the literate castes should have been leaders in the movement is not surprising, since their literacy made available to them currents of thought other than those generally accepted in Rajasthan. On the other hand, it is not self-evident that their leadership should have been directed towards social and political change. One of the most fascinating features of Indian political and social development has been the role of the Brahmans, guardians par excellence of tradition and the sacred order, as the bearers of the new political and social ideas. The vicarious authority which Brahmans and members of the other twice-born castes lent to innovation may help explain the relative ease with which India has taken to social and political change over the past 150 years.

Most of the prominent members of the literate castes in Rajasthan were attached to the bureaucracies of the princely states, or dependent on the court for trade and other patronage. But those who led the freedom movement had, almost without exception, some independent occupational base: as schoolmasters and lawyers they were not directly dependent on court patronage. If they were dependent, like Shastri (office superintendent under Finance Member Atal in Jaipur state) they left their posts before becoming active in the Praja Mandal. For the *most* part they were city men; the peasant castes and rural people were scarcely represented.

Members of the merchant castes were active in the freedom movement, especially in Jodhpur. Jamnalal Bajaj, one of Gandhi's most important financial supporters, was an important figure in Jaipur state as well as on the national scene. Gandhi's efforts to organize and encourage non-political social service organizations and through them his campaigns to prevent the sale or consumption of alcoholic drinks and even to aid untouchables appealed to the merchant castes, already attached by religion and custom to teetotalism and non-violence. In the mid-1930's members of merchant castes were particularly prominent as officers of the Harijan Sevak Sangh (Service Society for Untouchables).[59] Formally apolitical, it had strong reformist overtones and was explicitly connected to Gandhi's programme.

Some of those who joined the freedom movement did so because of their mobile sensibilities,[60] their capacity to imagine themselves and others under circumstances other than those which the traditional society prescribed; some joined because they had fallen from favour; some because a rebellious disposition made them unable and unwilling to 'succeed' under the conditions of courtierly behaviour required in a princely state. Even Rajasthanis who did not join the nationalist movement speak with bitterness of remembered humiliation, of being made to "feel small" in the presence of ministers, of not being offered a seat by those in authority, or of being required to express themselves in ways they found degrading. Some joined because they were idealists prepared to take risks. The Gandhian appeal made sense to these men because it did not demand the martial style which was incompatible with their non-Kshatriya aversion to violence. Instead, it proposed self-suffering of a kind long familiar to Brahmans, whose ancestors had fasted or immolated themselves in response to unjust exactions. It appealed to the instincts for pedagogy of the traditionally literate castes now in the roles of schoolmasters or lawyers, who were asked to carry their Gandhian and nationalist teachings to rural people, bringing the message of moral and material conditions as they were elsewhere and might be here too.[61] Still others, having been educated in British India, found the political climate in Rajputana incompatible with what they had learned.

The earliest activities of the freedom movement are difficult to isolate and identify. A variety of local issues just after World War I and, subsequently, during Gandhi's first civil disobedience campaign, took on added meaning from national events and concerns. In 1918, Manikyalal Verma and Vijay Singh Pathik organized a peasant *satyagraha* (non-violent resistance campaign) against forced labour at Bijolia, Udaipur. Verma's arrests in 1918 and 1922[62] vaguely united the political consciousness arising out of protests over local grievances with that of the larger nationalist movement. The Marwar Hitkarni Sabha (Marwar Improvement Society) formed in the early 1920's in Jodhpur state by Jai Narayan Vyas and other Jodhpuri political activists, aimed at freeing the state from the rule of 'aliens': a Chief Minister and other non-Jodhpuri officials both Indian and English. Its motto was "Marwar [Jodhpur] for the Marwaris" and its design to protect local interests from the effects of administrative reform.[63] The maharaja, happy to free himself from the implicit restraints which outsiders represented, gave the Sabha his blessing, while Vyas saw his role in it as his first contribution to the freedom movement. Such political ambiguity was not unique to Jodhpur.

In the "Sikar rebellion" of 1937, the backward-looking Rao Raja of the largest estate in Jaipur asserted the claims of feudal liberty against those of centralizing absolutism in resisting the maharaja's British officered armed forces. In this struggle between prince and feudal aristocrat, the middle-class Jaipur Praja Mandal to a degree backed the claims of Sikar in an effort to advance the fortunes of representative government and public liberties.[64] At the same time, the maharaja was inclined to be more sympathetic to the Praja Mandal under the Jaipuri leadership of Bajaj than was his government under the direction of a British chief minister.[65] Freedom movements affected by local patriotism and susceptible to palace influence were sometimes useful in dealing with pressures for administrative reform from the political department and a maharaja's own government.

Freedom organizations of a clearly anti-princely cast, however, faced grave obstacles. Jai Narayan Vyas, whose first organization, the Hitkarni Sabha, was banned in 1924,[66] became adept at shaping new ones as those he created were outlawed. He formed in quick succession the Jodhpur Praja Mandal, the Youth League, and the Marwar Lok Parishad. Whenever Vyas had trouble in his home state of Jodhpur, or was ordered out of other states in the areas,[67] he guided his movements from Ajmer, the British enclave in the middle of Rajasthan, or from Bombay. Ajmer played an important role throughout the nationalist years since British administration made it a haven for agitators expelled from the princely states. In 1921 and again in 1930–32, the civil disobedience movement of British India found its counterparts there.

The less political Rajasthan Sevak Sangh, a Gandhian non-political service organization, fared better, although its leaders sometimes engaged in political activities. It began at Ajmer in the late 1920's and even employed paid workers in some states.[68] Early activities in Bikaner, Kotah, and other states coincided with the civil disobedience movement of 1931–32 in British India. In Kotah, the Haravati Praja Mandal imitated the British Indian agitation by picketing liquor and foreign cloth shops in 1931 and 1932.[69] But even these associations tended to lead precarious lives since most states disapproved of any association which, in the words of the Bikaner Public Safety Act of 1932, was "likely to create disaffection against the Maharaja or his government".[70] Assembly, publication and speech were more restricted than in British India. But, the pattern of restriction varied: Kotah reports meetings of up to 300 persons in 1937–38, not insignificant for a small (population 7,00,000) state, and successive meetings through at least 1941 favouring responsible government, federation of princely and British India, compulsory education, and temperance.[71] In Bharatpur, the Praja Mandal sought "to secure responsible government under the aegis of His Highness the Maharaja". When it attempted to organize a campaign to withhold payment of land revenue from the state, the Mandal was declared unlawful in April 1937. Four hundred and seventy three individuals were detained in connection with the campaign and 212 were arrested – again, not a small agitation in a state containing only 5,00,000 people.[72] Jaipur and Jodhpur alternately forbade and permitted Praja Mandals and Lok Parishads to function. In Jodhpur in 1937, the Civil Liberties Union and the Praja Mandal were declared unlawful and their president, A.P. Sharma, arrested.[73] Since Seth Jamnalal Bajaj, the Jaipur leader, was a man of national stature and treasurer of the Indian National Congress, the Jaipur *durbar* was in constant embarrassment regarding methods of dealing with him, but eventually admitted both him and the Praja Mandal to public activity. In Bikaner, the Public Safety Act of 1932 acted as a strong deterrent. Udaipur banned the Praja Mandal in 1938, as soon as it was founded, and expelled its founder.[74] Sirohi and Alwar also had active movements, while Dungarpur and Banswara had developed a tiny but impressive service organization working in a Gandhian spirit among the Bhil tribes.

The life of the 'old nationalists' was not always easy, Manikyalal Verma came out of the non-violent resistance movement at Bijolia badly beaten, as did Gokulbhai Bhatt out of a Sirohi meeting in 1939.[75] Mrs Verma was imprisoned for two years in 1934.[76] Narottamlal Joshi, later speaker of the Rajasthan legislature,[77] was beaten twice on the same day by Rajput landholders of small estates for the effrontery of campaigning for political freedom and tenant rights in Jaipur's first election in 1945. He was attacked near a police station, the occupants of which remained inactive throughout the assault, and believes he escaped death only because his assailants stuck at Brahman killing. Unable to walk, he was tied to a camel and abandoned in a forest.[78]

The attempt to win responsible government did not succeed. In 1913 Maharaja Ganga Singh established what he liked to call the "Bikaner Representative Assembly". The organization had the power to pass bills. In reality, however, it provided no forum for criticism, much less for the exercise of power by representatives independent of the Crown, since the assembly was dominated by a majority nominated by the maharaja, and the climate of the institution was courtierly and placating. "I have nothing special to mention in connection with the budget," a representative said while speaking in the budget debate, "except that this year's budget is an occasion of great delight for us as it contains a provision for the estimated expenditure of the celebration of His Highness Sri Maharaj Kumarji Sahib's auspicious marriage, which auspicious marriage celebration has come after many years, and it would be an occasion of great delight for every loyal subject of the state".[79] The budget had been delivered to members on the day previous to the debate, and it passed in a few hours. The assembly met for three days in the year.[80] Similar bodies were introduced in Jaipur and Jodhpur in the 1940's, but until after the war their powers were insignificant. The Jaipur assembly saw a budget for the first time in 1946.[81] After the war, as independence rushed ominously closer and democracy began to loom as a real possibility, most of the states moved swiftly towards popular governments, which were soon superseded by the amalgamation of Rajasthan's 22 princely states into one.

In British India, the political associations and representative institutions of the nationalist era served as an important recruiting ground for post-independence political leadership. In Rajasthan, this function was indifferently performed. The experience which British Indian Congressmen developed in the Swarajist days of the 1920's when they joined legislatures, or in the short-lived provincial governments of the 1930's, or in district boards and municipalities, was missing altogether in Rajasthan, where there were no meaningful representative institutions, unless a few municipalities deserve the title. And, the Praja Mandals too were inadequate training grounds for later state politics. The small movements required devotion and idealism, but they did not develop new organizational and administrative skills on the part of their leaders. Because they were personal, comradely organizations, each coinciding with a princely state, they resembled the small state governments in that no high professional competence was required to manage them. The British Indian political movements, because they covered large linguistic areas, developed in their leaders a capacity to build rational and effective political structures, so as to co-ordinate diverse political interests, and to formulate and communicate policies. The Rajasthan political organizations, because they were very small operations, developed few qualities that would equip their alumni in later years to take over the large-scale unified government of the 22 states of Rajasthan. In fact, this early political experience may even have disqualified them for their later tasks. They carried the narrow horizons of parochial princely states into the politics of the larger state, failing to shift easily to the more abstract general perspectives required in the new circumstances. Many remained small-town politicians when faced with the responsibility of governing 15 million people in new Rajasthan. Yet, when independence came and the old order was superseded, they were the only ones available for the new politics.

Apart from the freedom associations, Rajasthanis did not form voluntary organizations of the kind that grew in British India and structured its emerging middle classes' turn to politics. The Rajasthani middle classes, such as they were, developed few modern institutional channels for action. The universities, the chambers of commerce, the bar, and a host of social, literary, cultural and political associations had given focus to the organized interests of British Indians in the days before a mass movement gave new strength to nationalism. Higher education in the princely states was feeble and dependent on the maharaja. The bar was weakly developed since much legal practice rested with the traditionally trained *vakils* (pleaders), and a modern legal profession had still to emerge. The merchantry was organized in caste associations, but not into any association cutting across caste on the basis of economic or civil interests.[82] Such associations as existed were mostly natural groups congruent with the old society and polity and felt no special reason to upset them. Thus, in 1912, at the silver jubilee of the maharaja of Bikaner, addresses were offered by the following groups: officials of the government, Maheshwari Sahukars (a merchant caste), Oswals (a merchant caste), Brahmans, Pushkarna Brahmans, Jain Swetamber Yatis (Jain holy men), Mohammedans, Sikhs, the Nagri Society, two secondary educational institutions, and the bar association.[83] They made no political demands, restricting themselves to requesting traditional favours, such as the maharaja's intervention in a serious caste dispute among the merchants or support for some new building or educational enterprise.

Neither the old corporate groups nor the new political associations explicitly demanded expansion of the political community, although that was sometimes a long-range objective. The cry for responsible government amounted rather to a demand for institutions that would make effective the influence of those who already had some claim to be de facto, though not *de jure*, part of the political community – the literate, the twice-born. For the most part, the Brahmans and Vaishyas (merchant castes) and Kayasths in the Congress appealed to others like themselves. But there were exceptions. In a few areas, for example in Jodhpur and Jaipur in the early 1940's, members of the peasant caste of Jats began to develop political consciousness, and elsewhere Congressmen who took seriously Gandhi's guidance went to the rural areas to preach social reform if not political participation.

The 1930's, however, brought one additional sign that the times were changing and that new groups were emerging at the edge of the political community. Census reports as far back as 1891, and other official records of much earlier vintage, record that in the British Indian provinces certain lower and middle castes were beginning to organize themselves to press courts, temples, and administrative bodies for recognition of rights, privileges, and higher status than tradition assigned them. These efforts foreshadowed attacks on the traditional order of castes.[84] The censuses of Rajasthan in the twentieth century, on the other hand, reported very few developments of this sort before 1930. In 1911, a Kayasth group tried to list itself as Brahman, as did the Bhargavas (another caste). Some individual members of castes made up of illegitimate descendants of Rajputs tried to have themselves listed as

Rajputs. But the efforts were sporadic and apparently involved very few people.[85]

The main agricultural caste in Rajasthan is the Jats: they comprise the largest single caste group in the state (9 per cent), and were, in the 1930's and even earlier, the most self-conscious and prosperous among the peasant castes. In 1935 their claims to certain privileges led to a series of clashes between them and the Rajputs, who resisted their attempts to revise accepted signs of status. The clash of 1935 is reminiscent of similar ones in other areas between lower castes on the rise and higher established castes.[86]

The Jat demonstrations broke out in Sikar, the largest *thikana* in Jaipur state, and involved both economic and social issues. The Jats in the area had formed two associations – the Sikarwati Jat Panchayat and the Jat Kisan Sabha – and had received some help and encouragement from the British Indian province of Uttar Pradesh. Some of these 'outsiders' were organizers for the socialist-oriented Kisan Sabha, which attempted to mobilize the peasantry in the 1930's in response to radical pressures in the Congress.

The initial demonstration in Khuri village on March 27, 1935 was occasioned by a social issue, whether a Jat bridegroom should be allowed to ride to his bride's house on a horse, a ceremonial act asserting higher station than Rajputs were prepared to concede. The Rajputs objected, the Jats insisted, fighting broke out, and an old Jat was killed. The incident led to further clashes, and the *thikana* police, the Sikar Lancers, under command of the English chief of the Sikar police, charged the Jat crowds with *lathis* (quarter-staffs), injuring many. This incident was followed by others as Jats in the area protested against the revenue collections and resisted and attacked Sikar revenue officials on April 22 at Bhaironpura and at Kudan village on April 25. The Sikar police killed four Jats while putting down this last demonstration and arrested 104 persons. The anti-rent agitation eventually involved some 21 villages, and local headmen were as active as any outsiders. A school where, according to the Jaipur *durbar,* unlawful doctrines were being preached by a Jat teacher from outside the state, was knocked down. The agitation had some effects. The Rao Raja of Sikar remitted all arrears of revenue previous to 1934 and promised to open schools, provide loans where needed, and embark on a permanent land settlement that would introduce some certainty into the vagaries of the *thikana's* revenue demand.[87]

There was some evidence that the more advanced peasantry were beginning to insist on some regulation of their land rights. Beginning as early as 1872 in Alwar, most states undertook survey and settlement operations in *khalsa* (crown lands), that is, they prepared records of rights and established regular revenue demands. In the judgment of an inquiry committee of high civil servants from British India that reported on tenant rights at the time of independence, "the tenant [of khalsa] has his rights defined and secured, and there is, on the whole, little cause for him to complain".[88] But in the *jagir* (nobles' estates) lands, which made up a substantial part of most states (about half), records were rarely kept, collection procedures remained arbitrary, and peasants had no protection. Only 32 per cent of the 16,780 *jagir* villages in all of Rajasthan had been settled (their revenue obligations officially specified and limited) by 1947.[89] A number of *durbars* tried to press settlement, but their efforts were strongly resisted by the *jagirdars.* No one doubted that tenants had customary rights, including in many cases rights of inheritance, mortgage, and fixed rents. But so long as these rights were not established by enforceable laws and administrative procedures, they were subject to the *jagirdar's* discretion; the nobles rightly regarded settlement as a diminution of his own powers. But it was a limitation that would in turn have conferred upon tenants rights most fundamental in a peasant society – rights in land.

Most *durbars* did not undertake *jagir* settlement before the 1930's and 1940's. Such operations as were undertaken in *jagir* lands proved dangerous, especially in small holdings where the landlord and tenant were not very far apart economically. In 1937, the Jaipur *durbar* pressed settlement in Udaipurwati, an area adjoining Sikar, where the Jat agitation had taken place, only to see its revenue officials chased out by irate small *jagirdars.*[90] In 1947, the Jaipur *durbar* passed enabling legislation for laying down rules concerning rights in land and for establishing procedures and principles fixing land rent in *jagir* areas,[91] a clear indication that the 1937 effort had not advanced far.

Legal procedures were regulated, at least as far as the maharaja's hand reached, by taking over British Indian legal codes with only minor alterations and by establishing courts at various levels to administer that law. A graduated court system with defined jurisdiction existed at Jhalawar and Jaipur in the 1870's, and written codes were taken over, at least formally, in most states by 1910–20. These changes marked an advance toward promulgated law which could be anticipated. It is difficult to say just how meaningful the adoption of the codes and the creation of courts was.[92] Most states were reluctant to have defendants bring in lawyers from British India to argue before these tribunals, a policy which may have been due to a feeling that the local system would not stand scrutiny, or to provincial fears that the local judiciary might be made to look foolish by 'slick' Bombay barristers, or both. In any case, the new law impinged less than in British India on the local, pluralistic caste and customary law, a circumstance that may have been congenial to Rajasthanis but that illustrates the restricted development of the legal power of the state.

The new conceptions of government were compelling enough to teach some maharajas how a respectable ruler conducts himself. Responsibility to the public welfare and effective performance were added to birth in judging the legitimacy of rule. Public reports of government action implied that princely expenditure amounted to a public budget, not merely a private household account, and thus favoured the differentiation of the public and private roles of the prince. They also implied that the prince in his public capacity was accountable to someone other than himself. Associations developed enough to introduce, at least in the minds of the literate, ideas of representation and consent and to undermine the self-evident quality of princely rule. Advances in administration, particularly fixing of the revenue demand, introduced the principle that government action ought to follow certain rules. The prince often consulted his fellow princes, or the political department, or his now more modern conscience. But his new sense of public responsibility, of effective performance, and regular procedures fell short of establishing a modern state or constitutional rule in Rajasthan.

The emergence of a modern state, the revision of traditional notions of legitimacy, and the growth of popular politics progressed too slowly under paramountcy to be of any real help to Rajasthan when it became part of India. The attempts to centralize authority and regularize administration did not carry very far and were often more formal than substantive. Compared to British India, the development of associational life in Rajputana was slight. No real concessions were made to political participation and institutional restraints on autocratic power. Important changes did occur, but, without roots in society and consciousness, they lacked substance.

Notes

We are grateful to the Ford Foundation for its grant under the Foreign Area Training Programme, which allowed us to visit Rajasthan in 1956–57. The library of the University of Rajasthan has holdings of the administrative reports of the princely states that make up Rajasthan, holdings that were taken over from the Residency at Mount Abu. Runs of these reports are partial and incomplete. We took advantage of our stay to record the recollections of a substantial number of persons who participated in the States Peoples Freedom Movement and in the social transformation of the last forty years. These have been cited as sources at the appropriate points. Since communications media in the princely states were sparse, these sources are more significant than they would be in British India.

The character of pre-British Rajasthan is described in James Tod, *Annals and Antiquities of Rajasthan, or, the Central and Eastern Rajput States of India* (2 vols. in 1; London, 1950). Our citations are from this edition. William Crooke's annotated edition in three volumes (London, 1920) corrects some of Tod's findings. Daniel Thorner's essay, "Feudalism in India", in Rushton Coulborn (ed.), *Feudalism in History* (Princeton, N.J., 1956), deals with Tod's Rajasthan. See also A.C. Banerjee, *Rajput Studies* (Calcutta, 1944) and *The Rajput States and the East India Company* (Calcutta, 1951); Alfred Lyall, "The Rajput States of India", in his *Asiatic Studies, Religious and Social* (London, 1881). pp. 181–228.

1. As Sir William Lee-Warner judiciously put it: "There are no collections of political rules, and no authoritative treatises to guide the inquirer. These matters are, according to some opinions, best left alone as the mysteries of the trade... the absence of any definite interstatal law must be recognized as depriving the states united to the Indian Empire of the safeguard which all law or system provides". [Sir William Lee-Warner, *The Native States of India* (London, 1910), pp. 2–3.]
2. "Reports of the committee on the relationship between the paramount power and the states" (Butler Committee), *Parliamentary Papers* (Great Britain, Reports of Commissioners, 1928–29), Vol. VI, Cd. 3302.
3. Coinage was still a function of several states in Rajputana in the 1870's when the *Rajputana Gazetteer* was compiled [*Rajputana Gazetteer* (3 vols.; Calcutta ca. 1870)].
4. For accounts of the general trends of paramountcy see Lee-Warner; H.H. Dodwell (ed.), *The Cambridge History of India* (5 vols.; Cambridge, 1922–60), Vol. VI, chap. xxvii; K.M. Panikkar. *Introduction to the Study of the Relations of Indian States with the Government of India* (London, 1927).
5. K.M. Panikkar, *His Highness the Maharaja of Bikaner* (London, 1937), p. 94.
6. Earl of Ronaldsbay, *Life of Curzon* (3 vols.; London, 1928), Vol. II; John Buchan, *Lord Minto* (London, 1924); Mary, Countess of Minto. *India, Minto and Morley, 1905–1910* (London, 1934).

7. See Lee-Warner for a broad survey.
8. Annual Report on the Administration of the Kotah State (hereafter cited as "A.K.S.") August 1896-July 1897, p. 3.
9. See Panikkar, *Maharaja of Bikaner,* p. 56, for a document outlining the conditions of rulership. The operative clause reads: "His Highness the Maharaja will not act against the Political Officer's advice in any important matter".
10. We are grateful to Major Thakur Raghubir Singh of Bissau, Raja Kalyan Singh of Bhinai, and General Thakur Nathu Singh of Gumanpura for descriptions of the atmosphere and education at Mayo College at Ajmer, the princes' and nobles' school for Rajputana. Their memories cover the 1930's. Mayo College was established by Lord Mayo, viceroy from 1869 to 1872. See W.W. Hunter, *A Life of the Earl of Mayo* (2nd ed.; 2 vols., London, 1876), I, p. 221.
11. See Rupert Wilkinson, *Gentlemanly Power* (New York, 1964), for an analysis of the relationship between such educational culture and the character of public men.
12. Jaipur and Jodhpur had British *dewans* (chief ministers), Beauchamp St. John at Jaipur and Peter Young and Donald Field at Jodhpur, in the late 1930's or early 1940's. Of Jaipur's eight major bureaucratic posts, six were held by Englishmen in 1937–38. Bikaner also employed a series of British officials in Maharaja Ganga Singh's era, but not for the post of *dewan (Report on the Administration of the Jaipur State* [hereafter cited as *"AJS"],* 1937–38, and the same for 1938–39; Panikkar *(Maharaja of Bikaner).*
13. Sir Arthur Lothian, *Kingdoms of Yesterday* (London, 1951), pp. 133–34.
14. "Report on Indian Constitutional Reforms", *Parliamentary Papers* (Great Britain, Reports of Commissioners, 1918), Vol. VIU, Cd. 9109.
15. In K.M. Panikkar, *The Indian Princes in Council* (London, 1936), pp. 18–20.
16. Among these men were Sardar K.M. Panikkar, Sir V.T. Krishnamachari, Sir Manubhai Mehta, Sir Mirza Ismail, and C.S. Venkatachar. Of these, Panikkar has given some idea of his activities in the works cited, as has Krishnamachari (see below). Sir Mirza Ismail gives an account in *My Public Life* (London, 1954).
17. A few states came into alliance with Britain after 1818.
18. Speech at Gwalior, November 29,1899. Cited in Earl of Ronald-shay, *Life of Curzon* II, pp. 89–90.
19. Tod suggests that a number of states were consolidating their military position independently of the nobility. This was true of Jodhpur, Jaipur, Bikaner, and Jaisalmer (Tod, *Annals,* II, p. 134, 162, 228, 351). It is evident from his report of the Maharaja of Jodhpur's dispute with his nobles that Tod favoured the diffusion of power. See letter from Rathor nobles to Colonel Tod (ibid., I, p. 160), and Tod's critical report of the maharaja's "overgrown establishments, to maintain a superiority over the feudal lords" (ibid., II, p. 134).
20. Lyall, "Rajput States".

21. Tod, *Annals* II, pp. 423–25.
22. See accounts of these states in *Rajputana Gazetteer.*
23. C.V. Wills, *A Report on the Land Tenures and Special Powers of Certain Thikanedars of the Jaipur State* (Delhi, 1933). For the response of some Jaipur nobles to the Jaipur *durbar's* claims see John Jackson, *A Reply to the Report on the Land Tenures and Special Powers of Certain Thikanedars of the Jaipur State (by C.V. Wills) on Behalf of the Panchpana Sardars (including Khetri) and Seekar* (Delhi, n.d.).
24. *Jaipur Gazette Extraordinary,* May 19, 1939, No. 4864, reports the *durbar's* decision.
25. Ibid., p. 12.
26. See Percy M. Sykes, *Life of Sir Mortimer Durand* (London, 1926), p. 172. They were later known as "Indian States Forces".
27. *AJS,* September 1947-August 1948.
28. Interviews with Raja Kalyan Singh of Bhinai, son-in-law of the Rao Raja of Sikar and with the Rao Raja of Sikar, autumn, 1956. The Sikar rebellion telescoped a feudal and a democratic nationalist interest in resisting the state of Jaipur. For a recent account of the rebellion, see Barnett Rubin, Feudal Revolt and State Building (New Delhi, 1983).
29. Panikkar, *Maharaja of Bikaner,* p. 89.
30. Conversation, summer 1961, with the late Sir Arthur Lothian, formerly the Resident in Rajputana.
31. Conversation with the same, summer 1957. The Maharawal of Dungarpur confirmed, in conversation in 1963, that he opposed such consolidation.
32. Panikkar, *Maharaja of Bikaner,* p. 70.
33. Ibid., p. 25.
34. Sir V.T. Krishnamachari, *Speeches of Sir V.T. Krishnamachari* (Jaipur, 1949), p. 46.
35. We collated educational data on 143 group A and B *tahsildars* (the rankings refer to the status assigned to them in the united civil service of the new state). These men had been originally recruited to the civil services of the various princely states. Ten per cent of twenty-nine men recruited in the 1920's held B.A. degrees or better; of the sixty-three recruited in the 1930's, 56 per cent; and of the fifty-one in 1940–47, 94 per cent [Government of Rajasthan, *Civil List of Rajasthan,* 1956 [(Jodhpur, 1956), pp. 72–90].
36. See Saranghadar Das, Bikaner; Report submitted to the President, All India States Peoples' Conference [Bombay, n.d. (ca. 1940)], p. 38.
37. Letter to the authors from Mohan Mukerji, lAS, special secretary to government, Rajasthan, Nov. 30, 1956. Mr Mukerji had charge of establishment matters.

38. *A.K.S.*, 1935–1936 (n.p., n.d.). By our calculation, Kotah spent Rs 7,87,647 on the palace and his highness's family, polo ponies, elephants, royal gardens, guests, rewards, marriages, and work on royal properties. According to the state's own report, the privy purse would have been nearer 10 per cent. A lower figure than ours, Rs 5,57,503, is listed in the report as having been spent on the palace and royal family. We have reached the higher figure by adding to the 'official' figure the other items listed above, which seem to be not clearly public expenses. Bikaner too claimed to spend only 10 per cent on the privy purse, but calculations like ours were made by Das (p. 75), and bring the figure higher.

39. *A.J.S.*, 1937–38.

40. See Das, *Bikaner*, p. 76. The figures relate to the mid-1930's. We have converted Das's figures for Bikaner into dollars, counting 5 rupees to the dollar. The official figure at the date of this writing is 4.7 to the dollar.

41. A.N. Sudarisanam, *Indian States Register and Directory*, 1932 (Madras, 1932), p. 245. The maharaja had succeeded to the *gaddi* as an eleven-year old minor in 1922.

42. Lothian, *Kingdoms*, pp. 193–94.

43. Interview with Mr Vyas, November 1956.

44. Pattabhi Sitaramayya, *The History of the Indian National Congress*. Vol. II, 1935–47 (2 vols.; Bombay, 1947), p. 78.

45. Article V of the Nagpur Constitution. See N.V. Rajkumar, *Development of the Congress Constitution* (New Delhi, 1949). For what the clause meant in practice, see the letter of N.C. Kelkar, president of the All India States Peoples Conference, to Gandhi, June 2,1934 [M.K. Gandhi, *The Indian States Problem* (Ahmedabad, 1941), p. 60].

46. Sitaramayya, *History of Congress* II, p. 79.

47. Gandhi to Kelkar, July 2,1934, *Indian States Problem*, p. 65.

48. Vallabhai Patel urged in 1935 that workers in Indian states "should do their work with all the limitations imposed by the state, and instead of criticising the administration, efforts should be made to keep up cordial relations between the ruler and the ruled" [cited in *Jawaharlal Nehru, an Autobiography* (new ed.; London, 1942), p. 533n.].

49. Ibid., p. 532.

50. Ibid.

51. Kathiawad Conference address, January 8, 1925 [reprinted in M.K. Gandhi, *Young India*, 1924–26 (New York, 1927), p. 472].

52. *Times of India*, January 25, 1939, quoted in N.D. Parikh, *Sardar Vallabhai Patel*, translated from the Gujarati (2 vols.; Ahmedabad, 1953), II, p. 299. Gandhi's movement toward a more interventionist policy was intensified by the difficulties of those pressing for reforms in Rajkot where his father had been Chief Minister.

53. "Congress Committees in the States shall function under the direction and control of the Congress Working Committee and shall not engage in parliamentary activity nor launch direct action in the name and under the auspices of the Congress. Internal struggles of the people of the States must not be undertaken in the name of the Congress. For this purpose independent organizations should be started". [Indian National Congress, Report of the General Secretary, March 1938-February 1939 (Allahabad, 1939), p. 7.]

54. *The Indian States Problem,* p. 117,157, 378. Details of the Jaipur Public Societies Regulation Act may be found in N.N. Mitra, *The Indian Annual Register,* 1938, I, pp. 321–22.

55. Kaka Kalelkar (ed.), *To a Gandhian Capitalist* (Bombay, 1951). The correspondence of January and February 1940 is on pp. 110–12.

56. There is as yet no published history of the Rajasthan political movements. We have based our account to some extent on interviews and biographical materials as well as the particular sources cited. [This is no longer true in 1983.]

57. For biographical data on Rajasthan leaders we consulted M.C. Dandia (ed.), *Rajasthan Yearbook and Who's Who.* 1961–62 (Jaipur, 1962); Rajasthan legislative assembly, *Who's Who* in *the Rajasthan Legislature* (Jaipur, n.d., published between 1954 and 1956) (Hindi); Rajasthan Pradesh Congress Committee, *Who's Who of Congress Candidates* (Jaipur, 1951) (Hindi).

58. On the participation by Jodhpur Oswals and Maheshwaris (merchant castes) see Richard Sisson, "Caste, Faction and Politics: A Case Study in the Rajasthan Congress" (Berkeley, Calif. 1965) p. 3 (mimeographed).

59. Sisson writes that the caste composition of presidents and secretaries of the Harijan Sevak Sangh in Rajputana in 1935 was Brahman, 43; Mahajan (merchant caste), 20; Kayasth, 3; Scheduled caste, 3; Jat, 2; Unknown, 13, Written communication to authors, May, 1965.

60. See Daniel Lerner, *The Passing of Traditional Society: Modernizing the Middle East* (Glencoe, III, 1958) for the phrase.

61. These generalizations emerge from interviews with and visits to the area of influence of Bhogilal Pandya (interview and visit), Haribhau Upadhyaya (visit), Manikyalal Verma (interview and visit), Jai Narayan Vyas (interview and visit), Hiralal Shastri (interview and visit), Gokul Bhai Bhatt (visit).

62. *Rajasthan Yearbook and Who's Who,* 1961–62, p. 256. Biographical material on Manikyalal Verma in sources cited and in ibid. (Jaipur, n.d.), pp. 105–6.

63. Anand Raj Surana and Bhanwarlal Saraf were active in the formation of the Sabha (interview with Jai Narayan Vyas; communication from Sisson, May 1965).

64. The immediate issue was the maharaja's insistence, supported by the resident in Rajasthan, Sir Arthur Lothian, that the heir of Sikar be educated outside Sikar, where it was feared he would be subject to morally reprehensible influences.

The larger issue was the maharaja's power over his noblemen (interview, Sir Arthur Lothian, summer, 1957).

65. So one may infer from the correspondence surrounding the arrest of Bajaj in 1939 (see n. 54).
66. Vyas interview.
67. In 1938 he was ordered out of Alwar (Mitra, *Annual Register*, 1938, II, p. 261).
68. Vyas interview.
69. See Das, *Bikaner*, p. 42, for Bikaner agitation; and *A.K.S.*, 1936–37.
70. Das, *Bikaner*, p. 42.
71. *A.K.S.*, 1937–38, 1938–39, 1940–41.
72. Report on the Administration of the Bharatpur State, November 1938–October 1939.
73. Mitra, *Annual Register*, 1937, II, p. 333, 350.
74. *Rajasthan Yearbook and Who's Who*, 1964, p. 38.
75. In 1939, a Praja Mandal meeting at Sirohi was forcefully broken up by the police (Letter from Gokulbhai Bhatt to Gandhi in *Indian States Problem*, pp. 376–77).
76. *Rajasthan Yearbook and Who's Who*, 1964, p. 106.
77. Interview with Narottamlal Joshi.
78. Similar patterns appear to have characterized events in the neighbouring state of Indore, which enacted a public meeting prevention act. Three political workers were deported for agitating against this act in 1938 (Mitra, *Annual Register*, 1938, II, p. 312).

    On the other hand, Gwalior, in 1939, repealed a circular which had required those who held political meetings to obtain the permission in writing of the *subhas* or *tehsildars* (local officers) or the inspector general of police and which had prohibited *hartals* (suspension of business as a protest), processions, burning of foreign cloth in public, saluting of the national flag, and picketing of liquor shops [Michael H. Brown (ed.), *Gwalior Today* (Bombay, 1940), p. 24].
79. Das, *Bikaner*, p. 84.
80. Ibid; p. 83.
81. Krishnamachari, *Speeches*, p. 2. The neighbouring state of Gwalior did better in this respect. The constitution of 1939 provided for a lower house with an elected majority and an upper house half elected, envisioned enfranchisement of up to 20 per cent of the population, and invested these bodies with the right of initiating legislation and discussing the state budget. The latter provision suggests that the maharaja did not wish to turn over financial power. He also retained the right to veto or pass, on his own initiative, any legislation (Brown, *Gwalior Today*, pp. 22–23).
82. The All India Marwari Federation, which operated outside Rajasthan, united the Rajasthan merchant castes. It lobbied, for example, in 1938, for the removal

of the disqualification of the subjects of the states in government service in British India (Mitra, *Annual Register,* 1938, I, p. 315).

83. Report on the Administration of Bikaner, 1911–12.
84. See Lloyd I. Rudolph and Susanne Hoeber Rudolph, "The Political Role of India's Caste Associations", *Pacific Affairs,* XXXIII (March 1960), pp. 5–22. See also Lloyd I. Rudolph, "The Modernity of Tradition: The Democratic Incarnation of Caste in India", *American Political Science Review,* LIX, No. 4 (December 1965), pp. 975–89.
85. Government of India, *Census of India 1911, Rajputana and Ajmer Merwara* (Ajmer, 1913), Part I, "Report", p. 248–49.
86. For example, the Shanan riots in the nineteenth century in Madras or the Namasudra riots in 1911 in Bengal.
87. *Amrit Bazar Patrika,* April 4, 1935; *Statesmen,* April 4 and 18, May 2 and 16, June 6, 1935; *Times* (London), April 30 and July 5, 1935. [Barnett R. Rubin, *Feudal Revolt.]*
88. Government of India, Ministry of States, Report of the Rajasthan Madhya Bharat Jagir Enquiry Committee (New Delhi, 1950), p. 36.
89. Ibid., p. 34.
90. Conversation with Mr Eric DaCosta, associated with the Jaipur court in the late 1930's; conversations with north Jaipur *jagirdars,* notably Narendar Singh, Thakur of Jobner, and Major Thakur Raghubir Singh of Bissau.
91. Krishnamachari, *Speeches,* p. 11.
92. For discussion of aspects of this question, see Lloyd I. Rudolph and Susanne Hoeber Rudolph, "Barristers and Brahmans in India: Legal Cultures and Social Change", *Comparative Studies in Society and History, VIII,* No.1 (October, 1965), 24–49. [The *articles* referred to in f.n. 84 and the present note are incorporated, in modified fashion, in Lloyd I. Rudolph and Susanne Hoeber Rudolph, *The Modernity of Tradition: Political Development in India* (Chicago, 1967).]

4

Dynamics of Change in Rajasthan Before and After 1947

Comment on a Thematic Focus Note for a Seminar

BHUPENDRA HOOJA

I congratulate the organizers of this national seminar*, which is intended to rediscover the dynamics of social, economic and political changes in Rajasthan before and after 1947. It is a wide field indeed which cannot be covered or compressed in a short two days' seminar. Besides, quite a few disciplines of social sciences and, to some extent, natural sciences are involved. In fact, what is required is a long-term multi-disciplinary study of the several themes and processes connected with the overall transformation and modernization of Rajasthan. May I suggest for the consideration of the academic and other authorities concerned that a separate centre for such studies or at least a multi-disciplinary course about the modernization of Rajasthan should be started not only in the University of Rajasthan but also in other state universities.

Wrong Slant to Rajasthan Studies

There are some 'unhistorical' and perhaps ideological assumptions which have prompted me to comment on the note entitled "Thematic Focus" circulated at this seminar. As has been mentioned under sub-heading *Relevance*, the background to our present discussions in the seminar happen to be a long 58-page note (Narain-Mathur essay) which has been included in the 1990 OUP publication *Dominance and State Power in Modern India: Decline of a Social Order* (New Delhi: Oxford University Press, 1990), edited by Prof Francine Frankel of

Text of the lecture delivered by the author at a national seminar on Social and Economic Dynamics of Rajasthan Politics at the Department of Political Science, University of Rajasthan, Jaipur on November 4–5, 1995.

USA and late Prof M.S.A. Rao of Delhi University. What adds current political significance to this thesis is the article in *Economic and Political Weekly*; (March 12, 1994) on the analysis of the 1993 Vidhan Sabha elections in Rajasthan by Rob Jenkins. In my humble view and the learned two scholars will kindly excuse me if I were to say that this is where the 'mischief' lies. I call it a mischief because there is a wrong ideological slant and misinterpretation of certain historical facts which have given rise to the concept of the 'Rajput polity' in Rajasthan having certain political, social and economic features, which lasted for about a thousand years. Further, it has been stated that this thousands years' Raj gave rise to what have been called the twin aspects of 'Regional Isolation' and 'Rajput Hinduism'.

By way of a personal note, I may mention that I had drawn the attention of one of the contributors of the above mentioned essay to the wrong interpretation or misplaced emphasis on the aspects of Regional Isolation and Rajput Hinduism during the so-called "Thousand Years Raj". Since the essay or its thesis is now being not only paraded or perpetrated through scholarly anthologies as also through the present seminar, I think, the time has come when the main thesis and its ramifications should be discussed threadbare. Let us start the process from today, right here and now; and may I invite social scientists of all disciplines to join in the debate.

Non-Rajput Annals and Aspects of Rajasthan

By way of a start, I may mention that while we have historical works about the origins of the Rajput (and other major communities of Rajasthan and tribes), it is only their historical and political role, largely in terms of the so-called 'princely order' and the military adventures in which they were involved that have been the general and main themes of such historical studies. But now, various other aspects of the socio-economic and cultural history of the diverse people of Rajasthan, with their beliefs, customs, socio-cultural relations and interactions and so on, have started emerging from the dust of history and the mists of mythology. As we explore through these 'new finds' of history and rediscover the medieval past of Rajasthan, we must also have the courage to properly 'qualify' and re-define the 'princely order' and its newly discovered attribute, the 'Cult of Hinduism'. Thus, the well-known work, the *Annals and Antiquities of Rajasthan* and other histories of the various princely states, taken separately or together, as well as our rediscoveries, have unfolded many hidden pages of the military, political, economic, social, cultural and religious history of the diverse elements of our traditional society, its castes, communities and tribes, especially during the medieval and pre-modern eras. More recently, the Anthropological Survey of India has also carried out its study, the report of which about the peoples and communities of Rajasthan is likely to be available in our local book shops and university libraries in the near future.

I have referred to this only to emphasize that since times immemorial and even during the era of Rajput political and military dominance there have also been other (non-Rajputs) castes and communities which have interfaced and interacted with the Rajput rulers and other contemporary tribes and castes to give the peculiar 'composite character' to the culture and policy of this region. In the context when we talk of the 'princely order' or the 'princely states' or what is called 'Rajput polity' (and now Rajput Hinduism) is only a narrow aspect of the social and cultural kaleidoscope. (However, we may stick to some of the terms like the 'princely order' etc. as has been the fashion for the sake of convenience.)

Rajput Polity of Rajasthan: Some Questions about Its Uniquity and Uniqueness

What about this 1,000 years *Raj*? Was it one *Raj* all over the region or many *Rajas* going to war with one another? And what for? And, for how long or in what manner was this an independent or sovereign *Raj* or groups of *Rajas*? These questions would need to be answered honestly and faithfully. Frankly, do we wish to prescribe that ideal or model as 'desirable' and 'sustainable' in the age of democracy? Or, do we mean to suggest that Rajput value system still dominates this land !

But when we come to some other aspects of the theses like "Rajput Hinduism", we must have the facts (and the honesty) to ascertain in what way has the so-called 'Rajput Hinduism' been different from 'non-Rajput Hinduism'. (There can be many other broad groupings of the various communities and castes domiciled in the Rajasthan region over the centuries and adhering to their own ways and rituals of Hinduism.) Should we in that case also coin and bring into currency terms like 'Jat Hinduism', 'Maheshwari Hinduism', 'Gurjar Hinduism', 'Bishnoi Hinduism', and the 'Hinduism' as practised by Scheduled Tribes or various Scheduled Castes (and now Backward

Classes)? I think the learned authors have made the mistake of trying to 'define' a certain aspect and features of Rajput 'princely' political order and their social customs and rituals as 'Rajput Hinduism'.

Secondly, even if it comes to the basic thesis, we may have to yield to situation where the so-called 'Rajput Hinduism' with all its codes of chivalry, valour and sacrifice or the prescribed and formalized codes of conduct in the Rajput *durbars* or the palaces (and with their imitation in the local *thikanas*) – the courtly culture of the ruling elites – may have to be accepted, at best, as symptomatic of the culture of the *durbars*, of the ruling minorities, as against the co-mingling and co-existence of the daily lives and customs and beliefs etc. of the other vast numbers of power-denied social groups, castes and communities.

Parallel Patterns of Political Behaviour

Perhaps another aspect of this matter is that this whole 'system' (with its institutions and codes of honour etc.) was not exclusively an innovation of the Rajputs of Rajasthan. The then rulers over the sub-continent or the successful military commanders or the leading landholders, whatever their caste and creed, would seem to be following almost similar and parallel patterns of political, social, cultural or court behaviour except for some differences in designation or nomenclature or some natural variation because of the caste and creed. What is accepted as Rajput culture broadly was also prevalent elsewhere in the sub-continent. In any case, what the Rajput *Rajas* and all would seem to have done was to copy and imitate what was happening elsewhere in their neighbourhood and, more important, in the capitals of northern India, i.e., Delhi and Agra.

That brings me to another question on which my humble objections may go contrary to the belief and assumption of the learned essayists. I refer to the long era of relationships or interactions between the several Rajput states or kingdoms with their fluctuating fortunes or frontiers amongst themselves and vis-à-vis the imperial power at Delhi, Agra or elsewhere. The tragic fact that we cannot (or should not) ignore is that through this so-called era of a thousand years of Rajput *Raj*, many of the so-called Rajput kings or princes were not even independent or sovereign. In any case, they did not exist in isolation, but, they were very much dependent on – if not virtually the 'creations' of – whoever ruled in Delhi or Agra (or elsewhere) wherever the fulcrum of military and political power was vested. This is not to deny the historic role or the spirit of adventure or valour because of which the Rajput 'kingdoms' came into existence in the first place and/or extended their territories in the vast wilderness or sandy tracts or the inaccessible valleys and hills of Rajasthan.

Nature of Political Subordination

But then came a time almost a thousand years ago, if we were to leave the earlier incursions of the Arabs and others from north-west, when small bands of adventures led by Ghaznvi and Gauri and, later on, the hordes of Mongols descended upon the imperial seats of power in north India, with some of them venturing into and overwhelming the territories of Rajasthan. Perhaps it would not be wrong to say that since after the defeat of Prithvi Raj Chauhan (of Ajmer and Sambhar) many of the old kingdoms and principalities of Rajasthan ceased to be free and remained subject to the sultans/kings/emperors of Delhi. During the Mughal imperial days, there was a new type of relationship, a new network (or a web perhaps) in which most of the Rajput states were drawn, with the exception of Mewar and Bikaner, the rulers of which could resist the Mughal embrace for a long time. Let us not forget that many of the noble princes of Rajasthan were also office-bearers or *Mansabdars* of the Mughal empire and in that capacity they functioned as military commanders or governors, mostly away from their home territory. They served the Mughals to the best of their ability because their status and destiny rested on their faithful service. A lot of work has been done on the Mughal-Rajput (master vassal) relationship in its various aspects and we need not spend much time on the era.

Towards the close of the Mughal empire, when the growing vacuum was being filled by the northward march of the Marathas or the westward march of the new British company of merchants and when repeated invasions from the north-west zones were giving death blows to the tottering and narrow-based empire of the Mughals, and even when the Rajputs, like other restive and rebellious communities, were striving for a 'place' of their own or were jockeying for power, the time came when Marathas were able to overwhelm them, defeat their designs and control 'independent' Rajput kingdoms, station the Maratha forces in their territory and even collect *chauth* and other levies. If the people of Rajasthan were called upon to pay *jaziya* and other tributes to the Mughals in Delhi/Agra earlier, or when the

Marathas could collect their *chauth* at will, are we in a position to say that these princely kingdoms were independent and sovereign?

It was the ultimate tragedy of the Rajput princes and their subjects in Rajasthan that, ultimately, the political paramountcy was usurped (and enjoyed over the next 150 years or more) by the East India Company and later the British administration in India. Rajput as well as non-Rajput princes were left only with their court's splendour and with a resemblance of 'internal' or 'local' independence subject to imperial control and interference. In fact, with the dawn of Indian independence, the princely order was ended and with it the position of 'servitude' that the princes were placed in. Under these circumstances, what is the Rajput polity or the princely order in Rajasthan that we are speaking about?

Princes and the Paramount Power

We may leave the final judgement of the future historians about the political status or independence of the native princes *vis-à-vis* the imperial/paramount power. No one will dispute that there was a 'special relationship' with the Viceroy and his Political/States Department and Political Agents etc. running the show; or with some native princes being conferred honours or shown special favours by the Imperial Majesties in London. Besides their gun salutes and other privileges or power, some of the princely states did also have their own 'state forces'; and in normal circumstances there was very little of day-to-day interference in their 'own' or domestic affairs of the state. But, the strings remained with the puppet master. Perhaps, the apparent difference was that while in British India there were the Governors, Commissioners and Deputy Commissioners-cum-Magistrates with their subordinate bureaucratic functionaries running the show, in princely India, only the princes or chiefs were watched, supervised and manipulated so long as they did not digress or deviate from the accepted or acceptable codes of personal or political conduct, or so long as there was no challenge to the paramount power from the princes and their subjects. Thus, one-third of India was outside the pale of direct British-India governments, and Rajasthan formed a big chunk of the princely territories.

Before I conclude, I cannot resist the temptation of a comment about the mistaken belief which many of our political leaders, social thinkers and opinion makers seemed to have made in the past about the 'independence' or 'sovereignty' of the Indian princes, especially the princes of Rajputana. Among others, Swami Dayanand Saraswati, Mahatma Gandhi and Pandit Madan Mohan Malviya, to mention a few, seemed to have cultivated the idea that the native princes were 'free' or 'independent'. Perhaps they did not have a clear idea of what 'paramountcy' meant. Even if the princes were comparatively free or autonomous or symbols of *swarajya*, their freedom was limited and always remained under the careful watch and scrutiny of the paramount power. Not only that, but as years passed and new waves of awakening or new institutions began to open up elsewhere in the world, as in British India, gradually we also saw their unfoldment or establishment in the princely state – in the fields of political, administrative, or judicial reforms, establishment of police and law courts, introduction of representatives assemblies or the introduction of modern education, transport and communication network etc. More and more, the politico-administrative, socio-economic and educational system in princely Rajputana came to be modelled on what was being done in the neighbouring areas of British-administered India. If at all, there was a time lag before reforms could be adopted or introduced in the princely states. That is what the princely barriers also meant.

Internal Politics in Rajput States: Protest and Change

However, all was not smooth within the states, sometimes nobles and the *Thakurs* were restive or resisted their princes so as to wrest some concessions or favours. Not only them, the common people (mostly non-Rajput) also stood up for their basic human or civil rights. If the *Samants* of Mewar or *Thakurs* of Bikaner could gang up against their rulers or, if during the Mutiny, in several princely states, the states forces or the peasantry could dare to throw in their lot with the rebel mutineers, or if, subsequently, social reforms movements like the Arya Samaj could take root in some of the princely states, or if a long run struggles for tenancy rights and protection of the peasantry could be launched in Bijolia, perhaps it would not be a fair to say (as has been suggested (in the Narain-Mathur thesis) that political awakening came from outside – from British India. There are so many other instances of people's unrest. We have by now quite a bit of literature about *Praja Parishad* movements in the princely states of Rajputana and the formation of the States People's Conference and its coming together with the Indian National Congress, which goes to show that at least from the close of the 19th century, and the beginning of the 20th century, the diverse people of this region were up on their toes; and step by step they did manage to win some concessions from their rules (for example, when representatives or panchayat bodies were set up, or some land reforms etc. were introduced). In fact, it was as much as the political awakening and upsurge of the state's people as well as the political compulsions of the national/international scene which brought about the end of the 'princely order' and the merger of the princely states and well as common people with the ret of the India.

Further, it was the local awareness and pressure from below which forced and enabled the new popular governments in Rajasthan to initiate the whole series of political, administrative, economic and socio-cultural reforms through which we have been passing since 1947–1949. Unfortunately, very little is known or much less appreciated of these bold initiatives and achievements (as well as their failures or lapses) in the academic circles or outside the limited spheres of government. It is my submission and earnest plea that what has happened in the modern state of Rajasthan during the last half a century or more, should become that subject of constant and continuous research, study, appreciation and understanding. Once again, may I repeat my earlier suggestion for having not one but several centres/courses of Rajasthan studies in historical, political, socio-economical, administrative and cultural aspects.

In sum, there was no ideology, even current or in vogue, that may be called Rajput Hinduism; and Rajput polity or the princely order remained, by and large, a subordinate or subject-system for most of the time during the thousand years raj; and what is more the Rajput polity was also not an independent political or social conglomerate.

5

The Aravallis as an Early Centre of Agriculture and Metallurgy

DILIP K. CHAKRABARTI

Dedicated to the memory of one who has spent the better part of his working life trying to contribute to the development of Rajasthan and whose daughter has just published, possibly under his inspiration, the most comprehensive introduction to the history of state, the present essay of mine will not be a purely professional academic paper. It will embody my personal reaction to how one of the most crucial issues of the archaeology of modern India, which has as its geographical context the Aravalli region of Rajasthan, has been handled by the professional archaeologists in our archaeological literature. I cannot keep the personal element away from this discussion because this development has taken place in my life time and possibly I have played a role in partly shaping it.

The discovery of the extensive scale of prehistoric and protohistoric antecedence of the county in the first two decades after independence is an important positive feature of the history of archaeological research in India. In Rajasthan, the first step in this direction was taken by R.C. Agrawala at Ahar in the early 1950s. The site was later taken up by H.D. Sankalia who however was not satisfied with knowing it as only an *Indian* site. As he believed, like most of his contemporaries and successors in the Deccan College, Pune, that all the elements of civilization in India were acquired from the people who migrated here from the West, he found similarities between certain designs incised on the terracotta beads of Ahar in the chalcolithic level and some designs found at a number of West Asiatic archaeological sites, Further, the fact that iron objects occurred as early as the period Ib at the site, i.e., soon after the beginning of its chalcolithic level and in association with its 'chalcolithic' pottery, was ignored by him. This curious lapse occurred because the general idea of the period was that iron-smelting came to India with the Aryans and thus its date could in no circumstances be early. There has been a continuous tendency on the part of the Deccan College archaeologists to justify this lapse by arguing that the iron pieces found in the Ahar chalcolithic levels indicated only 'disturbed' levels. The fact that these objects occur in a large number of trenches all over the site and the fact that iron has also been reported from the Harappan levels at Lothal in the neighbouring Gujarat are of no interest to them. It would have been nice if the archaeologists of the Deccan College, the most generously funded non-governmental centre of archaeological research in the country, could first learn how to appreciate an archaeological discovery in terms of the history of the nation without bothering about how it would be viewed 'internationally'. However, this is not the academic tradition of the people employed or trained by this institution. It is also of no concern to them that in their quest to be recognized as 'international scholars', they have reduced themselves to the position of lackeys of various neo-colonial elements among the 'South Asian archaeologists' of the international circuit.

Meanwhile, in the late 1950s, B.B. Lal of the Archaeological Survey of India excavated another protohistoric site, Gilund. An important excavation was carried out at the site of Bagor by V.N. Misra of the Deccan College, and true to the tradition of this institution, he sought typological parallels for the copper arrowheads from the Period II of this site among various sites of West Asia. This phase of protohistoric research in Rajasthan culminated in the Ph.D. dissertation of Rima Hooja who closely examined the distribution of these sites and sought ethnographic parallels to understand this distribution.

A new phase of research in this field began with R.C. Agrawala's excavations at Jodhpura near Kotputli and Ganeshwar, near Nim-ka-Thana. The importance of Jodhpura excavations was that the ochre coloured pottery of the site was radiocarbon dated to the 4th millennium BC (calibrated). His excavations at Ganeshwar yielded this pottery in association with a large quantity of copper implements which thus could be put in the 4th millennium BC as well. The point is that the discovery of a rich metallurgical site of this date in a copper-rich area of Rajasthan was a matter of great significance in Indian archaeology.

It could also be appreciated after the discovery of Ganeshwar that the copper arrowheads, which were earlier found in the Period II of Bagor, belonged in fact to the Ganeshwar tradition. Besides, the radiocarbon dates from this period of Bagor also gave the calibrated date of the 4th millennium BC, thus supporting the date obtained earlier for Ganeshwar. One has to note here that Ganeshwar lies in the northern part of the Aravallis whereas Bagor near Bhilwara lies in its southern part. What is clear is that as early as the later part of the 4th millennium BC, there was a rich copper metallurgical tradition along the Aravallis. Besides, comparisons with various copper object finds in the Harappan zone of Rajasthan, the copper hoard belt of the upper Ganga plain, and some chalcolithic sites of Malwa showed that the source of these finds was the early copper-manufacturing belt of the Aravallis. This was a very important conclusion and put the significance of this metallurgical development in Rajasthan in a new light. The full credit of realizing the important role Ganeshwar was likely to have played in the dissemination of copper implements in a large number of north Indian sites goes to R.C. Agrawala. Subsequently, Rima Hooja and V. Kumar published data showing that the famous Daimabad bronzes from the Deccan could have the roots of their art style in the copper-working tradition of the Ganeshwar phase.

After the retirement of R.C. Agrawala from the Rajasthan State Department of Archaeology and Museums, the site of Ganeshwar was subjected to renewed excavations by his successors, P. Chakravarty and V. Kumar. They found only microliths in Period I but a number of copper implements in Period II. In Period III the find of copper implements was singularly rich Microliths continued to occur throughout the sequence. It does not take much imagination to argue that the microlith-using Period I of Ganeshwar must have had an agricultural economy, because if it was producing copper objects in its Period II which otherwise is a continuation of Period I, the metal-producing level was likely to have been preceded by an agricultural and not hunting-gathering economy. In fact, the sequence is very similar to that of Bagor. Although Bagor I has yielded only microliths, its animal bones show the presence of domesticated sheep, goat and cattle, suggesting in turn the presence of an agricultural economy. When calibrated, the dates of Bagor I fall in the 6th-5th millennia BC, thus suggesting a similar date for Period I of Ganeshwar as well. The point is that there is now enough ground to argue for the presence of an agricultural economy in the Aravallis as early as the 6th-5th millennia BC and the presence of an extensive tradition of copper metallurgy in the same region as early as the 4th millennium BC.

In 1984 J.P. Joshi, M. Bala and J. Ram, in their list of Harappan sites in India in *Frontiers of the Indus Civilization* edited by B.B. Lal and S.P. Gupta, included the Ganeshwar-type sites of Jaipur, Sikar and Churu districts of northeast Rajasthan in the site inventory. The details of these sites have not been incorporated in this inventory. It is important that this inventory is carefully checked in the ground so that we obtain a picture of the actual distribution and other features of the Ganeshwar-type sites. In a number of his publications R.C. Agrawala pointed out that the Harappan and pre-Harappan or early Harappan levels of the Ghaggar valley in Rajasthan were getting their copper artifacts from the Ganeshwar area. This is not something which could be doubted for a moment. When in the late 1970s and early 1980s R.C. Agrawala was excavating Ganeshwar and reporting 'copper hoards' from various parts of Rajasthan and reporting them in *Man and Environment* I was associated with the printing and publication of the journal. I was privileged to get to know R.C. Agrawala in that context. It was indeed a privilege to be acquainted with a nationalist Indian scholar of his stature.

In my book *The Archaeology of Ancient Indian Cities* in 1995 I pointed out that the early metallurgical tradition of the Aravallis must have exported copper to the chain of mature Harappan and earlier sites in the Ghaggar-Hakra course through the Cholistan desert and that the intensification of craft activities as exemplified by this tradition was one of the causative factors behind the transition from the early to the mature phases of the Indus civilization. This has also the implication of arguing for the first time that the growth of the Indus civilization was not something which was exclusively related to the developments in the Indus-Saraswati plain and the region to its west; there was a significant contribution from the east as well.

By the late 1990s there were further developments in the protohistoric archaeology of Rajasthan. By this time, some radiocarbon dates were available for the newly excavated site of Balathal in southeast Rajasthan. On the basis of an uncalibrated date of 2600 BC, which took us to a calibrated point in the late 4th millennium BC, I published the following observation in 1999 in my book *India: An Archaeological History:*

On the basis of the present evidence we would argue that from the late 4th millennium BC onwards there were two distinctive but interrelated chalcolithic growth along the Aravallis in northeast and southeast Baluchistan. Metallurgically, and from the point of view of its contribution to the intensification of craft specialization as a major factor leading to the growth of the mature Indus civilization, the growth in northeastern Rajasthan has a very distinct character of its own, but the fact that there was another major contemporary chalcolithic village development in southeast Rajasthan categorically highlights the role played by the Aravalli region as a whole in protohistoric India.

More radiocarbon dates are now available for Balathal, and there should no hesitation to put its beginning in the 5th millennium BC thus substantially adding strength to the supposition I made earlier.

Further support of this hypothesis has been obtained by the still more recent excavations at Gilund. The earliest level at this site is related to the earliest phase of Balathal because the same type of reserved slip ware occurs in both. More interestingly, there is an AMS radiocarbon date of 5550 BC from the context of the aceramic and ceramic microlith-bearing 60 cm thick occupation level on the eastern face of Gilund 2. When the character of this microlith-bearing occupation is analysed, it is likely to be found that this indicates an agricultural economic level. On the whole, there are enough indications to argue that there was an agricultural beginning in the Aravallis as early as the 6th millennium BC. We have noted that Period I of Bagor with the evidence of its domesticated cattle, sheep and goat, suggests a village beginning as early as the 6th millennium BC and that Period I of Ganeshwar, which bears only microliths, is also likely to denote an agricultural phase of this period. The point is that this early agricultural beginning in the Aravallis shows that early agriculture in the Indian subcontinent did not begin only in Baluchistan. The Aravallis were on the present evidence likely to be a centre of early agriculture too. If so, its contribution to the make-up of the Indus civilization has to be carefully assessed in future along with a careful analysis of the process of this beginning. This premise has been strongly underlined in my *The Oxford Companion to Indian Archaeology: The Archaeological Foundations of Ancient India – Stone Age to AD 13th Century* published in 2006.

At this point, it is worth emphasizing that there is not an iota of truth in Gregory Possehl's and others' (cf. Vasant Shinde, the Deccan

College associate of Possehl) opinion that the terracotta seal impressions from Gilund are identical or comparable in any way with the designs of the Bactria-Margiana Archaeological Complex (BMAC). I have already pointed out in my *The Oxford Companion* that the BMAC seals are mostly metallic (not in clay like the Gilund material) and they cover a very wide time range, beginning in the second half of the 3rd millennium BC, if not earlier. Besides, comparisons of this kind are identical with the types of comparisons which Sankalia made for the Ahar terracotta beads. This also shows that despite the protestations of 'anthropological archaeology' the basic approach to the understanding of ancient India has not changed much among a particular section of Western archaeologists.

The excavations at Ojyana seem to have made us aware that there could be more in the protohistory of Rajasthan than the Ahar and Ganeshwar cultures, although the white-painted black-and-red ware – the ceramic hallmark of the Ahar culture – occurs in all the three phases of the site. What we find distinctive about Ojyana is the presence of a 1.8 to 2 m thick stone and rubble fortification wall (large stone blocks in the lower portion and rubble set in mud mortar in the upper portion) around this site of about 11 acres. The find of two straight parallel streets inside the habitation is another noteworthy feature. A Harappan-type faience bead occurs among the antiquities which also include a number of painted (in white and in black) terracotta bull figurines and unpainted cow figurines, the second group shown with udders. A faint imprint of Harappan planning and contact at this site near Ajmer cannot be denied, and one would eagerly look forward to knowing about its radiocarbon dates.

I have to point out one more important feature of protohistoric archaeological research in Rajasthan, especially along the Aravallis. I would point out the necessity of closely examining the many old shafts of the pre-industrial mining activities of this region. These old shafts occur in hundreds throughout the Aravallis, the two convenient points being Khoh Dariba in the north and Zawar in the south. From time to time radiocarbon dates of some old stuff found in the mining shafts have been published, but careful research on all aspects of old mining in the Aravallis is an important necessity. There are also a few ethnographic records of mining available from this region and collected in the second volume of *A Source-Book of Indian Archaeology*, edited by F.R. Allchin and me. The same volume also contains a detailed article on the techniques and dates of pre-modern mining in the Aguncha field near Bhilwara. That the issue of old mining in Rajasthan cannot be held separate from archaeological research is shown very clearly by the location of the modern settlement of Bairat, which lies on the top of an artificial hill built entirely of old slag heaps of copper-smelting. At the foot of this artificial hill lies the fortified early historic remains of the ancient city of Bairat. There is not a shadow of doubt that Bairat was a major metallurgical centre of both protohistoric and early historic India.

From whichever way one views it, the Aravallis of Rajasthan are one of the most fascinating areas of Indian history. That it has now proved to be an independent early centre of agriculture and metallurgy is a major achievement of archaeological research in the state. That it is also a very rugged but beautiful area where peacocks move about in great numbers and cowherds wear turbans made of fine red-coloured cloth makes it a very appealing region to do fieldwork in.

6

Archaeology in Present Time

Four Desert Temples of Rajasthan

MICHAEL W. MEISTER, LAWRENCE A. BABB AND JOHN E. CORT[1]

To excavate a living monument is to search for evidence in real time. Focusing on four temples in desert Rajasthan founded in the 7th-to-9th centuries CE, an interdisciplinary team, with support from the J. Paul Getty Trust, has, over a decade, attempted to reconstruct and understand relationships connecting phases of each temple's architectural remains and ongoing lives.[2] The title of our interpretive research proposal, when funded by the Getty Trust, was *Continuities of Community Patronage: Pilgrimage Temples of Western India*. We hoped to test whether the ancient temples we chose had persisted for centuries – remaining in some fashion alive – because of their connections with specific communities (defined in part by caste and in part by religious affiliation).

Temples we chose shared one crucial characteristic: they are functioning temples today that are also of very great antiquity. As we discovered, this does not necessarily mean that they have been continuously functioning throughout their existence, but it does mean they have long and complex histories that raise critical questions about the conditions under which temple institutions can sustain themselves. We selected four temples that could help us define this range of possibilities.

We had in part hypothesized that, unlike many medieval Indian temples that have survived only as archaeological ruins – even though in their origins they may have been grand edifices, erected through the landed power of a king or other local elite, or through the economic power of a wealthy merchant-prince – each of these particular temples in some way expressed a single community's identity strongly enough that the members of the community, rich and poor, local and distant, ensured the continuing life of the temple.

At the site called Khed, for example, far out on the Rajasthan desert towards Barmer, a complex multi-spired stone temple had been built in the 9th century dedicated to a form of Vishnu, called Ranchodji, especially valued by a Rajput royal elite. Its domed inner-hall ceiling was finally installed only in the 10th century, and its main deity was replaced by a larger marble sculpture perhaps a century-and-a-half later.

Early in the 20th century, this temple only limpingly was still in use, compared to other major pilgrimage temples on the desert, but there was enough local patronage to build a large compound, visitors, quarters, and a new gateway – all types of patronage we found also at other temples in this period – and to extensively polychrome the 9th century stone sculptures carved along the sanctum's walls.

Later in the 20th century, after Indian independence, a newly affluent merchant community of Agrawals from the neighbouring town of Balotra contributed large sums to decorate the hall ceiling with expensive glass mirror work, and they have established the newly required Public Temple Trust for its management and upkeep. Yet this monument today, with no longer any royal connections and with few pilgrims, has only what we concluded is "a somewhat constricted contemporary life". We had hypothesized that if the deity enshrined in a temple bore a sustained special relationship with one community, a relationship central to that community's self-identity and therefore deserving of continued devotion, veneration, obeisance and financial support, then, the institution could sustain itself over many centuries. What we found at Khed instead was a break from the temple's royal patronage, and vague if sincere attempts by other local communities at various moments to help identify themselves by associating with its stuttering flame.

Our long-term team research led us to see temples, deities and communities in far more fluid relationships, requiring a redefinition of 'continuity' itself. A case in point is certainly the Dadhimati-mata temple set among gypsum mines and mustard fields between Goth and Manglod villages near Nagaur. An inscription, perhaps from 608 CE, records patronage of a local Dahima Brahman community for a '*sthana*' or sacred place where the Goddess Dadhimati had emerged from the earth. What remains now is an ancient stone temple, built around that sacred '*sthana*', which became its sunk sanctum, only in the early 9th century.

But there was also a remarkable reformulation and expansion of this temple in the mid-19th century - surrounding that ancient stone structure with four courtyards or *cauks* - instituted by a Dahima *brahmacari*, Vishnu Das, with substantial patronage from the Maharana of Udaipur, Swarup Singh, who ruled from 1842 to 1861. This 'new' institution has its own history, including a century of competing communities intent on controlling the keys to its ritual store-room and expansion of pilgrimage spaces around the shrine, but also a history by which the Dahimas of today - spread across India and even the globe - have used this temple and its mythic history to reposition and define their community through the past century and into the 21st.

Not only do the patrons and prominence of temples change, deities may change as well. Each of our temples has had its own story to tell us of periods of prominence and near desertion. One of them - dedicated to Sacciya-mata at Osian - today has even become one of the more important goddess temples in Rajasthan. Like Dadhimati-mata, however, Sacciya-mata began (and still serves) as a local goddess. Her earliest 8th century stone image survives - a passively beautiful form of the goddess called Ksemankari. The original small Sacciya-mata temple's sanctum, which stood next to a companion 8th century temple that still stands, was replaced in 1178 CE by a much larger structure. The earlier image in the sanctum was at that time replaced by a fierce version of the goddess slaying the buffalo demon Mahisha. (It is this fierce form of the goddess that Jain legends then say converts to Jain ways.)

The goddess Dadhimati first emerged from the earth as an autochthonous stone (her scull or elbow depending on the source of the story), stopped from fully emerging by the surprised cries of a local cow-herder. This event is actually represented in a small relief on a not-too-distant 9th century temple to Padamata, along with a fully developed image of the Great Goddess in her demon-slaying form at the centre of the outer north wall.

As Clifford Geertz has argued, "cultural analysis is (or should be) guessing at meanings, assessing the guesses, and drawing explanatory conclusions from the better guesses". At the town of Osian, located in a desert hollow northwest of Jodhpur, two temples - among many others at the site – tell differing if intertwined stories. One is the goddess temple of Sacciya-mata. The other is dedicated to the Jain *tirthankara* Mahavira. First constructed late in the 8th century, this temple has served primarily a community of Oswal Jains. In the centuries after its founding, the Mahavira temple underwent definable phases of renovation, expansion, new patronage, neglect, near abandonment, and re-appropriation and renovation by Jains in the 19th and 20th centuries.

By contrast, the temple complex dedicated to Sacciya-mata as a local place-goddess has served a number of communities over time and at the same time, in changing circumstances and in multiple ways. In stories of Oswal origins, for example, the goddess Sacciya commits herself to Jain austerities by becoming a vegetarian; yet for other multiple communities she continued to receive blood sacrifices until quite recently; and for contemporary priests today, she continues to service a variety of local and trans-local communities in definable and successful ways.

Among my responsibilities as an art historian on this team was to document the standing monuments and their physical changes. Part of my reasons for proposing the project had in fact been the remarkable changes – physical and sociological – I had observed from my first visits to this region in the 1960s and which continue today. We could, for example, study in some detail the physical transformation of the Mahavira temple's complex from the 1970s to 1990s, with new patronage for renovation from the Anandji-Kalyanji Trust in Ahmedabad, changing local politics, a new government agenda for the Jain school, and an increase in facilities for pilgrims and tourism.

As an example of what we could accomplish, I can point to one 'archaeological' recovery: we were able to reconstruct the elevation and plan of the little documented double-storied entry hall to the Mahavira complex, which I had first photographed in 1968, and compare that to the temple's newly reconstituted single-story 'tourist reception hall' as it stands today. This *valānaka*, first built in the 8th century, renovated and expended in the 10th (with an important historical *prasasti* inscription) and 12th centuries, has once again been recreated with new patronage in the 20th century.

As a Jain scholar, my colleague John Cort has written that the Mahavira temple today, although acknowledged archaeologically as the oldest Jain temple in Western India, remains "more important for art historians than devotees". Yet, the histories of its rediscovery by local Jains late in the 19th century, at the same time the building of a light railroad made regional pilgrimage more easily possible, the building and maintenance of a Jain school to repopulated Jains in Osian early in the last century, and the struggles of teachers and local priests – in particular a converted non-temple worshipper named Jhansundar – to recover its Jain lineage and restore the temple to its rightful position through the 20th century are stories we could also recover and that John tells very well.

The Sacciya-mata temple – and the recent growth of its importance and patronage from pilgrims – also allowed us to recover complex and unexpected histories.

The communities that *today* are central to the patronage of each of our temples have not necessarily always played such a role, and we found ample evidence that each temple has been the site of extended contestations over access, ownership and proprietary rights. Oswal Jains, who are currently the dominant community among patrons of the Sacciya-mata temple, advance a set of medieval myths to bolster their claims to Osian, but in fact have gained (or recently regained) prominence in the multiple-community patronage of the Sacciya-mata temple only in the past few decades, and for unusual reasons. These major patrons today are *sthanakvasi*, that is 'non-temple worshipping' Jains, as they were in the 19th century, who have returned to Sacciya-mata in recent decades, finding her an auspicious cancer-curing goddess who has also helped (as a reclaimed tutelary deity) to reframe their community identity in the 21st century.

One result of this patronage has been the vast expansion of the complex to meet the needs of multiple users and new pilgrims since 1970. Earlier in the 20th century the ritual functions of the Bhojak priests of the Sacciya-mata temple were still quartered in a small compound toward the northeast corner of the fortified hill, built possibly in the 18th century. Now, their enlarged community descends the hill on the east (and are contesting the Temple Trust to keep their private gate open). Vast feeding and sleeping halls have been built; new stone gateways (with even newer aluminum ornaments) march up the hill; and a set of nine shrines to the Nava-Durgas are still in the process of being constructed beyond the old fortifications.

We might think that the deities enshrined in temples would be strong evidence of great stability, but an icon does not exist in autonomous isolation. Scholars of comparative religion use the term 'god' to refer to a 'bilateral relationship', a general type of experience in which people as individuals and in community experience in 'otherness'. Thomas Coburn has written that "[god] does not refer to the intrinsic qualities of an object, person, text, place, [or] act. ... Rather, it is refers to [each] in relationship to and [in] interaction with particular persons, ... individually or collectively". The 'deity' is located in these relationships; and as communities change, deities also change. Within the Sacciya-mata temple itself, and around Osian as a sacred *tirtha* – as also at Dadhimati – we found many layers of divinities and user communities, as well as many stories (and images) of enabling teachers, sages, even a cow-herder or so.

Here again, we found fluidity more than fixity. In large part this is because in no case is the primary deity of the temple the only deity enshrined. Each deity stands in a web of deities, and how worshippers enter into this web alters the relationships between devotees and deities, and therefore alters deities themselves.

Sacciya, Mahavira and Dadhimati are the goals of pilgrims who come from afar. Most pilgrims pay little attention to other deities in the shrine. But for regional and local pilgrims, other deities – the Bhairava located in the Mahavira compound, the Hanuman in the Ranchodji compound, the goddess Gangaur worshipped one day a year in the Sacciya temple – may have greater importance on a permanent basis, or on particular days of the Hindu and Jain ritual calendars.

We thus came to see each of these temples as elements in fluid theologies and fluid archaeologies. The stones of temples change as they are periodically renovated. The communities connected to temples change due to the fluctuations of power, wealth and migration. Deities change as their relational identities are redefined. Continuity does not imply lack of change. On the contrary, we came to see that temples continue to survive only as they are able to change.

I am struck also by re-established connections with the past and the means by which myth can function – like archeology – to make the past present. At Dadhimati, for example, reformulation of the temple in the 1850s attributed to the Maharana of Udaipur has now been connected with a hoary ancestry. Cheap books at the temple reset this 'foundation' (of the 19th century temple) in the far distant past, and place Maharana Swarup in the ancient time of the world-ruling king Mandhata. That this king once competed with Indra, claiming his throne, represented in a famous 2nd century CE roundel from the Buddhist *stupa* at Amaravati, is beyond the 'event horizon' of contemporary devotees, but not beyond what I have called 'archaeology in present time'.

I would like to end with a summary of comments offered by our team's sociologist and anthropologist, L.A. Babb. He emphasized that the notion of social identity was crucial to our research. He finds that functioning temples are confluence points for social relationships of every sort, and deities are emblems of social groupings of all kinds – lineages, clans, castes, and even village or regional communities. By supporting particular deities, and by making them a part of life-cycle rituals, groups enact their own sense of themselves as social entities, and project their identities into public space. Origin mythology is the usual medium through which connections between temples and social groups are established and reinforced. Such mythology transmutes questions of social identity into assertions about a given group's past: how it came to be the kind of community that it is. Part of what makes a temple live and allows it to survive for as many centuries as these have is that it is embedded in a community's self-understanding as expressed in historical or mytho-historical ideas. People narrate their own history, and because a temple is central to that history, they travel to, worship at, and maintain that temple. Our four temples dramatically illustrate these principles; therefore, group histories, told over and over, with many variants, as well as temples built and rebuilt, became central to our research.

The Oswal clan's origin myth as retold at Osian asserts that the goddess Sacciya was instrumental in the 'awakening' of the inhabitants of Osian to the truths of Jainism, which was how the Oswal caste was created. A ferocious and bloodthirsty goddess, Sacciya-mata in the form of Camunda, became vegetarian shortly after the town's people became Jains. This same body of myth maintains that the Mahavira temple was built at that time, and credits a goddess with the creation of the image enshrined there. Sacciya occupies the role of clan goddess for many Oswals today, though by no means all. She is also venerated as clan goddess by many non-Oswals, and there perhaps exists a reservoir of origin mythology of descent groups belonging to non-Oswal communities in which Sacciya also plays a role.

The richest trove of origin mythology we encountered was that of the Dahima Brahmans. Rendered into Sanskrit in their recently constructed caste Purana, but also circulating in folk versions, their origin myth centres on the goddess Dadhimati and her temple. It traces the descent of the entire caste to the Vedic sage Dadhici, whom the myth claims to have been goddess Dahimati's brother. This relationship is a feature of the temple's present sacred geography, for an image of Dadhici now sits in the compound of Dadhimati in a side-shrine constructed in the 20th century by a Dahima Brahman devotee.

The re-telling of this myth reaches deeply into the structure of the caste by accounting for the traditional 144 caste *gotras* as the multiplying progeny of the sons of Dadhici's twelve grandsons. This mytho-fact is vividly illustrated by a large caste genealogy mounted on one of the inner walls of the temple courtyard, but its promotion has been a construction of the 20th century. The change from Dahima (i.e., local) Brahmans – which go back to the 'Dahiya' Brahmans of the 608 CE inscription – to contemporary Dadichi (that is, Vedic) Brahmans in the latter part of the 20th century is only one of the multiple layers our 'archaeology' has been able to uncover.

There is nothing static about any of our temples, and the coupling of the Dahima origin myth to the temple, was, although ancient, at the heart of important transformations affecting both caste and temple in the late 19th and early 20th centuries. This was a period in which caste elites all over India were, in response especially to changes related to urbanization and the emergence of new economic opportunities, revising their sense of themselves as caste communities and their notions of the nature of caste as a social institution. When Dahima Brahmans migrated away from Dadhimati's rural hinterland, they found themselves in need of burnished Brahmanical credentials and, in the face of their increasing geographical dispersal, they also needed a symbolic focus for caste unity.

Dahima elites polished their Brahmanical pedigree by manipulating their caste genealogy and reshaped their caste's origin myth in such a way as to support their claim that Dadhimati and Dadhici Rishi had a unique relationship with the Dahimā Brahman caste community. Such a claim had little basis in the local tradition, for Dadhimatī had been the goddess of many communities in the region, not just the Dahima Brahmans. As a result, Dadhici Brahmans of today have increasingly come into conflict with other communities over control of the temple – with local Jats in particular, who take this goddess also as their clan goddess – a contest that is yet to play itself out as the temple enters its 1,500th year.

Notes

1. This summary of the Getty project undertaken by its three authors was presented at the 19th International Conference on South Asian Archaeology of the European Association of South Asian Archaeologists in Ravenna, Italy, July 2007, by the first author, and occasionally uses his first-person voice. All three, however, contributed to the text in equal collaboration.
2. For a final volume reporting on this project see L.A. Babb, John E. Cort and Michael W. Meister, *Desert Temples: Sacred Centers of Rajasthan in Historical, Art-Historical, and Social Contexts,* Jaipur: Rawat Publications, 2008. Earlier versions of the authors' collective and individual work has also appeared in Lawrence A. Babb, Varsha Joshi and Michael W. Meister, eds., *Multiple Histories: Culture and Society in the Study of Rajasthan,* Jaipur: Rawat Publications, 2002, and Michael W. Meister, ed., *Ethnography and Personhood: Notes from the Field,* Jaipur: Rawat Publications, 2000. The four temples discussed also have entries in Michael W. Meister and M.A. Dhaky, eds., *Encyclopaedia of Indian Temple Architecture*, Vol. II, Pt. 2, *North India: Period of Early Maturity,* Delhi: Oxford University Press, 1991.

7

The Identification of Vasudeva, Founder of Rajasthan's Chahaman Dynasty

Was He a Tigin Shahi Ruler?

K.K. MAHESHWARI

Sometime during the end of the fifth century AD or the beginning of the sixth century AD a coin series was introduced in India that closely followed the coin pattern of those of Firuz I, a Sassanian ruler of Persia/Iran. The Hunas imitated Firuz I's coins when they were in occupation of Central Asia. The imitations of Firuz when introduced in India were popularly labelled as Indo-Sassanian coins.

One of the coin types of this series depicts a portrait to right on the obverse with the usual fire altar with attendants on either side on the reverse. A letter 'sa' just above the crown on the obverse (Figure 1) distinguishes this type as a separate series within the Indo-Sassanian currencies.

Figure 1

Coins with a Letter 'sa' Above the Crown

As with the Indo-Sassanian coins, this type of the Indo-Sassanian series also does not have the name of the ruler that could have given us the clue to the issuer of the coins. The find spots of these coins are restricted to Rairh,[1] Sakhun (Dudu-Jaipur)[2] and Ajmer[3] – all areas close to Jaipur/Sambhar region of the present-day state of Rajasthan.

As the Sassanian imitations originated from the northwest in Central Asia, we have to look to the link between India and the northwest, inclusive of Kapisa, Gandhara and, in effect, modern-day Afghanistan, not only because of that area's strategic locale – standing as it did at the nodal point of commercial activities – but also because it provides us with a numismatic bridge between the Sassanian issues of Persia and what appear to be their imitations, which may have been a direct or indirect outcome of the politico-economic interaction of the frontiers of India vis-à-vis the aforementioned areas, and had a wide diffusion in late times.

A chronological reconstruction of the area will have to depend on the Chinese sources primarily, and also the writings of Al Beruni and other Arabian travellers. Al Beruni tells us that the founder of the Ash-shahiyya of Kabul (referred to as Turk Shahis by modern scholars) was Barhatigin, whose date may be established "to be about AD 666".[4] The end of this dynasty may be construed to have come about in AD 843, on the basis of the inscriptions of the Hindu Shahi period. Thus, this group of kings remained in power for approximately 177 years. The rule of the western branch of the Turk Shahis, the Rutbils of our sources – generally described as the rulers of Rukhkhaj and adjoining areas – lasted a little beyond this; the last of the Rutbils mentioned in history was captured in AD 870.[5]

After the decline of the Hunas in the Indian northwest in about AD 530, Barhatigin was one of the many petty chieftains who succeeded the once mighty Epthalite/Huna power. He appears to have attacked Kabul and proclaimed himself king thereof. Humbach has identified Barhatigin with Shahi Tigin.

We come to an interesting coin specimen with the name 'Vakhudev' or 'Vasudeva'.[6] It carries a close copy of Khushro II's bust, with post-Gupta Brahmi inscription in the field to the front and behind the head. The reverse, too, is more or less a replica of Khushro's coin. This ruler has been placed by Dr Mukherjee and others[7] as belonging to the Tigin Shahi family. The assumption that Vasudeva was a Tigin Shahi himself is, however, subject to some doubt. Unlike the other rulers of the Tiginshahi – Vahitigin, Tigin Shah, Barhatigin and Tekin-Shah, the title of Tigin is missing on his coins. Moreover, his coins refer to Zabulistan as his area of control. Since we know from sources[8] that Zabul and Kabul had become two distinct areas of control by AD 680, there are grounds to distinguish Vasudeva from the Kabul Shahis, i.e., Tigin Shahis. Alternatively, it may be suggested that Vasudeva was identical with Rutbil, ruler of Zabul. He may have been related to the Tigin Shahis, as the Rutbil is said to have been a brother of Barhatigin. This may account for the similar coinage traditions of the rulers of Kabul and Zabul.

Having glanced at the coin types in question, it becomes imperative to delve into the political/economic circumstances governing the area under study, and their possible repercussions in the Indian northwest from a numismatic point of view.

The Turko-Arab struggle for the Khorasan and Zabulistan areas was at its peak in the second half of the eighth century AD.[9] The Arabs are said to have become stronger and more secure with the passing of years. However, Vasudeva seems to have been in firm control of Zabulistan, Taki, parts of northwest India, Gandhara and Multan, as may be surmised from his coins, and should thus be placed prior to the ascent of the Arab power.

His adoption of the Sassanian type coin may easily be explained. We know for a fact that in AH 78 (AD 690), the Zabul ruler (Vasudeva?) was involved in a conflict against Khorasan/Sistan. There must have been an enormous booty, and very likely a large war chest came into the hands of the king of Zabul.[10] Quite possibly, the coins of Khushro II found their way to Zabul/Kabul in this manner. The expedition of the Zabul ruler to East Khorasan is documented by coins containing the title Yabgu of Baxi. As noted earlier, the Arabs proved a major challenge from the early eighth century onwards. Therefore, the Epthalites may have combined with the ruler of Zabul/Kabul (Tigin Shahi) against the Arabs. Gobl has identified a group of Epthalite coins, adopted on the pattern of Khushro II's coins.[11] These coins have mintmark HWRA (Khurasan), and are dated AD 685. The legend rwzorono (Guzgan) is also found on these specimens.

Vasudeva's Coins

Let us now consider the coinage of Vasudeva, as it is this series of coins that had its influence on a coin series of Rajasthan. The coin types of Vasudeva are many. This goes to suggest a long period of rule. All the obverse types, however, are direct copies of the coinage of the Sassanian ruler Khushro II (AD 590–628). This also indicates that he was a near contemporary of Khushro II.

On one of the obverses, the portrait is different in as much as it depicts a younger face (Fig. 2), and there is also a change in the motif above the bust. Instead of a globe within wings, here we have a letter, which very much resembles Brahmi letter 'sa' (Fig. 3). Interestingly, this coin also carries the Brahmi legend Sri Vasudeva in front of the bust, which would go to suggest that he perhaps ruled in, or very close to, the Indian northwest. There is some added evidence to confirm this presumption: coins of Vasudeva carry the marginal obverse legend Saf Tef Varsu Wahaman Multan Mulka (Sri Vasudeva, king of Bahaman and Multan), Tulkan Zaulistan (India Zabulistan), and on the margin Sapardalakashan. Significantly, the term 'Sapadalaksha' (literally meaning one lakh and a quarter) was an old name of Rajputana (present-day Rajasthan), said to have been derived from a large number of scattered hills in the region for which the expression is used.

Figure 2
Vasudeva's Coins

Figure 3
Enlarged Section of Headgear Showing 'sa' within Wings

The basic point that one is trying to make in the discussion is that at least a part of Rajasthan was quite possibly under the control of Vasudeva. The fact that his coins actually refer to this region would also suggest that his control was not merely a temporary intrusion; rather, it was permanent enough to be recorded on coins.

Vasudeva's coin legend leads us to surmise that a part of northwest India lay within his domain. The question as to the identity of this Vasudeva now arises who claims Rajputana within his domain.

D.R. Bhandarkar[12] has dwelt at length on the word 'Vahaman'. According to him, the word 'Vahaman' is commonly taken to be equivalent to Bahaman. Vasudeva is, therefore, supposed to have ruled over Bahamanwasi in Sind. On one type of Vasudeva's coin, the legend is simply Sri Vahaman and Vasudeva. Bhandarkar is of the opinion that here Vahaman does not stand for a city or a province as Sri is not prefixed to place names like Tukan, Zaulistan or Sapardalakshan. He, therefore, concludes that the name Vahaman must be a family or a tribe name to which Vasudeva belonged.

He then proceeds to enumerate the reading of Cunningham[13] of the word 'Bahaman', which was read as such by Wilson. Doubting the reading of Wilson, Cunningham tentatively read the word as 'Vangara' or 'Chandara'. According to Bhandarkar, the letters 'Va' or 'Cha' are so close to each other that one could easily be mistaken for the other.

Therefore, though, disputing Cunningham's reading of the next two letters 'ngara' or 'ndara', Bhandarkar agrees with the reading of the first letter as 'Cha' and attributes the correct reading of Bahaman as Chahman, which, stands for Chahamana (later more popularly known as Chauhan). If this argument is agreed upon, then, Vasudeva becomes a Chahamana (Chauhan) ruler.

Prithviraja-vijaya states that the first prince of the Chahamana family was Vasudeva. This Vasudeva had received a gift of the salt lake (Sambhar), which he put under the protection of goddesses Asapuri and Shakambhari. Further, he refers to Rajasekharasuri's *Prabandha-kosha*, which lists thirty-seven kings of the Sapadalakshiya-Chahamana-nripa-vamsha (the Chahamana royal family of the Sapadalaksha country). This list begins with Raja Vasudeva, who has been assigned to 608 VE. (AD 551). Thus, he concludes that Vasudeva of the coins be identified with Vasudeva, the Chahamana ruler.

Cunningham takes Vasudeva to be a later Huna, while Prof Rapson thought him to be a Sassanian ruler. However, Bhandarkar believes that based on the Sassanian Pahlevi legend on the coins he was a Khazar. He thus concludes: "this much is incontrovertible, that Vasudeva was of foreign blood, and consequently the Chahamana family to which he pertained was also a foreign tribe".[14]

The next earliest prince of this dynasty Samanta is mentioned in the Bijolia inscription[15] as a Brahman of Vatsa gotra; hinting that the Chahamanas belonged to some priestly class of foreign tribe. At some stage, they seem to have given up their priestly pursuits to martial merging with the Kshatriyas. This, at that time, was not uncommon. The Guhilots of Mewar, who were originally Nagar Brahmans, became Kshatriyas when they adopted the martial profession. The origin forgotten, the Vatsa gotra of the Chahamana was regarded to mean that they sprung from the eyes of Vatsa Rishi.[16]

As per the Bijolia inscription, Samanta was supposed to have come from Ahichchhatra. Mayursarman, of the Kadabma family, who had gone to the Himalayas, had, brought with him a colony of Brahmans from Ahichchchtra. Bhandarkar, therefore, concludes that this place was the original habitat of the foreign tribes before they migrated to other parts of the country. He identifies this with 'O-hi-chi-ta-lo' of the Chinese traveller Yuan Chwang.[17] Cunningham's identification of Ramnagar, about 22 miles north of Budaun, seems doubtful because Yuan Chwang describes this place as "naturally strong, being flanked by the mountain crags". A Jain work mentions one Ahichchhtra with Jangal as its capital, which, in Mahabharata is placed near Madreya situated between the Chenab and the Sutlej. The Jangal near Madreya can be located somewhere in the southern part of the Himalayas. Apart from this, there are two more Ahichchchtras. One, as mentioned in the Mahabharata, was to the north of Panchala, which was identified by Cunningham with a place near Ramnagar. The second was Adeisathra of Ptolemy, which must have been in the Adeisathroi territory. This, according to Bhandarkar, is to be identified with the Adhichhatra of a Pabhosa inscription.[18] While rejecting the identification of these latter two places, Bhandarkar says that the Achichchhatra, mentioned as 'O-hi-chi-ta-lo' by Yaun Chawng, was the only one which was flourishing in the medieval times.

Bhandarkar then proceeds to identify this country whose southern most limit was formed by the Siwalik (Sawalakh) range. This range, which at present runs parallel to the Himalayas for about 300 kilometres from the Beas to the Ganges, must have, in the early period, covered a far wider range. For the identification, Bhandarkar falls on the support of an inscription found at Gaya,[19] which mentions Asokacalla as the lord of the kings of Sapadalaksha mountains; and as the overlord of a tributary Purushottamasimha of Kama, in the Kumaoun country. Another inscription of this king was found in Garhwal. In his autobiography, Babur, mentions this range commencing from the Indus and running through many parts of Kashmir such as Pakhli and Sahmanak was called Sawalakh because it contained no less than 1,25,000 hills.

Further, to strengthen the argument that the Chahamanas settled in the hilly region of Himachal before coming to Rajasthan, Bhandarkar alludes to the Pahadi language, which is spoken from Chamba to Nepal and is considered as an off-shoot of Rajasthani by Dr Grierson. According him, bands of Rajputs invaded these hilly tracts and settled there, marrying the original inhabitants on whom they imposed their language. To this extent, Bhandarkar falls on the linguistic proposition of Grierson. But, he differs from Grierson's chain of events, which presumes that the Rajputs came to the hilly region from Rajasthan. Based on his theory, as enumerated above, the Chahamanas first settled in the mountainous regions from where they then migrated to Rajasthan.

The coin series under study now becomes very interesting as this can be attributed to the Chahamanas (Chauhans). We have seen that the coins imitating the Vasudeva coins with sa in place of the globe are found mainly near the Jaipur/Ajmer region. Even the later development of this coin type in 'sri ha' series are heavily concentrated in the narrow band in the region, which was once ruled by the Chahamanas, later known as Chauhans.

Of the origin of Vasudeva not being from the Sambhar region, we come across an interesting reference in the Bijholi inscription[20] which, while describing the guardian deity Sakambhari of the Chahamanas, mentions Vasudeva as having carved out his principality round the Lake Sambhar, considered the region as having become his mother or mother-country. Now, if Vasudeva was indeed a local habitant, there was no need for him to consider the region to become his mother-country.

It is, therefore, safe to presume that Vasudeva, the Chahamana ruler, first introduced this coin-type when he conquered Rajasthan and established himself in the Ajmer region near the Sambhar Lake. Thereafter, his successors continued with the type with variant. This coin series and its succeeding series would have been in circulation till such time that it was replaced by the 'bull and horseman' type coin.

Notes

1. P. Pokharna (1982), 'A New Variety of Indo-Sassanian Coins', *Numismatic Digest* 6, p. 56.
2. P. Pokharna (1996), 'Initial Bearing Indo-Sasanian Coins from Sakhun', *Shodak*, Vol. 25, Part A, No. 73, pp. 77–80.
3. Jan Lingen cabinet.
4. A. Rehaman (1976), The Last Two Dynasties, Ph.D. thesis submitted to the Australian University, pp. 45–47, 61.
5. Ibid., p. 46, 61.
6. In Vedic tradition, especially *Yajurveda*, *sha* retroflex is pronounced as *kha* which may explain the variation Vakhudeva.
7. N. Sengupta (1984), *Cultural History of Kapisa and Gandhar*, Delhi, pp. 34–37.
8. A. Rahman (1976), op. cit., p. 66 ff.
9. N. Sengupta (1984), op. cit., p. 61, n.161.

10. R. Gobl (1967), *Documente Zur Geschichte Der Schen Irani Hunnen In Bakterien and Indien*, Wiesbaden, p. 86.
11. Ibid., cf. em. 271/A.
12. D.R. Bhandarkar (reprint 1985), 'Foreign Elements in the Hindu Population', *Indian Antiquary* 40, pp. 7–37.
13. A. Cunningham (1894), *Late Indo-Scythians or the White Huns*, p. 290.
14. D.R. Bhandarkar (reprint 1985), op. cit., p. 26.
15. As cited in ibid.
16. F. Kielhorn (reprint 1981c), 'The Chahamanas of Naddula', *Epigraphia Indica*, 11, p. 74.
17. S. Beal (reprint 1982), *Buddhist Records of the Western World*, Delhi, p. 228.
18. A. Fuhrer (reprint 1983), 'Pabhosha Inscription', *Epigraphia Indica*, 21, p. 243.
19. V.V. Vidyavinoda (reprint 1982), 'Two Inscriptions from Bodha Gaya', *Epigraphia Indica*, 12, p. 3.
20. Akshaya Keerty Vyas (1941–1942), 'Bijholi Rock Inscription of Chahamana Somesvara: V. S. 1226, *Epigraphia Indica*, 26, p. 88.

8

Orientalists and Historians on the Early Settlement Patterns and History of the Ghaggar Region of Rajasthan

G.S.L. DEVRA

Noted archaeologists and historians Tessitori, Aurel Stein, Hermann Goetz and A. Ghosh did extensive survey works in the valley of Ghaggar river of northwest Rajasthan and all of them concluded that at least before the period of seventh century it was a region of extensive and prosperous culture.[1]

Tessitori, using rare material that he collected from different places located between Munda (east of Hanumangarh) and Suratgarh, designated the region as a centre of Graeco-Buddhist (Gandhara) art and culture. He identified several structures as Buddhist *Chaityas* belonging to Kushan and later Kushan periods and believed that a majority of the people from this area were followers of Buddhism. Aurel Stein did accept the impact of Graeco-Buddhist art and culture but he was of the view that both Hindu and Buddhist cultures had flourished side by side in these regions during the ancient period.[2] Hermann Goetz differs with the findings of these noted scholars. He suggests that the terracotta sculptures of this area in its approach come nearer to the Mathura rather than the Gandhara School of Art and, further, that not a single archaeological object can particularly said to be Buddhist.[3]

Ghosh has used the term 'Rangmahal culture' for the later Kushan cultural period in Rajasthan, after the name of an archaeological site situated near modern Suratgarh, from where the course of Ghaggar river takes a westerly direction, and from where excavated artifacts and associated debris have been unearthed. In fact, Ghosh considered that this Rangmahal Culture in modified forms is present in almost all parts of northern Rajasthan.[4] James Tod, though he never visited the site, cited local sources reporting Rangmahal as possessing the vestiges of a large town buried in sand.[5] Ghosh did not exactly name the originators of the Rangmahal culture[6] but some other scholars held that the Yaudheyas might have been the lords of this culture.[7]

Recent excavation works and studies draw our attention towards the figures of fully developed Hindu mythology, like images of Umā-Maheśvara, Krishna-Gopala (particularly Krishna's lifting of Mount Govardhana), and goddesses, especially *Mahisasuramardini*, from the later Kushan or early Gupta period.[8] R.C. Agrawal has noted a beautiful red clay plaque from Bhadarkali *Ther* wherein *Devi* (the Goddess) pierces the animal with a full-size trident held in her lower right hand and twists the neck of the demon with her lower left hand.[9] The availability of large numbers of terracotta figures of Krishna-Gopala shows that in the early Gupta period Krishna cult was popular in the region. Aurel Stein found a figure with some letters in Brahmi, deciphered as 'Yasoda Krti' (Yashoda being the name of the foster mother of Krishna), from Munda, near Hanumangarh.[10]

Both Tessitori and Aurel Stein did some path breaking work at Munda, a place-name that reminds us about the settlement of a people known as 'Marunda'.[11] Aurel Stein discovered several terracotta fragments that imply the presence of a temple of the Kushan period.[12] Tessitori, from the same site of Munda, found the relic deposit of a *stupa*.[13] He also noted the presence of two more large *stupas* at Bhadrakali and Badpol. Hanna Rydh, a Swedish archaeologist who did extensive excavation work at Rangmahal and Badpol feels that the leading religion of the people was Brahmanism though Buddhism also flourished side by side.[14] The figures and images of *Surya* (the Sun), found chiefly at Rangmahal and Bhatner, suggest that Surya worship was also prevalent in the area.[15] K.C. Jain holds that Jainism also penetrated the region during the medieval period and even today one can see a Jain temple as one of the surviving structures at Bhatner fort.[16] All these evidences suggest that up to Kushan and Gupta times a settled population occupied this part of the Ghaggar river valley greatly in excess of that living therein small-scattered hamlets and a few villages at the beginning of the 20th century.[17]

Further, these scholars suggest that over time the Indo-Scythian, Kushan, Kedarite, Murund and Yaudheya groups probably ruled over places, like Badpol, Munda, Pir Sultan, Sardargarh, Bhadrakali, and Rangmahal in the Ghaggar valley.[18] Coins discovered at Munda, Rangmahal, Pallu, *dhanis* (or hamlets) near Suratgarh support such assumptions.[19] Aurel Stein discovered a small sculpture of a well-modelled head of a man about 5 inches high, with straight nose and eyes, moustache and curly hair at Munda that, according to him, bore the impression of the Gandhara School. Satya Prakash had obtained another small sculpture from the same site, which was 10 inches high and 6⅓ inches wide, which Satya Prakash believed was the 'Virbhadra' form of Lord Shiva datable to the Kushan period.[20] In Rangmahal some terracotta human figures have goat-like eyes. V.S. Agarwal, who noticed such figures at Ahichhatrā too, believes that such images represent a racial characteristic of Sassanian Persians whose presence in India was known during the Gupta period.[21] Aurel Stein found a well-modelled terracotta head of a boar, which he believed reflects the presence of Parthians or Persian origin people in the area.[22]

In addition, there are several examples indicating the presence of the Śakas in this region. V.S. Agarwal noticed two Sun (or Sūrya) images with Śaka facial type on a Rangmahal pottery bowl. Besides this, a small votive tank and statues connected with the worship of mother goddess show Parthian influence. Near the second gate of the entrance of Bhatner fort (now better known as Hanumangarh fort), there is a seated image of the Sun god wearing boots and holding two lotus flowers in his hands.[23]

Many archaeological remains and terracotta figures of the Ghaggar valley are displayed in the Tessitori Gallery of the Government Museum at Bikaner. Besides these, Hermann Goetz had carried some terracotta figures and remains of potteries to the Vadodara Museum. These evidences chiefly belong to the later Kushan and early Gupta periods.[24]

It appears that Gandhara branch of Indo-Scythians had penetrated this region during the early centuries of Christian era, but the Yaudheyas who once ruled till the extent of Panjnand region of the north-west frontier regions of the Indian sub-continent and challenged the might of the Western Śaka Kshtrapas and later on the Kushans, were the lords of Ghaggar valley. Perhaps, they could not become sovereign of their land after the fall of Kushans but certainly, they maintained this status for few decades with the decline of the combined strength of the Indo-Scythians, Parthians and Kedarites.

We have no strong evidence about colonization by the Parthians or Persian people but fragmentary references indicate their presence. Besides that, there is some historical evidence to suggest the formation of a Scythian-Persian alliance against the White Huns, and ultimately victory over them, with the assistance of Western Turkish *Khakan* of Central Asia. This made the resurgence of Scythian power possible in the Punjab and Sutlej-Ghaggar region during the seventh century.[25]

On the other hand, literary evidences from Rajasthan suggest that between the period of fifth to seventh century new clans like Panwars (Parmars), Bhatis and Varhas inhabited these parts.[26] A Prince Bhati of Jadam clan, who once ruled over the frontier regions of the Indian sub-continent, is said to have founded the fort of Bhatner sometime in the middle of the fifth century.[27] James Tod, who felt that the Jats were Scythians or part of the Yu-Chi branch of the Scythians, considered this region as having Jat dominance, noting that the Jats not only fought against the Arabs in the eighth century but later also resisted Sultan Mahmud of Ghazana in the Panjnand area.[28]

Both epigraphic and literary sources confirm that at the time of the Chauhans of Ajmer-Sambhar, the Yaudheyas were the leading power in the Ghaggar region. Under their king Arnoraj, the Chauhans are believed to have carried their arms up to the Sindhu (Indus)-Saraswati (Ghaggar) and Vahika regions and the Chauhans thought it politically wise to make matrimonial alliance with the Yaudheyas.[29] Chauhans had dominance over the Pallu and its neighbouring parts, known as *Bagar*,[30] coins of Chauhan chiefs are found in the Suratgarh and Pallu regions of northern Rajasthan. Before the rise of Chauhan political dominance in this area, Bhatis and Varhas had moved away and settled in the southern sandy parts of Rajasthan and Sind. Panwars also failed to remain dominant.[31]

Unfortunately, both Cunningham and Garrick who came to Bhatinda and Sirsa for survey work missed the site of Bhatner and other important centres in Ghaggar valley.[32] Perhaps both these scholars became obsessed with the glory of Bhatinda or as popularly suggested '*Bhatti da Pind*' and forget to include other more important sites of the region.[33] In fact, recent researches have shown that Bhatinda (actually Vitheda during that period) was not so impressively inhabited and the place was a leading forest-post in the area of *Lakhi Jungle*. The identification of it with the Ohind or Tabarhind had already being successfully contested.[34] On the other hand, the region of Ghaggar valley, which is usually not considered a place of rich settlement after the decline of Harappan civilization or at the most after the disappearance of the Painted Grey Ware (or PGW) culture, had witnessed the rise and fall of several cultures in the area from the Mauryan period onwards.

We have already briefly discussed about the settlement of various tribes and clans from the Kushan period and now will highlight the importance of the archaeological sites of the *Ther*, or mound, of Bhadarkali temple, near Hanumangarh town, in support of such arguments. It is surprising that neither Tessitori nor Aurel Stein gave much importance to this site, which otherwise draws the attentions of visitors even from a distance. According to literary sources, the temple was an important religious site during the medieval period. Sometime in the early twentieth century, Maharaja Ganga Singh of Bikaner, who extended hospitality to both Tessitori and Aurel Stein, repaired and somewhat modified the structure of the temple. At that time one important inscription was removed from the site and shifted to the Bikaner Fort museum.[35]

Aurel Stein had noted that, "...after 4 miles there is a large *Ther* of Bhadarkali named after the shrine of the goddess which occupies its eastern end. It measures close to 300 yards in length and shows a maximum height of 43 feet. The much repaired, small temple raised on a massive platform is thickly covered with plaster and affords no clear indication of the age. But judging from the quantity of painted and relief decorated sherds, all of the Rangmahal type, strewing the surface of the mound, continuity of local worship at the site may be assumed".[36] In other words, he accepts that archaeological remains of the *Ther* date to the late Kushan or Gupta period.

The architectural details of the temple are not commonly seen in temples of other parts of Rajasthan, Haryana and Punjab, and speak of its antiquity. The top portion of the structure presents a picture of the famous *Chaitya* arches of Buddhist sites. The front is built in the frame of an arch window and behind the arch frame there is a vault-roofed construction that gives an impression of a big burial chamber. All the important features of *Chaitya* framed construction of Buddhist monasteries are seen in this temple.[37]

The Bhadarkali temple was originally a Buddhist *stupa* and it carries all the architectural features characteristic of the *Chaityas* of the early Buddhist period.[38] Hieun Tsiang, the famous Chinese traveller of seventh century noted that a good number of Buddhist centres and monasteries were in existence in the areas of north Sind and south Punjab precisely in the region lying between Multan and Bhatner.[39] Noted archaeologist Cunningham almost felt tempted to confirm that Bhatner was the real site of *Po-to-tu-spo* or *Bhatsthala* in northwest India, although he subsequently, without contradicting his earlier findings, changed this identification to Sirhind in Haryana.[40] Yet the account of the Chinese traveller clearly suggests the position of Bhatner or *Bhatsthala* as the possible site of Satardru (*She-to-tu-lo* or *Po-to-tu-lo*). His details of travels from Punjab to Mathura via Satardru and Pariyatra also go in the favour of the identification with Bhatner.[41]

There are evidences that during that period one main branch of the river Sutlej or *Ghara* was flowing through a channel of its old eastern bed, which is even now visible on the strip parallel to the Indo-Pak border in Sri Ganganagar district of Rajasthan. Local tales still carry the description of this flow of *Ghara* and George Thomas, who came to this area at the beginning of the nineteenth century, recorded these in his memoirs.[42]

Probably Hieun Tsiang visited Satardru in the month of September of the year AD 635, and during this time, the monsoon season must be on its last leg as he noted the river (Sutlej), was flowing in its extended form. This branch of Sutlej used to meet the river Hakra at a junction now known as Marot (a town in the Bahawalpur area of modern Pakistan). The fort and town of Marot was founded by Rao Manday Rai, a Bhati prince of the royal family of the erstwhile Jaisalmer state, sometime in the middle of the seventh century. This town was a principal urban centre of the Bhati kingdom known as Ramel during the seventh and eighth centuries.[43] The text *Chachnama* has thrown light on the position of this powerful kingdom of Ramel, which lay on the border regions of Hind and Sind.[44]

The description of Hieun Tsiang about Buddhism in the kingdom of Satardru is very interesting. He writes that about three or four *lee* to the east of the city, the Buddhist king Ashoka (third emperor of the Mauryan dynasty) built a 200 feet high *stupa* on a mound.[45] The antiquity of the temple and the description, directions and distances recorded in the account of the traveler go in the favour identifying it with the Bhadarkali *Ther*.[46] Thus, on the basis of Hieun Tsiang's account, it is possible that perhaps the structure of the Bhadrakali temple first came up during the time of the Mauryan emperor Ashoka. Hieun Tsiang noted a number of other *stupas* in the same place and as per his description; all of them belong to Sakya Tathagata and his disciples.[47] He further noted that "...There are *stupas* containing relics of the bodies of Sakya Tathagata and his holy disciples still existing in this place; to wit, of Sariputra, of Maudgalyayana, of Purnamaitreyaniputra, of Upali, of Ananda, of Rahula, and of

Manjusri. Every year, on religious festival days, priests and disciples assemble at these several *stupas*, according to their school, and offer religious worship and offerings".[48]

It is known that the Kushans and Indo-Scythians had embraced Buddhism. The Bhatis and Varhas who latter settled in these parts of Rajasthan, Haryana and south Punjab may also have followed Buddhism, but the Yaudheyas were not Buddhists. Since the Chaitya occupied only the eastern side of the *Ther*, it is possible that other religious structures existed on the remaining portion of the *Ther*. The discovery of a red clay plaque of Goddess *Mahishamardini* here supports such a conclusion.

Possibly both Buddhism and *Shakti* worship were popular at the site but subsequently Buddhism declined. Cunningham's description of *Bhatsthala* as *Banda* or *Bando* suggests that a settlement existed at the site before the foundation of the fort of Bhatner, and that it was on the side of Bhadarkali *Ther*.[49] Hieun Tsiang noted that land was quite fertile and fruit producing and it is possible that it had a well-developed irrigation system.[50]

Perhaps the northern branch of Indo-Scythians, who once ruled over the Indian sub-continent's frontier regions and Punjab, held sway over this part of Rajasthan after the decline of Kushan power. They also succeeded in forming a strong military alliance with the other powers of western India, like Kedarites, Parthians (Persians) and Marundas. Shalivahan of Punjab, from the Indo-Scythian Gandhara line, was a contemporary of the Gupta dynasty emperor Samundra Gupta and his son Chandra Gupta II.[51] It is interesting that during the post-Gupta period they are not addressed as 'Śakas' but their confederacy became more popular as 'Gandhara'. It is the same ruling group, which had close social links with the rulers of Kapisa, and all of them ultimately accepted the suzerainty of emerging *Khakan* of the Western Turks of Central Asia.[52] Al Beruni has recorded that the Guptas defeated the Śakas at the place known as Kehrur, a place located on the western side of the river Sutlej, in the area between the Sutlej and the old bed of the river Beas.[53]

This view has been corroborated by a number of modern scholars.[54] This suggests that Emperor Chandra Gupta II, before battling with the Śaka *Kshatrapas* of Western India, had a serious encounter with another branch of Śakas of Punjab and Rajasthan. The first verse of the famous Mehrauli inscription of 'Chandra' clearly describes that he resisted the combined invasion of enemies from the country of *Vang* or *Bang*. Generally, scholars identify *Vang* with modern *Bang* or Bengal, but in Puranic literature the country and people of *Vang* or *Bang* has also been listed in the group of the countries of *Uttarapath* or northern India. In the *Hamir Mahakavya* a text of the medieval period, the area of the south Ghaggar valley has been addressed as *Vang*. Significantly, place-names like Kalibanga or Pilibanga in this part of the region bears the testimony to it.[55]

In fact, the geographical features of the region of *Vang* or *Bang* has certain characteristics where rivers flow through various channels on a vast levelled ground, and during that period the river Ghaggar, after crossing Bhatner, used to flow in this form. Aurel Stein had observed that towards the north-east side of Rangmahal, near Manik *Theri*, the area looks like a large bay of the Ghaggar bed. Even today, after very heavy rainfall in the Himalayan mountainous regions, the Ghaggar creates havoc in Rajasthan and upper parts of Sind (Pakistan) by submerging dry lands. Now, it is commonly addressed as '*Nali*'. The width of this river Ghaggar or Hakra has always amazed archaeologists and historians. Near Kalibanga site it covers a very large area and after Suratgarh it often flooded like a great lake or ocean. Aurel Stein has discovered many sites on the river between Suratgarh and Wullar where once regular ferry was conducted.[56]

Perhaps at the time of his accession the king 'Chandra' of Mehrauli inscription defended his kingdom from the combined attack of Śakas and Kedarites and even of Yaudheyas. Later, on as the inscription records, he attacked the country of enemies (*Vang* and its adjoining territories) and after crushing their power reached the country of *Vahalik* or *Vahik*, lying between Sutlej and Beas, or at the mouth of *Sapt-Sindhu* or *Panjnand*, where at Kehrur a decisive battle with the Śakas and Kedarites was fought. From there he crossed the river Beas (old bed) and reached *Vishnudham* or Multan. On his return journey from *Vishnudham* he passed through *Mahavan* or the famous *Lakhi Jungle* of Punjab.[57]

It appears that the Gupta sword settled scores against their traditional enemies and returned after establishing political hegemony over their regions. As such, one may assume that Śakas, Murundas, later Kushans and Yaudheyas had once inhabited the regions of the Ghaggar valley and its surroundings. Also, epigraphic evidence suggests that the Yaudheyas, once residents of *Panjnad* area, later moved and settled in Rajasthan.[58] Literary sources of the early medieval period do not mention the presence of Śakas, Murundas or Kushans in these parts.

The reference of Yaudheyas is there but they are known by the name 'Johiya' and many scholars have stated that this is a localized form of 'Yaudheya'. The northern most part of the erstwhile Bikaner state till the advent of Rathores in the late fifteenth century was known as *Johiyavati*.[59]

Eighth to tenth century sources of western India talk about the rule of Mauryas, Chapas, Gurjaras, Guhils, Partiharas, Abhiras, Bhatis, Parmars or Panwars, Rashtrakutas and Chauhans in different parts of Rajasthan.[60] In contrast, Hieun Tsiang, in the seventh century, writes about the castes of the rulers of Rajasthan as belonging to *Vaishyas*, *Kshatriyas* and *Sudras*.[61] The *Chachnama* text of the 8th century refers to the activities of Bhati clans and Jat tribes in the border regions of Sind and Hind, and as noted above, refers to Ramel as the principal kingdom of this region.[62] Nainsi and other Rajasthani writers of late medieval period refer to the political rivalry between the Bhatis, Varhas and Panwars (Parmars), the principal clans of this region.[63]

New researches have thrown light on the movement of Jat and Gujjar communities in the various parts of Rajasthan during this period.[64] Most of the Jat groups came from Sind and *Panjnand* area whereas the Gujjars, perhaps, moved from the Punjab and north-west frontier regions. From the references, should one assume that the old inhabitants of the region either moved away or, as suggested, that they were absorbed in the local societies? In case they became integrated into the local or regional societies, were they recognized in the social set up with new identities? It appears that different groups among them settled down as agriculturists and pastoral people. At the same time, some of their groups found opportunities to remain as ruling clans at the political or administrative level.

Hieun Tsiang discussed Indian society more in terms of *varnas* or castes of the people. As far as the ruling clans of Rajasthan, Sind and Punjab are concerned he, with a few exceptions, referred to them as non-*Kshatriyas* and even included some *Sudras*. He sometimes identified the same family as both *Sudra* and *Brahmin*.[65] It appears that he constructed his views in the background of pan-Indian social situation, whereas the regions of western India, at that time, were experiencing a flow of migrations and absorption of various outside communities within the framework of local societies. Several such outside communities may not have found a position for at least some generations in the categories of the *varna* order. In the *Prayag Prashasti* (or Allahabad pillar inscription), of Emperor Samudra Gupta, the territories of such people have been termed as *Partayant*. Contemporaneous literature described them as *Mallechhs* (countries).[66]

Bhati records from Jaisalmer throw some light on the situation, and note that in the middle of the fifth century, Prince Bhati, son of Balband and grandson of Shalivahan of Punjab, founded the fort of Bhatner on the bank of Ghaggar river and after him, his descendants became famous as Bhatis. Before that, as Jadams, they were residents of Gandhara/Qandhar, Ghazni and Kapisa regions.[67] Similarly, Varhas, rulers of Vitheda and Bahawalpur areas, were descendants of either the later Kushan-Kedarites or the Huns.[68]

We do not know much about the origin of Panwars but one version about their descent is that they are Malavas and residents of the *Madra* land or 'pradesh', of south Punjab.[69] Researches now indicate that the Bhatis or Jadams were from the Indo-Scythian stock.[70] While these findings require further investigation, it appears that a strong historical link existed between the settlements of the old tribes and the emerging new clans in the areas of lower Punjab, north Sind and Rajasthan. Perhaps the archaeological remains of the Ghaggar valley, particularly of the Bhadrakali temple, offer some evidence in support of such understanding.

Until the period of seventh century, it remained a Buddhist site. After that, it became popular as a place of the *Shakti* cult. It is difficult to pinpoint exactly when this *Chaitya* became a Bhadarkali temple. The changeover may have coincided with the downfall of Buddhism in the Punjab and north-western frontier regions of the country. Moreover, *Shakti* worship in the region was already present from the Gupta period. From Bhati records it appears that Bhati rulers became ardent follower of the *Shakti* cult during the ninth and tenth centuries. The foundation of a *Shakti* temple at Tanot (near Jaisalmer) and Rao Bijay Ray's immense faith in the worship of *Devi*, the Goddess, testifies to such beliefs.[71]

The chroniclers of Mahmud of Ghazna noted that after the fall of the fort of Bhatia or Bhatner in AD 1004, its lord Bijay Ray fled to the nearby jungle and committed suicide there to save his honour. Bhati records note that after the defeat Bijay Ray left the fort and went to the temple of *Devi* in the nearby jungle, where he tried to sacrifice his life before the image of the Goddess, but the Goddess, after seeing the noble act, persuaded him not to do so. However, soon afterwards, his arch-rivals, the Varhas, killed him at Vitheda.[72] The nearby jungle referred to was part of the famous *Lakhi Jungle*, and looking to the surrounding situations, the site of the temple where the Bhati ruler went goes in the favour of the modern Bhadrakali temple. *Khyat* writings of Rajasthan also verify the location of a temple in the *Lakhi Jungle* near Bhatner.[73] Such incidents confirm that during the early medieval period, like many other famous Buddhist *Chaityas* of western India, this temple became a centre of worship of Hindu religion.[74]

Even in the adjoining parts of Bhatner, Shakti worship became very popular as may be illustrated from the example of the old *Devi* temple of Pallu, from where two famous Saraswati images have been discovered. Interestingly, the priests of Pallu temple are Bhati Rajputs.[75] Such developments suggest as to how the old inhabitants of the region, with the passage of the time, and under the new political and social situations, successfully changed their social identities, and thereafter assimilated into local societies. In the *Hamir Mahakavya* text, the rulers of Vitheda or Varhas (descendants of Turki Shahis of Kabul) are addressed as Gopals.[76]

Two small inscriptions placed on the front portion of the chamber of the roof of the Bhadarkali temple state that after the tenth century for some time the *Ther* became a place of Islamic faith. One inscription on a small slab is still there but the other one (as noted previously) was shifted during the reign of Maharaja Ganga Singh to the Bikaner fort (and thereafter town) museum. The name of 'Allah' in the *Kufi* (Arabic-Sindhi) script is prominently engraved on the slabs. It appears that after the fall of Bhati power, Bhatner or Bhatia came into the direct possession of the Sultans of Ghazna. Sultan Mahmud, in the course of his several campaigns to different parts of India, preferred the route of Bhatner from Multan or Uchchh. After the fall of the Ghaznavids, the fort at Bhatner and the region came under the influence of the Carmathians of Multan.

These inscriptions suggest that possibly Bhatner became a centre of Carmathian activities.[77] Sultan Mu'izz al-Din Muhammad Sām of Ghūr finally broke the strength of the Carmathians, and after the battles of Tarain, Bhatner or Tabarhind, too, became the part of Ghūrid Empire.[78] The Bhatis, after their defeat by the forces of Ghazna in AD 1004, moved towards the interior of the Thar and Cholistan deserts, while their rival Varhas, too, could not survive for long and finally after the battle of Tarain, they too migrated towards the south of Rajasthan and Gujarat. The Panwars met a similar fate and only the Yaudheyas or Johiyas remained to resist.[79] Over time, a good number of them converted to Islam. Otherwise, too, after the occupation of

Sind and Multan by Arabs, the Ghaggar valley came under the influence of Islam, and many people from tribes or clans like Bhatis (or Bhattis), Samas, Raths, Chayals and Chauhans accepted Islam.

During this period (c. AD 1000–1400), some major ecological changes occurred and aridity rapidly grew in the Ghaggar valley region. Because of such geographical and environmental changes, people started moving away. Although the Tughlaq dynasty rulers made some serious attempts for the restoration of environmental order and built canals, simultaneously, the clearance of the old *Lakhi Jumgle* in favour of agriculture opened new doors for the Thar desert.[80] However, as the river Ghaggar was still carrying some water in its channel beyond the rainy season, the region in and around Bhatner remained fertile and productive. Moreover, as Bhatner was located on one of the most important trade routes of the sub-continent, many important nobles of the Delhi Sultanate, including Malik Altunia and Sher Khan (a cousin of Delhi's Sultan Balban), asked to be posted here. It was from the military base of Bhatner that Sher Khan successfully checked Mongol invasions, before he was killed at Bhatner.[81]

Three images of *Devi* (in her form of Bhadarkali), placed in the main chamber of the temple, provide some important clues to the history of the region. The last image that is worshipped today was perhaps placed during the reign of Maharaja Ganga Singh and a new team of temple priests was called from Bikaner town. It is interesting that the first two figures of *Devi* are slightly disfigured but not broken. The first image of *Devi*, in its appearance and form, gives the impression that it belonged to an earlier period. We do not know when the second image was installed in the temple. We know that Delhi's Sultan Firuz Tughlaq, whose mother was a Bhati princess from Abohar, had assigned the fief of Bhatner to his maternal uncle, and perhaps it was at that time that the second *Devi* image was installed.

Though the Bhatis failed to retain Bhatner after the invasion of Timur,[82] it appears that temple not only survived but it became a popular centre of *Shakti* worship in the region. Even people who changed their faith did not forget to venerate the place. In the reigns of the Delhi Sultanate's Lodi dynasty Sultans and the early Mughal emperors, the temple had visitors from both faiths.[83] It is known that the Mughal Emperor Akbar visited the site, along with Prince Rai Singh of Bikaner,[84] and well before that, during the reign of the early Sultans of Delhi, a sizeable population of Sayyads had settled in and around Bhatner.[85]

Notes

1. Tessitori and Aurel Stein explored and sometimes excavated sites in Ghaggar valley in 1917 and 1940–41, respectively. For details see, Sir Aurel Stein, *An Archaeological Tour along the Ghaggar-Hakra River* (ed. S.P. Gupta), Meerut, 1989, pp. 14–25; Hermann Goetz did similar work in 1945 and subsequently in independent India (Hermann Goetz, *Art and Architecture of the Bikaner State,* Oxford, 1950, pp. 25–27); and A. Ghosh surveyed and produced a report on behalf of Government of India. For the report by A. Ghosh, see Stein's, *An Archaeological Tour along the Ghaggar-Hakra River* (ed. S.P. Gupta), Meerut, 1989, pp. 89–106.
2. Review of the findings of Tessitori by Aurel Stein, see, Sir Aurel Stein, op. cit., pp. 14–25.
3. Hermann Goetz, op. cit., pp. 26–27.
4. A. Ghosh, Sir Aurel Stein, *An Archaeological Tour along the Ghaggar-Hakra River* (ed. S.P. Gupta), op. cit., pp. 89–106.
5. Col. James Tod, *Annals and Antiquities of Rajasthan*, Oxford, 1920, Vol. II, pp. 1166–67.
6. A. Ghosh, Sir Aurel Stein, *An Archaeological Tour along the Ghaggar-Hakra River* (ed. S.P. Gupta), op. cit., pp. 105–106.
7. Hermann Goetz, op. cit., pp. 27–28; K.C. Jain, *Ancient Cities and Towns of Rajasthan,* Delhi, 1972, p.139.
8. Hermann Goetz, op. cit., pp. 26–27; R.C. Agarwal, "Ancient Sculptures and Terracottas from Rajasthan", *The Researcher,* Vol. I (Summer Number), Jaipur, pp.17–18.
9. R.C. Agarwal, "Mahishamasdini in Early Rajasthani Art", *The Researcher*, Vol. V–VI, Jaipur, 1965–66, pp. 11–12.
10. Aurel Stein, op. cit., p. 35.
11. Ibid., pp. 29–33.
12. Ibid.
13. Ibid., p. 31.
14. Hanna Rydh and others, *Rangmahal: The Swedish Archaeological Expedition to India 1952–54, (Acta Archeologica Lundensia, Series in 4°, No. 3)* vii, Lund: C.W.K. Gleerup: Bonn a. R.: Rudolf Habelt Verlag; etc., 1959, sw. kr. 100.
15. K.C. Jain, op. cit., p.146.
16. Ibid., p. 147.
17. Aurel Stein, op. cit., p. 25.
18. Hermann Goetz, op. cit., pp. 26–27; K.C. Jain, pp. 139–40.
19. Aurel Stein, p. 32; B.M.S. Parmar, *Numismatic Acquisitions (1965–1972)*, List is preserved in the Directorate of Archaeology and Museums, Rajasthan, Jaipur.

20. Aurel Stein, p. 31; Satya Prakash, "Ganganagar Jile ki eak Rochak avam Adhivitya Mrunmay Kalakarti", *The Researcher*, Vol. VIII–IX, Jaipur, 1966–68, pp. 85–86.
21. Discussed by K.C. Jain, pp. 142–43.
22. Aurel Stein, p. 23.
23. Discussed by K.C. Jain, pp. 142–43, 146.
24. Vadodara Museum and Picture Gallery, Vadodara, Series No(s) from 111 to 141.
25. B.G. Gafurov, *Central Asia: Pre-historic to Pre-modern Times*, Vol. I, New Delhi, 2005, pp. 316–17, 319. *Jaisalmer ri Khyat* (ed. by Dr Narayan Singh Bhati), *Parampara*, Part 57–58, Jodhpur, 1981, p. 32, (*Bhati Padihar mil re Judh kiyo*); *Tawarikh Jaisalmer* (Written by Lakhmichand by the order of Mohta Nathmal) Jodhpur, 1999 (Reprint), p.13–14.
26. *Munhata Nainsi ri Khyat*, Part 2 (ed. by Badri Parsad Sakaria), Jodhpur, 1984, pp. 18–19, 22, 25, 27–28.
27. *Jaisalmer ri Khyat*, op. cit., p. 31.
28. Col. James Tod, *Annals and Antiquities of Rajasthan*, Oxford, 1920, Vol. I, p.129; Vol. II, p.1164.
29. Dasharath Sharma, *Early Chauhan Dynasties*, Delhi, 1959, p. 13, 63 (Note 1).
30. B.M.S. Parmar, *Numismatic Acquisitions (1965–1972)*. List preserved at the Directorate of Archaeology and Museums, Rajasthan, Jaipur; Dasharath Sharma, *Rajasthan through the Ages*, Bikaner, 1967, pp. 252–55; Dr Pushpa Bhati, *Rajasthan ke Lok Devta and Sahitya* (Hindi), Bikaner, 1991, pp. 84–90.
31. J.N. Asopa, *Origin of the Rajputs*, Delhi, 1976, pp. 38–39, 150–53, G.S.L. Devra, Political Wilderness and Social Dismemberment – Varhas: A Forgotten Clan of North-West India (Pre-Medieval Period), Indian History Congress Proceeding, 2003.
32. Archaeological Survey of India, Report of a Tour in the Punjab and Rajputana of 1883–84, Volume XXIII, Varanasi.
33. Ibid., pp. 5–6.
34. G.S.L. Devra, *Poorva Madhyakalin Bharat Ke Abhigyan Roop – Tarain and Tabarhind* (Hindi), Jodhpur, 1995, pp. 9–10.
35. The inscription is lying in the Bikaner Museum though it is wrongly stated that the inscription belongs to the sixteenth century. The said inscription still regresses a clear screening: V.S. Srivastava, *Catalogue and Guide to Ganga Golden Jubilee Museum, Bikaner*, Stone Slab (594 B.M.), Size; 18"×25" (15th–16th Century AD Hanumangarh); The slab is inscribed 'Allah Ho' in Persian (?), Jaipur, 1960–61, p. 26.
36. Aurel Stein, p. 28.

37. G.S.L. Devra, *Bhadrakali Temple of Hanumangarh: A Buddhist Archaeological Site of Historical Importance*, '*Socio-Religious Movements in Rajasthan*' (ed. S.N. Dubey), Centre for Rajasthan Studies, University of Rajasthan, Jaipur, 1996.
38. Henry Cousins, *The Architectural Antiquities of Western India*, London, 1926, p. 12,13, 82. The design of Buddhist *Chaitya* at Ter in Andhra Pradesh looks similar to that of Bhadarkali, for the study see plate no. 9.
39. Thomas Walters, *On Yvan Chwang's Travels in India*, Delhi, 2004 (Reprint), Vol. I, pp. 297–300, Vol. II, pp. 252–55.
40. A. Cunningham, *The Ancient Geography of India, Delhi*, 1976 (Reprint), pp. 168–69. "The position of the celebrated fortress of Bhatner would suit the description of a small district bounded on the west by the Satlej and would also agree with the corrected distance from Kullu".
41. *On Yvan Chwang's Travels in India*, op. cit., Vol. I, pp. 298–301.
42. William Franklin, *Military Memoirs of George Thomas*, Calcutta, 1803, pp. 163–64.
43. *Jaisalmer ri Khyat*, op. cit., p. 35.
44. The *Chachanamah* (Tr. by Mirza Kalichbeg Fredunbeg) Delhi, 1979 (Reprint), p. 45, 53,160.
45. Thomas Walters, *On Yvan Chwang's Travels in India*, Delhi, 2004 (Reprint), pp. 299–300.
46. G.S.L. Devra, *Bhadrakali Temple of Hanumangarh: A Buddhist Archaeological Site of Historical Importance*, op. cit.
47. *On Yvan Chwang's Travels in India*, Vol. I, pp. 299–300.
48. Ibid.
49. A. Cunningham, *The Ancient Geography of India*, op. cit., p. 169.
50. *On Yvan Chwang's Travels in India*, Vol. I, pp. 299–300.
51. This inference has been drawn after a careful study of the Bhati records of Jaisalmer, *Jaisalmer ri Khyat*, op. cit. pp. 30–31. Also see, G.S.L. Devra, Presidential Address, Punjab History Congress (Political Zone vs. Historical Zone), Patiala, March 2001.
52. Bāna in *Harshacharita* has mentioned – ed. by P.V. Kane, Delhi, 1965 (Reprint), pp. 122–23; *On Yvan Chwang's Travels in India*, Vol. I, pp. 122–23, 198–99.
53. *Alberuni's India* (ed. by Edward C. Sachau), Delhi, 1989 (Reprint), p. 61.
54. A. Cunningham, op. cit., p. 277; Dasharath Sharma, "Mehrauli Pillar Inscription, The Location of Kartpur", *Journal of Indian History*, Vol. 15.
55. Nayan Chandra Suri, *Hammir Mahakavya (*Hindi translation by Nathulal Trivedi*)*, Jodhpur, 1997, p. 29 (Sarg 46–49). For the detailed discussion on the subject, see, G.S.L. Devra, *Chandra ka Mehrauli Stambh: Eak aur Adhyayan* (Hindi), Shodh Patrika, Udaipur, Ank 54/3–4, pp. 5–20.
56. Aurel Stein, pp. 22, 35–38.

57. G.S.L. Devra, *Chandra ka Mehrauli Stambh: Eak aur Adhyayan* (Hindi), op. cit.
58. For the study on these aspects, see, A. Cunningham, op. cit., pp. 281–3; D.C. Shukla, *Early History of Rajasthan*, Delhi, 1978, pp. 32–33, 66–67.
59. A. Cunningham, op. cit., pp. 282–83; Hermann Goetz, op. cit., pp. 28–29; G.S.L. Devra, *Rajasthan ki Prashasnik Vyastha* (Hindi), Bikaner, 1981, pp. 4–5.
60. For the study see, Dasharath Sharma, *Rajasthan Through the Ages*, op. cit., pp. 101–108; J.N. Asopa, *Origin of the Rajputs*, pp. 7–9.
61. *On Yvan Chwang's Travels in India*, Vol. I, pp. 299–300, Vol. II, pp. 248–55.
62. The *Chachnamah*, op. cit., p. 45, 53, 160; G.S.L. Devra and Shashi Arora, *Identification of Ramel, a Forgotten Empire of Early Medieval India*, IHCP, 2001.
63. *Munhata Nainsi ri Khyat*, Part 2, op. cit., pp. 18–19, 22, 25, 27–28.
64. G.S.L. Devra, "Social Formation and Stratification in Northwest India during the Early Medieval Period", published in *Sikh Society, Culture and Polity in Historical Perspective* (ed. by B.L. Gupta), Guru Gobind Singh Center of Sikh Studies, Rajasthan University, Jaipur, 2008.
65. *On Yvan Chwang's Travels in India*, Vol. II, pp. 248–55. Visitor describes the ruler of Chih-chito or Chittor as Brahman who became Buddhist and king of Sind as Shudra. In *Chachnama* of the eighth (next) century the king of Chittor has been suggested as a close relative of king of Sind, Sahasi, pp. 20–21.
66. K.D. Bajpayee, K.L. Agarwal and Santosh Bajpayee, *Aitihasik Bhartiya Abhilekh* (Hindi), Jaipur, 1992, p.148. For commentary on *Pratyant* countries, see, S.R. Goyal, *The Imperial Guptas*, Jodhpur, 2005, pp. 199–202.
67. *Jaisalmer ri Khyat*, p. 31.
68. G.S.L. Devra, Political Wilderness and Social Dismemberment – Varhas: A Forgotten Clan of North-West India (Pre-Medieval Period), Indian History Congress Proceeding, 2003.
69. D.C. Sircar, *Ancient Malwa and the Vikramaditya Traditions*, Delhi, 1969, pp. 1–4, 12, 18.
70. Hari Singh Bhati, *Annals of Jaisalmer*, Bikaner, 2002, op. cit., pp. 113–17.
71. *Jaisalmer ri Khyat*, p. 36, 37.
72. Elliot and Dowson, *History of India told by its own Historians*, Vol. II, Delhi, 1990, pp. 29–30; Muhammad Nazim, *The Life and Times of Sultan Mahmud*, Delhi, 1971 (Second Edition), pp. 100–01 (Footnote 8); *Jaisalmer ri Khyat*, p. 36, 37.
73. *Munhata Nainsi ri Khyat*, Part 3, op. cit., p. 17.
74. S. Nagarajun, *Buddhist Architecture of Western India*, Delhi, 1981, p. 86.
75. The village of Pallu is located on the road from Hanumangarh to Sardarshahar. Two beautiful images of Goddess Saraswati have been recovered from Pallu, which are now at the National Museum, New Delhi and Ganga Museum,

Bikaner, respectively. These images of Saraswati belong to the eleventh century.

76. Nayan Chandra Suri, *Hammir Mahakavya*, op. cit., p. 25 (Sarg 1-3).

77. Archaeological Survey of India, *Epigraphic India: Arabic and Persian Supplement* (ed. by Z.A. Desai), Delhi, 1965, p.1. (Kufi Epitaphs); For the influence of Carmathians of Multan, see, Farad Daftly, *The Islamic: Their History and Doctrine*, Cambridge, 1992, pp. 180, 478–80; G.S.L. Devra, *Identification of Bhatia*, published in *Prof Krishan Swaroop Gupta Abhinandan Granth*, Udaipur, 2008, pp. 260–66. In this matter I have taken the help from Dr Hasan Mahmud (M.S. University of Baroda) and N.M. Ganam (Baroda). Author acknowledges their valuable suggestions.

78. G.S.L. Devra, *Poorva Madhyakalin Bharat Ke Abhigyan Roop – Tarain and Tabarhind* (Hindi), Jodhpur, 1995.

79. G.S.L. Devra, *Poorva Madhyakalin Bharat Ke Abhigyan Roop – Tarain and Tabarhind* (Hindi), op. cit.; G.S.L. Devra, Political Wilderness and Social Dismemberment – Varhas: A Forgotten Clan of North-West India (Pre-Medieval Period), Indian History Congress Proceeding, 2003; G.S.L. Devra, *Identification of Bhatia*, op. cit., pp. 260–66.

80. *Desertification and Problem of Delimitation of Rajputana desert during the Medieval Period*, (*Rajasthan Ecology, Culture and Society)*; ed. M.K. Bhasin and Veena Bhasin, Delhi, 1999.

81. G.S.L. Devra, *Poorva Madhyakalin Bharat Ke Abhigyan Roop – Tarain and Tabarhind* (Hindi), op. cit.

82. Ibid.

83. *Munhata Nainsi ri Khyat*, Part 3, op. cit., pp. 17–18; *Teen Juni Vatan*, Parampara, (*Journal*, ed. by N. S. Bhati), Jodhpur, 1988, No. 73 (*Thakursi Jetsiyot ri Vat)*.

84. Abul Fazal, *Akbarnama*, Vol. II; (Tr. and Ed. by H. Beveridge), Delhi, 1972, p. 522.

85. G.S.L. Devra, *Poorva Madhyakalin Bharat Ke Abhigyan Roop – Tarain and Tabarhind* (Hindi), op. cit.

9

A Non-Historian's Personal Discovery of Tod and His Impacts

RAKESH HOOJA

Discovering Tod

My introduction to Tod's *Annals and Antiquities of Rajasthan* was perhaps better than that of many others. It was 1966. Our Jaipur school had a system of granting a long (2–3 month?) preparation leave to prepare for the school-leaving Senior Cambridge examinations. My father being posted as Collector and District Magistrate in Chittor (the original capital of Mewar), I spent the period there and it was arranged that to practice science practicals I would visit Chittorgarh's Sainik School daily. In between stints in the school's science laboratory – while the school's students were being coached in English, Hindi and other subjects – I would sneak into the school library (a window had been left unlatched by oversight) and read Tod on the exploits of Rajput princes and warriors. Since I was also simultaneously visiting Chittorgarh Fort two or three times a week, I could see some of the places that I was reading about in Tod and even try to imagine having been present myself at the historic sites when events described by Tod were actually unfolding. At times I accompanied my father on his tours within Chittorgarh district or on his visits to nearby Udaipur (which became Mewar's capital after Chittor), where Tod had collected much of his material that later led to his various publications including the *Annals...*, and again I could correlate what I was reading with actual sites. As a 15–16 years old school boy I was swayed by the tales of

---

This is the text, with minor editing, of the second half of the inaugural address delivered on December 29, 2005 by the author at the Fifth International Conference on Rajasthan, organized by Institute of Rajasthan Studies, Jaipur.

bravery and chivalry as well as betrayal amongst the Rajputs without really bothering about dynastic developments or trying to gain a sense of Rajasthan's history, or its socio-political background.

The fact that Tod had worked as an administrator like my father (the concept of Political Agent of the British to the princely states – or the fact that Tod was dealing with the fates of princely dynasty's rather than working solely as an administrator – were not then known to me) while he worked on his writings also fascinated me. (I am not sure whether I realized at the time that Tod's writings were mostly undertaken after his return at the age of 41 to Britain rather than during his stay at Udaipur – or even that Tod's Udaipur stay was a relatively short part of his life – four years out of twenty-two spent in India in the service of the East India Company.)

In any case that is when I first developed a desire to know more about the life of Tod.

I had not then known that I would eventually join the Indian Administrative Service (IAS) and thus, via the Indian Civil Service (ICS) of the days of the British Raj, become a successor to men like James Tod (the 'Men Who Ruled India' in the words of Philip Mason though Mason did not feature Tod as a 'Founder' in his two-volume work). Upon joining the IAS, I landed up in Ajmer in 1975 for my district training and was quick to avail of an opportunity to go to Todgarh located in a forest reserve in Beawar tehsil of Ajmer district. I do not remember much except that the small building generally looked like many a building from the days of the British Raj which could be seen in Rajasthan (North India) up to the 1950s, 60s, 70s – many of which have disappeared with time. As I recall not many at Todgarh (referred to locally as Tatgarh) had any idea of James Tod or his link with Todgarh. The last that I heard of a couple of years ago the old building was still standing at Todgarh – and is located in the premises of a non-governmental organization. Not (till very recently) having come across Bishop Reginald Heber's note from his 1826 visit that people in Bhilwara (now a district headquarters) felt that it should have been renamed Todganj due to Tod's efforts at reviving it as a commercial trade centre, I never tried to explore whether anything related to Tod survives in Bhilwara.

Much later, my wife getting posted in Udaipur gave me a chance in 2003 to see some artifacts related to Tod's life and Udaipur sojourn (1818 to 1822) in the City Palace at Udaipur. This generated a vague desire in me to write a life of Colonel James Tod – something very different from my normal official files or the semi-academic social science writing on themes related to development, administration and the rural delivery system, land-water management, democratic decentralization and Panchayati Raj, or governmental developmental schemes etc., which I often indulge in for journals, books etc.

But the latent desire to write a biography on Tod (similar to one to write a biography of Tessitori who had lived and worked in Bikaner) was tempered by the fact that I knew virtually nothing about Tod's life and had forgotten the details of what I had read year's ago in Tod's *Annals and Antiquities of Rajasthan*. (In fact, I do not even know whether the *Annals...* that I was originally introduced to were a reprint of William Crookes three-volume edited version first released in 1920, or of that edited by Douglas Sladen and issued in two volumes in 1914 with financial help from the Rao Rana or of Jhalawar, or the original versions that Tod got published 1829 and 1832, though the fact that Sladen's publisher Routledge and Kegan Paul had brought out a version in 1957 makes me suspect that it was what I read in Chittorgarh in 1966–67.)

Searching Sources on Tod's Life

I came across Gaurishanker Hirachand Ojha's *Suprasidh Itihaskar Colonel James Tod Ka Jeevan Charitra* (Life Sketch of the Renowned Historian Col. James Tod, apparently originally written in 1902) in a 2002 edition by Rajasthani Granthagar, Jodhpur at a book fair in Jaipur in late November 2005 followed almost immediately by the invitation from the Institute of Rajasthan Studies to attend the Fifth International Conference on Rajasthan with one of the focuses being Tod. I felt that instead of writing out a paper on a developmental theme as I had done for the Third International Conference on Rajasthan, I would take a look at whatever writings about the life of James Tod I could get hold of and give a non-historian's view as my perceptions about the impact of Tod as a Political Agent and as a scholar-administrator – without going into the contents of Tod's two books *(Annals and Antiquities of Rajasthan* and *Travels in Western India)* or Tod's other writings after he became Librarian of the Royal Asiatic Society in 1824, whose analysis can be left to professional historians and other academicians.

Having re-read John Keay's *India Discovered* (1981) in connection with preparing to introduce him for a lecture by him in Jaipur in

September 2005, I knew that there was about a chapter of material on Tod's life and achievements (including quotes from Bishop Heber) in the volume.

Introductions to Hindi translations of the *Annals*...and to Tod's second book *Travels in Western India* yielded very brief life sketches by Gaurishanker Hirachand Ojha (*Tod Krit Rajasthan Ka Itihas*, translator Keshav Thakur, editor Lokesh Sharma, published by Sahityakar, Jaipur, 2003 – though it appears an introductory life sketch by Gaurishanker Hirachand Ojha had first appeared in the second decade of the 1900s in a Hindi translation of Tod's *Annals*... that had been translated by Ram Garib Choube), by Kaluram Sharma (*Colonel James Tod Krit Rajasthan Ka Itihas*, translator Kaluram Sharma, published by Shyam Prakashan, Jaipur, 1988), and by Girdhar Shukla (*James Tod Likhit Paschami Bharat Ki Yatra*, translated by Keshav Kumar Thakur and published by Adarsh Hindi Pustakalaya, Allahabad, 1969).

The search (carried out as a layman not in contact with historians) was naturally hurried so as to be able to meet the deadline of the Fifth International Conference on Rajasthan (where I was asked at short notice to deliver the inaugural address) and more such introductory life sketches along with other Hindi translations may be available. (In fact, after my inaugural address at the Fifth International Conference, I came across Hukam Singh Bhati's edited book *Itihaskar James Tod Vyaktitva Evem Krititva*, published by Pratap Shodh Sansthan, Bhopal Nobles Institute, 1997 at a stall displaying books outside the seminar room on the occasion of the conference.)

I found that William Crooke had written a biographical introduction in his 1920 edition of *Annals*... and Vijay Kumar Vashishtha had contributed "James Tod as Historian" in *The Historians and Sources of History of Rajasthan*, edited by G.N. Sharma and V.S. Bhatnagar, Centre for Rajasthan Studies, University of Rajasthan, Jaipur, 1992. (Subsequently, upon hearing my inaugural address at the Fifth International Conference, Dr Vashishtha was kind enough to make available a copy of his article "Tod's Role as Political Agent in the State of Rajasthan" from the proceedings of the Fourth Session in 1970 of the Rajasthan History Congress. His paper is more critical of Tod's impact than the view I have formed.)

I also got to look at a draft research work "Serving Empire, Serving Nation: Tod's Rajasthan and the Life of an Imperial Narrative" by J. Frietag, which has apparently since been revised into a Ph.D.

thesis with a modified title. However, the draft manuscript is not in the public domain and as the title itself indicates it tries to place Tod's works within the imperial discourse and go into Tod's motivations for writing his books and undertaking his studies. I was more interested in a straight popular life sketch for the lay reader rather than for academics so that I could attempt an assessment of the impacts of his life. In any case I do not intend commenting further upon Frietag's draft except to say that it is both informative and interesting and any further comments upon it need to await its becoming available in published form.

Another piece looking at Tod's motivations and what may have influenced his writings is Lloyd I. Rudolph's "Producing and Reproducing Rajasthan: Why Col Tod Represented Rajasthan the Way He Did and Its Consequences for Imperial Nationalist and Rajput Historiography" in Varsha Joshi (ed.), *Culture, Communities and Change* (Rawat, Jaipur, 2002) which comprises papers from the Fourth International Conference on Rajasthan.

In fact, Lloyd and Susanne Rudolphs also circulated, and Lloyd presented for discussion, a paper "Writing and Reading Tod's Rajasthan: Interpreting the Text and Its Historiography" from Jos Gommans and Om Prakash edited *Circumambulations in South Asian History* (Brill Leiden – Boston, 2003) in the session following my inaugural address at the Fifth Conference. The arguments of this paper partly overlap those of the earlier Rudolphs paper.

Ideally, given a choice, I would have liked to have had access to comments/writing about Tod's life published in Britain about the time of the original publication of the *Annals* ... (1829) onwards to slightly after his death in 1835 by when he was known and respected for his writings. (Even Bishop Heber's travelogue including comments on Tod's work and impact as deduced when he visited Mewar within 3–4 years of Tod's departure is not readily available with me – though quotes and references are available in works that I have cited). I would also have liked to be able to get Hindi or English translations of the introductory life sketches in Bengali translations of *Annals and Antiquities of Rajasthan* because curiously enough more Bengali translations than Hindi ones (Rajasthan is considered a Hindi-speaking state) exist, which also is a matter worth looking into. And, of course, one would have liked to see biographies on Tod written in the 20th century (though I doubt if any book-length life did appear).

Tod has written a lot about happenings in his life in both *Annals...* and his other major work *Travels in Western India* (in the author's introductions and scattered throughout the volumes). However, in this exploratory piece, it is not intended to comment directly upon Tod's writings, but to deal with what I have picked up from life sketches written by others about his impact.

Impact of Tod

Let us start with some of impacts of Tod's East India Service, including as Political Agent at Udaipur.

- He is credited with significant contributions through his intelligence gathering and analysis (and his making available accurate maps that he had got prepared) in the British defeating the Marathas and controlling the Pindaris. With his informers and information gathers who travelled far and wide, he may be considered the precursor of intelligence services in British India.
- The dynastic mosaic of what was to become the Rajputana Agency (or group of princely states) in 1832, the same year that Volume II of his *Annals...* was published, was significantly influenced by Tod – he restored the power of Maharana Bhim Singh vis-a-vis the nobles of the Mewar Court (something he had itched to be involved in since his first visit to Udaipur in 1806 when apparently he decided to take up the Rajput cause; and I wonder whether if Tod had not visited Mewar in 1806 and been influenced by what he saw there including the Maharana feeling cornered and encouraging his daughter Krishna Kumari to take poison, would Tod have contrived and managed to get posted to Udaipur in 1818, and if not then would posterity have been deprived of Tod's *Annals and Antiquities?)*, was influential in Zalim Singh establishing the new state of Jhalawar which was carved out from Kota (interestingly, the only Rajput sponsoring of a work by Tod appears to be that by Zalim Singh's successor as Rao Rana of Jhalawar of Douglas Sladen's edited version of the *Annals...* of 1914), and he protected Sirohi from legal claims being set forth by the Jodhpur ruler. He also tried to superimpose his romantic ideas about English-Scottish feudal relations, and about how the Rajput princely states were in his perception managed in the past, on to the Mewar and other princely states of his day – leading to

tensions which had to gradually sort themselves out after he left in 1822–23.

- Being the first British resident located within Rajasthan, Tod set the pattern for ruler-Resident relationships and systems of princely state administration throughout Rajputana during the British era.
- As Bishop Heber (the same person who during his travels in "the upper provinces of India" had found Amber Palace incomparable), who visited the area shortly after Tod left, has attested that Tod also established standards for future administrators of ensuring peace, prosperity and economic reconstruction, stimulating local trade as well as getting public works (bridges etc.) built, and that he contributed significantly to the revival of Bhilwara as a thriving centre of trade and commerce and to peace and the economic renewal of Udaipur town.
- Tod's written testimony of 1832 to the select committee of Parliament regarding India and the governance of the East India Company (where his views were the counterpoint to those of James Mill who himself had written a six-volume *The History of British India*, without having visited India), along with his other writings and particularly the *Annals...* helped ensure that princely Rajasthan survived though under the doctrine of paramountcy rather than being absorbed into directly ruled British India and, as Lloyd Rudolph has stated (Varsha Joshi, ed., 2002: 31), Tod anticipated the post-1857 Mutiny policy of respecting the princes and relying on them as loyal feudatories of the Crown. This is despite the fact that Tod's immediate superior, when he was Political Agent, Ochterlony did not subscribe to views like those of Tod, and Ochterlony was responsible for Tod's charge of Agent to various princely states being reduced one by one till Tod was forced to leave India after only four years as Resident at Udaipur.
- Tod built up a picture of Mewar-Udaipur as the primary princely state of Rajasthan, which eventually resulted in the Maharana of Mewar being made Rajpramukh of Rajputana during the post-independence merger process. (Naturally, Tod's name evokes more positive reactions in Udaipur than in Jaipur or Jodhpur.)
- Some feel that his interaction with people wherever he went in Rajputana, as well as his various writings including the *Annals...* with its emphasis on Rajput honour, and by developing amongst

the Rajputs a sense of pride, brought the Rajputs closer to the British and thus eased the British imperial control over Rajputana.

As a scholar (or scholar administrator, who was not a trained historian but a collector of documents and other material available about the area and its history and who relied on translators to help understand much of what he collected), some impacts of Tod include:

- Coming up with the concept of Rajasthan as both a physical, as well as a cultural, area and contributing to the evolution of a Rajasthan specific identity, which would eventually lead to the creation of Rajasthan state in modern India.
- Tod was the person who launched Indian numismatics.
- Discovering of the Girnar inscription, whose script Princep later deciphered and which was subsequently discovered to be an Ashokan edict.
- He was the first outsider (European) to visit (discover) the now well-known Delwara Jain temples at Abu and to describe their "exuberant beauties".
- Getting physical surveys conducted and the geographical mapping of Rajasthan and Western India.
- Through his travel notes, collection of material, he also undertook what we can today refer to as the social and political mapping of the Rajputana of his days.
- Starting the Rajasthan tradition of collection of manuscripts, coins etc., and of documenting of monuments etc.
- Inspired numerous Rajasthan chronicles of history.
- *Annals...* and Tod's stories of Rajput valour were used as a source for Indian nationalistic writings, particularly in 19th century Bengal.
- He may be called father of domestic tourism in India as he stimulated initial Bengali interest in tourism to Rajasthan (precursor to today's domestic tourism) as many Bengali version of *Annals...* were printed and fired the imaginations of Bengal writers and the common folk alike, with stories like those about the Sonar Kila of Jaisalmer etc. being penned.
- He made the Rajputs known and admired in 19th century Britain and throughout India.
- He influenced the acceptance of the Rajputs as a martial race for purposes of recruitment to the army of British India.

Afterword

Many of the impacts that Tod wanted to achieve as a Political Agent were thwarted by his immediate superior at Delhi Major General David Ochterlony (through Tod's own tendency to ignore instructions from various superiors and to interfere to a much greater extent that the British East India Company desired in the internal administration of princely states also contributed to it) and eventually Tod resigned (on grounds of ill-health) and left India. Had he stayed on in India – Udaipur – he may have continued collecting his material and managing the British relations with Mewar, but he would never have got the time to write *Annals and Antiquities of Rajasthan* or *Travels in Western India* or the other scholarly writings that he produced after returning to the United Kingdom and becoming librarian of the Royal Asiatic Society. Thus posterity perhaps has Ochterlony to thank for Tod's writings and his consequent reputation. And it is Tod's books, perceptions and ideas, rather than the viewpoints of Ochterlony's official dispatches, which eventually prevailed in post-1857 India and even in England.

10

Origin and Evolution of Tribals in Rajasthan

Ancient Days to Modern Era

BHUPENDRA HOOJA

Who are the tribals? What distinguishes them from the non-tribals? At what point of time or stage of development, and under what circumstances, do the tribals cease to be tribals? What is or has been the tribal setting in Rajasthan? Where did they come from, if they (or most of them) were not indigenous? What has kept them away, and distinctly separate, from the 'non-tribal' society and why?

These and other allied questions need a deep probe and detailed study, if we wish to know something tangible and concrete about the tribals of Rajasthan and where they are going. An attempt has been made in this paper to attempt a partial or possible line of reply to these questions.

Even if we have a broad overall view of the tribal scene in the historical setting of Rajasthan, it is possible to make some general observations. There are only six 'scheduled' (or officially recognized) tribes in Rajasthan at present, of whom Minas and Bhils are the most important or significant from the point of view of their numbers and the widespread or large areas which they occupy, as also because of their important role in shaping the history of this land during the early and late middle ages. Next in order come Garasias, Saharias, Damors and Bhil Minas.

The population in Rajasthan of these scheduled tribes in 1961 and 1971 census operations was as follows:

	1961	*1971*	*Rate of Growth (in per cent)*
Mina	11,55,620	15,32,331	32.60
Bhil	9,06,705	14,02,943	54.70
Garasia	62,509	52,268	(-) 20.0
Saharia	23,299	26,939	15.60
Damor	14,534	14,795	1.80
Bhil Mina	2,063	17,076	7.27

These figures also indicate the decennial growth rate of these scheduled tribes which, on the whole, has been comparatively higher than the decadal growth rate. The overall total population was higher in the tribal dominated districts like Banswara, Dungarpur and Udaipur than in other districts.

As a result of these trends or growth rates, the percentage of scheduled tribe population to the total population of the state (as well as in the tribal dominated districts) has been steadily rising, so that from 11.67 per cent for the entire state population in 1961, it has become 12.21 per cent as per 1981 census. However, the general spread or concentration of the various scheduled tribes in certain specific areas has not changed much since 1961 when, on the basis of the census data, an Ethnographic Atlas was prepared by the Superintendent of Census Operations. For example, the *Minas* (who were not included among the scheduled tribes in Ajmer district in 1961, though they are found almost all over the state), have remained concentrated in Jaipur, Sawai Madhopur and Udaipur districts. In other words, most of the Minas are in the districts or areas bordering on the eastern slopes of the Aravalli ranges. It is estimated that nearly 50 per cent of the Mina tribal population of the state is in these three districts with a fair and strong concentration in other districts like Alwar, Chittorgarh, Kota, Bundi, Tonk, Dungarpur and Bhilwara in that descending order. Within these districts also, and particularly in the rural areas, Minas are concentrated in a few tehsils. For example, in Lasadia, Sarada and Salumbar tehsils in Udaipur district; Rajgarh and Lachhmangarh tehsils in Alwar district; Pratapgarh and Achnera tehsils in Chittorgarh district; Aspur tehsil in Dungarpur district; and Jahazpur tehsil in Bhilwara district.

Though there is now an increasing 'inflow' of Minas into the urban areas, and educationally, socially, culturally as well as economically, they have improved their lot substantially during the last few decades, most of their population is still very much settled in the rural areas. With nearly 60 per cent active workers amongst the Minas, almost 50 per cent of the total, may be more, are cultivators.

Bhils, on the other hand, have remained largely concentrated in the south-western districts or areas of Rajasthan, mostly in the remote reaches of the Aravallis, both on the eastern slopes as well as towards the west, in districts like Udaipur, Banswara, Dungarpur, Bhilwara and Chittorgarh; and Sirohi in the south or south-west and Barmer and Jalore in the west, and Jhalawar and Kota in the east. Nearly 68 per cent of their population was concentrated in the first three districts as mentioned above in 1961, and this proportion would not have changed much over the years.

Like the Minas, the *Bhils* are also concentrated or they predominate in some tehsils of each district. For example, in all the tehsils of Banswara and Dungarpur districts, Mandalgarh tehsil of Bhilwara district, Bhainsorgarh tehsil of Chittorgarh districts, Kherwara, Kotra, Phalasia, Girwa, Gogunda, Nathdwara, Kumbhalgarh, Mavli and Rajsamand tehsils of Udaipur district.

Garasias seem to be an off-shoot of the Bhils, who were over-powered and driven into remote pockets in the south-western parts of the Aravallis by the Chauhan Rajputs of Jalore about 600 years ago. Since then, they have been leading a very meek and difficult existence. Their total population in 1961 was about 62,500, which has not increased much (in 1971 it was actually less but at that time Rajput Garasias were also excluded). The percentage of workers amongst the Garasias has been slightly less than that of Minas and Bhils, and also the percentage of the cultivators. They have hardly any foothold in the areas in which they live, and socially, economically and educationally or agriculturally, they are very backward.

Same happens to be the position of *Saharias,* if not worst. About 100 years ago, they were considered to be a "little removed from savage life", and in 1961, "the most backward of all scheduled tribes" in the state. Their population, however, was not large – only 23,000 and odd, with the maximum concentration (almost concentrated and confined) in the Kota district and specially Shahabad Kishanganj area. Though the percentage of their total workers has been fairly high, i.e., about 55 per cent, there are less number of cultivators amongst them, and more of agricultural labourers.

Damors have been a very small tribal community, who seem to have shifted from Gujarat area and were concentrated in Dungarpur district, with some of them living in Udaipur and even some north-western districts like Ganganagar and Churu. (How and why they moved away so far to the north-west is a mystery). The percentage of workers amongst them is fairly high, about 51 per cent; also the percentage of cultivators, nearly 60 per cent.

Bhil Minas, mostly found in Ajmer district, are a very small group. By any comparative standard, they are and should be treated as a section of the Bhil community but to establish their status with the more developed Minas, they started calling themselves "Bhil Minas" about 50 or 60 years ago. Out of just about 3000 and odd number of Bhil Minas in 1961, about 10 per cent were found in the urban areas. The workers approximated 65 per cent, but in their case also, the percentage of cultivators was less than 40, while agricultural labourers approximated about 18 per cent.

The spread (or concentration) of the various scheduled tribes, as described above, has been based on the 1969 Ethnographic Atlas. Though their absolute numbers or percentages may have changed slightly since then, there has been hardly any change in their 'urban-rural ratio' or in the areas of their large or maximum concentration. They are still largely outside the pale of the established Hindu society and its culture. They are also comparatively untouched by the process of urbanization speeded up due to modern developments like the establishment of industries, better communications and transport systems, or the spread of education and health facilities and reformative impact of various measures for tribal welfare. They are still very much 'rural' based, very much linked up with and dependent on their land (through their primitive agriculture) and the available natural resources including the forests, except that Minas have been gradually and steadily bringing themselves up and out of their traditional tribal moorings.

In fact, a large section of the Minas, particularly the *Zamindar Minas*, are so much advanced in socio-economic (mostly agricultural) and educational or cultural field, that they may be considered to be passing through a phase of 'de-tribalisation' or 'sanskritisation'. But, the others, including *Chowkidar Minas*, are still 'tribal' in their socio-economic background and outlook, in their social customs, religious rites or rituals and ways of life. They are still very much cut off from the mainstream of the rural or urban communities belonging to or dominated by the other castes and tribes.

In this context, a question naturally arises. Whether the process of development and changes or modernization must necessarily mean their 'de-tribalisation' or being merged and through a process of what has been called 'sanskritisation' or 'acculturisation'? Must they lose their 'identity' and the distinctive features of their 'community life'? Or should they be allowed to remain as they are, where they are, be what there are and yet somehow take full advantages of all the modern facilities and services of 'welfare state'? Can they be accommodated in the modern world of trade, commerce, industry and technology without losing their separate or distinct identity? Our social scientists and reformers, development and change-oriented scholars, administrators and policy makers have to face and answer these questions.

From the location of the natural habitats of the important scheduled tribes in the state, it is possible to suggest that the Aravalli range, which divides the rhombus trapezium like state of Rajasthan into two 'unequal' parts (two-third area to the north-west, west south-west) being covered by desert lands, has been and can still be considered the main dividing line of the 'tribal world' from the rest. Perhaps, the only exception would be the dispersal in small numbers or pockets of course of the Bhils in some of the western and south-western districts, including Sirohi, Jalore, Jodhpur, Barmer, Pali and Jaisalmer. Otherwise, in the arid and sandy western and north-western desert lands or even in the north-eastern corner of the state, there are hardly any tribals left now.

Secondly, their geographical location seems to suggest that, all along and throughout the centuries, they have been hugging close to the safety and shelter of the Aravalli range and its offshoots or spurs, and well-protected green valleys, particularly in the south-west, as also on the plateau lands of the old Mewar and Haroti (Kota, Bundi, Jhalawar) states or in the Sawai Madhopur, Jaipur, Alwar, Bharatpur areas, as in the case of Minas in the state.

The fact that in the north-west, west or even south-west of the Aravalli range, the tribals, at least the scheduled tribes, are not found in large numbers (with the exceptions as noted above), also indicates that even if during the early pre-historic or historic period, some of the tribes were inhabiting these areas, west of the Aravallis, over the centuries they have been gradually pushed towards the east or from the north-eastern to the south-eastern parts. On the other hand, there is yet another possibility, which needs further detailed examination or scrutiny. Is it possible that instead of having been pushed from the north-west or west across the sandy wastes and the Aravalli towards the eastern parts of the state, the tribals of Rajasthan, and particularly the scheduled tribes as we know them today, have been living continuously in the present areas to the east or south-east of the Aravallis though their lands have been shrinking with increasing pressures from the north and north-west.

Or may be, since times immemorial, from the pre-historic and historic times, they have had some sort of close contacts and affinities with the tribals of north Madhya Pradesh and north-east Gujarat living in deep forests or inaccessible, remote corners of the Malwa plateau or the hilly areas in the north-eastern or the northern parts of Gujarat and Madhya Pradesh.

Looking at the ethnographic map of India, and in spite of the wide dispersal of the scheduled tribes, we are struck by the fact that, really speaking, the entire land area of central India stretching right up to Nagpur, Bihar and Orissa towards the east and going down south-wards through Orissa, Andhra Pradesh and Karnataka, or Madhya Pradesh and the eastern parts of Maharashtra has perhaps been the main tribal land of India, inhabited by different ethnographic groups or tribal communities since the dawn of civilization.

In any case, it seems that the scheduled tribes of Rajasthan have been concentrated in the areas of their present-day habitation for many centuries, and if at all ever in the past, they had some sway or position of importance as 'rulers' or masters of the other areas of the state, whether in the sandy desert lands of the west and the north-west or in the fertile plains of the north-eastern regions or the central high lands, then surely their days of such glory, control and importance have been buried deep or lost in the mists of time for many centuries so that, today, their past days or even tales of glory do not form a part of the living tribal traditions or their common tribal memory. Yet almost all the tribes claim a high or once regal ancestry as if once they were the unchanged master of what they surveyed and beheld.

No doubt, we have some historical references about ancient *Matsya* land of the Minas of Jaipur (Dundhar) region being displaced from power, or of the Bhils making way for other tribes and communities including the Rajputs in the *Medpat* or Mewar area. But, surprisingly, in the oral history or tradition of these tribes, there is not much significant mention of the period when these tribes might have been the sole or unchallenged masters of the areas from where they were eventually displaced.

We may look at the problem from a slightly different angle related to the movement of certain well-known ancient and historical tribes and communities along the vast region or areas now comprising Rajasthan and some of its neighbouring parts. We have the clear-cut tradition of the Aryans having come to occupy the fertile lands, particularly north of the river Sutlej (may be on both sides of the river) and its various tributaries, as also along the Indus river, when it was flowing along its ancient courses. Their south-eastwards movement has been quite well established, but not southwards. At least, there is no tradition or other record of the Aryans descending on the rather unwelcome landscape of Rajasthan.

We have, on the other hand, the tradition of the Pandavas spending considerable time of their exile in the *Matsya* land and at Virat Nagar (modern Bairath). There are archeological and historical evidences of Virat Nagar also being an important seat of Buddhist religion and culture besides some other sites on the fringe of the Malwa plateau.

Recent excavations have also identified a number of pre-historical or later sites, as also the various people of the ancient communities inhabiting these areas. For example, in the Ganeshwar or Kotputli area north-east of Jaipur or as far away south-west as Ahar outside Udaipur or Tilwara in Barmer or Noh near Bharatpur. In fact, when we piece together the recent findings or evidences from these important and other possible archaeological sites, which have revealed many interesting surface finds, it is possible to establish following broad generalizations or features of the changing situation, namely:

(i) Most of these sites are indicators of urbanized or at least settled agricultural centres.

(ii) Secondly, on the basis of the likely spread of the ancient archaeological sites, it is possible to demarcate the extent or area to which these past agricultural-cum-urban and well-organized civilizations had spread.

(iii) The border-lines between these 'land-settled' urban cultures and the tribal societies in the past would appear to be almost coterminus, if not overlapping, with the present divisions of their ethnographic watersheds, except that perhaps during the more recent intervening centuries, the tribals must have been often pressed and pushed deeper and deeper further into the hilly hinterlands or towards the unfertile and difficult plateaus or into the deep inaccessible forests.

Whatever their origin and whatever their past history or tradition, the fact remains that, for ages, the tribals have been very well and deeply entrenched in the areas where they are found even today. However, naturally, the geographical area under their direct control or occupation has gradually shrunk, as more and more outsiders or the more developed civilized or cultured communities have made their inroads into their once tribal territories. But, then, in the remote past, their numbers were small but lands were endless. Today, their lands have shrunk, but their numbers have swelled up. This is also a serious challenge to their existence.

Going back to the remote or pre-historic past, a journey of fascinating discovery made possible by recent archaeological explorations and excavations, we come across strong and scattered evidences of the stone age man remaining and rambling over almost all over Rajasthan. His reach or spread was perhaps as wide as deep were his roots.

In south-eastern Rajasthan, in districts of Banswara, Dungarpur, Bhilwara, Bundi, Kota and Jhalawar, paleolithic tools flakes and cleavers and hand-axes have been found along the Banas and its various tributaries such as Gambhiri, Berach and Wagan indicating the early settlements of man about one lakh years ago. Particularly near Chittorgarh tools found on the Gambhiri bank indicates that early man lived there on higher ground and maintained himself on wild fruits and roots and flesh of small animals like deer, pig, goat and sheep and cattle. Along the Chambal and its other connected river valleys also, stone age relics have been found.

Archaeologists working in the Vindhyan and Satpura ranges and along the middle reaches of Narmada, in the recent years, have also discovered many painted rock shelters, which seem to extend far into the southern areas of Rajasthan. Their hypothesis is that the early stone-man from central India may have moved to the north and then spread along the Chambal and Banas systems.

However, to revert to the discoveries in Rajasthan, in Jaipur and Indergarh area, quartizic hand-axes dating from about 2 lakh years ago have also been found. An ancient deposit of artefacts like hand-axes, cleavers, side and hollow scrapers has also been found from a site near Bhangarh district in Alwar. A similar site was located near Bairath (Jaipur district) in a nullah connected with river Sabi.

In western Rajasthan, evidences of stone age man's habitats have also been discovered along the Luni basin, which probably had a better climate then, as compared to our own times. Tools were of different materials from the tools of the early man in south-east Rajasthan and were based on flint-like jasper, fossil-wood and coarse rocks for smaller tools like scrapers etc. (for cutting, scraping and piercing the hides of animals, that, and printed tools like spear and arrow heads, which indicate the makers or users of these tools were very much in the hunting stage of development.

Microliths (or small stone tools) have also been found, both in eastern and western Rajasthan, with possibilities of a similar culture in the Saraswati basin area. Microlithic sites have been unearthed in Ajmer, Tonk, Bhilwara, Chittorgarh, Pali and Udaipur districts and in Jaipur (Bairath) and Jodhpur (Umed Nagar in Osian tehsil and Bilara areas). Ahar near Udaipur and Gilund on the Banas have also revealed microlithic tools. During these stages, the early (stone age) man lived in a wild state, without any permanent settlement and perhaps without any pots and pans for cooking or storage of food.

It has been rightly suggested that our early man, even in this period, was without permanent houses and settlements and did not have any vessels or pots and pans for drinking, cooking or storage of food. After this period, there is a long gap of centuries, perhaps thousands of years, in our sources of knowledge.

However, by about four or five thousand years ago, somewhat permanent settled sites seemed to have come into existence in the south-eastern and north-eastern parts of Rajasthan. Notable amongst these has been the site at Ahar which lies in a valley surrounded by hills. We have not been able to identify the community which first came to live here, or others who subsequently kept on using the site over and over again. (However, in the course of excavations, the settlement has revealed about 45 feet of deposits and at least 15 buildings levels.)

The site has revealed strong evidences of settled pastoral-cum-agricultural culture with permanent houses, storage jars and other pottery vessels and hearths for the kitchen fire. However, no stone age tools have been unearthed, but possibilities have been indicated of the use of copper implements based on copper ore (available at Debari, about 10 miles from Udaipur then as now). A copper sheet and three flat copper axes indicate signs of a "copper age". Terracotta beeds and semi-precious stones and some earthern toys of domestic animals and human figures have also been found. At least, at some later stage, the people of Ahar used to bury their dead with their heads towards the north.

Ahar culture had its extension all over south-eastern Rajasthan. Some sites like Gilund or Bhagawanpura (40 miles north-east of Udaipur) and other surface finds found extensively in that area have confirmed this proposition.

Were these people the early Bhils or their ancestors? If so, did they, later on, pass through along period of change and pushover, so that today they lag behind other advanced castes and communities in the region? And if so, what brought about their fall? Such queries seem to have some relevance.

In the extreme north or north-west corner of Rajasthan (and south-eastern Punjab) many Harappan sites have been discovered and identified along the ancient beds of Saraswati and Drishawati and the Sutlej rivers. With fertile soil, plenty of water and a tolerable climate, these sites seem to have been inhabited by some people even in the microlithic stage, though they later saw the flourishing of Harappan civilization. Kali-banga and Anoopgarh have been some of the notable sites in this area, though along the two dried-up river beds and in the plain between Sutlej and Yamuna, many other smaller sites of Harappan culture have since been identified. These discoveries have pushed back the ancient history of the region to the period of the Indus valley civilization.

It is generally believed that the Harappan culture was succeeded by the Aryan culture, but it is a moot point whether the Aryans had forcefully and violently overrun the Harappan people. For, all we know, they may have come into contact with each other more or less amicably and then peacefully co-existed. The issue remains open to controversy and speculation.

There is also the controversy about the Aryans, whether they had come from outside, from Central Asia through the north-western ranges? Or, whether they had developed or grown up indigenously like many other people or tribes of yore? The identification of the

Harappan people and their language or script, their religions, beliefs or social customs, still remain an enigma or an unsolved riddle of Indian pre-history, because unlike the Vedic Aryans, they have not left much of remembered knowledge or chronicles of their existence behind in the form of literature, folklore or tradition or what they may have left has since been obliterated by time. Is it possible that the Harappans, or at least some of them, found an eventual and natural sanctuary in the barren and harsh wastelands and jungle of Rajasthan?

In any case, the area of Harappan civilization, stretching between the south-eastern region of the Sutlej and Saraswati towards the east along the higher reaches of the Sutlej like at Ropan etc. and down south along the Yamuna in the east, and west and south-west of Multan towards the sandy plains of Sindh, seems to have played a very important part in the development of the Indo-Vedic cultural patterns or Indo-Aryan traditions, which have been acknowledged as formation of the foundations of the so-called Hindu culture, religion and philosophy.

We may, however, take note of some of the paleolithic and microlithic sites in Rajasthan and the rock shelters in Madhya Pradesh and in the Chambal area not in the order in which they have been unearthed, discovered or identified, but in order of the probable sequence of early man's adventures into these parts. We can then try to conjure up in our minds the extent of early stone age man's or pre-historic settlements in different parts and corners of the state, so as to trace out the possible beginnings or roots of the early tribal societies in this much-invaded and long battle-scarred territory, and co-relate the same with other circumstances or developments.

Some anthropologists have also done fairly remarkable work on the movements of various races and ethnic groups in India, especially in its north-western parts, during the pre-historic period. Philologists, especially those interested in a comparative study of ancient dialects and languages in India, have also supported these efforts. Yet, the picture of race movements, particularly in the areas comprising the present-day territory of Rajasthan or its tribal belt towards the south, has not yet become quite clear.

Noting the work of Dr B.S. Guha, then Director, Anthropological Survey of India, entitled "Racial Elements in the Population". We may accept the broad outlines of his thesis that in this connection among the first on the scene were the earliest *Negroid* races, though now almost extinct except in the Andamans and a few other far-fetched corners of south-west coastal India and the Assam hills in the east. They were then followed by the *Proto-Australoids* coming from the west. These groups of people pressed forward and passed on to the continent of Australia through Indonesia, Melanesia, or Polynesia. But they seem to have survived in India in large numbers as 'aboriginal people' especially amongst the lower castes and weaker sections of the people, even till today.

Then come the *Mongoloids*, with their peculiar head-forms and other typical features, whose descendants, particularly of the *Palaeo-Mongoloids*, are found even today amongst the tribal elements of Assam and in the hilly forest area along the Indo-Burmese frontier, while the descendants of the more advanced *Tibeto-Mongoloids* are found in Sikkim and Bhutan.

Amongst the next group of the *Mediterranean* people were many types of long-headed persons. Among them, traces of the *Palaeo-Mediterraneans,* slightly built or medium statured and dark-skinned are found today largely in the Kannada, Tamil Nadu or Malayalam areas, while the European-type *Mediterraneans*, somewhat taller or fairer, are found in Punjab or the upper Gangetic valley and amongst the 'Dravidians' of North India who later became Aryanised. The third Mediterranean group or the *Orientals*, sometimes wrongly called as Semitics or Jews, had longish noses and fair skins. People of these groups or physical features may be found in Punjab, Sindh, Rajputana, western Uttar Pradesh and many other parts of India.

The fifth group of *Brachyacephals* seems to have come from the Central Asian mountainous areas. Amongst them were the *Alpinoids* and *Dinarics* who spread over large parts of India. The latter group seems to have left its mark in areas as far away as Bengal and Orissa in the east and Kathiawad in the west and Kannada, Tamil Nadu and the Coorg tracts in the south, while the *Alpinoids,* with broad heads, are found along the western coast of India. These groups seem to have passed through the Gangetic valley and drifted into Central India, eastern Uttar Pradesh and Bihar and western Nepal. Among these groups, the last category was that of *Armenoids,* now represented by the Parsis.

Last of all came the *Nordic Aryans* who gave their name, social structure, language and culture to this land, and for long, cast their influence on a large part of the sub-continent, particularly in the north and west and most important they have left behind a living tradition of their memory.

With the *Aryans,* we step into the historical period, through the early and medieval parts of which periodic migration and invasions from the west or north-west continued unabated. Especially north-west and the *Madhyadesh* of the Indian sub-continent has been a melting and mixing pot of races, people, religions, languages and cultures through pre-historic and historic times. Small wonder, therefore, that the pure types of one of these races, whether Negroids, Australoids, Mongoloids, Mediterraneans, Nordics or Aryans, Indo-Greeks, Sakas, Huns, Afghans and Mangols are difficult to find.

Anthropologists and philologists or the linguists have, however, tried to study and compare the various dialects spoken in different parts of the country and have gone back to the olden or archaic times in their attempt to identify and locate common features or diversities in the common words, idioms and language structure to see whether or not these various racial groups ever came together, inter-mixed and then pressed on into different parts of the sub-continent, one after another, after long intervals and in a clear-cut sequence as suggested above. Such and other allied questions may be and still are open to discussion and dispute. But, the linguists, the sociologists and other scholars interested in the study of the beginnings of various religious rites and customs have indeed found various common strains or parallel features, in the names of articles of everyday use on places or human emotions and feelings as well as in certain surviving of religious rites and social customs, which broadly seem to establish the hypothesis of race movements and intermingling in the remote past, including the movement or migration of the Aryans, and the subsequent successive waves of migration in the historical era.

The facts that the Aryans occupying the land of the Saptasindhus (seven rivers) north of the Sutlej and Saraswati and Drishadavati rivers, later on moved towards the east where they seemed to have found a somewhat safer or more fertile and permanent place of abode, are well established through clear historical traditions and references in the early Vedic literature, though many controversies about contacts of the Aryans with the Harappans and the characteristics of the Harappan civilization, viz., about its being a proto-type of the Dravidian civilization, still remain. But, from the Vedic hymns and religious literature, we learn many interesting aspects and details of the coming together of the Aryans and the other local residents of north and north-western India. We can almost see slow transformation of wandering and warring pastoral groups or tribes into communities of settled farmers and cattle breeders and gradually develop their urban characteristics. From the available literature, it is also possible to work out the geographical details and features of the early Aryan settlements in India and their gradual advancement towards the east and south-east until they came to dominate the Gangetic plains and beyond.

We also find that the early Aryans not only overcame the vast stretched area of the Harappan civilization (in the region between Sutlej and Yamuna) but also came into contact with may indigenous people whom they chose to call the *Dasas, Dasyus* as well as *Nishads*, who were treated as 'outsiders' and lived on the fringes of the Aryan settlements and in many cases were treated almost as slaves. The Vedic literature of a comparatively later date also makes a brief mention of many other people residing in different parts of the sub-continent, some friendly, some hostile towards them but in all these descriptions there is no clear-cut or definite mention of any of the tribes with whom modern-day Meenas or Bhils or Girasias or Saharias of Rajasthan may have had some sort of an established or traditionally accepted affinity or ethnical ancestral, racial or cultural connection. unless we consider the Meenas to be the same people or people with common heritage and ancestry with the *Matsya* of the Epic Age who lived west of *Surasena* land (of Mathura) in the modern areas of Alwar, Bharatpur and Jaipur, or unless the *Dasas, Dasyus* or *Nishads* were the fore-runners of Bhils and other contemporary tribes.

There is no doubt that much further works need to be done in this respect before we can come to a definite finding or indication about the origin and ancient ancestry of the tribal people of Rajasthan.

However, in this connection, it may be also worthwhile to bear in mind the long existing or well-recognized physical or geographical features of a major part of the Rajasthan territory, viz., north-west and west Rajasthan. As is commonly believed and has now been well proved, perhaps thousands of years ago, the climate of Rajasthan was comparatively more mild or more wet than it is today. There is no doubt that even at that time, or when Aryans or even the earlier racial groups appeared on the scene and were on the move, they probably thought it prudent and wise (because of their own experiences and earlier traditions) to avoid the harsh and inhospitable and the rather awe-inspiring desert lands of the Thar. It is, therefore, possible that they may have by-passed these waterless desert and sandy lands, except when a group was overwhelmed and very much compelled and suddenly forced and pushed by a successive group to move down southwards into the recesses and sanctuaries of the desert and its shrub jungles and forests of the Aravalli hills.

But, as we have seen from the various findings of archeological excavations and explorations, these parts have also given shelter and sanctuary to many primitive or pre-historic tribes from the dawn of the stone age. May be, they were some indigenous aboriginal tribes whose origin and possible movements have not yet been plotted, and must remain mysterious. Or may be, they had some connections with the cavemen from the Central Indian plateau lands, as has been recently claimed. May be, the Minas and the Bhils were from some such primitive or aboriginal stock? Or may be, they belonged to the groups of *Dasas, Dasyus* and *Nishads* whose presence was noted by the Aryans. As is turned out the Aryans were the first chroniclers of the tribal scene in North India. Even after a lapse of thousands of years, perhaps we can even now detect notes of contempt and derision, and may be some pity in their reference to the suppressed, enslaved and the outcast tribes.

Yet, the Vedic age was itself indeed a tribal age. Thus, the *Dasrajana* or the battle of ten kings (or chiefs of tribes), referred to in some hymns of the *Rigveda*, seems to have been an important and unforgettable event of the age. *Viasvamitra* had then led a combination of 10 tribal chiefs, including the well-known tribes of *Puru, Yadu, Turvasu, Anu* and *Druhya* or the *Panchjanha* (the five people) and the lesser known five, namely, *Alina, Pakhta, Bhalanas, Siva* and *Vishanin* against the *Bharats* of the *Tritsu* who had settled in the *Brahmvarta* area. In the battle, the *Bharats* were victorious. Much later, the Bharat king (chief) Sudas fought and overcame some non-Aryan tribes, the *Ajas, Sigrus* and *Yakshas*, who had united under their king (chief) Bheda. (Were they the ancestors of the Bhils). And so the story of the Aryan tribes' advent and march into the heart of the land goes and other references add up.

Vedic scholars have also tried to suggest the local names of various events and tribes mentioned in the Vedic literature. But they have mostly covered the land of the *Sapta Sindhus* or the trans-Sutlej lords, the Saraswati and the Yamuna regions and the *Madhyadesh*, perhaps *Ajas, Sigrus* and *Yakshus* were the eastern non-Aryan tribes, while to the west of Mathura or what was then *Surasena* territory there were the *Matsayas*. Other lesser known tribes like *Pakhted, Bhalasans, Vishanina, Alinas* and *Sivas* have been identified as the "frontier" people living in hills of Afghanistan or other regions of north-west India. Between the Yamuna and the Vindhyas were the *Chedis*. Other tribes mentioned are the *Usinars*, living in the middle country with the *Vasa* and the *Kasis*.

Later, the *Gandharas* or the frontier people in the north-west Gandhar area, the *Prithu-Parshvah* or the Parthians and Persians have been mentioned as also *Paravatas* along the Yamuna, *Kikatas* who were non-Aryans and were perhaps located in *Madhyadesh* and the *Panis*, who have been mentioned along the *Dasas* and *Dasyus* as enemies of the Aryans and who were rich cattle owners and traders. They might have been aboriginal non-Aryan people unlike *Dasas* or *Dasyus*, who lived in fortified towns and had considerable wealth. *Asuras* have also been mentioned as the enemies of the Vedic people.

But going through these references to the various tribes and their geographical locations in the period of *Rigveda* or the later *Samhitas*, the *Brahmanas* and *Upanishads*, by which times new tribal names have appeared replacing many of the earlier one, we can be overwhelmed by the variety of their names and identities. In the process, we note not only the expansion of the Aryans deep into Indian sub-continent but also the gradual displacement, movement or dispersal of the tribes, of whom only the *Matsyas* and *Sahas* appear to have occupied parts of the present-day eastern Rajasthan.

It is a colourful account though many details or facts are still not clear. Traditional historical accounts, as reconstructed from the Vedic and Puranic literature and the great epics of Ramayan and Mahabharat, mention a large number of non-Aryan people or tribes, including aboriginal and hostile *Rakshas*, friendly *Vanars* and many others like *Asurs, Dattyas, Danavs, Nagas* etc., at different levels of development from the aboriginal to semi-civilized, who resisted the spread of the Aryan culture, so that they were termed as demons. *Nagas* were civilized to some extent, but the *Nishads, Dasas Dayus*, *Pulindas* and *Kikatas* were mostly primitive and savage, living in the hilly areas, e.g., *Nishads* in Central India and Vindyachal ranges, *Pulindas*, *Sahars* and *Mutibas* were towards the south, and *Kirats* in Assam and Nepal.

Later came the foreign tribes from the west such as *Sakas, Yavanas, Kambojs, Paras* and *Pahleyas*, but most of them got absorbed amongst the earlier or original settlers, many among the *Kshatriyas* of the Lunar dynasty.

Our purpose of making such references to the Vedic period and later to the period of Puranic literature is to suggest that most of the tribes mentioned in those days seem to have remained outside or at the most on the periphery of Rajasthan. Perhaps, the *Bhadras* or *Uttam Bhadras* would also come in the same category. However, there are references to some outsiders like the *Bahliks* or *Malechhas* or the *Yavanas* and *Sakas* who may have later and gradually moved into some of the areas of south-west Punjab or western Sind and also western Rajasthan.

There seems to be a long gap in our knowledge of the mythological, *Puranic* or historical references about ancient India (especially its north-western areas and the present-day territory of Rajasthan) about the tribal communities of the past. We first start hearing about them sometimes during the classical age and, in greater detail, much later. At that time, those people who stood outside the newly emerging caste system were often called *Malechhas* or the *Malechh-jajs*. Many of them probably represented the remnants of some earlier tribes and races like the *Yavanas* or *Indo-Greeks* and *Sakas* and *Hunas* etc., who had come into north-west or western India from outside – from Central Asia and beyond. There are indications of these invaders having come down deep into Rajasthan upto *Madhyamika* (Nagri) in Chittorgarh.

Later day Jain literature mentions many local castes and communities like *Sabaras, Kiratas, Khasas, Odras, Gonds, Pulindas Kochas, Bharruyas* and *Bhillas*, which were termed as *Malechch. Kvualayamala, Prasnavyakarana* and *Samaradhityakatha* mention many communities or ethnic and social groups such as:

(a) Foreigners or foreign immigrants: *Saka, Yavana, Ramosa, Paras, Marunda, Barbara, Sinhala* and *Arvay-Ḥuna*.
(b) *Advasins: Sabara, Kaya, Kirata, Khasa, Bhilla, Pullinda, Andhra, Kotha, Bharuga, Bokkasa* and *Lakusa*.
(c) Totemistic tribes: *Hayamukhas* etc.
(d) Miscellaneous: *Drevida, Kudakkha, Ketaya*, etc.

Similarly, *Vishnu Dharma Sutra* suggests that a country without the caste system (or a *Varna*) is a country of *Malechhas*, who are mentioned as beef-eaters. Some settlements of beef-eaters have been mentioned in *Brihat Katha Kosh*.

Some of these ancient (religious) books of Aryans, specially Jain sect, merely take note of the existence of these "outside" castes and communities, while others speak of them in derogatory and contemptuous terms. For example, Uddyotan Suri considers them sinful, cruel and fenocious.

Obviously, by this time, some of these outside castes or tribes had been driven into the interior hills and were forced to lead an unsettled and outcast, nomadic and rather primitive life, often indulging in attacks and acts of robbery on their more "cultured" neighbours. In *Samaraichchakaha* there is a mention of Sabar chiefs raiding their neighbouring settled areas and marching away with captives, but then releasing them on receiving some ransom.

About this time, the main indigenous or local tribes in Rajasthan appeared to have been Medas, who gave their name to (a) Medapat or Mewar (perhaps Ajmer-Merwara area also had their association), and the (b) Bhils, who from all accounts, should have had a very strong settlement near Bhillmala (Bhinmal) and spread out into the Aravalli hills and along its spurs. We can also presume that there were other tribes inhabiting these parts such as Jhallas, Mallas (Malvas? or Molois?) and Minas. According to traditions, which have come over to us, almost all these tribes were perhaps fighting with their backs to the wall (or the Aravallis) against the *Khatriyas* and other communities and later on the Rajputs.

Sometimes, the local tribes or their chiefs also played an important part in establishing a new dynasty. Many Rajput princes or adventurers owe their rise and consolidation to the *adivasis*. Medpat and Dhundhs or Amber dynasties of Rajputs were examples of such help.

In the Dholpur inscription of *Chandamahasena* (V.S. 899 or 942 AD) it is mentioned that on both sides of the river Chambal there were *Malechha* tribes and castes which paid their homage to him. These *Malechha* were probably some *adivasi* tribes. Similarly, there is a possibility that an *antyaja* who helped Lakshman Chouhan in establishing himself at Nadol could have been a member of some local tribe. Later-day Rajput history also mentions the role of Pabuji and his Thoris (now scheduled caste) and Ramdeva Tanwar and his Dhedhas (now scheduled caste).

Besides the *Malechcha jatis* mentioned above, there were many depressed classes or castes and groups of outcaste people who lived outside the city boundaries and were called upon to perform various jobs and functions, which were rather menial and dirty by their nature or which involved acts of cruelty etc.

In the *Kuvalayamala*, there is a mention of *Chandalas, Bhillas, Dombs, Saukarikas* and *Matsybandhas* as people who had no *dharma* nor were *arth* and *kama* their objectives. They were no better than *Malechcha*. The *Samaraichakaha* gives additional names of *antyaja, jatis* such as *Rajaka* (washerman), *Charmakara* (worker in leather) and *Sakuniak* (fuller). Another text, *Upamitibhavaprapanchkatha* gives a description of the manner in which some of these outcastes (*Matanga* and *Dombs*) lived in extremely poor and dirty conditions. Jinesvara in his *Kathakosa-prakaran* gives further interesting information about *Bhillas, Bekhasas* (?) *Khattikas* (present-day SCs) or fishermen, hunters and trappers as low class people without any *dharma*. Among the *adhams* were mat-makers, washermen and actors and *adham-dhams* were *Sankarik* and *Chandal*. Thus, by about 1,000 to 1,500 years ago, the caste system had emerged with many tribes and lower functional castes outside the main social grouping.

Further description by Jineshvar and Al Beruni also suggest that many of these low castes had grouped themselves into their own guilds (*Sremigatahas*). In other words, they were having their caste or tribal associations and panchayats. Fullers, shoe-makers, jugglers, basket or shield-makers, sailors, fishermen, hunters of wild animals and weavers have been mentioned to have had their guilds, but they were among the *adhams* or low castes, fullers or washermen, shoe-makers and weavers being lower among them.

Another big group of people outside the established caste system was that of the *Sudras*, who surprisingly were considered to be a part of the caste system (according to *Smritis*). They became *Sudras* because of the nature of their work and were not treated as *dvija* (or twice-born). Many mixed castes of agricultural labourers or agriculturists and members of craftsmen's guilds, who were neither *Malechcha* nor *Antyaja*, were treated as *Sudras* and these included *Kumbhakara* (potter) *Malakaras* (garland-makers), *Tambulikas* (betal-sellers), *Silukutas* (workers in stone), *Kallapalas* (distillers) and *Tailika* (oil-pressers) and *Mehras*, goldsmiths, silversmiths, carpenters, coppersmiths, barbers, Jabals, goatherds, *Suchikas* or tailors, *Kahars* and *Bhois* were also later on added to this list. Sometimes, *Ahiras* were also treated as *Sudras*.

It is indeed a sad commentary on the Indian social system through the ages that the bulk of working communities engaged in many essential services or those living their simple existence close to nature have been given such a low status or kept away from the mainstream.

Thus, these various descriptions from the religious literature and historical chronicles of the early middle ages clearly indicate that gradually over the years, and by the end of 9th/10th century many local or indigenous tribes and other castes or groups of people, who either belonged to the various wings or *varnas* of the Hindu society or those who came from outside or those who could not be assimilated or absorbed into the mainstream of the 'urban society' came to be treated as *Sudras, Antyajas* and *Malechchas* or if we want to go by the probable chronological order, they came in the reverse sequences.

While much more and definitive work needs to be done to cover the period from the Harappan-Vedic times to the middle ages, for the purpose of our study, we have only to note the drift of these developments and mentally visualize the circumstances in which these classifications leading to the segregation of various groups of people seems to have taken place. How it began? When it began? And how? And, when the Bhils, Minas, Garasias, Saharias came to be separated and cut off from the mainstream of society and how they came to be treated as outsiders even hostile or criminal elements? All these questions also need further detailed probe by historians and sociologists.

Unfortunately, as we have said in the beginning, there are no archaeological finds, artefacts, pottery-sherds, tools or arrow-heads, and palaces or religious platform and such other symbols which may have thrown light on the origin of the various local tribes. Nor are there any religious texts, historical chronicles or genealogies, traditions and folklores or folk-songs which may help us in studying the evolutionary process of this slow change-over during the centuries. Perhaps, the tribals did not have the knowledge or use of any alphabet. May be, they did not need that in there clearly knit of face-to-face society so that no inscriptions or epigraphs or even coins etc. have been left behind to unravel their mystery. At least, no such definite discoveries have yet been made.

But there is no denying the fact that by about the 7th to the 10th century AD that is by the time, the early Rajput kingdoms came to be established, the tribal communities had already been shown their place and had been pushed into the remote recesses of hills and jungles, where they have existed all through the subsequent centuries, except that they have been constantly under slow but steady pressure. Their existence or use for those in power has been recognized only very occasionally, sometimes on symbolic ceremonial occasions such as *Raj Tilaks* in Amber and Mewar and sometimes to give shelter to the fugitive warriors like Maharana Pratap.

Looking once again at the map of Rajasthan and the Ethnographic Atlas, as also to the location of various sites of archaeological excavations and surface finds of a varied nature and other historical references in Vedic and Puranic religious or classical or folk literature, we get some very strong impressions that for thousands of years, and more particularly during the historical times, there have been a series of mass movements of people with diverse origins, tribal communities and groups from the north-east and eastern parts into the present-day territory of Rajasthan.

Such movements seem to have been more pronounced or marked along the eastern slope of Aravallis and the north-eastern or south-eastern parts of the state, along the various river systems, and to a lesser extent on a western side of the Aravallis. May be, there had been movements from the west (say from the ancient coastal parts of West Pakistan, such as Baluchistan and Sindh and along the western coast of India) into the state, of which we have little knowledge. It is also possible that these movements from the north-west may have preceded the aforementioned north and north-east downward movements by a few centuries. There is no doubt that the proper sequence and the full and long range and reach of all these various movements have yet to be pieced together in a systematic manner and studied in depth. This is a challenge for the archaeologists, anthropologists, social scientists and historians who want to study the ancient and pre-historic history and progress of the people of this area.

But, as far as this sketchy overview is concerned, there are very strong evidences which point towards the gradual but steady incursion of people from the north-west and North India and plains of Sutlej-Yamuna and Ganga moving into the territories of Rajasthan in successive waves, thereby pushing the residents of long ago, the indigenous tribes or the earlier immigrants and local settled communities, pastoral and nomadic forest-dwellers further and further into the deep sandy and barren waste-lands. At least, from the times of the Indo-Greeks the Yaudhayeas and Sivis and the Kushans, Shakas and Hunas right upto the days of Rathores and Chauhans and later the

Afghans, Mongols and Mughals. There are clear evidences and vivid accounts of these mass movements and migrations, though we have not had much of local tradition of folk literature or folklore come down to us, which may give some idea of how the original or comparatively earlier indigenous people took these intrusions and the repeated shocks of these successive waves, or how they felt about them, and how they proceeded to defend themselves and their traditional ways of living. Known history of literature draws a blank there, presenting a void of almost a millennium and a half.

Whether there was a similar pressure from the south or from the south-west towards the north, is an open or moot question. At least, there are a definite, clear or well-marked archaeological or historical or even legendary or folk traditional references suggesting mass movements of the local indigenous tribes and communities from the Vindhyas and Satpuras pushing their way up towards the north into the territories of Rajasthan through the pre-historic, early historic and early medieval periods. Ethnographically, perhaps, the Bhil tribes of north-west Madhya Pradesh or north-east Gujarat and south-west Rajasthan must have been the links or off-shoots of one the same people in the very remote past. May be, they also managed to retain their close affinities and intra-tribal associations through the ages, except of course when they were separated from each other by having been subjected by different dynasties and different sets of rulers or by different princely states, in the past and then the creation of new political administrative units of the British and the post-independence eras.

In the past, we have clear and repeated mention of the kingdoms of Malwa, Vallabi and Gujarat or towards the east of Orchha and Bundelkhand as also of Gwalior. There is also no doubt that some important historical battles have been fought in the jungles and plateau-lands of Madhya Pradesh and Gujarat, as also in various parts of South Rajasthan. These battles, rather long-drawn struggles between various kingdoms and empires for supremacy over North and Central India, as also in the coastlands of Gujarat and the rest of India, particularly in the south, must have had very serious and significant impressions or impacts on the sandwiched or hamstring tribal community life and their social, cultural and political organizations. May be, some tribal chiefs considered it expedient to jump into the fray and side with one ruler or conqueror or other. Or may be, they became victims of encircling pressures from both sides. Or may be, they tried to keep aloof as much as possible from these battles and long-drawn wars for supremacy over the heartland of India, the Central India, which also commanded and controlled the traditional roads from north to south (and much later, the other way round). But, there is no doubt and no denying the fact that they were very much hard pressed from all sides and were crushed or harassed and subjected to all kinds harsh and oppressive measures.

Recent history suggests that the Marathas in their march towards Delhi came across a number of tribal strongholds and chiefdoms, which they tried to overrun and suppress. In fact, there are strong evidences that the tribals, particularly the Bhils, were hunted down like animals or criminals by them. The same became the fate of the tribals once again, when the British came into Rajasthan or advanced through Central India chasing the Pindaris and giving running battles to the Marathas and later, after establishing their sway over the princely states of Rajasthan or of Madhya Pradesh, Gujarat and Saurashtra through treaty alliances which gave them the position of a 'paramount power' and ruling the land of Rajputana through proxy, they had the onerous task of maintaining conditions of peace in these parts. Experienced as they were, they tried to control and suppress the 'freedom' loving tribals by winning away some sections and organizing their tribal units – Mina corps of Bhil corps – to fight the 'rebels' and to keep the 'peace' in their new area of peripheral control and political influence.

For more than a thousand years Rajasthan was the domain and the battleground of Rajput warriors and chiefs. Soon after they rose to power and attracted the covetous eyes of many intruders from far and near, their tales of war and supreme sacrifice, court intrigues and conspiracies, mutual fights and squabbles become subject matters of many a poet's songs and bardic sagas which have survived to this day. Their mythologies and ancient genealogies have a charm of their own. As also the strong forts and palaces they managed to build in spite of being so constantly out on annals or seasonal campaigns. Among them were soldiers, and statesmen, builders and architects, poets and painters of arts, scholars, saints and scientists, a varied and fascinating galaxy of men and women. In spite of their separate identities, they gave a particular character to their age and became the pillars of support for many occupants and aspirants for the throne of Delhi.

By contrast, the tribals of those days and their chiefs were a different lot. Away from the splendours and glamours of Rajput courts or complexities of cities, they seemed to love and enjoy a simple and self-contained community life. Their rare mention in the contemporary bardic literature or Rajput chronicles would seem to suggest that perhaps they did not count for much. Yet, in moments of stress and strain, even the mighty of the land went upto them for help.

An interesting feature of the tribal situation during the long period of Rajput history seems to have been that once the Rajput clans and princes had established their supremacy and carved out their kingdoms whether through cunning or connivance with the earlier rulers of their opponents or through conquests, they, almost all of them without exception, left the tribals in their domain to be on their own. No attempts were made by the rulers or their supporters and agents to enter into or penetrate the tribal areas or to interfere with their tribal ways of life, social customs or institutions. They were left to live for themselves.

Whether or not the tribals or their chiefs were called upon to pay tributes to the Rajput rulers, or to render them other social and customary services or to join the rank of the Rajput armies whenever the latter sought to fight each other or went on military campaigns under the Mughal banners are points, which need further detailed study.

But, the overall position seems to be that for almost a thousand years, no outside forces interfered with the tribal ways of life in the remote interior areas left to the management and control of the tribes. During the brief Arab incursion from the west, or in the face of the repeated onslaughts and invasions by the Afghans, Turks, or Mongols from the north-west or when the Mughals made their frequent marches southwards, often with Rajput support, through all these periods of turmoil and uncertainty, in a manner of speaking, the Rajput princes and their kingdoms acted as buffers or virtual shield, as far as the protection of various tribals was concerned.

Of course, there is no doubt that, now and again, when the Rajput princes and their kingdoms fell, the tribal areas must also have been over run. But perhaps under new adjustments after such events of victory or defeat, the tribal society seems to have reasserted itself and rebuilt its old, though slightly modified but community ways of life. Otherwise, perhaps by now, the tribal societies would have been either wiped out or absorbed without their separate identity into the rest of the multi-racial, multi-ethnic or multi-religious society.

After all, apart from its feudal structure and political links with the Mughals, the Rajput polity maintained a delicate balance between various tribal groups, clans and professional castes. Does it not suggest that the very survival and continued existence of various tribals of Rajasthan, particularly during the medieval period, deserves further detailed research, which no doubt will be quite fascinating and revealing?

Perhaps another interesting point to note is that all through the middle ages ending with the rise and fall of the Mughal empire, as also during the preceding pre-historic and early historic eras, the major thrust or direction of incursions and intrusions, invasions has been from the north-west. Why should it have been so is yet another unresolved riddle of Indian history from tribal point of view.

But, the point of interest for us to note is that almost all the invaders and intruders also basically represented their own particular type of tribal society from the Vedic times and perhaps earlier on and until the last Afghan invaders or adventurers including Ahmad Shah and Nadir Shah, the forces which came into north-India and subsequently some of them into the Rajasthan areas, were by and large themselves nomadic pastoral and tribal in character.

Perhaps what distinguished them from the indigenous communities, including many settled and well-entrenched or urbanized community of farmers and ruling castes, as well as the contemporary forest and waste-land dwelling tribals, was the relevant difference in the technology available to them. The technology of warfare and the firing power of their guns, the technology of transportation and movement of their fast horses, or the technology of art of their tribal system of administration based on the democracy of their tribal councils and perhaps above all, the sheer vigour and vitality of the tribesmen from the comparatively colder climates of north-west.

Similarly, perhaps what distinguished the local tribes from their comparatively more affluent and well-settled neighbouring farming communities or the native princes and their feudal supporters was again the difference in the levels of technology available in their respective societies.

Tribals lagged behind the others in their tools and technologies. Such difference has persisted to the present day. That is why, some of the well-known communities like Jats, Gujars, Mallis or Ahirs etc. (which no doubt still retain many of their earlier tribal characteristics) are acknowledged as very good farmers, devoted to their lands or well-versed in animal husbandry, while the tribals in the nearby areas seem to subsist or meekly survive with their backwards, traditional and primitive ways of life in rather inhospitable and harsh environments.

As we have seen, most of the Rajput rulers did not care to (or shall we say, dare to) interfere with the tribal ways or the tribal chiefs so long as the latter also kept within certain mutually agreed bonds, if not prescribed limits of conduct and jurisdictions of area. But, as soon as the Rajput power seemed to decline, as it did under the knocks it received from the expanding Maratha confederacy (once again based on a clannish or tribal unit and supremacy) or with the blows being delivered by the Pindaris without the Mughal empire in Delhi offering any protection, at least according to some available historical records and traditions, the Rajasthan tribes were once again forced into a renewed state of turmoil and turbulence. Some of them became victims of and restive against the Marathas and more so, when the British under the East India Company appeared on the scene, and in their own way, they sought to 'restore peace' and create conditions of 'law and order'.

Not only in various other parts of the country, but in Rajasthan also, perhaps the first ever signs of organized resistance or rebellion were offered by the local tribes, particularly the Bhils and to some extent by the Minas and the others. They were hunted out, hard-pressed into unremote and accessible areas and came to be treated as 'criminals' or 'outcast' brigands and robbers. And then some semblance of British supremacy or paramountcy built, the protection of the Rajput princely order came to be established over Rajputana territories.

But decades later, when social and political awakening came, at least in Rajasthan, it was the Bhil tribe which once again led the way of protest and resurgence.

These broad trends of events or developments have been mentioned here to indicate that for the local tribals their traditional ways of life, the so-called spirit of children of nature, their way of independent existence at peace with the surviving natural environment with the least amount of outside official or administrative interference has been something worth preserving and worth fighting for. It has been so since the days of Maharana Pratap when the Bhils had rallied to his support in spite of heavy odds against them.

The tribal world may well be a small world, but it has been and perhaps until is a self-contents and self-reliant world. At least, in the case of various Rajasthan tribes in the south-east and south-west, one can say that.

Throughout historical times, we do not come across any stories or chronicles of the tribals or their chiefs fighting each other for superiority and dominance. The attacks and invasions have invariably come from outside, from near and far and the tribes have resisted the same with all their might some resistance and a measure of success. At the same time, they have adjusted with the changing times, yet preserving something tangible and lasting from their original common heritage.

One more relevant point which comes to mind in this connection is that with the coming of the East India Company and the British system of administration, followed by this missionary zeal for liberal education and social reforms and dolling out the benefits of a civilized and modern society, perhaps for the first time, the Rajasthan tribes came face-to-face with a system or a society or a philosophy of life which was not basically tribal in character. Gradually, they became victims to the new communities of traders, contractors, missionaries, social reformers, educationists and 'integrationists' and referring to our own contemporary times, one may say to the 'developmentalist'. This is perhaps their biggest, and may be the last challenge. Already, Mina's in the Jaipur region have so advanced as to lose many of their tribal characteristics.

Perhaps, as we have seen in our own life time, modern means of communication or opening up of the interior areas, modern methods of agriculture, trade or commerce or industry and modern systems or networks of machines and public health or educational development, have all broken up the barriers of the age-old and traditional tribal isolation from the rest of the society. But that does not mean that a process of intermingling or intermixing has started. Even under the impact of so-called forces of change or factors of modernization, the untouched tribals have retained their own social affinities and cultural and even ethnic identities. Perhaps they will continue to do so for many years and decades to come, until the rest of the society other than so-called advanced and progressive castes and or communities begin to treat them as their equal and learn to respect their separateness of separate identity. The choice lies to some extent with the tribals themselves at least about what elements, of the new age, they pick up and honour.

However, perhaps, it is necessary to invite attention to at least two factors or forces which seems to have played a very significant part in the process of 'modernization' or 'de-tribalization' and to some extent the 'de-generation' of the tribals. We have earlier briefly referred to the phase or the broad course of events during which the tribals once again were hunted and chased and finally suppressed or some of their left-over and straggling groups were treated as criminals, robbers and outcastes. Among the so-called de-generated tribals, apart from those who were considered to belong to 'a criminal tribe' under the British colonial administration, there are quite a few other tribal groups now connected with the business or the romantic world of "entertainment" or those who continue to render some sort of menial services to the main cultivating communities. These are some of the stray and peripheral examples of tribal groups and intermediate sections of society passing through the phase of detribalization and de-generation.

But as is now being universally acknowledged perhaps, the biggest shock or damage to the tribal social system and the tribal identity came in the wake of the British Crown assuming overall control or ownership of the forest ranges throughout the country towards the close of the last century. This disturbed the tribal relationship with their habitat and natural resources.

A consequential follow up of that policy declaration was that in the Rajputana princely states, the rulers became the virtual owner or master of their forest lands.

If these steps had been taken to preserve and protect the forest as well as the social, culture and economical interests of the forest-dwellers or the tribes living and dependent on their natural forest environment, perhaps, things would have been different. But, ultimately, the net result of the policy of the forests passing under the direct control and administration of the government was that a new class of managers, intermediaries and exploitors, the forest contractors had to be created so as to exploit the natural forest wealth, manly in the form of timber and fuelwood. The process of exploitation attained its tempo as the railway network expanded all over the country, or as ship-building activities were speeded up in various parts of the country, its main parts or trade centres etc. urbanization and house building activities, besides trade and commerce, picked up some momentum.

On the other hand, a positive factor based on social reforms and welfare concepts of the religious or well-meaning liberal-minded missionaries, whether Christian or belonging to Hindu/Aryan faiths and also efforts of the so-called constructive Gandhian workers have also brought in signs of a big change in the social system among the local tribes. The "Bhagat" movement among the Bhils and the teachings or struggles of Govindgiri are some important landmarks in the recent social and political history of Bhils of Rajasthan and Gujarat.

New values, new concepts, new aims and objectives or goals of human existence and endeavour have been preached and practised sometimes in the name of social reforms and education, sometimes in the name of public health and hygiene and sometimes in the name of welfare or improving the lot of the poor, backward or primitive tribes. What the forest contractors and their lackeys or agents or the missionaries or the constructive workers could not do in a significant manner, has been consequently attempted by the politicians, administrators and development-minded sociologists and academicians who have gone into the tribal hinterland with their own messages or programmes or schemes of development so as to change the tribals in their own self-image.

In the process of change, the tribes have also attained a new political coverage and weightage which can influence their choice and tempt them to remain 'tribal' as long as possible.

Thus, the tribal society in Rajasthan is standing on the crossroads between tradition and modernization, between its self-identity and slow but certain assimilation; and is faced with a big question mark about their role and justification of being somewhat different from others. Will the rest of the society or the majority and the more vocal or affluent sections of the society let them be? Will the tribals be given a chance to choose and follow their own methods and programmes of advance from their present levels of development?

This is possible to some extent if the state government and the society at large chooses to treat the forest-bound tribes living in clearly identified or demarcated areas of their natural habitats in their simple and traditional ways, to have an opportunity to build their own lifestyles and organizations for tribal management as well as far managing or administering the natural resources of their areas. For example, if in respect of the forest lands it can be agreed that the tribal communities living in and dependent on those particular forest reserves or ranges, have their right (or at least as much of a right as the forest department) to decide what should be done by way of range management, and if in the bargain, they are also given full backing of technical know-how or financial and material resources with outside interference reduced to the minimum, then perhaps some semblance of tribal ways of life based on "their links with the forest lands" can be preserved in respect of the Bhils, Saharias, Garasias etc., and allowed to develop even in the future.

Similarly, in respect of agriculture or trade and commerce, particularly in the tribal areas, which have not yet been clearly thrown open to outside commercial influences or institutions and organized efforts by other sections of society, perhaps what can save the tribal ways of life and their self-identity to some extent, would be the introduction and strengthening of a genuine cooperative movement or a movement for group action and mutual assistance by them.

Similarly, another instrument to safeguard the interests of the tribal society and preserve its inherent and internal coherence or unity would be the revival and strengthening of their panchayat movement on the basis of the old established traditional group life (rather than the present-day statutory system based on elected panchayats with limited functions).

Last but not the least is the socio-cultural sphere with its social customs and rituals, natural art forms of self-expression and communal fairs and festivals. These need to be preserved not as 'museum pieces' but as living traditions and protected against the high charged onslaughts of modern urban and commercial culture.

If we may turn our mind to the prevailing sociological scenario in Rajasthan, perhaps, we will find that even some of the well-established and settled communities in areas where the land and cattle owning cultivators or traders, bankers or financers have come to dominate the rural scene, they have, especially the cultivators, retained some sort of tribal institutions, customs or practices in spite of the adoption by them of improved technologies and even modern methods of working, organization, management and administration. Jats, Ahirs, Malis, Gujars, and even Rajputs, retain some of their 'tribal' influences and social institutions. For example, in dealing with outside groups or forces, they tend to get together and act in their 'brotherhood'.

The society in Rajasthan is not only pluralistic, but it is also fragmented and fractional. That is why, even today, we have so many separate and distinct communities. For example, the scheduled castes and tribes, Brahaman groups or *gotras*, or numerous clans or groups amongst the Rajputs or groups of professionals or middlemen among Kayasths or trading communities or similarly amongst the cultivators there are many groups and castes and even amongst the poor and the non-landowning sections of agriculture labourers and workers. These diverse social groups, castes and communities come into contact with each other on many occasions. They interact with each other mostly at individual level when they have their business and professional work to do, but in certain respects, in their social customs, religious beliefs, rituals or marriage ceremonies and such other daily or occasional points of contact, they have learnt to keep their traditional distance or aloofness and manage to remain within the prescribed limits.

In such social settings, if the tribals also strive or endeavour to maintain and preserve their own social system or beliefs, institutions or ways of life, can they be blamed for trying to keep their identity and to go their own way? The process of social interaction or social and economic advances need not start with their assimilation, absorption or subjugation or merger of their identity. It can as well start with a similar process of mutual adjustment and cooperation between them and many other more advanced, enlightened or affluent sections or communities.

11

Remaking a State Polity

Ganga Singh to Sadul to Karni Singh and the Accession and Merger of Bikaner[1]

RIMA HOOJA AND BHUPENDRA HOOJA

The present-day administrative unit of Rajasthan took form when 19 princely states and two chiefdoms of erstwhile Rajputana (whose rulers had previously signed individual 'Instruments of Accession' to the newly independent nation-state of India in 1947), were merged together between early 1948 and April 1949. Subsequently, the previously British-administered Ajmer-Merwara, Abu taluka and a few other 'enclaves' were amalgamated and merged with this Greater Union of Rajasthan on November 1, 1956, in accordance with the provisions of the States Reorganisation Act, 1956. The territories and boundaries of the erstwhile princely states and chiefdoms of Rajputana, and of Ajmer-Merwara, were adjusted upon integration to facilitate better administration within the new State of Rajasthan.

Along with the merger of the erstwhile princely states came the process of democratization. This applied specially to the democratisation of feudal institutions and attitudes – for example, land reforms and the abolition of *jagirdari* in 1959, and so forth. However, it may be relevant to take note here that some attempts (howsoever limited) at partial democratization within certain erstwhile princely states of Rajputana had begun during the early decades of the 20th century itself.[2]

For example, during the early part of the reign of Maharaja Ganga Singh of Bikaner (b. 1880, r. 1887–1943), a legislative assembly – originally styled as 'Representative Assembly' – had been inaugurated by 1913. The motivations and catalysts for such changes were many, including people's movements, and advice by the British authorities. These, and other, aspects have been written about and debated in recent years.[3]

Ganga Singh of Bikaner ruled his state (and his family) in the manner of a patriarch – according to some, a rather despotic patriarch.[4] Obsessed with what he perceived to be the greater good of his people and the upliftment of his state, by today's lights Ganga Singh may be called a benign autocrat who ruled over a feudal state – a stark contrast to our current notions of democracy and people's rights. But those close to him insist that he tried to live according to his notion of a 'good' Indian king,[5] combining the better aspects of traditional Indian kingship with a 20th century outlook towards modernization.[6]

One of the outstanding men of his generation,[7] Maharaja Ganga Singh has been described as a sagacious statesman and a gifted administrator, who transformed Bikaner into one of the premier modern states of the Indian subcontinent during the course of his long reign. Appalled by the spectre of recurring famine and the accompanying suffering it brought to the people of his state, Ganga Singh pursued an irrigation scheme to secure water for Bikaner in the form of a perennial canal. His dream was partially realized in 1927 when water from the Sutlej river first flowed through the Gang Canal – then the world's longest concrete-lined canal – into the dry sandy terrain of northern Bikaner. (The subsequent Rajasthan Canal – now known as Indira Gandhi Canal – was part of the Maharaja's vision.) Alongside this, 883 miles of railroad tracks were laid and market towns established all over the state. The capital-city of Bikaner became the centre of a well-run modern administration, with hospitals, schools, colleges, and small industries. The development of democratic institutions remained slow, however, and political activities were actively discouraged.[8]

By the end of Ganga Singh's long reign in 1943, the days of India's princely order were numbered. [We shall not digress here, however, by discussing the events and happenings that made this inevitable – for example, the First Round Table Conference of 1930, where the idea of a self-governing federal India (with a responsible government at the Centre and provincial autonomy) made up of British India and princely India was mooted by Tej Bahadur Sapru, and supported by Maharaja Ganga Singh.][9] Soon after the independence of India, and its division into two separate nations – the Dominions of India and Pakistan – in 1947 was accompanied by the accession of Bikaner (and other princely states) to one of the two new nations.

The present paper attempts to look at the transition in the erstwhile Rajputana's important princely state of Bikaner from a feudal social and political system into an active constituent of the new democratic order mainly from the perspective of one of the 'royals' who was a close observer to the events and happenings, namely, Karni Singh, at the time the Maharaj-Kumar and later the Maharaja of Bikaner. As a 'concerned party', Karni Singh's perspective may be considered to be subjective to some extent, but it does provide additional details and viewpoints to the overall picture concerning that period. Furthermore, with a degree in History and Political Science from Delhi University, and later a Ph.D. on Bikaner's relations with the 'Central Powers', Karni Singh's did try to consciously present an unbiased view according to his lights.

Karni Singh (1924–1988), the eldest grandson of Maharaja Ganga Singh, and the heir-apparent to Maharaja Sadul Singh (r. 1943–1950), was the 23rd (and last) formally recognized[10] ruler of the state of Bikaner, before the abolition of privy purses and titles as per the 26th Amendment to the Constitution in December 1971.[11] Karni Singh also served as an independent member of Parliament (Lok Sabha) for 25 years between 1952 and 1977.[12]

The independence of India initiated perhaps the most drastic of changes for the various princely states (including Bikaner) and their people. Within the next quarter of a century India's princely order would be relegated to the pages of history. For, with independence in sight, the majority of India's princes had (with a few exceptions) acceded their states to either the Dominion of India or to the new Dominion of Pakistan. It should be noted here that the decision regarding accession rested entirely with the rulers of the States concerned. It was a decision of consequence for all the princes.

The individual 'Instruments of Accession' signed by the rulers expressly reserved and retained sovereignty and continuity of different State Governments, while at the same time binding them either to independent India or the newly created Pakistan.

Maharaja Sadul Singh of Bikaner was the first to sign the Instrument of Accession on the 7th of August 1947. In his speech, delivered at the state banquet on 15th August, 1947 to celebrate India's independence, Sadul Singh of Bikaner clarified that, "With the lapse of paramountcy, it was open to the States of India to stand aside and refuse to associate with the new Dominion. Legally we could all have been independent today, for the suzerainty which we had surrendered to the British Crown had reverted to us under the Indian Independence Act and we could have stood aside and not accede[d] to the Indian Dominion. A moment's consideration would show how disastrous the consequences would have been. It would have meant India breaking up into small fragments...From the beginning my mind was made up. With full knowledge of its implications, I decided without hesitation to cooperative with those elements in India which were working for the establishment of a stable central government and oppose with determination any forces that might come in the way of such consummation".[13]

At a crucial stage in Indian history, when the whole-hearted and willing cooperation of the princes, rather than their obstinate adherence to issues of their legal and ancestral rights and prerogatives, was the need of the hour, Sadul Singh played a part appropriate for Maharaja Ganga Singh's son. Thirty years earlier, Ganga Singh's statesmanship at the Imperial War Conference and the War Cabinet meetings in London in 1917, had led Austen Chamberlain, the then Secretary of State for India, to ask him to write a Minute on Indian issues. In response, during his stop-over at Rome enroute to India, Ganga Singh prepared the note which was to become widely known as the 'Rome Note'. On 15th May, 1917 this was forwarded to Chamberlain.

In it Ganga Singh stressed a four-point programme in the context of the then prevailing situation. This was: "[firstly]...the announcement at the earliest possible opportunity that the ultimate objective of British rule in India was the grant of self-government within the empire; secondly, further liberal reforms in the constitution and functioning of the provincial legislative councils as well as the Imperial Legislative Councils; thirdly, the grant of greater autonomy to the Government of India and the provincial councils; and lastly, the establishment of a Council of Princes for dealing with matters concerning the British Government and the Indian States".[14]

For Ganga Singh there was nothing incongruous in a ruling Indian prince, who offered allegiance to the Empire, to also demand self-government for India! According to Karni Singh's analysis, three loyalties had constantly and simultaneously worked in his grandfather.[15] One was his loyalty to the Crown which had almost acquired a religious sanctity with Ganga Singh because he held that the treaties which were entered into with the British government during the early 19th century, due to the then existing circumstances, by the ancestors of the modern Indian princes, were plighted words which must be respected. Another was his loyalty to his mother country which sustained Ganga Singh's sincere belief in India attaining its full political stature. In keeping with this, Ganga Singh made it very clear that the Indian princes, while belonging to the princely order, were very much 'sons of the soil'.[16] And the third was Ganga Singh's absolute loyalty to his state of Bikaner and his subjects. This love of country, loyalty to one's land of birth and people, and belief in both doing one's duty and honouring a pledged word was a basic facet of Maharaja Ganga Singh's attitude towards kingship.

In his lifetime, Maharaja Ganga Singh tried to live up to all these three loyalties in fact, he tried to blend them together as a ruler of a state which did its best to help the British Government/Empire in the two World Wars, in his service to the people of Bikaner state, and as the leading voice in the Chamber of Princes as its first Chancellor (1921–26). In his turn, his successor, Maharaja Sadul Singh, during the years leading up to Indian independence, played a vital role in the Chamber of Princes (the *Narendra Mandal*). Besides his work in the Chamber of Princes, Sadul Singh also played a decisive role in various other negotiations between the Indian rulers and the British government, which have been documented in full by his older son, Karni Singh.[17]

While other events were taking their course and the nationalist leaders of British India were making efforts towards India's 'tryst with destiny', the Standing Committee of the Chamber of Princes appointed Maharaja Sadul Singh in 1944 as the Chairman of a Committee of Rulers to formulate proposals and recommendations for more efficient administration in the princely states. From c. 1943 onwards, the pace of constitutional reforms in different princely states was gradually increasing. The process was to continue till 1947–48, but was often deemed too slow as far as the establishment of representative popular government in the Princely States was concerned.

In fact, in Bikaner itself, where Maharaja Ganga Singh's government had for long actively discouraged political activities,[18] by July 1942 a *Bikaner Rajya Praja Parishad* had become established, even though the Bikaner government was unsympathetic to it. The stated objective of this organization was to get a responsible government under the aegis of the Maharaja (at that time Ganga Singh). Eventually, one of the Parishad's leaders, Raghubar Dayal Goel was externed from the state. The Quit India Movement did not have much impact in Bikaner, and (despite the attempts of people like Magharam), the hoisting of the tricolour was regarded as a seditious act.

Even though the early years of Sadul Singh's reign did not see a drastic change in the established state policy, as early as March 1943 – within a month of his succession – Sadul Singh had announced the desire to associate the people with the administration to a greater degree. Certain changes were made in the functioning of the Legislative Assembly of Bikaner, though these were less than what the Praja Parishad and *kisan* (agrarian movement) leaders were looking for.

Aware of similar feelings and desires for responsible government in various states, the Bikaner Committee, headed by Sadul Singh made certain valuable recommendations. In September 1945, in a speech to the Informal Princes Standing Committee, Sadul Singh stressed that before very long the princes would be faced with the issue of how the states were going to fit into the future constitution of India. He also warned his brother-princes that unless the smaller states formed into groups which could provide necessary amenities to the people and march with the times, they were likely to be wiped out. In retrospect, it seems that the ruler of Bikaner tried to look into the future with a clarity of vision and the caution of wisdom – as the subsequent events revealed.

Karni Singh, a first-hand witness to several of the meetings and decisions that were to be crucial for India's future course, commented: "Soon after, the Maharaja reiterated his convictions in a confidential circular to the princes wherein he said that the passing of time would convince them whether or not his views were sound, and emphasized that the policy of drift and delay would be suicidal to them. His foreboding soon came true".[19]

Meanwhile, there were a number of instances of *jagirdar* and/or official repression against Praja Parishad led and/or local agrarian movements and public meetings at places like Kangar and Dudhwa-Khara[20] during the 1945–46 period, as well as at Sadulshahr, Lallgarh etc. These had some repercussions on political and constitutional developments within Bikaner state.

At the 7th session of the All India State People's Conference (AISPC) held at Udaipur (the capital of the state of Mewar), during December 1945 to January 1946, under the presidentship of Jawaharlal Nehru, had reiterated its long-held demand for the establishment of 'responsible government' based on representative institutions in the states – including the states of Rajputana. (In 1948 the AISPC was to merge with the Indian National Congress.) On 26th January, 1946, Independence Day was celebrated for the first time in Bikaner state, and the demand for responsible government was once again voiced.

On 24th March, 1946, the Cabinet Mission arrived in India to hold discussions and break the deadlock between the British and the Indians on the one hand, and the Congress and the Muslim League on the other. At this time, the Chamber of Princes made it clear that its loyalties lay with the country and that they supported self-governance for India. Karni Singh' perception of this period is as follows: "After discussion and correspondence with the Chamber of Princes and its representatives, the Cabinet Mission issued a memorandum dated 12 May, 1946 wherein it said that the Chamber of Princes had confirmed that the Indian States fully shared the country's desire for the immediate attainment by India of her full stature. ...And in the Cabinet Mission's plan announced on 16 May, 1946 the proposals, so far as they concerned the Indian states, were that there should be a Union of India comprising both of British India and the Indian states which should deal with foreign affairs, defence and communications and that the states should retain all subjects and powers other than those ceded to the Union...The states unanimously accepted the plan but not without internal difficulties, and it was as a result of the efforts of Maharaja Sadul Singh that unanimous decision was possible".[21]

"The Standing Committee of the Chamber of Princes having, by its statement of 10 June, 1946 agreed that the Cabinet plan offered a fair basis for negotiations both as to the representation of the States in the Constituent Assembly and as to their ultimate position in the Union, set up a State Negotiation Committee for the purpose".[22]

The Cabinet Mission plan was eventually not accepted, however, and, over time, various events and actions fanned the embers of communal passion. These were to leave the Indian sub-continent partitioned into separate countries – India and Pakistan.

In the interim, on 21st June, 1946, Maharaja Sadul Singh announced that a responsible government would soon be set up. Around this time, the externed Raghubar Dayal Goel re-entered the Bikaner state, despite the ban placed on him. On 30th June the Praja Parishad held a session at Raisinghnagar, under the chairmanship of Satya Narayan Saraf. There was a *lathi*-charge and firing by the police, and one of the Parishad leaders, Birbal Singh, was killed. Thereafter, through his proclamation of 31st August, 1946, Maharaja Sadul Singh announced the reconstitution of the Bikaner Legislative Assembly on a more popular basis. To achieve that end, he appointed a Constitution Committee and a Franchise and Constituency Committee. (Some people have doubted Sadul Singh's intentions in this matter of democratization,[23] but Karni Singh's writings and cassette-recorded views indicate that the attempt was not a ploy or pretence.) [24]

According to Karni Singh, while the proclamation was generally well received by the people at large, the Bikaner Praja Parishad, the counterpart of the Indian National Congress, entertained doubts. Despite that, the Praja Parishad leaders announced in the press that they would not precipitate matters, and the Parishad's working committee and workers' convention opted to cooperate with the Bikaner government in the Constitution and Franchise & Constituency Committees.[25] As a result of these efforts, in due course, the Bikaner Constitution Act was promulgated on 4th December, 1947.

Meanwhile, following the swearing-in of an Interim Government in British India on 2nd September, 1946, the countdown towards freedom had gained momentum. In February 1947, Prime Minister Attlee announced in Parliament Britain's intention of quitting India by June 1948, and transferring power to a responsible Indian government. That March, Lord Mountbatten replaced Wavell as the Viceroy of India. Soon afterwards, Maharaja Sadul Singh of Bikaner made a historic walkout from a meeting of the princes which was to influence the shaping of contemporary history. Ironically, this is scarcely recalled today!

According to Karni Singh, "During the meetings of the Princes Standing Committee held in Bombay in April, 1947 the agreements arrived at by the two negotiating committees (the States Negotiating Committee and its counterpart set up by the Constituent Assembly) were taken up for ratification and approved. However, a difference of opinion arose between the Chancellor [of the Chamber of Princes, Nawab Hamidullah Khan of Bhopal (b. 1894; r. 1926–1960)] and the Maharaja (Sadul Singh of Bikaner) over the time when the states should join the Constituent Assembly. The Chancellor and the majority of the princes were in favour of the states entering the Constituent Assembly at a stage when the Union Constitution was being framed, whereas Maharaja Sadul Singh and his group were in favour of joining immediately. Finding that it was not possible for him to make the princes realize the gravity of the problem, the Maharaja staged his historic walk-out leaving a note for the Chancellor wherein...he stated that his views on the problems then facing the rulers and the country at large were totally different from those of the Chancellor and majority of the Standing Committee, and neither could he remain silent nor did he wish to speak anymore on his point of view which he had stressed many a time before Their Highnesses".[26]

Karni Singh further writes: "The Maharaja issued an appeal to his brother princes the same day stressing that the only safe policy for the States was to work for the creation of as large a section of India as possible which would safeguard both the states and British India in the vacuum that would be created on the withdrawal of the British and which would maintain peace, order and good government and prevent civil strife...He, therefore, urged that the princes should rise to the occasion and be hailed as co-architects of India's independence and greatness...This historic walk-out by the Maharaja broke 'Bhopal's game' of evolving a third force and the action was not only acclaimed by all sections of the press but was also eulogized by eminent British Indian leaders".[27]

Karni Singh believes that, at this stage, "guided by the most patriotic of motives Maharaja Sadul Singh kept up his own plighted word of seeing India attain independence as also provided the much needed courage to his wavering brother princes".[28] As a direct consequence, on 28th April, 1947, Bikaner's representative, K.N. Panikkar, took his seat in India's Constituent Assembly.[29]

According to Karni Singh's account, Bikaner was fully aware, apparently, that with the prospect of the partition of India looming large, if "the states chose to adopt any path other than that of cooperation following Attlee's announcement of 20 February, 1947 regarding the lapse of paramountcy, the dangerous possibility of Balkanisation indeed existed".[30] Thus, when in July 1947 Sardar Vallabhbhai Patel, the Minister incharge of the newly created States Department, appealed to the Indian rulers to hand over matters regarding defence, foreign affairs and communications to the interim government, retaining other departments themselves, Maharaja Sadul Singh welcomed the motion and urged his brother-princes to support the step.

Since the task of negotiating with the princes was entrusted to Mountbatten (in his capacity as the Crown's representative), the

Viceroy summoned a full meeting of the Chamber of Princes on 25th July, 1947. Karni Singh, who was a spectator at this meeting, notes that the Viceroy "made out a strong case for the States acceding to the appropriate Dominion (i.e. India or Pakistan) in regard to the three subjects, assuring them at the same time that this would involve no financial liability and that there would be no further encroachment on their internal sovereignty. The Viceroy's persuasions succeeded and a majority of the princes signed the Instrument of Accession, Maharaja Sadul Singh being the first to do so".[31]

A Standstill Agreement which provided for the continuance, for the time being, of all subsisting agreements and administrative agreements in matters of common concern to the state and the Dominion of India, was also signed about the same time.

(Sadul Singh's role in taking the lead was later publicly acclaimed by Lord Mountbatten, Governor-General of independent India, in January 1948, during the course of his visit to Bikaner, accompanied by Lady Mountbatten. In his speech at the Investiture Durbar at Lallgarh Palace on 15th January, 1948, Lord Mountbatten stated: "His Highness (Maharaja Sadul Singh) was the first ruler who realised the part which the princes could play in the future by sending representatives to the Constituent Assembly to help frame the new constitution of India. Likewise, His Highness was the first ruler to support my proposals for obtaining the accession of States to their neighbouring Dominion. ...The statesmanship and patriotism displayed by the Maharaja of Bikaner in giving a lead in announcing his accession to the Dominion of India without a moment of doubt or suspicion cannot, therefore, be praised too highly").

Meanwhile, during July 1947, the imminent partition of the land into two separate countries brought a major threat for Bikaner. There were strong possibilities that the Ferozepore headworks located in the Punjab, which controlled water supply to the Gang Canal, could be awarded to Pakistan. If this came to pass while Bikaner remained in India, there was every chance that the interests of Bikaner would be 'prejudicially affected'. Put bluntly, the area could lapse into its pre-Canal condition and revert to being a desert-land. At this stage, Sadul Singh of Bikaner played a crucial role in ensuring that the Ferozepore headworks stayed in independent India, instead of going to Pakistan. The Maharaja even took recourse to his personal friendship with the Viceroy.[32]

Karni Singh has documented how, "when it became known through private sources that the Muslim League was likely to put forward claims for the control of regulation of waters from the Ferozepore Headworks, the Prime Minister of Bikaner addressed a letter to Sardar Patel...He also added that over one thousand square miles of Bikaner territory was irrigated by the Sutlej Valley Canals and if the Muslim League's claims were accepted, the interests of the State would very much suffer. He, therefore, urged upon the Sardar both as the Minister incharge of the States Department as also Member of the High Council of Partition, to ensure that the Ferozepore Headworks were entirely controlled by India. The Maharaja also sent telegrams to the Viceroy, Pandit Jawaharlal Nehru, Dr Rajendra Prasad and Sardar Patel on 7th July, 1947 requesting that in the arrangements that were being made, it might be ensured that the interests of Bikaner State were not interfered with".[33]

In his reply by telegram and letter dated the same day, Sardar Patel assured Sadul Singh that appropriate steps were being taken. Shortly afterwards, at the suggestion of Viceroy, the Bikaner Maharaja sent a telegram to the President of the Punjab Boundary Commission at Lahore, asking for an opportunity for the Bikaner state to present its case. Lala Kanwar Sain, then Chief Engineer (Irrigation) of Bikaner state, and Bakshi Tek Chand, a renowned Punjab-based lawyer and jurist (whose career highlights had included the position of Puisne Judge of the Lahore High Court from 1927 to 1943, and who was subsequently to serve as a Member of India's Provisional Parliament of 1950–52, prior to first General Elections of 1952), were deputed to present the case. Additionally, on 25th July, 1947, a memorandum was presented to the Punjab Boundary Commission.

Events were now moving rapidly. On 10th August, 1947, upon "...news reaching the Maharaja that the Boundary Commission was likely to award Ferozepore Tehsil to Western Punjab [Pakistan], the Maharaja again telegraphed the Viceroy stressing the importance of retaining the Headworks at Ferozepore in India as the economic life of the State depended entirely upon it urging that his Prime Minister and Chief Engineer Irrigation, might be afforded an opportunity to place facts before the Viceroy. It must be said to the credit of Lord Mountbatten especially, and to others concerned as well, that the efforts of Bikaner were finally crowned with success and a just cause upheld. Ferozepore remained in India".[34]

Thereafter, came the day when India became independent. Bikaner state's official celebrations to mark India's Independence Day has been described by Karni Singh in his book, *The Relations of the House of Bikaner with the Central Powers – 1465–1949* (based on his Ph.D thesis). He noted that, "The country-wide rejoicings on the attainment of Independence were celebrated with full enthusiasm in Bikaner on 15 August, 1947. The flag hoisting ceremony was performed by the Maharaja personally[35] at the stadium. In the evening a state banquet was held at the Lallgarh Palace to celebrate the function at which Panikkar, while proposing the Maharaja's toast said: 'We are all proud that the Maharaja has been one of the architects of the independence of India'. The Maharaja in his reply said that the day's celebrations were in honour of a great and historic event and that he had done his duty of India, to the states as a whole and to his State and his beloved people".[36]

With the euphoria of India's independence on 15th August, 1947, also came the traumatic partition of the subcontinent. Bikaner, itself untainted by communal madness, became a transit-point for many who took that route to travel across the newly created national boundaries of India and Pakistan. Karni Singh (then undergoing training at Bikaner, in his capacity as heir-apparent of Bikaner), has recorded how "...*kafilas* [caravans] of ten lakhs of people moved from India to Pakistan and vice-versa, and my father's orders were that not a single person should be harmed, and the moving humanity, irrespective of caste or religion, should be given total protection. But the story on the other side of the Bikaner state, in what was then called *Angrezi Raj* or British India, was quite different".[37]

Maharaja Sadul Singh appealed to the Bikaneris not to leave their homeland and cross the border into Bahawalpur. Guaranteeing safety to all his subjects, he urged those Muslims who had fled Bikaner to the return back. He also ensured the return to such people of all the property they had abandoned when they had left their ancestral homes. Besides this, the Maharaja ordered that the refugees using Bikaner for their passage – Hindus and Muslims alike – were to be given every feasible assistance. (A majority of the rulers of Rajputana took similar steps to protect their subjects as well as refugees transiting through their respective states. That was not the case in every Princely State, however.) Sadul Singh also placed his Sujangarh residence, with its vast grounds, at the district town of Sujangarh, at the disposal of the refugees.

As a result, "when the communal holocaust began to subside in both countries, the Bikaner state could proudly look back with satisfaction at a major humanitarian task so well done. Only one stray incident of assault had taken place. Even so, there had been no loss of life for refugees of either side who crossed the border through Bikaner", Karni Singh has recorded. "...Father was congratulated for his great work by both the leaders of India as well as the Prime Minister of Pakistan".[38]

Not long after, Mahatma Gandhi was assassinated in Delhi on 30th January, 1948. Karni Singh has documented how "as soon as the Maharaja [Sadul Singh] heard of the tragic news... he ordered state mourning and the holding of mass prayers at the stadium at 4.00 P.M. on 31 January, 1948. The Maharaja led the prayers personally and...wore a white turban, a symbol of mourning and which is only worn by the ruler in the case of the death of an elder from the immediate members of the family, and never otherwise".[39]

Meanwhile, the work of both, Bikaner's Constitution Committee, as well as its Franchise & Constituency Committee, had continued unabated. This led (as already referred to above) to the promulgation of the Bikaner Constitution Act in December 1947. The 1947 Bikaner Act brought in a bicameral legislature for Bikaner, and the administration, with certain reservations, was entrusted to a council responsible to the legislature. Through the proclamation of 4th December, 1947, it was further announced that the Act also contemplated the introduction of full responsible government, under the aegis of the Maharaja, within a period of two years. The pace of change was not rapid enough for the Praja Parishad, though.

Maharaja Sadul Singh issued another proclamation on 2nd February, 1948, announcing his decision to establish responsible government in April 1948 and dispensing with the interim arrangements. A month later, on 18th March, 1948, he announced the formation of an interim coalition ministry with Jaswant Singh of Daudsar as the Prime Minister. The coalition ministry, made up of both Congress representatives and the Maharaja's nominees on a fifty-fifty basis, replaced the Maharaja's Executive Council. It was charged with carrying on routine administration during the period pending elections. These were fixed for 23rd September, 1948.

According to Karni Singh's perception:

> For some time the work went smoothly. But it was noticed after some time that the dissident group in the Congress, i.e., the group which did not favour the formation of the coalition ministry began to agitate against the state. In order to refute the allegations of the agitators, a public meeting was called in the Sunaron-ki-Gawar at Bikaner and was addressed by K. Jaswant Singh, the Prime Minister, when other ministers including the Congress nominees were also present. The meeting, however, ended in rowdysim and the Congress ministers, instead of trying to quieten the mischievous elements and restore order, deserted the meeting.
>
> The agitation continued and the Congress dissidents now raised their voice for the merger of the state. The Maharaja brought these activities of the dissidents to the notice of Sardar Patel, and in view of the fact that the Bikaner state had been classified as a viable unit and also that the Maharaja was not only anxious to introduce more responsible government in the State but had actually taken steps for its implementation and the general elections were not far off, he asked the Sardar to see that the agitation was stopped forthwith and, in fact, the agitation did stop.[40]

Throughout this period (mid-1946 to mid-1948), Karni Singh was present at Bikaner undergoing the administrative training which his grandfather, Maharaja Ganga Singh, had originally planned out in keeping with the prince's eventual role as a future Maharaja of Bikaner, and which Maharaja Sadul Singh had continued with. Regular Council meetings either at the office of the *Mahakma Khas* or at Shiv Vilas, discussions with ministers and officials, Revenue Board meetings and related activities were the order of the week. Besides these, time had to be found for meeting private individuals and attending public functions. Occasionally, he attended the law courts too.[41]

Karni Singh frequently accompanied Maharaja Sadul Singh to Delhi to take part in meetings too. "I would sit behind my father and listen to all the discussions which took place with the leaders and Princes", he later recorded. "I remember one time when we went to meet Mr Jawaharlal Nehru ... to discuss with him the question of the Bhakra dam, as the waters were needed in Bikaner. Father also took up the matter with Sardar Patel and Mr Gadgil. ...Then I went with father to Mr C. Rajagopalachari...[and] discussed the Bhakra dam with him. As a result of these efforts, father was assured by the Prime

Minister...that he would do everything in his power to see that the Bikaner state got its share in the Bhakra dam project".[42]

In the summer of 1948, even as Bikaner prepared for the elections due that coming September, Maharaja Sadul Singh left for England for medical treatment. He placed his heir-apparent, Maharaj-Kumar Karni Singh, in charge of the state, with the aid of Bikaner's Maharani Sudarshan Kumari. To assist Karni Singh in the discharge of his duties, Mehar Chand Mahajan was named as Advisor.[43] There were problems in the coalition ministry while Maharaja Sadul Singh was away. Then, in August 1948, while work was proceeding towards the elections scheduled for 23rd September, the State Congress Committee abruptly demanded the postponement of the forthcoming elections. As Maharaja Sadul Singh had not yet returned from England, Karni Singh apprised him about the situation.

The young Maharaj-Kumar had "...explicit instructions from the Maharaja to ensure that the work of granting responsible government by the time stipulated must not be allowed to suffer under any circumstances". Further, "...as no cogent reasons were advanced for the desired postponement of the elections by the Congress", Karni Singh felt that "...he could not accede to the request to put the clock of democracy back".[44]

In an attempt to solve the imbroglio, pending his father's return to Bikaner, Karni Singh held protracted discussions with Congress leaders of Rajasthan like Hiralal Shastri (later to be the first Chief Minister of Greater Rajasthan, when that was formed – which post he would hold till January 1951), and Gokul Bhai Bhatt.

In his view, "Whatever explanation the Bikaner State Congress Committee might have given for the basis of their demand, and these were later duly refuted by Maharaja Sadul Singh on his return, in a press communique, the fact remained that the Bikaner State Congress Committee wanted to gain time as it was not sure of its hold on the people...The intention not to contest the elections and face a show-down was understandable particularly when the States Peoples Conference had tried to convince the world that they had complete control over public opinion in the States. Whether this claim was justified in the case of Bikaner and Jodhpur is a doubtful matter. ...As it is, the Bikaner State Congress Committee, by its resolution of 28 August, 1948, created an impasse by deciding not to participate in the general elections and also by calling upon its representatives in the coalition ministry to tender their resignations... This created an unfortunate situation; and the Maharaja, who was constantly being kept in touch by the heir-apparent, returned to Bikaner on 31 August, 1948. He immediately set himself to the task of resolving the tangle if he could".[45]

Sadul Singh secured an appointment with Sardar Patel and went to Delhi to discuss the subject with him (over lunch at the Sardar's house). Maharaja Sadul Singh was advised to discuss the matter further with V.P. Menon, Hiralal Shastri, Jai Narain Vyas and Gokul Bhai Bhatt, all of whom were in Delhi at the time. Eventually, the Bikaner Maharaja was advised to postpone the elections.

The Maharaja returned to Bikaner on 6th September, 1948. The Congress ministers had tendered their resignations and the Maharaja had "...no option but to accept them, dissolve the interim ministry and postpone the elections...At the same time, the Maharaja also announced his intention to appoint a Prime Minister from outside the State so that no one may have any genuine case for complaint and...C.S. Venkatachar, I.C.S., former Dewan of Jodhpur, took over in October, 1948".[46] (Venkatachar continued as Prime Minister right up to the Integration of Bikaner, and several of the 'Private Property Settlements' bore his signatures.)[47]

While these events were taking place in Bikaner, the Government of India had started to integrate some of the Indian princely states. The logic given was that the people of these states desired the same measure of freedom and democratic rights etc. as enjoyed by the people in provinces and centrally administered parts of the country. Secondly, the rulers of the smaller 'non-viable' states were not in a position to bring about the desired administrative reforms for want to resources. Consequently, it was decided to group them into sizeable units by merging them with either the neighbouring provinces, or converting them into centrally administered areas. Very soon, this process was extended to encompass the major States too, by creating new 'viable units' through the formation of unions of states. (Such an eventuality had already been foreseen by Sadul Singh.)

In Karni Singh's view, this "was going back upon the solemn assurances given at the time the accession of the states was sought for. The tide of times had changed. The process of integration started avowedly with the consent of the princes, but a consent which circumstances did permit them to withhold... Even the eighteen states which the

Government of India had at first declared as those satisfying the conditions as viable units of the Indian Union and whose names were listed in the relevant schedule of the Draft Constitution placed before the Constituent Assembly, ultimately lost their separate entity as the process of integration and merger progressed and in good time before the Constitution was adopted. Bikaner State was among these eighteen viable states".[48]

The process of integration had begun with the rulers of the Chhatisgarh and Orissa states ceding to the Dominion Government full and exclusive authority, jurisdiction and powers for and in relation to the governance of their States by agreements signed on 14th December, 1947 and subsequent dates. At a conference attended by several Indian rulers and Lord Mountbatten on 7th January, 1948, V.P. Menon, Secretary in the Government of India's States Department, assured the Princes present that the principle of merger would not be applied to those States which had individual representatives in the Constituent Assembly. (Bikaner being one such state.) "And yet what followed soon belied these professions", Karni Singh later commented. "The sudden switch in the policy of the new Government of India in respect of the larger States, which had even in the draft Constitution been declared as viable units, and which could maintain their separate identity, is rather hard to explain".[49]

The Government of India's shift of stance left Sadul Singh feeling extremely let down, even betrayed. Carried away by the euphoria of Independence, Maharaja Sadul Singh had taken the lead in signing away his traditional inheritance for what he perceived to be the greater good of the people of both Bikaner and India. Additionally, he had also played a vital role in persuading many of his brother-Princes to follow his example. This role had been acknowledged not only by all his contemporaries, it was to be publicity reiterated, a few years after the death of Maharaja Sadul Singh, by no less a personage than the President of India, Dr Rajendra Prasad.

Speaking at the unveiling ceremony of a statue of the Maharaja Sadul Singh at Bikaner on 2nd September, 1954, the President of India stated that:

> When the British Government decided to leave India, they declared that after their departure all treaties and agreements between the British Crown and the Princes and States of India would cease to operate. The result was that a large part of India, comprising about 600 States,

> scattered all over the country, became free after the departure of the British to remain either with India or seek to retain their separate entity. It was a crucial problem on which depended the unity and the very future of India...
>
> The great move for the unification of India could materialize primarily because of the goodwill and ready willingness of Princes like Maharaja Sadul Singhji to participate in Constitution making and to send their representatives to the Constituent Assembly of India. It was a difficult task, too difficult to be described in words because but for this kind of wilful cooperation, India might have remained split in several bits. It rebounds to the credit of the late Maharaja of Bikaner that by his bold decision he gave a correct and timely lead to other Princes. This eventually resulted in the accession of not only Bikaner but also other Princely States to India. Therefore, India is, and will remain indebted to him. When the history of that period is written, it will be recorded therein that at a time when India was faced, on the one hand, with the calamity of partition and, on the other, with the dangerous possibility of Balkanisation, Maharaja Sadul Singhji, prompted by farsightedness and the most patriotic of motives, stood firm like a rock and averted that possibility.
>
> ...By placing the interests of the country before their own, the Princes played a memorable part in the process of India's unification. The help which the late Maharaja Sadul Singhji gave in this connection, has been thankfully acknowledged by the great Indian leader and Minister of States at that time, namely, Sardar Vallabhbhai Patel.

When the process of integration was initiated, Maharaja Sadul Singh could not believe that the great leaders who had brought about Indian independence could go back on their solemn assurances within such a short period of time. According to Karni Singh, his father had "...placed his faith and trust in the words of our great leaders that they would not be interested in annexing the states. Then a sudden shift started which became a whirlwind almost when, without any apparent reason, the Government of India started shifting its stance and going in for integration of states and finishing them of".[50]

A noting made by Sadul Singh on a file which Karni Singh preserved, clearly expressed the Maharaja's bewilderment and anguish at the shape the future was taking. "Why this sudden change?", Maharaja Sadul Singh queried. His heir recalled that "A big meeting was held in Bikaner at which the people said they didn't want to merge and then the whole thing was rail-roaded through. My father felt let down...and he died soon after. It was the fact that assurances had been given and that they went back on their word".[51]

As is well known now, Rajputana's integration was completed in several stages. "The three old established major and viable States of Jaipur, Jodhpur and Bikaner, together with the ancient State of Jaisalmer, stood out till the last. The Ministry of States, therefore, soon initiated negotiations for the merger of these major and viable States for the formation of a Greater Rajasthan Union. The negotiations were protracted, several meetings took place jointly and severally between the three rulers and V.P. Menon, representative of the Ministry of States, at Delhi, Bikaner, Jaipur and Jodhpur ...[Karni Singh was present at most of these meetings]. It soon became apparent that the merger was inevitable and in the interests of the people of the States and the greater good of the country these four rulers agreed to form the Greater Rajasthan Union. On 14 January, 1949 Sardar Patel announced at a public meeting at Udaipur that the rulers of Jaipur, Jodhpur and Bikaner had agreed in principle to integration".[52]

On 7th April, 1949, Bikaner State was formally integrated into the Greater Rajasthan Union - the United State of Rajasthan - and the administration of the State of Bikaner was handed over to the new Government of Rajasthan.

A cash balance of Rs 4.87 crores, the highest amount amongst all the states of erstwhile Rajputana, was transferred to the new Government. In addition to this, all the assets of the Bikaner State Railway were also made over. The transfer included about nine crore rupees worth of railway line and rolling stock to the Central Government, and over a 1,000 miles of rail track. (This was a clear indication that Bikaner had been a well-administered and 'viable' state by any standards of reference.)

The Instruments of Merger and the Covenants, which transferred power from the ruler, also detailed the rights, privileges and so forth that had been fixed for them and their successors. In addition, these provided for the retention of their private properties by the Princes, and guaranteed to them privy purses and succession to their *gaddis*. According to Karni Singh,[53] "Steps were taken to define the private properties of the rulers as distinct from those of the States, and settlements were arrived at in a spirit of compromise with the due regard to the safeguarding of public interests. In the case of Bikaner, a list of the private properties so agreed upon to be retained by the Maharaja was received from the States Ministry by their letter dated 17 February 1949 to Maharaja Sadul Singh. As Bikaner was a large and viable unit, the Maharaja's Privy Purse was fixed at 17 lakhs and 10 lakhs for his successors".[54]

In the opinion of Karni Singh,[55]

> In order to appreciate this second phase of wiping off the entity of Indian States in the name of unification of India, it is necessary to...examine the workings of the minds of those at the helm of affairs in the States Department. When Sardar Patel was sceptical about the rulers of the Indian States agreeing to accede to the Indian Union and expressed his doubts about the same to V.P. Menon, he at once pointed out that the rulers could not refuse to accede. Menon's contention was that the lapse of paramountcy was a blessing in disguise for India because with it ended the many privileges which the princes enjoyed under the various treaties and engagements and which carried with them certain obligations which they would have been obliged to honour if paramountcy had been transferred to them. According to him, they were now free. He even told the Sardar that in case of political or communal agitation in the States or in case of the people rising up and demanding freedom or to join India or in case of popular agitation beginning to threaten the rule and even the lives of the rulers, who else would they have to look up to for protection other than the Indian Government. He said that it was now their turn to say how the princes behaved. And, the Sardar was not slow to catch the point, which in plainer words meant that any of these conditions could be created to achieve the desired end. And instances are not wanting...
>
> Thus, when soon after the states had acceded to the Indian Union, in respect of the three subjects of common concern, namely, Defence, Foreign Affairs, and Communications, the curtain was lifted for the second act of complete merger of over five hundred states. A lurking doubt was created in the minds of the people if the builders of free India were completely honest with the rulers and whether they did not actually negotiate accession as a first step with mental reservations to bring about total integration a little later on. The argument that the smaller states could not have a high administrative efficiency as required by the people after independence, and hence that there should be a move to merge the smaller states into groups, or with the adjoining provinces, or into centrally administered areas, was understandable. In fact, Maharaja Sadul Singh had advocated the formation of sizeable units of States much earlier so that they could keep themselves abreast with

> administrative reforms... The question of the merger of larger viable units, however, was a different matter".
>
> The two issues of accession and merger should never be confused. Accession of the states meant bringing into India under one flag nearly 1/3rd more of India at a time when a third force was possible and the Centre was somewhat weak due to transfer of power from British to Indian hands and due to the upheaval caused by partition. Maharaja Sadul Singh's strong lead to bring about accession was thus a most patriotic move. The merger issue, however, was an entirely different proposition as this envisaged boundary changes within the country with the head of State from a ruler changing over to a life – Rajpramukh. In fact, the question of monarchical governments continuing as constitutional heads had been accepted in principle subject to the people's approval by all the freedom fighter leaders including Gandhiji, Jawaharlal Nehru and Sardar Patel".[56]

Karni Singh later expressed criticism "not to the merger of the States themselves, but to the way in which it was brought about after assurances to the contrary given *ad lib* by the top-most leaders of India...Forcing of merger on the people of the states without taking their opinion was hardly democratic. It would have been much better had the Government of India at the time of the accession of the States to the Indian Union declared their policy that the ultimate merger of the states would be their goal, immediately or in progressive stages".[57]

With integration, a major chapter closed on the long history of the kingdom of Bikaner. It was the end of an era.[58] An end of five centuries of hereditary Rathore rule over a tract of land, which finally culminated in a peaceful transfer of power to the newly constituted State of Rajasthan within the forward-looking, eager and vigorous 20th century nation-state of India. It also marked the commencement of a new phase in the history of Rajasthan (erstwhile Rajputana), which focussed on the democratization of feudal institutions and mores, on economic and political reforms, on social transformation, on a move towards industrialization, and a range of other issues. Some of these remain centre-stage even at the start of the 21st century.

Notes

1. An earlier version of this paper was presented at a national seminar on 'Democratisation in Rajasthan (1950–2000)', organized by the Department of Political Science, Maharshi Dayanand Saraswati University, Ajmer and the ICSSR-NRC, New Delhi, on 25th and 26th March 2000.
2. It is outside the scope of the present paper to discuss the nature of the pre-1947 kingdom-State and its governance, the relationship between the ruler and fief-holders (*jagirdars* etc.), and between fief-holders and local peasants, and so forth. Those aspects have a major role to play in understanding the progress and process of 'democratisation' within the erstwhile States of Rajputana prior to 1947 (see Hooja, *A History of Rajasthan*, New Delhi, 2006).
3. See, for example, various works on people's movements in Rajputana and British India, including M.S. Jain, *Concise History of Modern Rajasthan*, New Delhi, 1993, pp. 152–188; and also *Rajasthan State Gazetteer* (Vol. Two), 1995.
4. For example, he did not allow the Arya Samaj to spread in Bikaner State (though it gained a foothold at Sujangarh). Similarly, people like Swami Gopal Das (1882–1939), who had established a *Hitkarini Sabha* at Churu in 1907 to work for socio-economic upliftment, were among those who earned the ire of the state and were arrested, following the distribution of pamphlets criticising Bikaner State's administration, at the Second Round Table Conference in London, by a deputation of the All India State People's Conference (AISPC). [Established in 1927 as the Indian States Peoples Conference (ISPC), this merged with the All India States' Subjects Conference in June 1931 to form the AISPC.] The 'Bikaner Conspiracy Case' is another case in point.
5. In 1902 Maharaja Ganga Singh had set aside a fixed privy purse to meet the personal needs to himself and his family.
6. See, K.M. Panikkar, *His Highness the Maharaja of Bikaner: A Biography*, Oxford University Press, London, 1937; also Rima Hooja's *Prince, Patriot, Parliamentarian: Biography of Dr Karni Singh – Maharaja of Bikaner*, Harper-Collins India, New Delhi, 1997.
7. Ganga Singh represented India at several conferences, and was a signatory to the Peace Treaty of Versailles after World War I. A delegate to the Round Table Conference, 1930–31, he was a prominent member of the Chamber of Princes.
8. For details, among others, see Jain, 1993, pp. 153–188.
9. See Hooja, *Crusader for Self-Rule: Tej Bahadur Sapru and the Indian National Movement* (Life and Selected Letters), 1999.
10. His succession was formally recognized by the President of India, Dr Rajendra Prasad, vide letter dated 18 October 1950.
11. When the Constitution 26th Amendment Bill was moved in the Lok Sabha for consideration on 2nd December, 1971, Baroda's Fateh Singh Rao Gaekwad told Parliament: "Twenty-two years ago on this very floor we were referred to as co-architects of Indian independence. Today, we are branded an anachronism

and reactionaries obstructing the path of building an egalitarian society..." The Constitution 26th Amendment Bill was adopted by the Lok Sabha by 381 votes to 6. A week later, amidst the Indo-Pakistan war, the Rajya Sabha passed it by 167 votes to 7. On 28th December, the President of India gave it his assent.

12. An evaluative study of the role of Karni Singh as a parliamentarian from 1952–1977 provides interesting insights and points of reference regarding the all-round social, cultural, political, economic integration of the state and people of Bikaner with the broader Indian socio-political order (see Hooja, 1997). That is, however, outside the scope of this present paper!
13. In Karni Singh, *The Relations of the House of Bikaner with the Central Powers – 1465–1949*, New Delhi, 1974, p. 309.
14. Ibid., p. 211.
15. Ibid., pp. 276–277.
16. Not many realize that nationalist leaders like Pandit Madan Mohan Malaviya were close friends of Maharaja Ganga Singh, and that for many years the Bikaner Maharaja was a major patron as well as Chancellor of the Benares [Banaras] Hindu University.
17. Singh, 1974, pp. 281–349.
18. For example, from the early 1930's onwards, (Pandit) Magharam Vaidya had provided leadership to a small but growing movement of dissent. Similarly, from about 1932 the cultivators around Dudhwa-Khara began voicing issues and problems under the leadership of Hanuman Singh of Dudhwa Khara.
19. Cited in Hooja, 1997, p. 99.
20. See, among others, Pande, 1974 [rep. 1998], pp. 72–77.
21. Singh, 1974, p. 301.
22. Ibid., p. 303.
23. See also, Jain, 1993, p. 183.
24. See Karni Singh's views in Hooja, 1997.
25. Ibid., p. 108.
26. Singh, 1974, pp. 304–305.
27. Ibid., pp. 304–305.
28. Ibid., p. 306.
29. This had been functioning from 9th December, 1946.
30. Ibid., p. 308.
31. Ibid., p. 310.
32. The friendship between Maharaja Sadul Singh and Lord Mountbatten dated back to their childhood days; see Hooja, 1997.
33. Singh, 1974, pp. 312–313.
34. Ibid., pp. 313–314.

35. Along with the unfurling of the India national flag – the tricolour – at this ceremony, the Bikaner state flag had also been unfurled. This was later to arouse some controversy and adverse comments in political circles.
36. Singh, 1974, pp. 311–312.
37. In Hooja, 1997, p. 104.
38. See Hooja, 1997, pp. 104–105.
39. Singh, 1974, p. 322.
40. Ibid., pp. 292–293.
41. The judicial system, overhauled and modernized during the early part of Maharaja Ganga Singh's reign, was modelled on that prevalent in British India. Significantly, Bikaner was the first princely state in northern India to establish a 'Chief Court', later upgraded to a High Court.
42. Singh, 1974, pp. 106–107.
43. Karni Singh handled his work with enough competence for Maharaja Sadul Singh, upon his return, to transfer Rs 1 lakh from his privy purse to his heir's account, noting in his letter of 19th September, 1948, that this was "...in appreciation of the excellent manner in which you conducted the administration during my absence in Europe and also to help you with the construction of your [Karni Bhawan] house" (cited in Hooja, 1997, p. 108).
44. Singh, 1974, p. 294.
45. Ibid., pp. 294–296.
46. Ibid., pp. 296–297.
47. Hooja, 1997, p. 111.
48. Singh, 1974, pp. 323–324.
49. Hooja, 1997, p. 112.
50. In Hooja, 1997, pp. 113–114.
51. Hooja, 1997, p. 114.
52. Singh, 1974, p. 326.
53. See Hooja, 1997, p. 115.
54. Following the death of Sadul Singh on 25th September, 1950, the Bikaner privy purse was reduced from Rs 17 lakhs to Rs 10 lakhs, as per the provisions of the Merger Agreement.
55. Singh, 1974, pp. 333–335.
56. Ibid., pp. 333–335.
57. Ibid., p. 341.
58. A few months after integration, when Sadul Singh returned to Bikaner from England and went by car to the Sri Lakshminarayan (locally also known as the Lakshminathji) temple, he received a tumultuous public welcome. Karni Singh, who was in the car, later described it as "a reception the like of which is not

often come across. The normal half hour run took five hours because the enthusiasm and love of the people was so great".

Select References

Hooja, Rima. 1997. *Prince, Patriot, Parliamentarian: Biography of Dr Karni Singh: Maharaja of Bikaner*, Harper Collins India, New Delhi.

—. 1999. *Crusader for Self-Rule: Tej Bahadur Sapru and the Indian National Movement* (Life & Selected Letters), Rawat, Jaipur and New Delhi.

—. 2006. *A History of Rajasthan*, Rupa, New Delhi.

Jain, M.S. 1993. *Concise History of Modern Rajasthan*, Wishwa Prakashan, New Delhi.

Pande, Ram. 1974. [ref. 1998]. *Agrarian Movement in Rajasthan*, Shodhak, Jaipur.

Panikkar, K.M. 1937. *His Highness the Maharaja of Bikaner: A Biography*, Oxford University Press, London.

Singh, Karni. 1974. *The Relations of the House of Bikaner with the Central Powers – 1465–1949*, Munshiram Manoharlal, New Delhi.

Vashishtha, V.K. 1995. *Rajasthan State Gazetteer (Vol. Two – History and Culture)*, Directorate, District Gazetteers, Government of Rajasthan, Jaipur.

12

Between Old and New

Modernization or Marginalization of the Princely State of Tonk, 1765–1947

BHUPENDRA HOOJA

Before its merger with the evolving state of Rajasthan, with some parts going over to Madhya Bharat/Madhya Pradesh, the erstwhile princely state of Tonk not only had its own distinct identity, but also some importance in the comity of the existing Rajputana states. The importance may not have compared with the almost dominant position it had commanded [or rather its founder Nawab Amir Khan (1765–1834) could command] about a century-and-a-half earlier, but none-the-less, it was an important state with a character of its own. With the merger and increasing integration and under the process of 'modernization' (or as we call it 'planning and development'), Tonk – now a district or whatever was left of the original state, as a part of Rajasthan – moved into the backwaters of history and took a back seat in the arena of development and progress. Why should that have happened is a question which the historians and students of modern social sciences like economics, sociology, political science and public administration must answer.

MERGER AND INTEGRATION (1947–1952/1956)

At the time of merger, soon after the dawn of Indian independence, Tonk state consisted of six districts called *Nizamats* viz., Tonk, Aligarh, Nimbahera, Chhabra, Pirawa and Sironj. The first three districts were parts of Rajputana, while the last three were parts of the then Central India. The total area of the state was 2,556 sq. miles (*Imperial Gazetteers-1908, and Administrative Report of the State for the Year 1352 Fasli-1944–45*). In the local administrative parlance, the term *Nizamat* was used for a district in British India. Aligarh was a *Naib-Nizamat*, or a sub-district. Each *Nizamat* or district had tehsils for revenue administration. Thus, Tonk had two tehsils; Sironj had three; Nimbahera had two; while Pirawa and Chhabra had one tehsil each.

It may be noted that, at that point of time, the state was fairly well administered not only in respect of revenue matters or land management, but also in several other respects. It could stand on its own, and at par with some of its neighbouring States or territories.

In the process of merger, Tonk state, first, joined with the other nearby princely states of Banswara, Bundi, Dungarpur, Jhalawar, Kishangarh, Kota Pratapgarh and Shahpura – we have listed them in the alphabetic order – on the March 25, 1948, into a new and large entity of what is now called "Former Rajasthan". This merger was the precursor of a continuous and sustained process which, through several stages and combinations, ultimately evolved into the formation of present-day Rajasthan. It may be noted that some of the states in this first merger were immediate close neighbours, though at different levels of political administrative and socio-economic or cultural progress. The essential point to note, however, is that there are no indications whatsoever that this was a 'forced' merger, or that any compulsion was used either from New Delhi or from the Rajaputana States' Agency (and their successor authorities). The process of merger or integration, however, soon picked up a new momentum, and before one merger or union could settle down, there was another yet another, until – except for Ajmer and a few territorial adjustment which came later (in 1956) with the states reorganization measures – the present-day larger state of Rajasthan had appeared on the scene. A special feature of Tonk needs to be taken note of at this stage; while almost all the princely states had Muslim *minorities,* Tonk was the only *Muslim* state, so to say, that is where the Muslim rulers and leading administrators, officials and land-holders and so on had held sway.

Thus, the old (erstwhile) Tonk state had ceased to be, and Tonk, once the seat of a princely court, became a district headquarters. It lost the prominence of a 'state capital' with all the trappings and institutions a state capital usually has, and also the control mechanism of various departmental hierarchies under its State Council and the ruler. On a hindsight basis, we can say that temporarily, 'Time' came to a stop as Tonk lost its prominence, its direction and, perhaps, dynamism too.

TONK STATE: GENESIS AND GROWTH (1765–1867)

In the beginning came a soldier of fortune, as has been the story of many a kingdom under dynastic rule. In this case, the soldier of fortune was Amir Khan (b. 1765), whose Afghan ancestors of Salarzai clan had come to India in the reign of Mohammed Shah Ghazi, and who after invading Rohilkhand had finally settled at Siwai Turin near Sambul in Moradabad. Since his childhood, Amir Khan was a restless youth; and at the age of 20, left home to offer his services to the French adventurer De Boigne, then recruiting forces for the Scindia army.

A Soldier of Fortune (1785–96)

Rejected, because of his youth, Amir Khan then visited Delhi to seek some favour under the Mughals and, little later, joined the retinue for Bijai Singh of Jodhpur. Soon he moved on to Baroda and took service with Holkar, with about 300–400 men. The Baroda connection, however, did not last long; and after a time of difficulty and hardship, he and his faithful band entered the service of Dulip Singh, Zamindar of Ranode in Ahirwara on the north-west frontier of Malwa.

Amir Khan was much sought after during 1794–96 by the rival factions then fighting for the control of Bhopal, after the death of the Nawab, Mohad Yasin, *alias* Chatta Khan. He had mixed luck; and was often forced to withdraw into the safety of Sironj, a convenient refuge for many adventures in the region. His association with Sironj was to become life-long, as this became his refuge as well as a launching pad for adventures in later years.

In 1796, he joined the forces of Durjan Lal and Jai Singh of Radhogarh, then deposed and expelled from their territory by Daulat Rao Scindia. This association did not last more than a year, but he was in command of 500 men, and a person of importance.

His next employment was with the Maratha chief, Balarao Inglia, military commander in the state of Bhopal, where he was called upon to command a garrison of 1,500 men of the fort of Fatehgarh overlooking Bhopal.

Under Holkar's Wings

In 1798, he was approached by Jaswant Rao Holkar with more favourable terms, which included *equal* sharing of their conquests and plunders; and Amir Khan undertook never to desert Holkar. This mutual bond of association remained in vogue until the latter's defeat at the hands of the East India Company forces at Deeg and Farukhabad in 1804. However, when there was rebellion in Holkar's army, and Amir Khan was called upon to pacify them, especially the Mohammedan troops, he had to remind an evasive Holkar of his earlier commitment, and was granted the districts of Piwara and Tonk in addition of Sironj, which had been assigned to him in 1798. Holkar also entrusted to him the collection of tribute from Kota state. Nimbahera and Chhabra were added to his territories in 1809 and 1816 respectively.

His ambitions would seem to have been realized – from a fortune seeking adventurer, he had attained, through his military zeal, the rights to these territories – his trophies. His might and status had grown and so also his influence. By 1806, he had thirty-five thousand soldiers under his command and 115 guns.

Yet they were called and continued to be treated as 'free-booters' perhaps because they operated – all over Malwa, and therebouts – in small mobile bands, and their services were borrowed or hired by several Maratha chiefs. Thus legends of (or fears from) Pindaris came to be woven in the people's imagination and these were blown up by the merchant-soldiers of the East India Company. Such was the charm in their chief Amir Khan's name and prowess that, by 1812, there were nearly 6,00,000 so-called Pindaris under his command.

A Man of Destiny and Power (1806–17)

During this period (1806–1817) Amir Khan was in a position to intervene in the inter-state affairs of some of the leading states of Rajputana, e.g. in the struggles between Jaipur and Jodhpur over the hand of the ill-fated young princess of Mewar, Krishna Kumari. For some time, he sided with the Raja of Jaipur, when Raja Man Singh of Marwar was defeated and Jodhpur was besieged. But when he found that the resources of Jaipur had depleted, he allowed his troops to rout the Jaipur forces and himself went over to the side of Raja Man Singh of Jodhpur. In 1810, when he was away on a campaign against Nagpur, the British (E.I. Co.) invaded his stronghold at Sironj. Meanwhile, with Jaswant Rao Holkar being afflicted with a serious brain sickness leading to his insanity, Amir Khan had also to look after the affairs/territories of his long-time ally. His troops did meet the British, but there were no engagements; and a truce – rather uneasy – prevailed.

Towards the close of this period, the East India Company forces having outmanoeuvred and overcome almost all the contenders for power in Central North India, and being in a position to assert their own 'paramountcy' thought it prudent and opportune to pacify the so-called Pindari hordes – free-booters, marauders and what not, as they called them. Amir Khan rushed back to protect his territories, from his siege of the fortress of Madhavarajpura in Jaipur; but before any skirmish could occur, there was an 'alliance' or an agreement with the Company. Amir Khan was allowed to retain his forces and control over territories given to him by Holkar as *jagir;* but he had to surrender his artillery, and to restore to their original owners the territories he had occupied. Historians may like to answer the questions as to what considerations of advantages the Company had out of this agreement and what Amir Khan gained from it. Question arises: Did the Company want the new chief Amir Khan as a shield cover or a wedge between the Marathas and the Rajputs on the one hand, and amongst the Rajputs and the Mughals, but not too close to Delhi, on the other?

A Nawab's Kingdom (1799–1834)

The districts of Sironj, Pirawa and Gogala Nimbahera were confirmed in his possession and his descendants; and the fortress of Tonk Rampura, with subordinate territories, was added to his possession as a special favour. He was granted a sum of Rs 3 lakh in cash, and his son the life *Estateship* up of Palwal (near Delhi) to cover the expenses of his/their maintenance. The Palwal area, however, remained under the Company's possession, but a sum of Rs 1,50,000 out of its annual revenues was to be reimbursed in monthly instalments of Rs 12,500 each to the Nawab. Amir Khan delayed the signing of the agreement for some time, when he was watching the changing scene; but, when in the battle of Sita Buldi, the East India Company emerged victorious against the Bhonsle of Nagpur, he accepted the new situation of the ultimate victory of the Company's rule and signed the document.

He chose to make Tonk his seat of government. Perhaps he felt more secure here than at Sironj or elsewhere in Central India. Perhaps the conditions in Rajputana were more favourable, peaceful or less turbulent than in and around Malwa. However, he soon set himself to the task of administering his territories after a long life of tramping around, marching up and down, and making his presence and prowess felt. No doubt, he proceeded to be a successful ruler, respected and feared by all concerned. Before his death in 1834, he could consolidate his kingdom and live a peaceful and pious life.

Mutiny and After

The most important event half way through the 19th century was the 'Mutiny' or the widespread revolt of the sepoys of the Company and the peasantry, often fanned and led by dispossessed and disgruntled elements of the old feudal regimes in different parts of the growing domains of the Company. The ruler of Tonk, Amir Khan's eldest son, Wazir Mohammad Khan, sided with the Company authorities (or tried to sit on the fence), but at Nimbahera, his official, Bakshi Ghulam Mohiuddin, actually sheltered the mutineers from the nearby Neemuch cantonment. When routed by the Company's forces, he escaped to Agra to join the rebels. On the other hand, the mutineers were invited by the Nawab's troops to visit Tonk on their way to Agra, placing the Nawab in a rather delicate situation, almost a dilemma, the gravity of which was aggravated when, in large numbers, his disaffected troops deserted him on the grounds of their arrears of pay, and went over to Delhi.

The Nawab was put into a further tight corner, when the rebel leader Tantia Tope crossed the Chambal on his way to Jaipur and beyond, towards Agra and Delhi. Intercepted en route, Tantia Tope diverted his march towards Tonk, and was joined by Nawab's troops in large numbers, though the Nawab himself remained shut in his citadel, with his faithful adherents.

After the second Nawab's death in June 1864, his son Mohammad Ali Khan succeeded to the *gaddi,* now once again secure. But some time later, he got embroiled in a unsavoury dispute with his feudatory, the chief of Lawa. Originally a part of Jaipur, this old fiefdom dating from the Mughal times had been transferred to the Nawab of Tonk when Amir Khan was installed and recognized as the ruler of these territories. Against the advice of the Agent to the Governor General, Mohammad Ali Khan attacked Lawa (1865) but was repulsed. Later he resorted to a different stratagem. He invited the Lawa Chief, Dhirta Singh and his uncle Rawat Singh and had the latter murdered along with his retainers while a force was despatched to capture Lawa. This led to his downfall in 1867. He was deposed and sent to Banaras by the British

Government of India where he died in 1895. Meanwhile, Lawa was taken away from Tonk and its chief put under direct British protection. Tonk also lost its 'status' or rank with the ruler's gun salute being reduced from seventeen to eleven.

The ousted Nawab's eldest son, Hafiz Mohammad Ibrahim Ali Khan was placed on the *gaddi* in 1867. During his minority, there was a Regency Council of five members, including his uncle and the British Assistant of the Agent to the Governor General as members. The Nawab was invested with his full powers on January 1, 1870. In 1875, he attended on the visiting Prince of Wales at Agra, and the Delhi *Durbar* in 1877, when the salute the 17 guns was restored for his lifetime and, later, for good thereby rehabilitating the Nawab's status.

Towards Modernization and Political Awakening (1867–1939)

During the long reign of Nawab Mohammad Ibrahim Ali Khan, from 1867 to 1930, Tonk state took several steps to modernize its administration: through the enforcement of revenue and police codes, reorganization of courts, start of land settlement operations, attempts to reduce indebtedness of *Jagirdars*, particularly in Sironj, and prescribing limits etc., for loans to them so that no *Mahajan* could lend to a *Jagirdar* more than his monthly income.

However, before his life came to an end in 1930, Nawab Mohammad Ali Khan's reign also witnessed some unrest and agitation too, particularly during the Congress non-cooperation and Khilafat movements. In 1921, the Tonk areas of the state were affected by an unrest due to abnormal rise in prices of food-stuffs (even the low-paid armed forces were agitated) and growing ill-feeling against the merchants of Ratlam (Central India) who not only supplied grain to the state, but were also the state financiers. The role of the Dewan was also being questioned in these matters. There were other grievances too. For example, the Nawab had stopped the reading of *Waaz* (sermon) in the mosques. These were also the days of the pro-Khilafat and non-cooperation movements throughout the country, in particular the north-western Indian sub-continent. In such an agitated and surcharged atmosphere, the clemency shown by the Nawab to his jailed *Parchanavis* (or confidential reporter) was also resented, all the more because the Nawab had banned the entry of political agitators of the Khilafat and non-cooperation movement in British India.

Mass Unrest

The mob feelings in the state capital were on a high pitch of resentment and protest. On one or two occasions, the Nawab and his entourage were mobbed, as for example on January 14, 1921, when the Nawab came for prayers at the Jumma Masjid. On this occasion, high prices and the Dewan's conduct were the rallying points. Things took a dramatic and violent turn on 16th, when a mass meeting was called despite the ban orders by the Nawab, and the state army and policemen disobeyed the orders. The attempt by the IGP to deal with the situation with a small band of police force, facing an angry crowd of 4,000 carrying flags of the Crescent and the Star, led to much confusion and mutual assaults. There was a second meeting the same day, with the mob more armed than before. An unnerved Nawab decided to meet a delegation of the agitators, who submitted their petition of grievances in the presence of the British Agent of Haroti and Tonk. The Nawab yielded and accepted all the demands, except two, viz., about the removal of the Dewan, and cancellation of the monopoly of Ratlam merchants in the supply/purchase of foodgrains. It was agreed to fix the price of *jowar* at 8 seers to a rupee and to remove state levy on import of grains. Dewan Moti Lal was, however, granted leave for six months.

Hardly had the Nawab escaped this tangle of mass unrest, when he was faced with another problem. On a visit to dinner with Qafla Sayyads of Tonk (a few days after the first mass meeting) the Nawab was mobbed again, and threatened with abusive language, while the hosts remained silent witnesses to the ugly scenes. Naturally, the Nawab suspected their connivance in the incident; and since the Sayyads of Tonk were known to be in touch with their main branch in Rai Bareilly, then the centre of socio-religious protests, the Nawab had their local premises searched, when some objectionable material, incriminating letters and seditious newspapers etc. were found. The documents also established links of the agitators as far afield as Delhi and Kabul. The Tonk Sayyads were then expelled.

British Intervention and Nawab's Proclamation

The situation had by now taken a distinct religio-political complexion. Agitations continued and British help was sought by the Nawab while the Khilafat-Congress Committees of Ajmer took up cudgels on behalf of the agitators. Press and political opinion outside Tonk increasingly turned against the Nawab and he was advised by the Agent to the Governor General to set up a Committee of Enquiry. Also, at the suggestion of the Agent, 33 'political' prisoners were released on bail.

However, the main result of these episodes of unrest and agitation was the *Proclamation* issued and read out at a mass meeting on February 23, announcing the setting up of a Consultative Committee to go into the public grievances and seek advice and opinion of the concerned people for the future legislation. A *Rubkar* (order) was also issued which allowed: (i) meetings of more than five persons on political issues, (ii) preaching of sermons or reading of *Waaz* in the mosques, but restricted only to religious subjects or themes, (iii) entry of outsiders into the State that had been forbidden so far, on condition that these were not 'seditionists', and (iv) the re-opening of Arabic schools. No doubt, all this meant a considerable gain for local/civil and religious rights.

The atmosphere continued to be charged not only in Tonk, but also outside the state boundaries, so that, as late as November 1928, when the Rajputana States' Peoples' Conference met in Ajmer, not only Abdul Irfan Faizi, a local leader, was elected to the Executive, but a resolution was also adopted condemning police-administrative repression in Tonk (besides some other states like Udaipur, Sirohi, Bundi and Jaipur, where also there had been some political agitations).

A Season of Change (1931–32)

The desired and much sought-after changes in Tonk state came in 1931–32, during the reign of Hafiz Mohammad Saadat Ali Khan, the second son of the late Nawab Mohammad Ibrahim Ali Khan, who died in 1931, his eldest son having predeceased him in 1927. It was on the intervention of the then Viceroy, who had received strong representations from the State's People's Conference that the old policies were continuing unabated; there was hardly any freedom of speech or press or association in the state; deportations and internments were continuing; properties were being confiscated and so on, that Nawab Hafiz Mohammad Saadat Khan realized that it was time to relent, and change with the demands of the time.

In the widesweep of changes, the new Nawab announced, there was the setting up of a State Administrative Council with powers to review annual budgets; Departments of Public Works and Forests etc. were created; and Customs and Excise Department was reorganized.

Efforts were made to have a more competent and 'independent' judiciary. But perhaps more significant were measures to constitute the *Majlis-i-Amma* (Council of People) besides municipalities and panchayats.

The *Majlis-i-Amma* was set up by a *firman* (ruler's decree or order) on November 23, 1939. It comprised of 26 official and non-official members. Among the official members were: members of the State Council and other nominated members. Among the non-officials, 12 were (to be) elected by panchayats and the District Council representing urban and rural areas in equal number, five were to represent varied interests such as the *Sahibzadas* (sons of nobles) and backward classes etc. It was so arranged that from each urban and rural constituency, one Muslim and one non-Muslim representative were elected by rotation.

The *Majlis-e-Amma* was to tender advice on all matters of legislation relating to taxation, health, education, commerce and industry. Non-official members could move amendments on bills related to these matters. The President of *Majlis* was also the Vice-President of the State (Administrative) Council.

Popular Representative Institutions

By way of concomitant action, a Municipal Act was passed in 1939, enabling the *parganas* of Tonk, Sironj, Nimbahera, Chhabra and Pirawa to have partially elected (on communal basis) and partly officially nominated members of the various municipalities.

In December 1939, the State Panchayat Rules were promulgated for panchayats (five members for each village or group of villages with population of 2,000 and above). The panchayats had small cause, civil and criminal jurisdiction; and their Sarpanchas formed the electorate for the elections of the *paragana's* representative on the *Majlis-i-Amma*.

There was, thus, a semblance of popular, representative institutions in the administration of the state for a few years before the State opted to join the bigger and an enlarging entity of present-day Rajasthan.

REVENUE ADMINISTRATIVE AND OTHER REFORMS

It may, perhaps, come as a surprise to many that the first regular (and uniform) land settlement of all the six *parganas (Nizamats)* of the state was conducted during 1887 and 1891. The operations covered 951½ *khalsa* villages and 374½ villages under *jagir, istmirar* and *muafi* tenures.

In the process, forest areas were demarcated, and if large enough, these were also mapped. Records regarding proprietary etc. rights, village maps, lists of wells and tanks, irrigated lands (with source) and nature or class of soils etc., were duly noted, besides human inhabitants and cattle population etc. The history and customs etc. of each *(halat-deh)* were also recorded.

Because of the way in which Pindaris and Nawab Amir Khan's camp followers had come to settle in these parts, the different pockets or parts of the then spaced out and spread about state had different types of land management/revenue systems. During first settlement these were got put together into a common shape and design. Incidentally, the estimated revenue receipts from all these six areas was about Rs 8,20,000 in 1850. In the 1887–91 settlement operations, the survey was done for all the villages, but assessment of land revenue was restricted only to the *khalsa* (government) land.

The second regular settlement followed in 1911, without any fresh survey, but with due correction of village maps where necessary. *Jagir* villages, including resumed *jagirs,* were also covered. The settlement completed in 1914 came into force from 1922–23 *(Fasli Year* 1330). Next round of settlement operations began in 1939–40, and completed in Tonk and Aligarh areas by the time of merger. Meanwhile, several administrative and structural changes and promulgations of rules and regulations had also taken place.

It should, thus, be noted that towards the end of the 19th century and the early decades of the present century (and by the time of merger), Tonk state had initiated steps towards the creation of a 'modern' state/administrative set-up to deal with revenue and agrarian affairs in keeping with similar efforts in other princely states as well as in several parts of British India.

Scarcity Conditions and Land Resources

Much of the prosperity of the people of the state (including its far-flung and scattered territories) as well as the fiscal resources of the state accrued from its land resources, viz., land revenue, and incomes from cattle breeding and allied activities or the management of forests, minor irrigation works, mineral deposits and the like. Since the Rajputana parts of the state territories were subject to frequent and serious visitations of rain failures, scarcity conditions and famines, the state administration had, over the years, evolved its own local strategies to cope with these calamities and to provide relief measures, as was done at the time of the failure of *kharif* crops in 1868, or during the much more severe scarcity conditions during the great famine of 1896–97, and again in 1901–02. By and large, the state managed its relief operations and supplies of essential commodities fairly well. Those days, there was no 'dependence' on 'outside help or relief', either on the Indian administration or the neighbouring state areas as happens to have become the general rule these days. Usually, other nearby states or territories were also equally or similarly affected; and, in any case, there was no hope or possibility of receiving any 'central' support. The state administrations and the people had to deal with each such calamity or scarcity situation on their own resources and on the basis of self-reliance.

In the long term, irrigation through wells and small or medium-size storage dams could provide some sort of a protection, and ensure steady production of crops. The state had also worked out some measures for the protection of livestock, and for improved agriculture. In the field of animal husbandry, Tonk had its first veterinary hospital in 1939. In the closing years of the princely regime, there was a qualified Agriculture Officer and a department to help and guide the cultivators through 'research' and 'extension' in its then existing version, in crop management and through improved tools and implements, manures, fodder, seed multiplication and dryland farming.

The state had also participated in the Grow More Food Campaign launched in the country during the last years of the Second World War, when the Agriculture Department's budget was doubled, and seeds of improved varieties of wheat, vegetables and potato were introduced/distributed, besides several supportive steps. The Revenue Department, for example, remitted its collections for the first six years of any new cultivation of food crops. It also distributed *tacavi* loans, and allotted disused government wells to the cultivators.

HOW BACKWARD WAS TONK?

The foregoing measures show that in the promotion of agro-economic activities in the primary sector, the state did not lag behind. We need to discard any notions about the erstwhile Tonk state being 'backward' or 'non-progressive'. Within its limitations and in the context of the then existing state of knowledge and practices, the state (at least in the parts of Rajputana) was going ahead in the right direction.

Backwardness was there, no doubt, in the secondary sector, and in the fields of trade and commerce or the services sector, and in terms of the basic infrastructures like power or energy, transport and communications, and in the fields of social security education, health and medical services, and in the social security coverage or what we now a days generally group together under 'social welfare'. To some extent, these shortfalls and lapses were inherent in the political, administrative, socio-economic or cultural situation and in the domain of technology.

Industrial Scene

A glance-back at the industrial scene prevailing in the Tonk sate at the end of the World War II would be revealing. Since the beginning of the 20th century, cotton cloth weaving on a small-scale or as a village industry had come to stay in the Tonk and Sironj areas of the state. Woollen felt rugs (*namdas*) and saddle clothes were also made at Tonk. Nimbahera was known for its manufacture of plated utensils for daily use. A cotton press and ginning factory had also come up in Nimbahera in the first decade of the 20th century. Wood and ivory-inlaid items of handicrafts were made in the Central Indian parts of the state.

Sandstone quarries for building stone were operating in Tonk and Nimbahera. Earlier, there were a few small-scale iron mines at Amli (in Aligarh), near Dungla (in Nimbahera) and at Lakheri (in Sironj) which were closed by about 1850.

However, Tonk state did benefit from the late and somewhat unplanned boost to industrial growth in the closing years of the 1939–45 war (as did many other business-industrial houses in some of the neighbouring princely states like Jaipur as well as in the province of British India). According to the 1945–46 Annual Administrative Report, there was a state weaving factory in Tonk; the same year, a woollen yarn and a carpet factory were established in Tonk; and a rice mill at Pirawa. Some handloom weaving units and a few confectionaries had come up or were permitted at Nimbahera. There were a couple of small stone-crushing/roller units in each district/*Nizamat* of the state, while jail-based industries were engaged in the manufacture of woven *durries*, compressed felt *namdas*, carpets and coarse cloth, pottery, *chick*- making, rope-twining and caning of chairs etc.

In the case of minerals, there was a mica mine on contract, which brought in reasonable royalty; both raw mica and cut mica were being produced. Mica mining was improved and expanded after 1940.

Infrastructure

The main drawbacks were in respect of basic infrastructure, especially in the domain of power generation, despite small diesel sets later installed in Tonk and one or two other places. There was not much of road transport and communication system; and, to top it all, the state capital was not connected with the rest of Rajputana or India on the railways network; the nearest facility available was several miles away at Niwai on the Jaipur State Railway's Jaipur-Sawai Madhopur line. Incidentally, this is a handicap from which Tonk district continues to suffer even today.

Yet another major weakness was the almost total absence of entrepreneurial and business or commercial and banking support. This was partly due to the nature or character of the state, its widely scattered territories, its comparatively smaller size as compared to the neighbouring State of Jaipur touching on the borders of Tonk, or Mewar area which flanked Nimbahera, or other parts in the vicinity of Bundi, Kota and Jhalawar. Nor were there any venture – some local traders or businessmen like 'Marwari' in Western states or the enterprising businessmen from the Shekhawati area who had gone ahead to seek their future destinies in distant parts and the new growing industrial or commercial cities of India. It is for the historians and economists to explain why the industrial or commercial progress was slow and stunted in Tonk. Was it due mainly to the constraints of resources, lack of markets and entrepreneurial skills or opportunities or was it because those who should/could have come forward were hesitant because of the Muslim rulers of the state, in whom they did not have full confidence?

Yet, there was not much wrong or amiss with the administration and the direction in which the state was going in tandem with the other 'larger' and 'old established' neighbourly states or with the rest of India at that point of time.

State Budget (1943–44)

As an indicator of the pre-freedom affairs of the state, let us have a fleeting look at the State Budget for 1943–44.

The total revenue receipts (including extraordinary receipts by way of loans (Rs 17.00 lakh) and deposits (Rs 23.06 lakh) came to Rs 74.25 lakh, a considerable sum according to then existing standards and value of the rupee. Some of the major heads were: Land Revenue – Rs 12.88 lakh; Customs – Rs 11.03 lakh; Excise – Rs 3.08 lakh; Forests – Rs 2.3 lakh; Art & Industry – Rs 0.64 lakh; Stamps – Rs 0.57 lakh; Judicial Receipts – Rs 0.22 lakh; Salt Compensation – Rs 0.20 lakh; PWD – Rs 0.15 lakh; Miscellaneous Receipts – Rs 0.65 lakh; and other smaller receipts from Registration, Police, Jails, Gardens, State Garage etc.

It is not surprising that there were only nominal/negligible receipts from the fields of education and hospitals, and the Army. How one wishes that similar heads of Expenditure Account were also before us. But even then Receipts Account can give us a clear picture of the health of the state administration, and its finances. Lands, forests and customs (on imports) contributed the most revenues. We have also to note the two items regarding loans and deposits. Perhaps these were to overcome some temporary fiscal needs or may be loans and deposits were called for/encouraged to give a boost to the State Budget as well as its economy. Deposits could have been due to a near total absence of banking facilities in the state, except for the state treasury.

There was a Finance Department of the state under the charge of the Finance Member of the State Council (who was also Vice-Chairman of the Council). He was assisted by the Secretary to the Finance Department and the Budget Officer or *Bakshi.* The department looked after customs, excise, forests and agriculture among other field agencies/activities.

Law and Order

From the early years of the 20th century, the Police Department was under the charge of the Home Member (of the Council) who, at times, also functioned as the Police Chief – I.G., Police. There was not much of a police organization. The force comprised of a superintendent, a few inspectors, some *Thanedars, Hawaldars, Sepoys* and *Chowkidars.* Its equipments, including weapons, were rather old-fashioned; and mobility was limited. In 1916, a British Officer (then S.P. of Ajmer) took over as I.G., Police at Tonk and set about reorganizing and modernizing the police force/department.

A question may be asked as to what had compelled the state to reorganize its police force? Was the law and order situation deteriorating? Or, were there other (external) threats? However, on the pattern of the laws in British India, the Tonk State Police Act was formulated to follow the British Indian procedures and with provision for regular parades, training in laws, and state-paid uniforms.

There were now two superintendents – one at Tonk, mainly for the Rajputana parts of the state, and the other, at Chhabra for Chhabra, Sironj and Pirawa. Later, their number was increased to three – one for Tonk and Aligarh; another for Sironj and Chhabra; and the third for Nimbahera and Pirawa. Such was the demand and logistics of the changing situation. Police Lines at Tonk (set up in 1916–17) and police housing elsewhere were provided. Recruitment and training programmes were improved/modernized. A reserve force was created to combat dacoits. There was also a posse of mounted police (with camels and horses). A finger-printing section was started.

Earlier, the state had a military force consisting of cavalry, artillery, infantry and sappers, but it was mainly employed on watch and ward duties. In 1940–41, one company was disbanded. Instead, a company of military police was created and put under the I.G., Police.

Judicial Reforms

Administration of justice and the development of a proper judicial set-up (to cope with the changing demands of the modern age) have had a long and chequered story in Tonk. Though the *Diwani*, *Faujdari* and Revenue Courts had existed before 1885, a Code of Civil Procedure (on the same lines as operated in British India) was drafted that year. But, the ruler did not give effect to it, on the ground that these elements/practices were foreign to the local people who might view them with suspicion and disaffection. The less ambitious scheme, to set up *Munsif* courts in place of the old *Amils*, was, however, accepted, and in, 1887–88, the powers of each court were defined.

What is more, the *Shara Sharif* courts, dealing with *Shariat* laws on both civil and criminal matters, hitherto exempt from supervision, were brought under the Judicial Department, and their civil powers were restricted.

As the years passed, several Acts on the lines of laws prevailing in rest of India were incorporated in the Tonk state judicial system. Reorganization and expansion of judicial administration went on apace so that, by 1910–11, the state had six criminal courts (at Tonk, Aligarh, Nimbahera, Chhabra, Pirawa and Sironj) and six civil courts with the

Sadar civil court at Tonk and *Munsif* courts at other five places. Appeals from these courts lay with the Appellate Court, State Council and, ultimately, to His Highness' Vernacular Officer.

There were also four Mohammendan Law Courts at Tonk, Chhabra, Pirawa and Sironj, where cases relating to dower, marriage, inheritance, gift, divorce, endowments etc. could be instituted and disposed of according to Muslim Law. In the Sadar court at Tonk, there was a jury of five *Muftis* to deal with cases under the Muslim Law, while at other three places, there was a *Mufti* or Muslim Law Officer. This special dispensation for Muslim subjects or separation of judicial jurisdiction should have worked to the satisfaction of all concerned, and was perhaps an indication of the 'secular' nature of judicial functions of the state.

In due course of time, the State Council took over the functions of a High Court and the Sessions Court. The Council heard appeals from the orders and decrees of the Judicial Member, who acted as the first Appellate Court. Under the 1931–32 Reforms or reorganization of the judicial system, the State Council was divested of its judicial powers, while a separate District and Sessions Court was created with jurisdiction covering the entire state, the court meeting at each *Pargana* headquarters to deal with sessions cases. The Chief Court was also created in August 1932, with the Judicial Member of the Council working as Chief Judge. In cases of heinous crimes, another member of the Council was nominated by the ruler to assist the Chief Judge and form a Bench.

The ruler retained the power of confirming death sentence or hearing mercy petitions. In civil matters, he had the powers of the Privy Council. In 1944–45, the Chief Court became the High Court with a permanent Puisne Judge to assist the Chief Justice.

By the Act of 1945, the High Court (at Tonk) became the largest Court of Appeal, the ruler only retaining the privilege of mercy. The powers of the High Court and other courts were redefined; the post of Judicial Member was abolished; and Puisne Judge was given the powers of the legal remembrance and of drafting legislations.

An attempt was also made to separate judiciary from the executive by appointing purely judicial officers, though some *Nazim* and *Naib-Nazims* continued to enjoy magisterial powers. The land law suits and revenue matters continued to be dealt with by the respective Revenue Courts.

Earlier, under the 1931–32 reforms and restructuring of courts, in Tonk *Pargana* area (the state capital) there was a *Nazim Diwani* for civil cases, while two officers, Magistrate with first class powers and Magistrate with second class powers, dealt with criminal cases under their jurisdiction. In other parts/*Parganas* of the state, the *Nazims* exercised first class powers; and second class powers were with a Special Officer, who also dealt with civil suits not exceeding Rs 5,000 in value. Suits of higher values were sent to the *Nazim Diwani* at Tonk. It may also be mentioned that in forest cases, the Forest Officer of the state enjoyed powers of the third class magistrate.

POLITICAL/STATE ADMINISTRATIVE SET-UP

The foregoing brief recount of several facets of the administrative set-up in Tonk state should suffice to indicate that the state administration was by no means antiquated or out of step with developments elsewhere. Over the years, more responsive and, to a large extent, responsible administration had gradually evolved, though it was not yet quite fully representative.

Perhaps two other features of the changes that had occurred or the system that existed on the eve of merger would complete the picture.

Council of State

At the apex level, to assist the ruler, there was a Council of State which consisted of a Vice-President and three members. While the departments/functions of the army, *Shikar Khana* (hunting) and matters connected with the *Khandan* (royal family) were under the direct control of the ruler, the other departments were looked after by the other four members of the Council. These included: land revenue, finance, customs and excise, price control (during the war) jails, judicial, police, medical, education, agriculture, forest, audit, municipal committees and industries.

The State Council met every week, and matters requiring the orders of the ruler were submitted to him in *Arzdaashts* (petitions or notes) read out to him by the Council's Secretary and explained by the member concerned at the time of the weekly *Peshi* (audience). After his orders, the members had to ensure a faithful implementation of the ruler's orders.

As noted earlier, the state had been divided into five *Nizamats* (districts) and one *Naib-Nizamat*, each further divided into *Tehsils* (nine in all). *Nazims and Tehsildars,* though primarily responsible for revenue collection, also enjoyed magisterial powers although there were separate judicial officers/magistrates to look after the judicial work of their respective areas. Regular police officers and police force were posted at the district headquarters to assist in the maintenance of the law and order. Each district had a treasury, with sub-treasuries at some tehsils. Deposits or withdrawals of government money could be handled under orders of the competent authorities.

In the *fasli* year 1347 (1939–40) a State Public Services Commission was also set up for appointments to government posts with its approval.

Under the 1943 Tonk State Forest Act, to look after forests and forest produce, a State Forest Officer was put in charge of the department with six forest rangers under him and subordinate staff of deputy rangers, foresters, guards, *Beldars, Chaukidars* and *Chaudharis* in each range to deal with forest offenses, trespass cases and reserved forests etc.

Local Self-Government

It might surprise some of us that Tonk had its first Municipal Board in 1886 – to supervise streetlighting and conservancy arrangements in the state capital. In 1904–05, four members were nominated to the Board. Aligarh had its municipality in 1908–09.

Those days, *Abkari* income was placed at the disposal of the municipalities by the Nawab. As time passed, the municipal responsibilities increased, and to meet their expenses, they depended more and more on state support, besides their income from road tax charged on carts exporting grains.

The Tonk State Municipal Act, 1939 introduced an element of elections. Six wards, three each for Hindus and Muslims, sent in their elected members against four nominated and two *ex-officio* members with the Revenue Member of Council as Chairman. They discharged a wide range of municipal functions besides managing *Nazool* lands and upkeep of city walls, markets, public streams, water supply, municipal roads, lighting and conservancy.

By an order of October 21, 1943, Tonk Municipality had an elected Chairman. Its income accrued from the levy of light tax, slaughter house tax, *tehbazari* tax (rent etc. from municipal lands) *hundabara,* and hackney charges on vehicles and road tax, and, of course, government budgetary grants.

Panchayats made their 'official' or formal appearance in Tonk state in 1940–41 after Panchayat Rules were promulgated. An elected Panchayat of five members was constituted in every village or group of villages with a population of 2,000 and above. Tonk *Pargana* had 22 such Panchayats and Aligarh had seven. A Sarpanch was chosen by the Panchayat from among the members who could read and write Urdu. The Panchayats had some 'judicial' functions/duties: to try money suits up to the value of Rs 100, criminal cases of theft, if property involved did not exceed Rs 5 and ordinary cases of assault or cattle trespass, besides matters relating to village uplift, sanitation, village paths and tracks, water supply, small dams and cattle improvement.

Sarpanchas of the state collectively elected a certain number of members who constituted, besides the nominated members, the *Majma-i-Aamaa* – an advisory council of 33 members to advise on all matters of legislation relating to taxation, public health, education, including rural education, commerce and industry. The *Majma* comprised of both Hindu and Muslim members.

EDUCATION, HEALTH AND CULTURE

A few words on these aspects of social life will also be in order.

To start with, education was in the private domain and was channeled through the traditional *Maktabs* or *Madrsas, Paathashalaas* and primary schools. The oldest school was established near Motibagh, in the reign of the founder Nawab (1817–34). Under his successor, Nawab Mohammed Ali Khan (1834–67), 14 similar schools were opened in different parts of Tonk town. Two private schools for advanced education in Persian and Arabic were also opened. Teachers of the *Maktabs* were also awarded *jagirs* by way of encouragement.

There were similar parallel institutions for Hindu boys. Besides, the learned *Maulavis* and *Pandits* also held classes privately at their residences. Through these efforts, somewhat organized but largely through local initiatives, the study of Urdu, Persian, Arabic, Hindi and Sanskrit was being promoted along traditional lines. There was, however, no educational facility for girls until much later.

Education on 'Western lines' was introduced during the long reign of Nawab Ibrahim Ali Khan (1867–1930) with the opening of the first primary school in 1870 to teach English, besides Oriental languages, especially Persian and Arabic. Though the school was opened originally or primarily for Muslim boys, it could attract only five Muslim students. The shortfall in the number of Muslim students was perhaps due to the existence of *Madrasaas* attached to every *Masjid* (mosque) so that even 15 years later, in 1885–86, the Hindu students far exceeded the number of Muslim students. This sort of discrepancy continued for a long time. Because of the large number of Hindu students, Hindi was also introduced. At the same time, efforts to introduce or continue with the teaching of English were also aborted, when during the period 1887–92, the Political Agent failed in his attempt to popularize English through the services of a Headmaster brought in from the North-Western Provinces (modern-day Uttar Pradesh).

Since the sons of the Nawabs were sent to study at Ajmer (Mayo College), a boarding house was built there in 1878.

In the state, however, a new chapter in the spread of education opened in 1884, when two schools were opened on January 1 – the Central High School and the Noble School, the latter for the sons of the rich. Next month saw the opening of two other smaller schools at Tonk – Tonk School and Amirganj Branch School.

Education for girls received a fillip during 1885, with the opening of four schools in different parts of Tonk, with an enrolment of 100 girls. Two more such schools were opened seven years later.

By 1892, Tonk city could boast of about 898 students at schools – 762 boys and 136 girls. Next year, while the number of boy scholars had exceeded 1,000, there was a decline in the number of girl students. As per the 1904–05 Annual Administration Report, there were 15 institutions in all under State management, of which 10 were at Tonk, including all the five institutions for girls, where English was being taught. The Tonk Central High School prepared students for the entrance examinations to the Allahabad University, and also for *Munshi* and *Maulavi* examinations of the Punjab University. This arrangement came to a stop in 1906–07, when only students of the Oriental College, Lahore, were eligible for these qualifications.

In all the state-managed schools, primary education was free. Various improvements, innovations and administrative reorganizations were attempted as the years rolled by, so that by 1930–33, the primary schools covered a four years' course, the middle schools were for six years, and, at the high school level, there were options available for subjects like geography, Persian, Arabic, Sanskrit, Urdu and Hindi.

By way of some earlier experiments, during 1904–05, a *Patwari* section had been opened in Central High School, later transferred elsewhere in view of the lower educational standard of *Patwaris*. In 1906–07, two schools offered the study of the *Quran* for Muslim students and two others were for instruction in Hindi for Hindu students.

In 1907–08, the control of schools was transferred from the Revenue Member to the Headmaster, Durbar High School, who was also able to make some inspection visits. The high schools at that time were affiliated to the U.P. Board, and the middle schools prepared their students for the Rajputana Middle Schools Examination. These were quite significant arrangements linking the Tonk state's education system with the United Provinces/Rajputana courses as well as in raising standards.

However, the 1930–31 Annual Report lamented that "Education is at a low ebb in the state. There is no inspection staff and the existing (teaching) staff is inefficient and ill-paid."

It was another decade before the post of an Inspector of Schools was created in 1940–41, and other functionaries placed under him. A physical instructor was also employed, and some adult education centres were opened. At the time of the merger of states, the Home Member was also the Director of Education, as overall in charge.

In addition to the network of 'normal' schools, there were several 'religious' schools – 23 for boys, eight for girls and four state-aided private schools. For advanced religious education, there was the Ameriya School. Besides the *Madrasa Nasariya* and *Madrsa Faquania* (which prepared students for the Persian and Arabic examinations of the U.P. Education Department), there were the *Madrasa Khadewal Musalmeen,* a Hindi *Paathasala* and *Khadem-ul-Musalmeen* institution providing religious education.

What may, however, be of some significance is the interest in the introduction of English and the opportunities provided for the teaching/learning of Hindi and Sanskrit in the state-managed or state-aided institutions, albeit on a smaller scale. Also, there was no enforced or compulsory stress on the teaching/imposition of Persian and Arabic or for that matter even Urdu, though as an official language, Urdu had its pre-eminence. Should we call it a 'secular' approach towards education in terms of our present-day idioms or manners of speech?

All said and done, education remained at a low level of development and spread, even in the state capital.

Higher education through colleges/university was some decades away. Even the sons of the nobles and the rich who went to the Mayo College, Ajmer, were not very much interested or involved in higher education. There was also no facility for any kind of professional or vocational education. These were some handicaps and causes as well as symptoms of the socio-cultural and educational backwardness of the state, which have kept the successor communities backward and handicapped.

Medical and Health

As regards medical and health facilities, once again, the state continued to lag behind in the fields of modern medicine and hospital facilities, though in respect of the *Unani/Tibbi* and *Ayurvedic* systems, both the private practitioners and the state (in respect of the *Yunani* system) continued to encourage and promote these. We may take this to be another example of how, in the long run, the adherence to traditional and indigenous knowledge or skills could hold back the state and especially the professional communities from the portals of new knowledge and opportunities being opened by modern science and technology.

Tonk: Lost in the Mainstream?

As we have seen, at the time of merger, Tonk state stood delicately poised before the old traditions and new challenges of modernization. Its decision to throw in its lot with other similarly placed states and, later on, in the larger entity of new Rajasthan was, no doubt, a step in the right direction. Was there any other choice open to the state and its ruling elite or the sections who could see the future, think and act?

But, if the state had been strongly placed in the respect of its economic development, or if it had more developed and advanced infrastructures, or if its administrative and psychological equipment in terms of education, public health and similar features of social services had been more assuring, perhaps it could have played a somewhat more pronounced and significant role in the post-merger situation. Or it had been a bigger state like Jaipur, Jodhpur, Mewar or Bikaner, it could have influenced the future course of development. But that was not to be. So, the identity of (the smaller and once scattered) Tonk state was to be fragmented in due course of time, with the other local princely states' reorganization, and was, eventually, submerged and, if one may add, lost in the sea changes that came about. Given a proper size or infrastructural and economic growth level, given the resources and social advancement, and so on, with its central location – almost in the middle of modern Rajasthan – at least the central part of the erstwhile state – Tonk could have hoped to play a more useful and important part in the new comity of the state of Rajasthan.

Lack of Antiquity

We may also note the inescapable fact that the state of Tonk, as we have known and observed its growth and evolution, did not enjoy the hoary ancient traditions and charisma of some of the other big and old-established states like Mewar, Udaipur, Jodhpur and Bikaner (in that chronological order) with traditional and historical links dating back to 6th–7th, 8th–9th and 14th–15th centuries, and claiming pre-eminence or superiority on account of their legendary/mythological Rajput genealogies.

Tonk state was a creation of the East India Company, no doubt a reward or compensation or a sop to a brave soldier of fortune and his restless followers, as a price for co-operation and submission to a new paramount power. By the time of merger, it was only a century and three decades old. The new rulers could not fall back on any earlier heritage or nostalgia. To an extent, it was an advantage too, because the state and its ruling elites could experiment or adjust themselves more easily and comfortably to the changing situations. Nonetheless, a long heritage and a rich legacy have their own advantages, which Tonk lacked.

The Nawabs' Non-Communal Outlook

We should also note that Tonk was a 'different' state in comparison with others. It was not a Rajput or a Jat domain; its rulers were Muslims, though they had not opted (could not have opted) for a 'theocratic regime', partly in view of the complexion of the state's population, partly due to the 'overlordship' of the British masters, and partly because the times had changed. Not that they, the rulers did not lean in favour of their Muslim brethren in faith, but they could not openly discriminate against 'their non-Muslim/Hindu subjects', who were there in large numbers, and who did have a strong presence in the state's socio-economic life.

According to the *District Gazetteer (1970)*, the majority of the subjects of the Tonk state were Hindus. According to the 1941 Census, in the towns, the Hindus had formed 45.9 per cent of the total population while in 1951, a few years after merger and the reorganization of district, when parts of Jaipur and Ajmer-Mewar joined the reorganized and compacted district of Tonk, Hindus constituted 88.3 per cent, Muslims 9.4 per cent and Jains 2.3 per cent (of the population). Subsequently, the percentage of Hindus did rise slowly and steadily. The slow but a marked shift in the complexion of the communitywise population has had its own logic.

Partition and Communal Harmony

It should also be noted that Tonk state was, by and large, spared from the tragedies and horrors of the post-partition madness, which overwhelmed north-western and eastern parts of the Rajputana states close to New Delhi. The people and the administration of Tonk state could stand united and firm in the face of these unfortunate challenges of communal disharmony and mistrust. We do not have the figures about emigration of people migrating to the domain of the Pakistan, but we know, as per 1951 and 1961 Census data, that only 1,500 to 2,000 persons, mostly traders, had come into the state (Tonk district area).

After the dark clouds of 1946–47 had passed, it was indeed sagacious and wise on the part of the state's ruler and the advisors/administrators to join in the merger process without any fear or hesitation. Did they have any questions or doubts in their mind? Any qualms or fears? One would say, not: Yet, in the so-called popular mind, there had been a lurking mistrust about the Muslim rulers and the ruling elite of the erstwhile state. It is, indeed, a pity. Let us also boldly go on record here that there was hardly any untoward incident or overt tension in the Tonk state during those dark days of partition and after all that happened in the subcontinent. Soon, things had settled down to a state of normalcy.

Communal Tensions After 1947

Only recently, a few years ago, Tonk district had to pass through very tense days, when communal passions were roused and violent incidents occurred at some places, largely due to the intolerance and overbearing postures of some sections among the majority community. The lesson for those who indulge in such misadventures in the name of religion should be clear from the record of the Tonk state during the 130 years of its existence.

In fact, if one were to look at the career of Nawab Amir Khan and his meteroric rise from the time he joined as a military adventurer and fortune-seeker offering his services to De Boigne, then recruiting forces for Scindia's army, later under Bijai Singh of Jodhpur and, still later, under the Gaekwads of Baroda and so on, from one alliance to another, until he joined forces with Holkar, one cannot help but notice that military exploits and adventurism were his ambitions and goals, rather than religious exclusiveness or supremacy. He had spent many years of his active life in the service of the Marathas to serve and further their cause. His life and rise to a life of adventure and fame are chapters which appear prominently to us at this stage; but his indifference to religious or communal alignments and his eclectism or spirit of tolerance should interest us, since that was also his legacy to the state he came to found and nurture. That was his legacy to his people and to his successors who did not fail him.

Tonk after 1947: Community, Setback or Slow-Down?

Our main effort through this note has been to delineate some of the measures which should together confirm that the small state of Tonk in the heartland of Rajputana was well on the way to modern developments in the years preceding its voluntary merger and integration in the entity of Greater Rajasthan.

We may now look back (in our minds) over the journey of development during the last 4–5 decades (after merger) and decide how far have those pre-1947 potentials and trends of development in Tonk have been pushed forward? Or, whether there has been a setback in the pace?

Tonk in Rajasthan (India): Non-Realization of Pre-1947 Potential

It is our contention that, as one of the many districts of Rajasthan, away from the mainstreams of history and modern progress, Tonk has not grown or changed according to its pre-1947 potentials and the prospects. To mention a few hard facts: Tonk is still not connected with any railway network; the seriously damaged Frazer Bridge (for road traffic) has taken several decades for a replacement; no large or major industry has come up in the area; the few agro- or wool and leather-based units, whether in state sector or private, have floundered; higher/technical or professional education and training in skills have still a long way to go; and so on. There are promises to keep, but the pace has been slow and progress erratic. Meanwhile, located on the once perennial Banas river, now almost drained dry, Tonk is growing into a dusty bowl of backwardness in the shadows of barren rocks. That is a new challenge for us and for the local citizens.

13

Theatre in Rajpootana

RANBIR SINH

The word 'Rajpootana' is derived from Rajputs. In 3100 BC, when Manu, the law giver, became the first king and established himself at Ajoydhaya, he introduced the four *varnas*, viz., Brahaman, Kshatriya, Vaishya and Shudra. In the later years the Kshatriyas came to be known as Rajputs. *Raj* as kingdom, *putra* as sons, and thus the sons of the kingdoms, and their place of abode came to be known as Rajpootana. Different dynasties established different kingdoms: Sisodiyas – Udaipur, Dungarpur and Banswara; Rathores – Jodhpur, Bikaner and Kishangarh; Kachchawas – Jaipur and Alwar; Chauhans – Kota, Bundi and Sirohi; and Bhatis – Jaisalmer. Later, in the times of the Mughals, the Jats became a power and established the states of Bharatpur and Dholpur, and in the British times the state of Tonk was formed. All these states constituted Rajpootana.

By the times these different dynasties came to Rajpootana, the Sanskrit theatre had come to an end. The death knell of Sanskrit theatre was sounded when in the year 940 AD Krishna III, king of Rashtrakut empire, had attacked Malwa and Gujardesh. In the foreword to "The Age of Imperial Kannauj", K.M. Munshi says, "the two raids of Rashtrakutas had unfortunate results for the whole of India. Madhyadesh lay mauled and bleeding. The empire of South tottered to a fall. The feudatories of both declared independence one after the other. The country was prostrate and defenceless, and the Aryavarta consciousness was submerged by parochial sovereignties".

The 'parochial sovereignties' were busy in finding new grounds to re-establish themselves, and had no time and finance to patronize theatre. The period of 974–998 AD was that of anarchy. It was then that the ancient India ended and medieval India began. The medieval age was the age of invasions, battles, infighting between different dynasties, each trying to oust the other and extend its own territories. It is important that for the theatre to exist and develop it must have an enlightened, cultured and socially aware society. There are references of music and dance at the courts of the Rajput rulers, but there is hardly any reference of drama. It is also difficult for drama to exist in feudal days, because theatre besides being a vehicle of entertainment, is also a weapon of social change. It places the mirror in front of society which reflects the true picture. This is not tolerated by the autocrat rulers. One of the earliest records that we possess is the *Nritya Kosh*, written by Maharana Kumbha, which talks about music, dance and drama. But, there is no reference at all which says that there was a drama repertory or *Natak Mandali* at the court of Maharana Kumbha, which was subsidized by the state exchequer. It appears that the Maharana has based his work on *Natya Shastra*, and has not offered any new directions or has even followed the directions of *Natya Shastra* of establishing *Natak Mandalis*.

Folk Theatre

Whatever folk theatre was in existence in those days, it was strictly practised by the Adivasis in their remote inaccessible areas, without any interference from the state or participation of other persons. It was strictly their personal religious and social expression performed by themselves for their own people who participated in it as a community.

There were other forms of entertainment presented by the travelling artists, such as, Pabuji ki Phad, Devnarain ki Phad, Nats (acrobats), storytelling (Baatposhi) etc. Also, in the olden times, there used to be groups (*mandalis*) of dancers in the villages, who were known as Khayalia or Nachania. On the various celebrations, such as Holi, Gangaur, and other social functions, these Mandalis were invited to perform. This dance was known as 'Khela Dance'. There is a reference of it in 'Kumarpal Devras':

भेरी भूंगल ढोल घणा, घघमई बीसाणा।
खेला नाचई रंग भरे, नव नव सुजाणा।।

When the victorious armies returned, and the soldiers and other people celebrated by dancing and merrymaking, this was also known as 'Khela':

खेलै महाकाली दे दे ताली नाचै वीर खेला।
हेला मुण्डमाली पढे संचे हार हेत।।

It is probable that when in the 19th century folk theatre evolved, then it took the name of "Khayal". There are three different forms of Khayal: Kuchamani Khayal, Shekhawati Khayal, and Alibuxi Khayal.

Kuchamani Khayal

The first playwright of Kuchamani Khayal was Lachchiramji (1867) who was a resident of Kuchaman, and thus the Khayal came to be known as Kuchamani Khayal. He was patronized by the Thakur of Kuchaman and also received support by the people. The artists belong to the same area and most of them are from Didwana and Nagore. The language of the plays is Marwari and are written in the Parsi theatre style. The music of Kuchamani Khayal is based on the folk tunes of the area.

Shekhawati Khayal

The area of Shekhawati is known after the dynasty of Shekhawats, who at one time were independent and were the Mansabdars of the Mughal court. They were greatly influenced by the etiquette and manners of the Mughal court and most of them had professional (Mirasi) singers attached to their courts. It was customary that in the evening when the lamps were lighted the musicians gave recital of classical music at the durbar.

The first playwright of the Shekhawati Khayal was Nanu Ramji (1827) who came from Chidawa. Both Lachchiramji and Nanu Ramji were almost contemporary. The texts of the plays of both Kuchamani and Shekhawati Khayals are more or less the same as that of Parsi theatre. It is evident that they have been influenced by the style of production of Parsi theatre. The music of Shekhawati Khayal is highly classical.

Alibuxi Khayal

Alibuxi Khayal was completely different from the other two mentioned above. The founder of this form was Nawab Alibux of Mundawar and thus it came to be known after his name as Alibuxi Khayal. Although a Muslim, Alibux was an ardent devotee of Lord Krishna. Most of his plays were based on the episodes from the life of Krishna and as songs had Bhajans written and composed by Alibux. The language of the text and of Bhajans was Braj. The plays were mostly musical and had lot of influence of Raas Leela.

These Khayals at one time were very popular and received the patronage of the Thakurs, Seths and the people. They were travelling troupes. But it was most unfortunate that both Kuchamani and Shekhawati Khayals did not produce any playwright after the death of Lachchiram and Nanu Ram. They were the first and the last playwrights. Alibuxi Khayal virtually came to an end after the death of Alibux as his descendants refused to patronize it. Today, there are a few very old singers living but they are not in a position to perform. The future of Shekhawati and Kuchamani Khayals is also not very hopeful. The end of both is evident.

Ramayan Mandalis

The other very popular form that emerged in the 20th century was the performances of theatre mandalis, which used to tour from one village to another and put up their plays. They were known as Ramayan Mandalis but in fact they used to present various other plays which most of them were from the repertoire of the Parsi theatre. Basically, these mandalis were an offshoot of Parsi theatre. It is of interest to know that the performance of Ramayan Mandalis were based on the Ramayan written by Radhey Shyam Kathavachak, a very popular playwright of Parsi theatre.

It is most unfortunate that the tradition of Khayal and Ramayan has almost reached the end of its glorious journey and their resurrection seems almost impossible.

Since the end of Sanskrit theatre, till 1843 AD, when *Sita Swayambar* was written by Vishnudas Bhave in Marathi, and *Radha Kanhaiya ka Qissa* in the same year in Hindi by Wajid Ali Shah, the Nawab of Awadh, there was no theatre. Both these plays were confined to the respective courts of Sangli and Awadh. There was a big cultural vacuum. In 1853 Amanat's play Inder Sabha, which in fact was the first people's theatre, played a very significant role in the Indian theatre. But theatre in Rajpootana only made its appearance in the 19th century once again influenced by the Parsi theatre.

Jaipur

It was Sawai Ram Singh, the ruler of Jaipur, who probably had witnessed the performances of the plays staged by various theatrical companies in Calcutta. In Jaipur he witnessed the performance of Inder Sabha presented by Rustam Pestonji at Jaleb Chowk on V.S. 1935

Kartik Badi 8 Saturday AD 1876. He was greatly impressed and decided to have a theatre hall, whose foundation was laid at Rajamal ka Talab opposite Chandi ki Taksal on Baisakh Badi 9 V.S. 1935 AD 1876. It opened on V.S. 1935 Sawan Badi 13, Thursday AD 1876, with the performance of Inder Sabha. Later in 1880 AD a proper professional repertory or Natak Mandali was formed under the able direction of Ratanji Dhoondhi, who was paid a salary of Rs 978, plus rail fare Rs 100, making a total salary of Rs 1,078, with a house and a horse carriage. Regular performances of plays from Parsi theatre were staged. When Maharana Sajjan Singh of Udaipur visited Jaipur in 1879–80, he visited Ram Prakash Theatre and witnessed the performance of "Badra-I-Munir", "Alladin's Chiragh", "Laila Majnu" etc. The theatre was completely subsidized by the state and was open to the public. After the death of Sawai Ram Singh, the Natak Mandali was disbanded and the theatre was closed. Although there is a mention in the records that when New Alfred Theatrical Company visited Jaipur in 1932, it staged plays at Ram Prakash Theatre. Sir Mirza Ismail, who was the Prime Minister of Jaipur state, tried his best to convert the theatre into an institution of music and drama, but he failed. Ram Prakash Theatre was then converted into a cinema house. For almost 30 years now the building is locked up and its future seems to be indefinite.

Several Indian princes of Rajpootana came under the influence of Parsi theatre and patronized it.

Bharatpur

Maharaj Kishan Singh established a theatre company at Bharatpur. Several plays were regularly staged till 1928, when the British government deposed Maharaj Kishan Singh for his anti-British activities. Lala Suraj Bhan purchased the entire assets of the company and went to Tonk where he established a company known as "Bharatpur Dramatic Society". But it lasted only for a year and went into liquidation.

Tonk

The dramatic activities in Tonk were started by Lala Suraj Bhan's "Bharatpur Dramatic Society". But theatre flourished in the reign of Nawab Saadat Ali Khan. Several Parsi theatre companies were invited to stage their plays, and Nawab Saadat Ali much impressed by them instituted a theatre company named "Sarkari Theatre Company" which was completely subsidized by the state. Actors, musicians were employed from Jodhpur and Bikaner. Hafiz Muhammad Umar "Jam", a well-known Urdu poet and writer, was appointed as the director of the company. The plays were staged in a theatre which was specially made for the company. Today, the hall is known as Raj Talkies which in the later years was converted into a cinema house.

Besides the popular plays of Parsi theatre, plays written by Hafiz Muhammad "Jam" (who wrote about 30 plays) were staged. But, all the plays were written and staged in keeping with the style of Parsi theatre, whose themes were historical and mythology. They had several songs and scenes with painted curtains.

With the death of Saadat Ali Khan in 1947 theatre lost its patronage, and theatre activities came to a close.

Jodhpur

The regime of Maharaja Takhat Singh during the regency of Sir Pratap Singh did not provide a congenial atmosphere for theatre in the state. After the bifurcation of Bengal in 1905 the Parsi theatre in particular and the rest of the regional theatre joined the national movement and the entire Indian theatre became a weapon for political change. It thus became difficult for the Indian princes who were loyal to the British Raj to patronize theatre. It is because of this that right from the beginning when Jamadar Theatre Company visited Jodhpur in 1897, theatre was supported by the people. Impressed by the performance of the plays presented by Jamadar Theatre Company, Laxmandas Dangi formed a theatre company of his own, known as Marwar Natak Company. The first play staged was "Draupadi Swayanbar" at the Haveli of Thakur of Ahore. In the absence of royal patronage and not much scope in Jodhpur, most of the artists migrated to Calcutta and joined various theatre companies. Among them the most famous was Manik Lal Dangi who owned Shahjahan Theatre Company. His younger brother Ganpat Lal Dangi and Fida Hussain were among the actors employed in the company. Large exodus of actors, dancers, musicians, directors, painters, playwrights from Jodhpur and Bikaner was a notable contribution to Parsi theatre.

Alwar

Alwar also came under the influence of Parsi theatre and in 1916 some of the youths got together and produced a 'Swang' and took it round the city. Dwarka Prasad Bhargava, a well-known lawyer and social worker encouraged these youths to stage Ramlila. A group was formed, which was named as "Shri Hari Kirtan Samaj" and in 1917 some scenes from Ramlila, most probably from Ramayan of Radhey Shyam Kathavackak, were staged. Maharaja Jai Singh, who was popularly known as "Prabhu", witnessed the performance and was greatly impressed. He was a very learned and enlightened person and he could foresee that in time to come several groups would emerge and jealousy and infighting may result. He therefore brought all the smaller groups together and founded "Shri Rajshree Abhai Samaj". The Samaj predominantly staged the plays from the repertoire of Parsi theatrical companies, in a hall which was constructed by the state. The Samaj also received subsidy from the state. The hall in later years was converted into a cinema hall. The fate which almost all old theatre halls were subjected to. Today, Tej Talkies as it is known is laying vacant, eager to be converted again to its past. Shri Rajshree Abhai Samaj is still in existence, but has withdrawn itself to staging only one play "Brahatrihari" once a year in an attempt to keep up the tradition of Parsi theatre.

Dholpur

It was during the rule of Rana Nihal Singh (1873–1901) that theatre came to Dholpur. Under the royal patronage "Indian Imperial Theatrical Company" was formed, under the direction of Hafiz Abdulla, who was a well-known playwright. The Company achieved success and received popular support from the people. But it is a well-known fact over the centuries all over the world, no theatre worth the name can successfully exist without the state patronage, artistic leadership, repertory or mandali of professional artists, and above all a permanent theatre. It was unfortunate that no theatre hall was made and after the death of the Maharaja and Hafiz Abdulla, there was no one left who could keep up the tradition.

Jhalawar

The state of Jhalawar was fortunate in having Maharaj Bhawani Singh (1886–1929), who was intelligent, well versed in English literature, and interested in fine arts, music and drama. He patronized poets and dramatists in his court. As it was the order of the day most of the Indian princes having received education at the public schools were attracted towards Shakespeare. Maharaja by the royal orders formed "Shakespeare Dramatic Society". He encouraged and patronized translation of the plays of Shakespeare. Pandit Purshottam Surya translated Midsummer Night's Dream, Julius Ceasar, King Lear, Merchant of Venice, and Macbeth. It is of interest to note that all these plays were translated or adapted by the playwrights of Parsi theatre, but Pandit Purshottam Surya's translation is his own. The language used in Parsi theatre is a judicious mixture of Hindi and Urdu, popularly known as Hindustani, which was easily spoken by the actors and understood by the audience. For the presentation of the plays a theatre hall was made which similar to Ram Prakash in Jaipur was designed on the lines of Victorian theatre.

Jaipur, Tonk and Jhalawar were the only states where the playwrights were encouraged to write new plays, or translate the classics from the West. It will be a useful effort if these plays are edited and brought into one edition for the benefit of the present theatre. Sayyad Muhammad Razvi, one of the prominent writers of his time, under the royal patronage, wrote a book on Urdu drama. It was published in 1904 AD under the title "Urdu Drama Par Ek Daqeeq Nazar" (Urdu Drama From a Critical Eye).

The death of Maharaj Bhawani Singh in 1929 brought the curtain down on the stage. The theatre hall still stands with empty stands, abandoned stage, to remind people of the past glory.

When one reflects on the past theatre in Rajpootana, one realizes that a vibrant and socially relevant theatre does not exist in large buildings, and mindless spending of large funds, but it needs wise, sincere and generous patronage of the state, a team of professional actors, directors, playwrights, and a theatre where permanent creative theatre performances are presented for the benefit of the people at large. If not, then, it remains, "a tale told by an idiot, full of sound and fury, signifying nothing".

14

People's Movements in Rajputana and their Role in India's Struggle for Freedom

RAM PANDE

Rajpootana – a composition of 19 princely states, three chiefships and one centrally governed province – has administrative and socio-economic variations. The people of the state were subjected to three-tier exploitation of Jagirdar or Zamindar, the prince (Raja) and the paramount power of the alien British rule. This province has witnessed revolutionary activities of Barhats – Kesari Singh, Zorawar Singh and Pratap Singh, Gopal Singh of Kharwa, Bhoop Singh alias Vijay Singh Pathik, Arjun Lal Sethi etc. under Ras Behari Bose. The first non-violent peasants movements are peculiar and unique landmarks in the history of India's struggle for freedom. The defiance of Amrita Devi of Khejadli against mighty autocracy of Rathores of Jodhpur in 1730 AD is, though very little known, but unique where 333 people lost their lives at the hands of prince's henchmen. The Meghwal uprising of 1775 in Churu thikana of Bikaner state is also a forerunner. The Peasants Movement of Bijolia, which continued for 50 years, was non-violent and first of its kind. Mahatma Gandhi observed in 1915 that he has taken a lesson to launch peasants' cause through peaceful means. Emancipation from human bondage, which was protected by law under different princely regimes, was also attempted first of all in the country. The Praja Mandal movements were unique of their trends. It was a fight for obtaining responsible governments under the aegis of their respective princes on the one hand and emancipation of India from foreign rule, on the other.

The freedom movement in the princely states of Rajputana was basically agrarian movement. Praja Mandals and Praja Parishads, which were formed between 1931 and 1945, also took up agrarian character of their movements. The first agrarian movement in Rajputana may be traced to the Bijolia unrest in 1897 culminated in the abolition of Jagirdaris/Zamidaris/Bisvedaris etc. after independence.

Bijolia: The Pioneer

Agrarian movement in the states of Rajputana started much before any such movement in any part of the country. As early as 1897, in Bijolia thikana of the state of Mewar, a pioneering non-violent struggle began, which continued for 50 years and also spread to the Bhil areas of Sirohi, Idar, Dungarpur, Banswara etc., besides other parts of Mewar and Bundi. This movement was started by Sadhu Sitaram Das and later on was led by Vijay Singh Pathik after 1915. He (Pathik) was a revolutionary by conviction, who in an orderly way organized the kisans for a non-violent agrarian struggle. The movement was a predecessor of the one launched by Mahatma Gandhi in Champaran in the year 1921. It can be said with some conviction that Gandhiji had the full knowledge of this movement, and perhaps derived inspiration from this for the peasant uprising that he subsequently led. Even in the national movement Bijolia played a pivotal role.

The Bijolia movement in its turn also inspired other movements, at Begu, Bundi and the Bhil movement. The Praja Mandal and the Lok Parishad led the peasant uprisings during independence movement on the lines of Bijolia.

Leadership

The question of leadership is of vital importance indeed. Basically, the problem with the peasant uprising is, as the experience of such struggle around the world amply demonstrates, that the peasantry on its own is incapable of leading them. And, therefore, for all practical purposes, the leadership was an external contribution.

Ronald Mousier, in his book *Peasant Uprising in the 17th Century France, Russia and China*, has concluded that it was the vested interests of certain people which ultimately led to such peasant uprisings. Same type of views have been expressed in *The Social Origin of the Democracy and Dictorshi* (author unknown) and *Peasants Wars in Germany* by F.M. Engels. An Indian author, Vinay Bhushan Choudhary, after carefully recording and reflecting on the peasant uprisings in Bengal, has expressed similar opinion in his article "The Study of a Peasant

Revolt in a Bengal District" (*Bengal: Past and Present*, Vol. XCII, ii, 174).

Rajputana was no exception to the above rules whether in Bijolia or in Begu, Sirohi, Dabra or Dudhwa Khara or Bharatpur, etc., and all the uprisings were led by persons not from the ranks of kisans or peasants. The leaders were external elements, certainly with political motives. Vijay Singh Pathik was a Gujar, not engaged in cultivation. Similarly, Manik Lal Verma was a service class person, in service of Bijolia thikana. Jai Narayan Vyas, Mathura Das Mathur, Dwarka Das Purohit, Ram Narain Chouwdhry, Nenu Ram Sharma, Magha Ram Vaid, Professor Kedar, Kishan Lal Joshi, Laduram Joshi, Tarkeswar Sharma etc., came from classes other than the peasant and had wide political ambitions.

After independence the state of Rajasthan witnessed two major agrarian struggles: (i) "Ganganagar Struggle" led by Y.N. Handa, a Communist leader. Peasantry did not come in the vanguard at all (ii) In Bharatpur the same kind of uprising was led by Pandit Ram Kishan, a socialist worker and political leader and not a peasant by profession. This shows that the peasant of the country and especially of Rajasthan was not so aware, if at all he was, of his rights and to fight for the cause. It is significant that the well-known Champaran movement (1921) was led by Mahatma Gandhi and Dr Rajendra Prasad, who too were not peasants or farmers by occupation but ambitious political workers.

Nature of the Movement

The greatest task of any historian surveying the movements of this era is to determine their nature. Precisely whether these were in the nature of agrarian or they ought to be described otherwise. In all these movements, whether it was Bijolia or Dudhwa Khara, etc., one factor was demonstrably present: they were, by and large, part and parcel of the freedom movement launched in the country, though the Bijolia peasant movement was purely agrarian in the beginning or say, till its leadership was assumed by Vijay Singh Pathik.

An analysis of these movements reveals sufficiently that the struggle was more often than not designed to convey the grievances to the Jagirdars, and not intended to overthrow their authority. In none of these movements is there any sign or symptom which may show that the leadership was committed to the uprooting of the feudal system. The feudal overlord, the Thakur, at the same time, enjoyed very good relations with certain kisans, but some others were alienated. The leadership always had this in their sub-conscious while they launched any movement. The nature of the movements was absolutely non-violent, although state occasionally took to violence.

India is an agricultural nation. The majority of its population live in the rural areas. For a national movement it was essential that the villagers be taken into confidence. This is what was precisely contemplated by the leaders of these movements, who foresaw that without their active involvement the struggle could not assume the gigantic proportions that they thought would make any mark. In Rajpootana the problem was of a different nature, for here the struggle was against the triumvirate of the Raja, the British and the Jagirdar. It was, therefore, quite essential for a struggle to have a substantial involvement of the rural peasantry.

In all these movements leadership never demanded overthrow of monarchies but demanded responsible governments under the aegis of the Maharaja.

The movements in the beginning were for economic and social reforms. Mostly after 1938 they assumed political shape under Praja Mandals and Praja Parishads. One of the main leaders of these movements declared that to secure independence was the aim of the Indian National Congress. The aim of Praja Mandals or Praja Parishads was to secure responsible government under the aegies of the monarchs. In the beginning the rulers of the states did not react to it. Jhalawar was first to establish a representative council. Bikaner, Jaipur, Jodhpur and few others granted responsible governments but they never became truly public representative in nature. In 1946 the demand for responsible government with affiliation to Indian Federation was raised.

Religion and Caste

In India, religion and caste have played a dominant role since time immemorial. Once when Vivekanand was asked in America as to what language was easily comprehended by Indians, he replied, the "Language of Religion". In Rajasthan also religion and caste have played a decisive role. For we find again and again that the leadership has made use of these twin tools for conveying their radical message to the peasantry. For example, the Samp Sabha was created by one Sadhu

Govind Giri. The movement of Bijolia was also started by one known as Sadhu Sitaram Das.

Arjunlal Sethi started his activities through Jain Vardhman Vidyalaya ensuring the expected role of Jain community. Precisely worth mentioning is, those who led the movements for political reform were basically Brahmin school masters, along with some lawyers and journalists of other communities. It should be regarded as one of the most interesting features of Indian social and political reforms that the Brahmins, the guardians of tradition, even in conservative form, have also been in its vanguard. Being educated persons, they had earliest and the most direct access to modern ideas and opportunities. The people's movement was most successful since it was led by the Brahmin who enjoyed traditional, prestige and authority. Important leaders like Jai Narayan Vyas, Hira Lal Shastri, Tika Ram Paliwal, Harideo Joshi, later Chief Minister Rajasthan, Bhogi Lal Pandya, former Minister, Narottam Joshi, later Speaker of Rajasthan Legislative Assembly, Ram Karan Joshi, former Minister, Gokul Bhai Bhatt, later President, Provincial Congress and a freedom fighter and quite a large number were Brahmins.

The Bhils were taken to temples of Kalaji, etc., and made to take a vow in front of the deity for continued struggle by the leaders. This is a unique case in the annals of the history that violent tribesmen were made non-violent agitators through religious and social reform movements of various leaders. The Bhagat Movement of 1905–1908 at Mana hills was most notable in this respect. Religion was thus used as a tool by various leaders. In Shekhawati the role of religion was very vital. Under the religious grab of the Arya Samaj, the leaders prepared the peasants for any movement they wanted to start.

That religious and social reforms have played a notable role. Rajasthan is indebted to two personalities – Swami Dayanand Saraswati and Swami Vivekanand. The former aroused the masses through his Arya Samaj activities, which aimed on Swadeshi, Swadharm and Swabhsha through his social and political reform movements. The later left powerful impact on the educated youths.

Arya Samaj is not only significant as socio-religious movement, it went a long way in promoting patriotism and nationalism. The second edition of his work *Satyarth Prakash* was revised and enlarged by Swami Dayanand Saraswati during his stay at Udaipur as Maharaja Sajjan

Singh's guest. He clearly mentioned in this edition, "whatever one may do but the kind of rule administered by his own people is the best".

The volunteers of Ajmer Arya Samaj also played an active part in spreading the spirit of nationalism through their Bhajans and songs composed in an exceeding communicative diction.

Caste has similarly played its role. In Bijolia there was a caste of peasants known as 'Dhakars' whose sentiments were evoked when 'Dhakar Panchayats' were created, placing Dhakar at their heads. In Marwar the Jat Sabha was created with B.R. Mirdha at its head, Marwar being inhabited mainly by the Jats. In the Shekhawati the Jat Sabha was a premier organization of the kisans. Strangely, Tarkeshwar Sharma, a Brahmin leader, was leading Jat Sabha. In the movement from 1931 onwards even Jat leaders were called from outside. For instance, Chajju Ram and Chhuttan Lal from Haryana and Thakur Desh Raj from Bharatpur were invited to join the struggle. The leaders of Dungarpur and Banswara such as Bhogi Lal Pandya, Gauri Shankar Upadhyay, Harideo Joshi and Bhopendra Nath Trivedi, Jani Mani Shankar Nagar with exception of Dhulji Bhai, a Chhipa etc. of Banswara state, were Brahmins.

Role of Mahajans

The study of these people's movements reveals an important aspect of the economic situation and the role of Mahajans in the agrarian sphere. It is evident from this study that sometimes it was the Mahajan who was ruling the area instead of the Thikanedar. He lent money to the thikana and in return was authorized to realize some lags in lieu thereof. So he collected the revenue of lag. The kisan also often borrowed money from the Mahajan of the village, and the Mahajan received his money back in the form of crop produce and also exploited a kisan's resources. This gave birth to mass resentment slowly and gradually. But some Mahajans supported peoples movement by donating their belongings, example like Narsingh Dass Babaji may be quoted.

Role of Panchayats

India is a traditionally democratic country and the primary unit of its democratic set-up is seen in the existence of panchayats. The system in Rajasthan has long existed according to the ancient culture, heritage and polity. It is significant that local traditions and customs were respected, and the local law was definitely shown regard. The Rajasthan peasant was not a serf of European type. It is evident that he enjoyed more freedom than the serf of Europe. Perhaps this was the reason why Russian or Chinese-style socialism could not take root in India.

Fight through Social Reforms

It is a unique case that the movements were fought through social and economic reforms. The leaders established schools, *chatshalas* and boarding houses for the spread of education. Adult education movement was also launched. Rajasthan Seva Sangh was much ahead of all these activities. It made its workers self-sufficient in the economic matters. An unmarried worker was paid Rs 15 per month and those who were accompanied by their spouses were getting Rs 30 per month for their livelihood. The activities carried on under various voluntary organizations such as Rajputana-Madhya Bharat Sabha, Hitkarni Sabhas, Vanvasi Seva Sangh etc. are a clear proof of fight through social reforms.

Revolutionary Activities

There have been revolutionary activities associated with Rajasthan. The main figures of such activities were Thakur Kesari Singh Barhat, his son Pratap Singh Barhat and brother Zorawar Singh Barhat, Arjun Lal Sethi, Vijay Singh Pathik, Rao Gopal Singh of Kharwa, Seth Damodar Das Rathi of Beawar, Bisan Dutt of Benaras etc. They all operated under some samities like Bir Bharat Society, Mahamandal etc. They were guided and directed from British Indian revolutionary centres. Jodhpur bomb cases of 1942–43 and Dogra shooting incidence of Ajmer are also worth noting. However, they all fizzled out gradually. Most of the leaders later on joined non-violent struggle which was going on in those days. Though communist movement is also visible but very little.

Congress Party in Rajputana

It is generally believed that Congress was never organized in the states and was limited only within the territories of the British province of Ajmer-Merwara. There are ample records to show that the Congress party was working in all states of Rajputana and Central India since 1928. Though its activities were limited but it was active, they too on agrarian front.

The study of the nature of the people's movements in Rajasthan would reveal that the movements were mostly for redressing the local grievances, responsible governments in the princely states, agrarian reforms etc. These movements helped the people in carrying on reforms in the fields of education, social caste, religion, agrarian, land etc. But with agrarian base.

Students Agitations

We had students federation of India's branches. All India sessions were also held. The strike of local colleges such as Maharaja College, Jaipur's strike of 1939 is also reported.

Role of Women

The womenfolk of Rajasthan did not lag behind. Anjana Devi Choudhary, Rama Devi Joshi, Durgavati Sharma, Bhooti Devi Bajpai, Rampyari Sharma, Ratan Shastri, Saraswati Devi Pandey and Sumitra Devi Khetan are some of the names who participated in the people's movements along their spouses. Name of Kamla as student of Banasthali participating in pickets demonstration in 1942 is worth mentioning. Above all is the name of Kalibai, a girl of a 12 years of age, who laid down her life in Dungarpur thus became martyr.

Tribals

The Managarh incidence where thousands of Bhils were shot dead was predecessor of Jalianwala Bagh incident. The role of Bhils, like Nanakji, Nana Bhai and Senga Bhai is praiseworthy. The role of Bhil women introduced Gandhi to the Bhil masses through their folk songs.

Rajputana-Madhya Bharat Sabha

Many historical studies have taken their nucleus from freedom struggle in the various erstwhile kingdoms of Rajpootana. The treasure of historical importance is very vast so it is very likely that all the available material for recounting the history of people's movements in the princely states has not been used. The material, which is being presented here, is among the records which have been used scarcely.

Rajputana-Madhya Bharat Sabha was founded on the occasion of Delhi session of Indian National Congress on 28 December, 1918 with late Jamana Lal Bajaj as its Sabhapati. The headquarters of Sabha was stationed at Ajmer in the British territory in Rajputana. Its last session was held at Ahmedabad under the chairmanship of Rai Bahadur Govind Lal Pitti and Kunwar Chand Karan Sharda of Ajmer happened to be its Secretary.

The main objectives of Rajputana-Madhya Bharat Sabha were:

(i) Establishing Seva Samitis in the various areas of the states of Bikaner and Jaipur.
(ii) Organizing various conferences of Sabha at the different places like Nagpur, Delhi, Ahmedabad, just to seek the co-operation of the other Rajasthanis residing at these places.
(iii) Assisting the Bhils of Sirohi and other areas (Bundi etc.) in their struggle against the oppression of the ruling chiefs.
(iv) It has also been pronounced that the Sabha's one of the aims was to establish the schools for untouchables.
(v) To stage an agrarian *satyagraha* in Bisau, Pisangan and Khetri against the highhanded oppressions of local authorities, Jagirdars, etc.

All India States' People Conference

The policy adopted by the leaders of the Indian National Congress towards Indian states and their people has passed through various stages. The Congress attitude towards states' people's aspirations was sympathetic and helpful yet guided by calculated caution, which the leaders could follow with the Congress gradually gaining strength and importance in the political scene of India. The attitude of the Congress towards the states and their people could be seen in three different phases. The first phase, which goes up to 1919 AD, is clearly marked with Congress' indifferent attitude towards the state's people. The second phase, from 1920 AD to 1937 AD showed the limited interest of the Congress in the affairs of the states, and this was followed by the third and final phase between 1938 AD and 1947 AD, when an attitude of total identification with the rising aspirations of the states' people merged. This resulted in the two organizations working with close cooperation, Congress in British provinces and All India States' People Conference (ATSPC) active in the Indian states respectively. Their combined power not only compelled the British to quit India but also resulted in the establishment of a united India with a strong central government.

Vijay Singh Pathik became the Vice-Chairman of ATSPC. He was incharge of Publicity Division of AISPC. Records reflect his working, conditions of Indian states and Round Table conference, etc. Overall the view of strong and united India is supreme in these records. The birth of AISPC is due to amalgamation of two conferences. Pathik had played an important role in it.

Pathik wrote a book on *Indian States* through which he enlightened the elites of Britain, U.S.A. etc., about the miserable conditions of the Indian states' people. It attracted the attention of the friends of India and Indians who were fighting for Indian independence basing themselves abroad.

Role of Press

The press rendered a yeoman service in creating political awareness and also warned the princely states against the mischievous designs of British rule. As early as 1856 Master Kanhaiya Lal was publishing his bilingual weekly *Roze-ul-Talim* and *Rajputana Samachar*, from Jaipur. In one of its issues of 13th October, 1856 carried charges of corruption against a British engineer. It made a request to the Maharaja Ram Singh to punish the delinquent. *Rajputana Gazette*, *Rajputana Malwa Times and Rajasthan Samachar* created awakening in the masses. Agrarian movements in various princely states paved the way for political awakening in Rajasthan. The newspapers like *Uparmal ko Danko*, *Navin Rajasthan*, *Tarun Rajasthan*, *Tyagbhumi*, *Sangram* etc. played heroic role by opposing not only local chiefs but also the rulers of the princely states and encouraged the people's rise against exploitation and injustice. These newspapers spread the spirit of nationalism.

The role of press, laureates and *pravasi* (non-resident) Rajasthanis' contribution towards people's movement is also of vital importance.

II

Amber

The Prelude to Jai Singh II and Jaipur

15

Amber

Erstwhile Capital of Dhundhar's Kachchwaha Rajputs

RAKESH HOOJA AND RIMA HOOJA

> ...a small ruinous town, overgrown with trees, and intermingled with towers and temples, and over it...a noble old fortified palace, connected by a long line of wall with tower, with a very large castle on the highest part of the hill. The town which almost entirely consisted of temples had few inhabitants.... I have seen many royal palaces, containing larger and more stately rooms - many, the architecture of which was in a purer taste, and some which have covered a greater extent of ground but for varied and picturesque effect, for wild beauty of situation, for the number and romantic singularity of the apartments, and the strangeness of finding such a building, in such a place and country, I am able to compare nothing to Amber.
>
> —Bishop Heber (1828)

Amber, with its palace on the hillside, the fortress of Jaigarh above it, the habitation and temples as well as Maota lake below it, and Sagar lake and its attached little village/hamlet behind it, and battlement walls on the surrounding hills to protect the entirety, was the capital of the Kachchwahas till Jaipur was founded in 1727, 11 kilometres away from Amber. The name of Amber was first mentioned by Ptolemy. It is believed to have been founded by the Minas (also spelt Meenas), and is generally held to have been taken over around AD 1037 by the Kachchwaha Rajputs. It was to be almost seven centuries before Amber was finally supplanted as the primary city of the kingdom of Dhundhar by the newly founded city of Maharaja Sawai Jai Singh II - the city of Jai Nagar or Jaipur.

After the shifting of the capital by Sawai Jai Singh II, the older Amber palace-complex and parts of Amber town were largely deserted, but not fully abandoned. Thus, old records and unwanted artifacts continued to be housed in the old, locked, chambers within the Amber palaces; descendants of old retainers or minor members of extended (joint) families continued in possession of the slowly crumbling mansions and humbler homes in the old Amber town; hereditary priests continued to perform rituals in some of the temples; and various successive rulers continued the practice of staying at Amber for nine days, twice a year, during the religiously important *Navaratra* period. This practice was stopped during the reign of Maharaja Madho Singh II following the advent of the motor car, which facilitated easy visits from Jaipur to the Amber palace-complex and temples. It is only with the advent of tourism after India's independence that the Amber fort and palaces slowly began to be frequented afresh by a large number of daily visitors.

Approaching Amber

Nowadays, the fort and palace-complex of Amber resounds to the sounds of countless visitors coming in busloads and air-conditioned vehicles, as also tempos and auto-rickshaws, as tourists and picnickers to the palace, or as visitors to the Shiladevi temple. However, it is interesting to see what people wrote in earlier centuries about approaching Amber.

Writing in the second half of the 19th century, G.W. Forrest has this to say: "Emerging from the north east gate [of Jeypore] we found ourselves on the white sandy road running through luxurious gardens and garden houses, the trees glittering with their broad leaves in the sun; parrots all awake chirping, screaming, flashing from branch to branch, peacocks, blue and white, sunning their tales on the walls. Then we come to a large lake covered with waterfowl, and alligators basking in the sun.... On the bank of the lake the road passes through an ancient gateway in an embattled wall, which connects the two hills that enclose the valley of Amber. Here, we find the elephants sent by the Maharaja to complete our journey, for the road now becomes too steep for carriages. ...When loaded [the elephant,] rose, and rolled slowly up the steep hill like some ungainly, fat dame. On reaching the summit we passed through another gateway, and below us lay a deep, glen, where by the margin of a small lake, a blur of hot colour, sleeps the ancient capital of Amber, a city of ancient temples and ruined palaces, a city of the dead. The crests of the hills on either side are glorified with castles built of pink sandstone, the relics of the old Rajpoot story. Above the lake on its western side rises the old fortified palaces, whose white and yellow facade is broken by balconies and verandahs. The elephant rolled through a winding street of ruined houses and miserable huts till a sloped paved ascent leading to the palace was reached. Guarded on either side by embattled ramparts, and having at every turn a massive red sandstone gateway, it is a fitting entrance to the home of a Rajpoot chief".

Similarly, Francis Brunel wrote: "This ancient city lies in a cleft between two ranges of the Aravallis; it originally belonged to the Minas, and was dedicated to Amba Mata, goddess of the earth and fertility. ...The fort and palace proudly overlook Lake Maota, its Moghul garden, and the city below. It can be entered on elephant-back accompanied by a smiling minstrel playing enchanting airs on his *ravanhata,* or lute. A paved ramp leads to Jaipol, the Victory Gate, which opens on to a large courtyard in the centre of which stands the magnificent Ganesh Gate. The Hall of Public Audience, Diwan-i-Aam, has a dome supported by a double row of exquisitely carved pillars. Several other edifices lie within the palace precincts, including the Diwan-i-Khas and the Jai Mandir. The Hall of Private Audience has its walls and ceilings inlaid with a myriad small mirrors arranged in decorative patterns, producing remarkable scintillations when a flame is lit. Sukh Niwas is the Pleasure Palace. The Surya Puja Room with its sundial altar, the royal apartments, the terrace open to the sky where dances were performed, and the interior gardens – all form part of the palace-complex, as does the silver-doored Temple of Kali, the tutelary goddess of the Jaipur family. Standing on a high peak, the Jaigarh fort overlooks the palace and the city of Amber lower down. It was a defensive strong-point in former days, and its vaults housed the royal treasure. ...In the ancient city below the spires of several Hindu and Jain temples point skywards. The Jagat Shiromani Temple is very richly carved... [and]... the white marble *chattris* of Raja Man Singh and Mirza Raja Jai Singh are at Amber".

Rise of Medieval Fortress Towns like Amber

The period between c. AD 1000–1500 saw the establishment or further development in Rajasthan of many urban centres, forts, religious and market towns, and trading posts, under various rulers, minor chiefs and landholders. Among them were centres like Amber. Shops, temples, step-wells, houses, public buildings, gardens and palaces were basic features of such towns. Traditional principles, with due recognition to local requirements and trends, were a factor in determining their overall location and architecture.

High fortified walls punctured by gates and defences were an important feature for practically all the medieval towns and forts for reasons of security. Records tell us that these were regularly strengthened and repaired by successive rulers. When closed, such gates kept invaders and other unwelcome visitors out. Amber had seven gates – Birai Gate (named after the Varahi form of the group of *matrika* mother-goddesses), Kundlab Gate, Kheri Gate, Delhi Gate, Ghati Gate, Susawat (Seshawat) Gate and Mathura Gate. Most of these gates, unfortunately, have not been able to withstand the ravages of time and are in a rather dilapidated condition. Among the better preserved ones are the Ghati Gate and Kheri Gate. The emphasis on protection undoubtedly motivated the re-use (with occasional renovations of defences) of strategically located sites over several centuries. Such sites include the fortress-towns of Amber and Dausa, and some medieval hill-forts were built over older, pre-medieval, remains.

The Land, the People and the Prominent Structures of Amber Town

Lying as it did on the trade routes from Delhi and Agra to Gujarat, the Deccan and to Malwa, and being proximate to the Imperial Mughal twin-capitals of Delhi and Agra, affected the planning, defence and growth of Amber town. Rugged terrain and scanty rainfall made the people of Dhundhar state sturdy and hardworking. In the absence of rich mineral deposits, they made agriculture their main occupation, and wheat, millet *(bajra)*, barley, and lentils or pulses like *moong* etc., were amongst the main crops grown here. The farmers chiefly depended on rainfed cultivation, though wells and step-wells (or *baori)*, tanks and ponds were also constructed and used. The land was fertile and the nearby Banas and Banganga rivers provided water enabling the inhabitants of the region to be self-sufficient in agriculture production during the heydays of Amber city.

The Kachchwahas followed the established regional system of distributing landholdings, or *jagirs* and *muafi* lands and so forth, in lieu of civil or military services rendered to the ruler (in the form of payments to the royal treasury and provision of horsemen in times of war). The *jagirs* could be confiscated by the ruler, though this was seldom resorted to. Over the centuries, the majority of the people of

Amber were mostly Vaishnavites, followed by Shaivites, Jains and Dadu-panthis. Other faiths and sects were also known, but were less dominant. The society being agriculture-based, the religious fairs and festivals were often associated with crop husbandry and particularly the sowing and harvest times. Accordingly Holi, Diwali, Gangaur, Teej and Basant Panchami were amongst the main festivals.

In common with ruling groups through the centuries, matrimonial alliances were often used as a means of enhancing the political power and sphere of influence of rulers (and the ruling elite). This, in part, led to the Maharajas and members of the upper classes practising polygamy, with Raja Kuntal having five wives, Prithviraj nine, Bharmal ten, Bhagwant Das thirteen, Man Singh I thirty one, Mirza Raja Jai Singh six and Sawai Jai Singh II twenty seven wives respectively. This led to a system of one of the queens of the Maharaja being designated as the chief queen or *Patrani,* who was usually - but not necessarily - the mother of the heir-apparent. It also frequently contributed to feuds between the supporters of rival half-brothers at the time of succession to the throne.

Construction of the Amber palaces atop the hill - in contrast to the smaller old palaces that lie near the Sagar and Narsimha Temple area in the bowl of the valley below - had begun in 1558 during the reign of Bharmal. While most of the more spectacular structures were built by rulers like Man Singh I, Mirza Raja Jai Singh and Sawai Jai Singh II, other rulers also made some additions. Among the older structures and palaces that lie on the slopes below, is the mansion of King Prithviraj, with the temple of Narasimha near it. In contrast to the earlier Amber palaces, the 16th (and post-16th) century hilltop Amber palace-complex is built on a high ridge overlooking the Maota lake with Dula Ram ka Bagh - also referred to as Dalaram Bagh - and occasionally as 'Dil-Aram' Bagh (constructed at the order of Mirza Raja Jai Singh around 1664) on the one side and the lake garden called Kesar Kyari or Mohan Bari, on the other. It is commonly held that Dula Ram (or Dalaram) and Mohan were two main architects - artisans used by Mirza Raja Jai Singh - Bharmal's 17th century descendant, for work on some new palaces within the Amber fort-complex, and that afterwards the two architect-artisans laid out two separate gardens alongside the Maota lake.

Dula Ram ka Bagh is regarded as a fine example of 17th century Rajput garden architecture. The Bagh contains octagonal *chhatris* with a curvilinear roofed pavilion of red Agra sandstone at its north-east and south-east corners, and also houses a small museum of local artifacts. The Mohan Bari garden is popularly called the Kesar Kyari, and is said to have formerly had saffron growing in its finely laid out symmetrical rows upon rows of hexagonal, stone-trimmed, flower beds.

A steep road from the old Amber town leads to the Suraj Pol Gate, which is the main entrance for the hilltop Amber palace-complex. The Suraj Pol Gate leads to a huge courtyard with square gardens, known as Jaleb (also Jalebi) Chowk. On the south-west corner of the courtyard is a row of steps leading to the double gatewayed Singh Pol, and on through it into the large Diwan-i-Aam, which was built during the reign of Mirza Raja Jai Singh.

The Diwan-i-Aam stands on a raised platform supported by a series of 40 columns, with the outer columns being made of red sand stone and the inner columns of whitish marble. Rousselet says that this building aroused the envy of the Mughal Emperor Jehangir. Consequentially, Mirza Raja Jai Singh got the pillars covered with stucco and it was much later that they re-acquired their original colour. From the Diwan-i-Aam a tall gateway, the Ganesh Pol, also constructed by Mirza Raja Jai Singh, leads to the inner portions of the palace. Though the visitor can be misled by the single façade, Ganesh Pol actually consists of two stories. The upper portion of Ganesh Pol is the Suhag Mandir (a small pavilion limited in size to the span of Ganesh Pol), which on the inner side of the palace overlooks the courtyard of the Sheesh Mahal or Jai Mandir – also known as Diwan-i-Khas, which was intended for private audiences.

The Sheesh Mahal consists of two beautiful halls with low arched entrances and elaborately decorated niches. These halls contain intricate carvings, floral designs and mirror-work on the walls and ceilings. Both halls are surrounded by a corridor with double columns made of alabaster. An inner room contains such mirror-work that a single lit candle can glitter to form thousands of twinkling stars as the mirror-work reflects the light. Above the Sheesh Mahal is Jass Mandir, which is an oblong chamber, with splayed corners and a curvilinear – or *bangaldar* – roof, flanked by two octagonal domed side-rooms. The structure has a polished lime floor, and delicate marble *jali* work on the windows. Facing the Sheesh Mahal is the Sukh Niwas, which is a large chamber with side-rooms, fronted by a verandah, overlooking a courtyard garden. The rear wall of the main chamber has a pierced marble slab over which water cascades when required, before flowing out through the chamber and out into the garden through a marble water channel. The garden also has small fountains inset in the channel.

A long and narrow passage from the courtyard leads to the Zenana, which was mostly built by Maharaja Man Singh I. The Zenana contains high walls, towers and long galleries as well as covered balconies and corridors leading to numerous apartments of the royal ladies, and has apparently been modified over time by the addition of several small courtyards etc., as well as a pillared *Baradari* in the centre of the quadrangle. The high walls and the ring of balconies and corridors enabled the palace ladies (with their scores of servitors and retainers) to remain in *purdah* – or behind a veil. The Zenana also contains smaller apartments for the servants and other staff. The centre of the Zenana courtyard contains the *Baradari*, which is a twelve arched pavilion hall, which seems to have been a later addition to the courtyard, which was originally empty of structures.

The best known of Amber's temples is that of Shila Mata inside the palace. The idol of this temple, as well as the priests who perform the associated religious rituals, were brought by Maharaja Man Singh I from his Bengal campaigns in 1604. Both, the rulers and the general public of Jaipur, used to obtain the blessings of Shila Mata on occasions like birthdays, marriages, while going on journeys and for military campaigns etc. These days students also visit the temples before examinations. The *Navaratras* are a special time for the people to visit this temple.

The north-west portion of the Amber complex contains another known temple – the Jagat Shiromani Temple (now also known as Mira Mandir), which is the largest temple at Amber, and is located at what was once the main road leading from Amber town to the palaces above. Constructed by Kanakvati, the queen of Maharaja Man Singh I, in memory of her son Jagat Singh (Man Singh's eldest son), the temple stands on a raised platform, and has a small porticoed *Garuda Mandap* in front of the entrance to the shrine. The idol of Lord Krishna inside this temple is commonly said to have been brought from Chittorgarh and its original ownership is attributed to Meera Bai.

There is also a temple of Narasimha (also spelt Narsingh – an incarnation of Vishnu), near the Jagat Shiromani Temple. This was constructed to house the image of Narasimha in the form of a holy ammonite or *Shalagram*, which was given to Queen Bala Bai, wife of

Amber's King Prithviraj, by the saint Krishnadas 'Payahārī' of the Ramananda sect. Krishnadas 'Payahārī' deputed his disciple, Parbat, to act as hereditary priest at the temple. It is said that the coronation *teeka* or *tilak* – or the crowning ceremony of the Kachchwaha rulers used to be performed here. One may also note a famous legend associated with this temple. Apparently, the saint had predicted that as long as the image of Narasimha remained within the temple, Prithviraj's dynasty would hold Dhundhar, but if the idol was taken out of the shrine, they would lose their hereditary kingdom. Interestingly, the idol was stolen just before the time that erstwhile Jaipur state merged into independent India's new state of Rajasthan!

The town of Amber below contains the Ambikeshwar Mahadeo Temple, which is said to have been constructed by King Kakil shortly after the establishment of Kachchwaha rule at Amber. It is devoted to Lord Shiva but has lost some of its importance in recent years. Among other shrines at Amber, the temples of Kala Hanuman and Kalyan Rai-ji in the town below the palace are known for their architecture. The latter is believed to be a late 8th century AD structure, which was partly renovated in later centuries. Another well-known temple is the Lakshmi-Narayan (also called Sitarama) Temple dedicated to Vishnu, which was built by Queen Bala Bai.

Amber's famous Surya Mandir, or Sun Temple, is situated on the slope of the Amber hill, to the west of the present main fort and palace-complex. Facing the east, the small temple is supposedly the oldest surviving temple of Amber. It has a square sanctum sanctorum, with a vestibule and an open pillared hall. An inscription on the second pillar of the first row of pillars is dated Vikram Samvat 1011 (AD 954), suggesting that the temple itself was perhaps built in the 10th century. Amber also contains Jain temples like the temple of Lal Saheb, and the temple referred to as 'Sanghi Jhuntharam ka Mandir'. (Sanghi Jhuntharam was a 19th century minister of Jaipur state). However, it appears that the Sanghi Jhuntharam Temple predates the infamous minister, for an inscription in the Amber museum records that the temple was originally built by one Mohandas in Vikram Samvat 1714 (AD 1657).

Besides these, to the left of the road going past Amber to Delhi lies the Akbari Mosque (less commonly called the Jama Masjid), which is among the oldest structures of Amber. It was built in 1569–70 by Haji Tawachi Bashi at the command of Raja Bharmal for the Mughal

Emperor Akbar to offer prayers when he passed through Dhundhar on his way to Ajmer – and to the Sufi shrine or Dargah Shareef there. One may also note, albeit briefly, the existence of *Kos Minors* near Amber.

A number of buildings, especially havelis, in old Amber town have recently been catalogued and some of them are apparently being restored. In this context, the privately owned 16th century Chanwar Palkiwalon-ki-Haveli has recently received a UNESCO award for conservation. Old Amber town's several other surviving structures (including unrestored havelis) include the 16th century Bhatt Haveli with a painted first floor chamber, and the 16th century Ranchordasji-ki-Haveli, as also the Chomu Haveli, Bengali Para, and the Old Nizamat building. Many of the structures of old Amber town are, unfortunately, in a dilapidated condition today.

Besides the numerous palaces, temples, pavilions, fortificatory walls and bastions, and wide range of now ruined dwellings at Amber, there are also several water bodies. One of these, of course, is the Maota lake, below the hilltop palace-complex of Amber. Another is the old Sagar, situated in the valley to the rear of the hilltop palaces. Among other tanks, reservoirs and step-wells, the Khalsa Baori – a three-tiered step-well, with arches and walkways, is noteworthy. Among the other water structures at Amber is the Panna Mian ka Kund – also referred to as a *baori.* Built by Mian Panna, reportedly a eunuch in the service of Bishan Singh and his son, Sawai Jai Singh II, this structure has four octagonal *chhatris,* and a double-storey verandah.

Among the cenotaphs or royal memorial *chhatris* at Amber are included those of King Kuntal and his queen, Ladan Devi, which are both sited near the above-mentioned Panna Mian Kund. Prithviraj's cenotaph is near the Ambikeshwar Temple, while Man Singh I's cenotaph is in a different part of old Amber, and is located along the road going past Amber to Delhi.

Jaigarh and Nahargarh: Sentinels of Jaipur

Associated with Amber, and perched on the highest ridge of the Amber-Jaipur hills, stands the fort of Jaigarh. It is believed that Kakil Dev, the first Kachchwaha ruler to hold Amber after taking over the area from the Meenas, laid the foundation of a fort at Chil-ka-Tola in AD 1036. This Chil-ka-Tola seems to have been the fore-runner of the present Jaigarh fort. Prior to the time of Sawai Jai Singh II, Chil-Ka-Tola was also referred to simply as Amber fort, after the name of the capital-town of Amber. It was Sawai Jai Singh II who added some palaces and other buildings inside the fort and renamed it Jaigarh.

Jaigarh is about 3 kilometres from north to south and 1 kilometre from east to west. It has three approach gates: the Awani Gate constructed in the 16th century to connect the fort to the Amber Palace below, the Sagari Gate towards the lake Sagar, which had originally served as the main entrance to Jaigarh Fort and the Doongar Gate constructed by Maharaja Man Singh II in 1942. All the approach gates are linked to the huge courtyard known as Jaleb Chowk, which has two long galleries on either side. These were used as stables up to the 16th century but later became garages for cannons.

The fort contains the seven-storey Diwa Burj from which signals could be sent to the five watchtowers on the fortified outer walls of the entire Amber complex. The Subhat Niwas structure inside Jaigarh's palace is an 18 pillared hall, open from three sides, meant for addressing the soldiers. It is connected to the Khilbati Niwas, where the rulers met their ministers, generals and other confidantes. Thus, this also served as a hall of private audience.

Another building, the Laxmi Niwas Palace, was constructed by Mirza Raja Jai Singh, to with additions being made during the reigns of Sawai Jai Singh and Maharaja Ram Singh II. This building has a unique system of central-heating. It has long tunnels under the floor connected to a furnace which opens in the north-west corner of the building. The burning furnace enables heat to permeate through the tunnels, keeping the floor warm during winters. The ceiling of the furnace opens into a boiler tank above the bathrooms of Laxmi Niwas. Accordingly, one of the bathrooms had a provision for a steam bath, and other bathrooms had provisions for hot and cold water.

Among other structures, the temple of Ram Hari Har was built in 1225 AD. Besides this, there is the Lalit Mandir, or the summer palace, which is a double-roofed building having a number of bedrooms with *jali* work and *jharokhas.* The open terrace facing Lalit Mandir provides a lovely view of the Aravalli range and of Amber's Sagar lake. Aaram Mandir, or the garden house, has square gardens and fountains. A three-arched doorway constructed by Maharaja Man Singh II provides a picturesque view of the hills. There is also the Vilas Mandir, which was meant for get-togethers of the royal ladies, or a Zenana Majlis.

The fortress complex contains a puppet theatre designed for the traditional puppet shows of Rajputana. The old Zenana apartments and

Ranawat Chowk lie between the puppet theatre and the Surya Mahal. They are the oldest buildings in the fort having been constructed in the 11th century. The royal court or durbar used to initially be held in the Ranawat Chowk, while the Vijaygarh structure was used as an armory. The Tilak Chowk faces the Vijaygarh.

There is a 295 feet passage connecting Laxmi Vilas and the puppet theatre, and there are numerous underground passages or tunnels linking every part of the fort as these were a strategic requirement during the medieval days when the fortress could be subject to attack at any time.

Jaigarh fort is self-sufficient in water. Rainwater from the outer reaches of the Aravalli range were channelized into small canals or plastered channels, connected with the main tanks inside the fort. Structures similar to silt traps had been constructed to ensure that the dirt and filth settled in such traps and only fresh water reached the tanks. The fort contains five big tanks – three in the northern courtyard and the other two in the north-east corner of the fort. Four of these tanks were covered to prevent evaporation, as also the growth of bacteria. The largest tank in the fort is 158 feet long, 138 feet wide and 40 feet deep. Amber's Sagar lake and other small dams also supplemented the water for the people inside the fort.

It is said that Man Singh I, who was Akbar's army commander, picked up technical know-how regarding the casting of cannon while serving in Kabul. He brought this knowledge to Amber, and his father Bhagwant Das, who was then the ruler of Amber, constructed a local gun foundry in 1584. The earliest cannons to be found inside the fort date to 1587. The gun foundry at Jaigarh Fort comprises of a furnace and a drilling complex, and covers an area of 162 feet by 57 feet. The cannon named 'Jaivana', constructed in 1720 at the gun foundry of Jaigarh, is reportedly the biggest cannon on wheels in the world, with its barrel being 20 feet long and its weight being about 50 tonnes. Tradition holds that it has been fired – which seems to be corroborated by the fact that its barrel too indicates that it has been fired. Even today it is a major attraction for visitors to the fort.

Some distance from Jaigarh, atop another hill, the Nahargarh or "Tiger Fort" looks down at the sprawling city of Jaipur below it. A large part of Nahargarh was built by Sawai Jai Singh II shortly after the founding of Jaipur. Originally called Sudarshangarh, it became known as Nahargarh because, it is said, the ghost of one Nahar Singh had to be appeased before it could be constructed. Subsequent rulers, particularly Madho Singh II of Jaipur, who built seven of the nine palace buildings there, added to the fort from time to time. Madhvendra Palace was built in the 19th century. Nahargarh's palace-complex is a maze of terraces and courtyards, and there are separate chambers for nine maharanis (queens). Most of the chambers have painted rooms with floral designs and beautiful stained glass windows.

Shift from Amber to Jaipur

Much has been written about the founding of the new city of Jaipur by Sawai Jai Singh II, and there are speculations regarding the motives of the ruler. One of the possible reasons for the move appears to have been because by the first quarter of the 18th century the scope for further expansion was getting limited at Amber the then capital of the Dhundhar state of the Kachchwahas. As such, administration and commercial activity was shifted from Amber to Jaipur because that provided more space, away from the small hill-girt valley of Amber that had served the need of a different era. This was not much different to the case with the shift of the capital of Marwar from Mandore to Jodhpur nearly 300 years before the founding of Jaipur. Furthermore, the relative era of general peace brought about during the height of the Mughal empire may also have enabled Sawai Jai Singh II to think of a capital in the plains rather than in the naturally better protected Amber.

Without going further into the issue, one may conclude by noting that with the founding of Jaipur in 1727, and the eventual transfer of the capital of Sawai Jai Singh II, the fortune of Amber changed in no small measure – and almost permanently. Henceforth, Jaipur was to see a rise to eminence that has led to it becoming one of the well-known cities of the contemporary world.

16

The Kachchwahas of Amber from Dulha Rai to the Founding of Jaipur

Dynastic Succession, Military Campaigns, Architecture, Literature and the Arts

RIMA HOOJA AND RAKESH HOOJA

Origins of the Kachchwahas and the Displacement of the Meenas by Dulha Rai

The origin-myth of the Kachchwaha clan (also spelt and pronounced as Kachchawa or Kachhawa), which came to rule the Dhundhar (or Dhoondhar) region of Rajasthan, has its share of romanticism, in common with many Rajput dynasties. Bardic literature and popular tradition holds that the founder of Dhundhar's Kachchwaha dynasty, prince Dulha Rai - popularly referred to as Dhola Rai - was a descendant of a branch of the solar dynasty that traced its origins back in time through King Kush, one of the twin sons of King Rama (the hero of the epic *Ramayana*). Popular belief holds that it was from Central India that Dulha Rai came to Rajasthan. Some genealogies, and literary works like the *Kachhavamsha Mahakavya* and *Kurma-Vilas*, assert that 'Dhola' came from Gwalior, while writers like Nainsi, Bankidas and Tod maintain that he came from Narwar (near Gwalior). There are several theories regarding the clan name of 'Kachchwaha' or 'Kachhawa'. Apparently, the term became more popular from about the late 16th century during reign of Raja Man Singh of Amber. Thus, poets like Amritraj in his *Mancharitra Kavya* composed in AD 1585, Narottam in his *Mancharitra*, and Murari Das in *Man Prakash Kavya*, have used the terms *Kurma* or *Kurmhha* for Raja Man Singh's dynasty.

James Tod has provided the traditional view, as understood by him in his *Annals and Antiquities of Rajasthan*. According to Tod, "The Cuchwaha or Cuchwa race claims descent from Cush, the second son of Rama, King of Koshula... Cuch, or some of his immediate offspring, is said to have migrated from the parental abode, and erected the celebrated castle of Rhotas, or Rohitas, on the Soane, whence, in the lapse of several generations, another distinguished scion, Raja Nal, migrated westward, and in S 351 or AD 295, founded the kingdom and city of Nurwar, or classically, Nishida. Some of the traditional chronicles record intermediate places of domicile prior to the erection of this famed city: First, the town of Lahar, in the heart of a tract yet named Cachwagar, or region (*gar*) of the Cuchwahas; and secondly, that of Gwalior. Be that as it may, the descendants of Raja Nal adopted the affix of Pal (which appears to be the distinguishing epithet of all the early Rajpoot tribes), until Sora Sing (thirty-third in descent from Nal), whose son, Dhola Rae, was expelled from the paternal abode, and in S. 1023, AD 967, laid the foundation of the state of Dhoondar".[1]

Precise details about Dulha Rais arrival in Dhundhar – and even the date – remain a matter of dispute. One version holds that Sodh Deo, Dulha Rai's father, established his hold over the Khoh-Maach area of Dausa on *Kartik Badi* 10 (i.e., the 10th day of the dark half of the month of *Kartik)* in the year *Vikram Samvat* 1023. This date converts as October 14, AD 967. After a long reign of 40 years, 3 months and 12 days, Sodh Deo was succeeded by his son, Dulha Rai, on *Magh Sudi* 7 (7th day of the bright-half of the month of *Magh), Vikram Samvat* 1063, i.e. January 29, AD 1007. These dates are by no means without controversy, however. For example, V.S. Bhargava believes that "... Sod Deo with his son Dulha Rai (whose real name was Tej Karan) left Gwalior around 1128 *V.S.* (1071 AD) and entered the territory of Dhundhar, subdued the Badgujars and Minas and settled at Dausa, 50 km east of Jaipur".[2]

Tod's version, based on Amber-Jaipur's genealogies, is more romanticized. He wrote:

> ...On the death of Sora Sing, prince of Nurwar, his brother usurped the government, depriving the infant, Dhola Rae, of his inheritance. His mother, clothing herself in mean apparel, put the infant in a basket, which she placed on her head, and travelled westward until she reached the town of Khogong (within five miles of the modern Jeipoor), then inhabited by the Meenas. Distressed with hunger and fatigue, she had placed her precious burden on the ground, and was plucking some wild berries, when she observed a hooded serpent rearing its form over the basket. She uttered a shriek, which attracted an itinerant Brahmin, who told her to be under no alarm, but rather to rejoice at this certain

> indication of future greatness in the boy. But, the emaciated parent of the founder of Amber replied, 'What may be in futurity I heed not, while I am sinking with hunger', on which the Brahmin put her in the way of Khogong, where he said her necessities would be relieved. Taking up the basket, she reached the town, which is encircled by hills, and accosting a female, who happened to be a slave of the Meena chieftain, begged any menial employment for food. By direction of the Meena Rani, she was entertained with the slaves. One day she was ordered to prepare dinner, of which Ralunsi, the Meena Raja, partook, and found it so superior to his usual fare, that he sent for the cook, who related her story. As soon as the Meena chief discovered the rank of the illustrious fugitive, he adopted her as his sister, and Dhola Rae as his nephew. When the boy had reached the age of Rajpoot manhood (fourteen), he was sent to Dehli [sic], with the tribute of Khogong, to attend instead of the Meena. The young Cuchwaha remained there five years, when he conceived the idea of usurping his benefactor's authority. Having consulted the Meena *d'hadi*, or bard, as to the best means of executing his plan, he recommended him to take advantage of the festival of the *Dewali*, when it is customary to perform ablutions *en masse*, in a tank. Having brought a few of his Rajpoot brethren from Dehli [sic], he accomplished his object, filling the reservoirs in which the Meenas bathed with their dead bodies. The treacherous bard did not escape; Dhola Rae put him to death with his own hands, observing, 'He who has proved unfaithful to one master, could not be trusted by another.' He then took possession of Khogong...[3]

Though the historicity of Tod's tale has been questioned by scholars, similar popular versions continue to be re-told in Dhundhar even today. So much so that, according to some Kachchwaha elders, the erstwhile Jaipur Court's tradition of wearing black clothes and head-gear (albeit, with gold brocade), during rituals connected with the festival of Diwali is intended to commemorate the Meenas who originally ruled over the territory.

The historian Jadunath Sarkar, in his officially sponsored history of the erstwhile Jaipur state, noted that there were many conflicting versions of the origins of the "Kachhwa settlement in the land they now hold", and that these had been written down from oral tradition only in the eighteenth century.[4] According to Sarkar, "...Sodo's father, Ishwar Singh, gave away his ancestral estate of Narwar to his younger brother and Gwalior to his sister's son, and retired to the life of a religious recluse...northwest of the Chambal river, on the route from

Malwa to Rajputana. On his death, his son Sodo crowned himself at Nadarabari, but he seems to have been already aged, and continued as a *roi fainéant*, while all the activities of his State were guided by the insatiable ambition, dauntless spirit, inborn leadership and organizing genius of his heir, Dulha Rai, the real conqueror of Dhundhar. He was a youth of remarkable beauty and valour, for which he was called Dulha Rai or 'the Bridegroom Prince'. His fame attracted to his banners the voluntary support of all the spirited chiefs in that neighbourhood. Dulha married the daughter of Ralhan-si, the Chauhan rajah of Lalsot district, and received as his wife's dowry half the share of the fort of Dausa (and its adjacent district) which his father-in-law owned. The other half belonged to a Bar-Gujar [Badgujar] family".[5]

It appears that the initial path to state-building was facilitated for Dulha Rai when he married Kumkum-dey, the daughter of Ralhan-Si, the Chauhan chief of Lalsot (about 57 miles south-east of modern Jaipur). According to M.L. Sharma, "In order to seek the support of a powerful chief against his Badgujar rivals Ralhan-si offered the hand of his daughter to Dulha Rai of Gwalior...[and] to make Dulha Rai continuously interested in the affairs of Dhundhar, ...Ralhan-si gave him a part of his chiefship with half the town of Dausa. This town was then the capital of the surrounding districts which belonged partly to Ralhan-si and partly to a Badgujar chief. The latter resided at Dausa and held under him half of the town".[6]

Following the matrimonial alliance, the Chauhans encouraged the young Dulha to subdue the Badgujars of the area. Thus, on behalf of his father-in-law, Dulha Rai attacked the Badgujars and wrested the portion of Dausa held by them. In appreciation, Ralhan-Si handed over the newly acquired portion of Dausa and its surrounding territory to Dulha. This helped establish Kachchwaha dominion in that area.[7] Dausa now became the capital of Dulha Rai, and over the centuries, it was to remain a major centre of the Kachchwahas.

Tod's account is somewhat different. He writes that soon after taking possession of Khogong, Dhola "...repaired to Deosah, a castle and district ruled by an independent chief of the Birgoojur tribe of Rajpoots, whose daughter he demanded in marriage. 'How can this be,' said the Birgoojur, 'when we are both Suryavansi, and one hundred generations have not yet separated us?' But being convinced that the necessary number of descents had intervened, the nuptials took place, and as the Birgoojar had no male issue, he resigned his power to his son-in-law. With the additional means thus at his disposal, Dhola determined to subjugate the Se'roh tribe of Meenas, whose chief, Rao Natto, dwelt at Mauch".[8]

Bearing in mind that matrimonial alliances have long been a means of strengthening or getting political power, it is possible that Dulha Rai may have married the daughters of both the locally prominent Chauhan and Badgujar chiefs, thereby gaining two powerful clans as kinsmen-allies. Probably it was after securing his position that Dulha eventually turned his attention to other territories that were held by various local Meena chiefs.

"At this time the country south-west of the present city of Jaipur was parcelled out among five family groups of ruling Minas, known as the *Panch-wara* or Confederacy of Five, who prided themselves on being of the purest blood among their fellow caste-men. But these people were not united into one political body. Each fort with the hamlets grouped around it for protection lived its isolated life and warred with its neighbours even when peopled by men of the same blood. A vague and ineffectual headship of the Mina caste was nominally acknowledged in the Mina lord of Amber hill. Here and there the Mina holdings were dotted with the forts of the Bar-Gujars, and...the Minas used to appeal when in distress, to the Bar-Gujar rajah of Deoti, as a suzerain".[9]

Having established Dausa as his base, Dulha Rai went on to attack the Meena stronghold of Machi, then under a chief named Meiwasa. According to some accounts, his first campaign failed, but his next, which took place on the day of a festival of the Meenas, was successful. Machi was subsequently renamed [Jamwa] Ramgarh (whose lake presently supplies some of the drinking water to contemporary Jaipur). In thanks-giving for the victory, a temple dedicated to goddess Jamwa Mata was erected at the site, which is still venerated by the clan, besides other worshippers. The fort of Deoti (some 16 miles west of Dausa), held by a powerful Badgujar chief, was also invested by Dulha soon afterwards, as were two other forts held by the Badgujars.

In his continued bid for kingdom-building, Dulha then moved successfully arms against the Meenas of Khoh (6 miles east of Jaipur), then ruled by a Meena chief called Chanda. Next it was the turn of the Meenas of Jhotwara (3 miles west of modern Jaipur), and Gaitor (2 miles north-east of Sanganer), to face the arms of Dulha. Having successfully wrested these two strongholds, held by chiefs Jhota and Gaita respectively, from the Meenas, Dulha found himself in possession of a tract of land that was perhaps 50 miles long and 30 miles broad. For practical reasons, the capital was now shifted from Dausa to Khoh.[10]

Sarkar believes that the Kachchwaha occupation of Dhundhar "...could not have taken place in one lifetime nor been completed by one stroke...And there were also temporary fluctuations in the fortunes of the conquerors. We can readily believe in the tradition which tells us that Dulha Rai, after his first success over the Minas, was defeated by them and left for dead on the field, and that he retrieved the disaster...Lastly, the Kachhwa leader made a statesmanly compromise with the vanquished race by granting to such of the aboriginal chiefs as offered him allegiance and promises of loyalty for the future, some landed estates, which have been held in hereditary succession ever since. Dulha also kept the rank and file of the Mina youths out of mischief, by employing them as watchmen and permanent servants of the State".[11]

Interestingly, the tradition has long survived that the Meenas of Kali-Kho, who were displaced from their position of local supremacy by the coming of the Kachchwahas, were entrusted with the protection of the state treasures of Kachchwaha-ruled Dhundhar, and the person of the Rajput ruler. According to some 19th century records, formerly, the privilege of applying the *Raj Tilak* or mark of coronation on the forehead of the Kachchwaha kings had vested with the Meenas of Khoh, though later the custom went out of vogue.[12]

The Immediate Successors of Dulha Rai

There is insufficient information about the early rulers of the Kachchwaha dynasty. Various local traditions and genealogical tables suggest that the successive rulers after Dulha Rai were as follows: Kakildev, Hanu[t]-dev, Janhad, Pajvan, Malesi, Bijaldev (Jildev), Rajdev, Kilhan, Kuntal, Jannsi (Joonsi), Udaikaran, Narsingh, Banbeer, and Chandrasen. The Royal Asiatic Society's 'Tod Collection' manuscript no. 9, titled as *Hakikat,* lists Dulha Rai's successors as follows: Kakil, Jahnu, Janhar-dev, Panju, Malesi, Bijalsi, Rajdev, Kilhan, Kuntal, Jayensi, Udaikaran, Narsingh, Banoeer, Udai Raj, Chandrasen, and Pirthiraj.

Kakil and the Founding of Amber

Dulha's successor, Kakildev apparently continued to strengthen the nascent state. One of the dates tradition has ascribed to Kakil is *Magh Sudi* 8 (8th day of the bright-half of the month of *Magh)* of *Vikram Samvat* 1093 (i.e., 28 January, AD 1037) which marks his formal coronation. Kakil is credited with taking the area of Amber from the Susawat Meenas whose chief was Rao Bhatto, habitations held by Nandla Meena, and the territory of Med and Bairat held by Yaduvamshi/Yadava Rajputs.[13] During his short reign, "troubled by frequent Mina revolts...all of which were in the end, suppressed",[14] Kakil laid the foundations of the fortified walls of the future Kachchwaha capital of Amber, founded a new fort called Kakilgarh, and built the temple of Ambikeshwar Mahadev at Amber. (Amber's c. 10th–11th century Sun Temple is among that site's earliest extant monuments).

Pajvan to Prithviraj

It seems that Dhundhar's early Kachchwaha rulers may have offered allegiance to the Chauhans of Shakambhari-Ajmer. Thus, Pajvan (Pajjun), the fifth in descent from Dulha Rai, is described in the *Prithviraj-Raso* as a feudatory of Prithviraj Chauhan III. It is said that when Prithviraj defeated the Chandella king Parmardin, Pajvan was made Governor of Mahoba. The *Prathviraj-Raso* holds that Pajvan, a veteran of sixty-four battles, fell fighting for Prithviraj Chauhan in the battle of Kanauj, while his liege-lord, Prithviraj, carried away princess Sanyogita to Delhi. The correct history of Dhundhar and its ruling dynasty between the time of Pajvan and Rajdev, who made Amber his capital, is inadequately known. It appears that these early chiefs consolidated their local hold in the face of frequent conflicts with the local Meenas, Chauhans, Badgujars, and neighbours like the Yaduvamshi Rajputs, who collectively held dominance across many parts of the Alwar-Bharatpur area.

Pajvan's son and successor, Malesi, is said to have consolidated the clan's position in Dhundhar, particularly through a large number of judicious marriages. Several of his thirty-two sons are believed to have carved out landholdings for themselves from adjoining tracts. There are indirect references to a possible attack by Sultanate troops during the reign of either Malesi or his successor, Bijaldev. According to some versions, Malesi gained a victory over the ruler of Mandu at the battle of Rutroli. However, the matter of dating remains a problem. For example, Dasharatha Sharma believes that the *Kurma-kshiteesh* killed by king Jait Singh of Ranthambore (father of the famous Hammir of Ranthambore), who is mentioned in the Balvan Inscription is probably identifiable with 'Kalyan'[15] (or Kilhan, the son of Rajdev), whereas other calculations would place Kilhan' s reign somewhat later!

Kilhan's successor, Kuntal, was called upon to protect his small state against the invasion of Sultan Mohammed Tughlaq of the Delhi Sultanate. After Kuntal came Jannsi (Joonsi), who was, in turn, succeeded – probably around V.S. 1423, or AD 1367 according to some historians-by his son, Udaikaran (r. circa 1367–1389). Sometime between V.S. 1439 and 1467, Udaikaran defeated the Kyam-Khanis of the northern Baggar region (an area now more famous as Shekhawati), and incorporated that area into the territories of the Kachchwaha state of Dhundhar. His successor, Chandrasen, is also attributed with several military victories. It was probably around this time that Mewar's Rana Kumbha triumphed over Amber and successfully obtained tribute from the Amber Kachchwahas. Two of Chandrasen's queens are known to have built temples to Siva at Amber and Mahar, while Chandrasen's daughter-in-law, Apurva Devi, is credited with the construction of Amber's Lakshmi-Narayan Temple.

Prithviraj to Bharmal, 1503–1574

Greater information about Amber and its Kachchwaha rulers is available from the period of Dhundhar's King Prithviraj (r. 1503–1527) onwards. Prithviraj, the son and successor of Chandrasen, was a contemporary of Rana Sanga of Mewar. Prithviraj fought alongside Sanga at the Battle of Khanua (1527), as part of the 'Rajput Confederacy' organized by Sanga against Babur. As such, he is sometimes described by later chroniclers as a feudatory of Sanga.

This issue of feudatory-suzerain relationship should perhaps be viewed in the light of dominant kingdom versus smaller states, and not as the relationship between an absolute sovereign versus a subordinate feudal chief. The former kind of relationship seems to have a long history in the region. A cycle seems to have existed, of the stronger power gaining the 'homage' of lesser powers, and frequently tribute at pre-determined intervals from them, in the form of gold, or food-grains, or other material goods, or the promise of warriors and weapons in times of crisis.

In the case of the status of Prithviraj of Amber vis-a-vis Sanga of Mewar, it should be borne in mind that one of the queens of Prithviraj was a Sisodia princess from Mewar, who also happened to be the sister of Rana Sanga. Thus, it appears that Prithviraj-like many an independent chief accepting the nominal suzerainty of a more powerful neighbour – was perhaps not wholly the subservient 'feudal' chief in the sense that is understood by contemporary political scientists and historians, but rather a junior ally of Sanga.

Prithviraj assigned land-grants to his sons and close kinsmen, and is traditionally regarded as the initiator of what has come to be known as the *Bara Kotri* or 'Twelve Households' of the Amber Kachchwahas. (A *Kotri* means, variously, a chamber, or branch, section/segment). The select group of royal and aristocratic kinsmen classified into these twelve *Kotris* were assigned areas over which their respective descendants long held sway-albeit as subordinates of successive Amber rulers. The holders of these *Bara Kotri* formed the highest category of Amber's nobility.

It was during the time of Prithviraj that the *Kan-phata* Jogis of the Nath sect, which had once been predominant over the Dhundhar area, with their base at Galta, near Amber, lost their position to the Vaishnavite Ramanandi sect. Prithviraj himself, formerly drawn to the Naths, and a near-disciple of the *Jogi* Chaturnath who used to meditate in, and give discourses at, Amber's Ambikeshwar temple, later withdrew his patronage from the Naths. This was apparently under the influence of his favourite queen, Bala Bai (daughter of Rao Lunkaran of Bikaner), who was a Vaishnav when she came to Amber as a bride, and subsequently became a follower of Krishnadas 'Payahārī' of the Ramananda sect, when the latter arrived in Dhundhar. There are many local tales about the miracles performed Krishnadas as he asserted his supremacy over the Naths and made Galta the seat of the 'Ramanandis'. Possibly the influence of Queen Bala Bai and *guru* Krishnadas led King Prithviraj to have the idols of Narasimha and Vishnu installed within the Narasimha-ji and Sitarama temples at Amber.

Prithviraj was among those who are eulogized for having fought valiantly at the battle of Khanua in 1527. When Sanga was struck on the head by an arrow and became unconscious on the battlefield, Prithviraj was among the party of warriors and princes that carried him off to the safety of Baswa. Prithviraj died on November 19, that same year, and a period of internecine struggle for the throne seems to have followed his death. Prithviraj had nominated his second son, Puranmal (r. 1527–1534), as his successor, possibly because Puranmal's mother, Bala Bai was Prithviraj's favourite queen. Even as neighbouring rulers exploited the situation of internal strife, there are even suggestions that Humayun helped in Puranmal's accession.[16]

However, Puranmal's reign was short. According to one version, Puranmal laid down his life fighting Mirza Tatar Khan around c. AD 1534, while according to another, he died at the battle of Anaseri in 1534, fighting against the Mughal prince Hindal (brother of Emperor Humayun). Hindal had been granted the fief-hold of Alwar and its surrounding Mewat area, and needed to resort to the sword to take possession of his grant. He followed up his campaign against the Mewatis by forays into Kachchwaha-held lands, and attacked Amarsar (then held by Raimal of the Shekhawat sub-branch of the Kachchwahas). Shekhawat accounts note that Amber's Raja Puranmal laid down his life helping Raimal at the battle of Anaseri, near Shikhargarh, Amarsar. Yet another version holds that around c. 1533–34 Prithviraj's eldest son, Bhimdev (Bhim Singh), seized the throne and capital from Puranmal and deposed his younger brother.

Bhim Singh (r. 1534–1537) also had a short reign. He was followed by Ratan Singh, who ruled for some eleven years (r. 1537– 1548). In 1544 Emperor Sher Shah Suri, already master of much of Marwar, and portions of Mewar, Sirohi and Ajmer, attacked Dhundhar. Possibly taking his cue from Rana Udai Singh of Mewar, who had yielded up the keys of Chittor fort to the Afghan, Ratan Singh of Amber too found it prudent to accept Sher Shah's suzerainty. Meanwhile, Ratan Singh's paternal uncle, Prince Sanga – the fourth son of the famed Prithviraj – had established control over a substantial portion of territory, and founded the township of Sanganer (later also renowned for its block-printing on cloth). Upon Sanga's death, Bharmal (also called Biharimal by some writers), who was one of the younger sons of the late Prithviraj of Amber, succeeded his brother as the next chief of Sanganer. Meanwhile, the Amber ruler Ratan Singh was poisoned in 1548 by his half-brother, Ashkaran, who managed to hold the throne for only 16 days before being deposed by local feudal lords. Some historians believe that this could have been done at the instigation of Bharmal, who now became the new ruler of Amber.

Bharmal was over 50 years old by now, and a seasoned political survivor of the long-drawnout intra-family struggle for power. The reign of Bharmal (r. 1548–1574) was to see a new political equation between Amber and the Mughal Empire, which soon catapulted the Kachchwahas to the centre stage of pan-Indian politics, diplomacy and administration as Mughal feudatories. This was based only in part upon the oft-discussed matrimonial alliance between Emperor Akbar and a Kachchwaha princess.

In his initial period as ruler of Amber, Bharmal was faced with considerable opposition. This came not just from various relatives, who were rival contenders to the throne, but also from Haji Khan Pathan, a former slave who became a military commander of Sher Shah Suri, whom Bharmal managed to placate, as well as from the Mughal *Subedar* (or Governor) of Mewat, Mirza Muhammad Sharif-ud-din Hussain. Hussain, supporting the cause of Prince Suja, a son of King Puranmal, attacked the Dhundhar capital in 1558, and Bharmal was forced to sue for peace.

Despite a peace treaty, Bharmal remained insecure. This could have been one reason for his taking the opportunity offered by Emperor Akbar's visit to Ajmer in 1562 AD to consolidate his position. Bharmal waited on the Emperor in person at the Imperial halt at Sanganer en route to Ajmer. This meeting at Sanganer in 1562 was to have momentous consequences, both for the Kachchwaha dynasty as well as for the Mughals. Bharmal not only entered into an alliance with Akbar, he also cemented their new friendship by offering the hand of his daughter in marriage to the Mughal Emperor. [She is called Jiya Rani, Maanmati, Harika, and 'Shahi-Bai' in different sources, but is popularly referred to as 'Jodha Bai'. According to the writings of Abul Fazl and Nizam-ud-din Ahmad, she was princess Harika, Bharmal's eldest daughter, and her mother was Bharmal's Solanki clan Queen, Rani Chandravati (see also Bhargava, op.cit., 1979, p.13, fn. 2)]. The marriage ceremony, which included full Hindu rituals, seems to have been solemnized at Sambhar. Akbar bestowed the title of 'Mariam-uz-Zamani' (d. 1622) on his Rajput queen. Following the marriage, Bharmal, accompanied by an entourage that included his sons, Bhagwant Das and Jagannath, and twelve-year-old grandson, Man Singh, proceeded to the Imperial Court at Agra.

The alliance with Akbar influenced the subsequent pre-eminence of the Kachchwaha ruling house of Amber at the Mughal Court. Raja Bharmal received a *mansab* rank at court, and the princes Bhagwant Das, Jagannath Kachchwaha, Man Singh and the latter's younger brother, Madho Singh, obtained ranks of importance in the Imperial Army. Various other members of Bharmal's entourage at Agra also soon proved their worth in their respective fields. The association would remain mutually beneficial over the next several generations, with Kachchwaha arms, administrative skills and loyalty proving an asset to the mighty Mughal Empire, just as was the recognition, high honours, territorial stability and economic prosperity that followed in its wake for the kingdom of Amber.

By the time that Raja Bharmal died in 1574 AD, he was a trusted and favoured member of the Mughal Emperor's court, holding a *mansab* of 5,000. It is said that Bharmal earned the confidence of the Mughal Emperor to the extent that whenever Akbar left his capital he used to place it in the charge of Raja Bharmal of Amber.

Bhagwant Das

The capability of Bharmal's successor, Bhagwant Das (r. 1574–1589 AD), as an administrator, warrior and diplomat, received suitable recognition at the Mughal Imperial Court. A prominent participant of several imperial military campaigns and expeditions across Rajasthan, Gujarat, Kashmir and the Punjab (including the conquest of Ranthambore in 1569, and the battle of Sarnal in 1572), Bhagwant Das was given the title *of Amir-ul-Umra* by Emperor Akbar, and a *mansab* rank of 5,000. Following the policy adopted by Bharmal, in 1585 Bhagwant Das too opted to strengthen Amber's geographically vulnerable position vis-à-vis the Mughals through the marriage of his daughter, princess Man Bai (also Mani Bai or Manbhavati, afterwards known as Sultan-un-Nisa), with Akbar's eldest son, the Mughal Prince Salim (later Emperor Jahangir).

Like many a contemporary raja, who had accepted Akbar's supremacy, Bhagwant Das spent many years on imperial service, away from his ancestral capital and his kingdom. In 1578 he was posted to the Punjab and north-western areas of the Mughal Empire. In 1583, towards the latter part of his life, Bhagwant Das was made *Subedar* of Punjab, where he served for seven years till his death in the winter of 1589 at Lahore. A keen builder, he encouraged the construction of temples, palaces and pavilions at his capital of Amber, as well as at places like Fatehpur Sikri, Agra and Lahore.

Man Singh

The next of the Kachchwaha rulers was Bhagwant Das's eldest son, Man Singh (r. 1589–1614). Man Singh had served a long apprenticeship as soldier and administrator during the reigns of his grandfather and father, Bharmal and Bhagwant Das, respectively. Born to Bhagwant Das's chief queen, Rani Bhagwati Panwar, on 21 December, AD 1550 *(Palish Vadi* 13, V.S. 1607), Man Singh was 12 in 1562, when he entered the imperial service, along with his grandfather's entourage. The subsequent training enabled the young *Kunwar* (prince) Man Singh to become familiar with traditional Rajput as well as the Mughal techniques of warfare and tactics. In fact, first as a prince and then the ruler of Amber, Man Singh took part in as many as sixty-seven important Mughal military campaigns and battles that took him from Kabul, Balkh and Bukhara in the north-west to Bengal in the east, besides the southern and central part of the sub-continent.[17]

Early in his fighting career, Man Singh took part in several battles and imperial campaigns, including Emperor Akbar's conquest of Chittor (1568), siege of Ranthambore (1569), and the conquest of Surat (1573). Man Singh commanded a small Mughal force that marched to the Mughal capital from the Gujarat campaign by a route that took it through the Vagar part of Dungarpur. In April 1573, when confronted by Rawal Askaran of Dungarpur (r. 1549–1580) and his forces, the Mughal Imperial Army inflicted a defeat on Askaran and plundered the land. Man Singh is believed to have gone on to Mewar after this. Here he met with Maharana Pratap but his mission of convincing Pratap to acknowledge Akbar's suzerainty proved unsuccessful. In 1574, Man Singh formed part of the Mughal expedition, led by Emperor Akbar, against the rebellious Daud Khan of Bihar and Bengal. Abul Fazal's account records that Akbar took along Raja Bhagwant Das of Amber and his son, *Kunwar* Man Singh, besides over seventeen other noted generals and commanders. After a series of successes, the Emperor (along with Man Singh and the others), returned to Fatehpur Sikri (the new capital), leaving Munim Khan to deal with Daud Khan, who was finally defeated and killed in a battle near Rajmahal in July 1576.

Bengal was attached to the Mughal Empire, but within a few years the harsh policies of Akbar's *Subedar* of Bengal, Muzaffar Khan

Turbati, which came on top of Akbar's revenue and military reforms that had left many officials disgruntled, gave rise to fresh rebellion in Bihar and Bengal. (Later, Akbar posted Man Singh first as governor of Bihar, and then Bengal, to deal with the situation, as we shall see below.)

Meanwhile, in 1576, Man Singh was told to lead the imperial campaign against Rana Pratap, the ruler of Mewar, who had refused to accept the sovereignty of Akbar. This culminated in the fiercely fought battle of Haldighati between the forces of Rana Pratap and the imperial forces. Following Pratap's leaving the battlefield (at the insistence of his officers), some versions insist that Man Singh forbade the Mughal Army from pursuing and harassing the Mewar forces and their supporting troops. This action drew the Emperor's displeasure and censure on Man Singh's head for a time, but Akbar later admitted his unrepentant Rajput *Farzand* (son), back into his favour. Meanwhile, Man Singh went on to capture the fort of Gogunda, and consolidate the position of the occupying Mughal armies across much of Mewar.

The Amber prince was then given the task the dealing with the rebellion in Khinchiwara, which lay to the south of Bundi and Kota. Records tell us that Man Singh proceeded from Amber with a strong contingent, and subdued recalcitrant chiefs along the way. Having put down the trouble in Khinchiwara and established military outposts to safeguard imperial interests, Man Singh next marched towards Malwa, conquering the principality of Oond on the way. His efficiency in putting down dissension and establishing good governance in Malwa so pleased the Emperor that Man Singh's *mansab* rank was raised to 3,500.

Next, along with his father, Bhagwant Das (by then Raja of Amber), Man Singh was posted to the Punjab and north-western region along the still-fluid frontier of the Empire. Both men, with their retinues, took up their new duties in Punjab by April 1578. Over the course of his long stay in the Punjab and the north-western part of the Empire, Man Singh was part of numerous campaigns, including against Badakshan, Kashmir and other areas. For a time, Sialkot in the Punjab was his headquarters, and tradition states that Man Singh repaired the old fort and beautified the city as *jagirdar* of Sialkot. His major achievements included chastising Sulaiman Mirza – an ally of Mirza Muhammad Hakim, the ruler of Kabul and Emperor Akbar's half-brother and rival. In January 1580, Man Singh Kachchwaha was given the task of managing the law and order situation of the north-western frontier part of the Mughal Empire in the regions around the river Indus. That December, Man Singh inflicted a severe defeat on the forces of Shadman, another of Mirza Muhammad Hakim's allies, who had attacked the fort of Neelab.

When the *Nazim* (administrator) of Sindh was perceived as having mismanaged affairs, Man Singh was sent to replace him. Meanwhile, Mirza Hakim, the Emperor's half-brother, once again took up arms against Akbar and advanced south-eastwards from Kabul, attacking Punjab, and for a time besieging the fort of Lahore. On hearing this, the Emperor deputed various commanders, including Bikaner's ruler Rai Singh, and one of the Amber princes, Jagannath Kachchwaha, to assist Man Singh. In February 1581, Akbar personally marched against his half-brother. On learning this, Mirza Hakim retreated towards his capital, sped on his way by Man Singh and the other imperial commanders. Afterwards, Man Singh formed part of the imperial expedition sent against Mirza Hakim in July 1581 under the command of Akbar's second son, Prince Murad. Mirza Hakim was defeated and fled towards the northern points of his realm. Kabul lay before the imperial army. In August 1581, Akbar entered Kabul but returned to his own capital later that year, leaving Man Singh to hold charge of the Indus region for the next few years. The situation altered with the death of Mirza Muhammad Hakim in mid-1585. Akbar moved his court northwards, where it stayed till 1598. For a while the Emperor was based at Hasan Abdal (near Taxila). Man Singh was commanded by his Emperor to proceed to Kabul without delay and bring that area and its people formally into the fold of the Empire. Man Singh crossed the river Indus, accepting the submission of the area of Peshawar and other regions that lay en route, and then marched into Kabul and established Akbar's sovereignty.

Pleased with Man Singh's achievements, Akbar appointed him *Subedar* of Kabul. Man Singh discharged his duties with great vigour, earning the grudging respect of the Afghans and Pakhtoons (or Pathans, as they are better known) as a warrior and commander. Man Singh was faced with the task of subduing the formidable Roshanias. Besides fighting the Roshanias and other frontier groups, Man Singh assisted in suppressing the Yusufzai tribe of the north-western region. The Yusufzai had been responsible for the death of Raja Birbal, along with about 8,000 imperial troops, during an ambush in February

1586.[18] Man Singh was placed under the overall command of Raja Todar Mal, another of Akbar's valued ministers and counsellors.

With the aim of having an operating base for launching an offensive against the Yusufzai, Man Singh promptly ordered the construction of a strong fort between the Buner Pass and Ohind (Wahind), which could also be used for defensive purposes. Satisfied with the preparations and strategy adopted by the Amber Prince, Todar Mal left him in charge of future operations against the Yusufzai and returned to the court in March 1586. Man Singh's offensive against the turbulent tribe inflicted defeats, which temporarily blunted the zeal of the Yusufzai. During the latter part of the year, Man Singh continued the imperial campaigns against the Roshanias, Tarikis, Ghori and other frontier groups, and in December 1586 inflicted a crushing defeat on them. Around the same time, Akbar reorganized his administrative structure. As part of this, Man Singh was confirmed in his previous appointment as *Subedar* of Kabul, with Zain Khan Kokah appointed his deputy, Nizam-ul-Mulk as the *Dewan*, and Khwaja Shams-ud-din as the *Bakshi*.

The five-coloured flag of the Amber state (which continued to be used until after Dhundhar's integration into independent India) is said to have been designed by Man Singh during this period, with the colours taken from the pennants of the main Afghan and Pathan groups defeated by Man Singh. It is believed that having defeated the tribes, he duly presented their flags and other booty to Emperor Akbar. The latter authorized Man Singh to use the colours as his own, as he had fairly won them. To these, Man Singh added the white already used in the pennant of his dynasty – and thus was created the famous Dhundhari *Panchranga* – or five-coloured, flag.

Man Singh's long and successful stint along the northern and north-western reaches of the Mughal Empire ended in March 1587, with his recall from Kabul. Abul Fazl's writings indicate that Man Singh was given a fresh assignment as the presence of the ever-victorious Man Singh and his warrior Rajputs in the *Suba* (province) of Kabul was proving galling to the proud Afghans and Pathans. Whether or not that was the sole reason for his recall from Kabul, it cannot be denied that by the beginning of 1587 Man Singh had successfully established the imperial might (for the time being) over the major local tribes of the areas under him, and simultaneously established Mughal administration across the recently subdued province of

Kabul. Being one of the best commanders of the Mughal Empire, Akbar now opted to use Man Singh's services in other areas.

That December, Man Singh was appointed *Subedar* of the province of Bihar, where several recalcitrant chiefs and landholders, including Afghans and Pathans, were proving a problem to Akbar through persistent dissensions and uprisings. Man Singh held charge of the province from December 1857 to March 1594, during which time he was successful in establishing stable administration and putting down scores of rebellious chieftains. Abul Fazl noted that "when the Raja was sent from the Court to the province of Bihar, he united ability with courage and genius with strenuous action. By His Majesty's fortune, he administered the province excellently".[19]

Within a couple of years of his taking up his office in Bihar, Man Singh ascended the *gaddi* (throne) of Dhundhar, upon the death of Raja Bhagwant Das at Lahore on 13 November 1589. On hearing the news, Man Singh returned to Amber, where he was enthroned. The formal coronation ceremony of Man Singh, to which Emperor Akbar sent the ceremonial coronation *teeka* recognizing his accession, along with an order conferring the title of 'Raja' and a *mansab* of 5,000 took place on February 14, 1590.

Soon afterwards, Man Singh returned to his post in Bihar. Man Singh's major achievements in Bihar included a successful expedition against Raja Puranmal of Gidhaur. Puranmal gave several elephants and other precious articles as tribute for the Emperor, and also offered the hand in marriage of his daughter to Man Singh's brother, Prince Chandrabhan. Man Singh next marched against Anant Chero of the Gaya district and forced his submission, as he did in 1590 with Sangram Singh of Khadagpur, who was defeated. The Sayyids of Sambhupuri were similarly subdued.

While in the district of Gaya, Man Singh founded a new town, located across the Phaglu near the town of Gaya. This was named 'Manpur' – or the city of (Raja) Man. Man Singh subsequently marched against Raja Gajapat of Hajipur, and the latter was forced to quit his estates. While Man Singh dealt with the *zamindars* and *rajas* of southern Bihar, two strong rebel chiefs from Bengal, Sultan Quli Qalmaq and Kackewa, attacked Purnia, Tajpur, Darbhanga and adjacent areas of eastern Bihar. Man Singh sent his eldest son Prince Jagat Singh, against them and the invaders were forced to withdraw, leaving behind considerable booty.

With Bihar secured to the Empire, Man Singh turned his attention to the neighbouring area of Orissa, which at the time was virtually under the control of Afghans led by Qutlu Khan and his son, Nasir Khan. Prince Jagat Singh was sent into Orissa, but he was defeated and captured. Man Singh now prepared to march in person, but before his campaign got underway, Qutlu Khan died of an illness. As Qutlu Khan's followers and his son, Nasir Khan, proved amenable to a peaceful resolution, Man Singh negotiated an agreement with Nasir Khan and the Afghans of Orissa, by which they accepted the sovereignty of the Mughal Emperor. One hundred and fifty elephants formed part of the large tribute that was yielded up by them. They also agreed to cede the famous temple of Lord Jagannath at Puri, along with the surrounding districts. During the lifetime of Isa Khan, who was the *Vakil* of the late Qutlu Khan, the contract was maintained in good faith. After Isa Khan's death, the Orissa Afghans rose against the Empire in October 1591. Man Singh marched back from Bihar into Orissa, and by early 1592 had conclusively beaten the Afghans. One of his more striking victories was against the powerful Usman Khan, who held Sarangarh. The defeat of Usman Khan and the taking of Sarangarh by Man Singh drove several lesser Afghan chiefs into surrendering before the Amber ruler. The town of Jaleshwar too was taken from the Afghans by Man Singh and Mughal authority established there.

Meanwhile, Raja Ramchandra, who had his stronghold at Khurda and was ranked amongst the more powerful of the Orissa *zamindars*, accepted imperial authority in June 1592, but his subsequent attitude later drove Raja Man Singh of Amber into besieging Raja Ramchandra's stronghold of Khurda. The siege was lifted shortly afterwards at the command of the Emperor, and Ramchandra surrendered and offered personal homage to Man Singh. The latter gave the administration of the Jagannath Puri temple into Raja Ramchandra's hands. (Ramchandra's descendants have continued to hold the charge over succeeding centuries). Man Singh also had a temple built here.

Through his military campaigning, Man Singh Kachchwaha ensured that dissension and rebellions in both Bihar and Orissa were subdued, and Mughal suzerainty was acknowledged in both regions. In March 1594, Man Singh was appointed Governor of the adjoining province of Bengal, where Mughal suzerainty was being seriously challenged by recalcitrant nobles, *zamindars* and others. Man Singh proceeded to Bengal in early May 1594 and took charge as the new

Subedar. At the time, Tandah was the capital, but a number of reasons convinced Man Singh to contemplate shifting to a new capital. Man Singh selected Rajmahal to be his new capital. At the time this was a *mahal* or sub-division of *Sarkar* (district) Tandah (later part of Bihar's Santhal Parganas area). Rajmahal was located on the banks of the Ganga, and was strategically placed for Man Singh's purposes. In November 1595 the capital was moved from Tandah to Rajmahal, and the new capital named 'Akbarnagar' after the Emperor. Man Singh erected a strong rampart, strengthened with bastions, around the city, and started a mint, which was authorized to strike gold, silver and copper coins.

Later, having subdued the Afghans of eastern Bengal, Man Singh built the fort of Salimnagar, near Mymensingh (now in Bangladesh). The following year, the kingdom of Cooch-Behar acknowledged Mughal supremacy. The ruler of Cooch-Behar, Raja Lakshmi Narayan, had found himself faced with the challenge of Pat Kunwar, a rival claimant to the throne. As the latter had forged an alliance with Isa Khan against Raja Lakshmi Narayan, the Raja, in turn, sought imperial assistance and offered his formal submission to the Emperor's Governor in Bengal. Raja Man Singh accepted his submission, along with the proposal that he marry the Cooch-Behar ruler's sister, princess Barbhavati. The extension of imperial authority over Cooch-Behar provided Man Singh with a convenient base for further action against recalcitrant chiefs. In May 1597, Pat Kunwar was defeated conclusively, but that September it was the turn of the imperial army to face defeat. Isa Khan joined hands with Pat Kunwar and inflicted a severe defeat on Man Singh's forces at Katrabu, near Dacca. One of Man Singh's sons. Duljan Singh, was among those killed in this battle. Another son, Himmat Singh, also fell in combat during Man Singh's tenure as *Subedar* of Bengal. Some time after this, Isa Khan surrendered to Man Singh. The powerful Afghan chief died two years later, in September 1599, and with his death ended one of the major rallying forces against Akbar's authority in eastern India.

Close on the heels of Isa Khan's death, came the death of Man Singh's eldest – and possibly favourite – son Jagat Singh, in November 1599. (The prince's mother, Rani Kanakvati, later erected the Jagat Shiromani Temple in his memory at Amber, which is considered an architectural trendsetter for its times, as it used certain stylistic features typical to eastern Indian architecture.) Deeply troubled by his personal loss, Man Singh temporarily returned to Rajasthan, leaving the administration of Bengal in the hands of his grandson, Maha Singh, a son of Prince Jagat Singh.

In April 1600, the Afghans of Bengal, under the leadership of one Usman Khan, rose in rebellion against the Mughal Empire. Maha Singh was unable to deal with the rebellion satisfactorily, and Man Singh returned to Bengal to handle matters in person. In February 1601 he led the imperial forces to a crucial victory over the Afghans at Sherpur Atai (district Murshidabad), and followed it up by suppressing the rebellion of Kedar Rai, the *zamindar* of Shripur (south Dacca) and Vikrampur, later that year. In addition, the rebellion of the *zamindar* of Magh, in the Arakan area (now part of Myanmar), was crushed. Jalal Khan, Kandarpa-narayan of Chandradvipa (Bakarganj) and King Pratapaditya of Jessore were among the various other chiefs subdued by Man Singh during his governorship. It was in the course of his Bengal campaigns that the idol of the patron-deity of the Amber ruling family, goddess Shila Devi, was brought to Amber from Bengal, and the image was established in a specially built temple. By 1604, Man Singh had succeeded in imposing imperial authority across Bengal.

In August 1605 the Emperor honoured Man Singh at the Imperial Court of Agra. His *mansab* honour was raised to 7,000 *zat* and 6,000 *sawar* – an honour which till then had been bestowed exclusively on Mughal princes of the blood royal! Other court honours came his way too as they had on previous occasions. Emperor Akbar, who had bestowed the title *of Farzand* (son) upon Man Singh prior to the march against Pratap of Mewar, eventually granted him the title of *Mirza Raja* as well. Man Singh's triumphant return to the court and the honour of holding a *Sapt-hazaari mansab (mansab* rank of seven thousand), confirmed Man Singh's position as one of the most powerful military commanders of the Mughal Empire, and one of the most important individuals of the era.

The failing health of Akbar encouraged Man Singh in his hopes of seeing the Emperor's grandson, Prince Khusrau (b. 1587), who was the nephew of the Amber Raja, as the next Emperor, in place of the eldest Mughal Prince, Salim. These hopes were shared by the *Khan-i-Azam* Mirza Aziz Kokah, who happened to be one of the most powerful courtiers of the Empire, besides being the father-in-law of Khusrau. Desiring the absence of the Prince Salim from the Imperial Court to ensure a clear field for furthering Khusrau's chances, Man Singh now prevailed on the Emperor to appoint Prince Salim the next Governor of Bengal. The plan fell through as Salim refused to move from Allahabad to take up his charge in Bengal.[20] Meanwhile, the Emperor had fallen ill. Man Singh and the *Khan-i-Azam* unsuccessfully tried to persuade him to leave Agra for the other bank of the river Jamuna, and when this could not be managed, tried to hustle through a formal declaration making Khusrau the Emperor's heir, but failed in this attempt as well.

Man Singh, in collusion with the *Khan-i-Azam,* now tried to arrange the capture of Salim, but the latter was able to elude the snares set for him. Undaunted, Man Singh tried to enlist the support of other powerful court nobles at a gathering convened in one of the halls of Agra Fort. His passionate appeal failed to convince the bulk of the nobles. Man Singh now made his final attempt to gain the throne for his nephew by trying to take possession of the Imperial Treasury, but found that he had been pre-empted in this by Sayyid Khan Barha and other supporters loyal to Salim. Prasad notes: "The only course left now to the Kachhwaha chief was resorting to the sword for deciding the issue. Raja Man Singh had a faithful army at his command which he could have utilized for installing Khusrau on the imperial throne. But Raja Man Singh had become so broken-hearted on account of the failure of all his plans that he did not wish to seek a solution in the whirlpool of blood. Hence, being thoroughly disgusted, Raja Man Singh decided to proceed to Bengal along with Prince Khusrau. Consequently, Salim was declared as the Emperor of the Mughal Empire and it was approved by the dying monarch Akbar also".[21]

The death of Akbar on October 15, 1605, and the accession of Salim as Emperor Jahangir (r. 1605–1628), marked a new phase in Man Singh's life. Man Singh had held the highest of offices during Akbar's reign, but he had also had the audacity to try interfering with the succession to prevent his own brother-in-law, Prince Salim – the Emperor Jahangir – from ascending the imperial throne. His actions could rightly be regarded as seditious by the new Emperor. In the opinion of many, therefore, Man Singh's future hung very much in the balance! However, though Jahangir remained cautious and carefully monitored Man Singh's activities, he apparently thought it prudent to let matters rest, and included the Amber ruler in the general amnesty announced upon his accession. Man Singh was confirmed in his charge as Governor of Bengal, and asked to take up his duties speedily.

Discussing Jahangir's reaction towards Man Singh, Prasad emphasizes that "Raja Man was the most outstanding personality of the Mughal Court. He was at the head of the strong Kachchwaha cavalry...Besides, Jahangir had not yet established himself firmly on the Mughal throne and it would have been inexpedient and unwise to remove and humiliate a powerful noble like Raja Man Singh. Moreover, the Raja had rendered immense services to the Mughal Empire and he was popular among the rank, and file of the Mughal Army. Had Jahangir done anything to harm the Raja, the latter would have openly backed up the cause of Khusrau and drawn the country into the vortex of civil war. There was another reason for adopting a liberal attitude towards Raja Man Singh...Usman Khan, an Afghan leader of Bengal was creating great trouble there. Raja Man Singh, who had earned great experience in Bengal affairs, could be safely depended upon for suppressing the Afghan leader, Usman Khan. Thus, the continuance of Raja Man Singh as the *Subedar* of Bengal was the result of mature deliberations and keen foresight".[22]

In June 1606, Man Singh was posted to Rohtas Fort, where he remained till 1607. He was then directed to proceed south to join in the imperial campaigns led by the *Khan-i-Khana* in that part of the country. Before marching south, Man Singh made what was to prove his last visit to his own state. Here, he dealt with matters relating to local administration etc., including making allotments of *jagirs.* Man Singh left Amber in July 1609 and went to the Deccan. However, unlike his spectacular successes in Punjab, Afghanistan, Bihar, Orissa and Bengal, his successes in the Mughal Army's southern campaigns were more modest. It was while serving in the Deccan that the long and distinguished career of Man Singh came to an end, as, following a short illness, the Amber ruler died a natural death at Elichpur on 6 July 1614.

Regarded as one of the nine jewels *(nav-ratna)* of Akbar's Court, Man Singh was recognized not just for his skills as a warrior and general, but also as an administrator and diplomat. Amber traditions describe him as an enlightened ruler, who encouraged scholarship, literature, poetry, architecture, and the arts. It was also during his reign that aspects of the imperial administrative pattern, like the use of the *pargana* as a land-unit, approximating a modern 'district', was introduced. Each *pargana* comprised of a large number of *mauza.* The size of Dhundhar's *parganas* varied, with some made up of 400 to 1,000 villages.[23] Well-versed in Sanskrit, Persian, Rajasthani and Hindi, Raja

Man Singh was himself a poet, a man of letters and a patron of learning. He was familiar with all the noted litterateurs and poets at Emperor Akbar's Court, including poets like Dursa-ji Adha, Holrai, Brahmabhatt, Gang and others as well as other contemporaries like Tulsi Das. His Amber Court too attracted writers and talents of the stature of Rai Murari Das, Pundarik, Dalpatraj, Narottam Kavi, Amritlal (also Amritraj), among others. In fact, the once-magnificent private library of the Amber-Jaipur rulers - the *Pothikhana* (Royal Library) - to which many subsequent rulers added, owes much to the collection put together during Man Singh's reign. The munificent raja is said to have granted his chief bard, Rata Barhat, a hundred elephants, besides other honours. Narottam Kavi and Amritlal's contemporaneous texts on Man Singh (both titled *Man-Charitra*) provide considerable information about Man Singh's reign, down to aspects like musical instruments played at the Amber Court.

Possibly influenced as much by the art trends at the Mughal Court, as by existing Rajput traditions, Man Singh also encouraged the painting of murals on the walls of his palace at Amber. The themes reflected a blend of Mughal tastes and local sensibilities, with Mughal-style floral motifs and birds as well as panels depicting scenes from Lord Krishna's life. The predominant colours at this time appear to have been variants of reds, yellows and greens. The Amber-Jaipur School of Painting probably dates to Man Singh's reign as well. Extensive frescoes of what one some people call the 'early Jahangiri style' have been noted at Mauzamabad (Man Singh's birth-place), Bairat and Amber. Some texts from the period contain illustrations, which the subjects including the *Rāga-mālā*, various scenes from the Indian epics, the seasonal depictions of *Bārā-māsā*, etc. An illustrated copy of the *Bhagvat-Purana*, prepared at Ahmedabad in 1598 is described as being among the material preserved in the *Pothikhana* collection of the rulers of Amber-Jaipur. There are suggestions that a copy of the *Geet-Govind* of c. 1550 AD, containing numerous miniatures in the '*Chaura-Panchasika*' style once formed part of the kingdom's old *Pothikhana* collection. However, at present little real information about miniature paintings dating to Man Singh's time (or that of his father and grandfather) is available.

Man Singh proved a great builder too - an activity possibly helped by the immense wealth and booty which had been bestowed on the Commander-in-Chief of the Mughal forces by his not ungrateful

Emperor. Among the architectural legacies left by Man Singh are the palaces within Amber Fort, Man Mandir, Man Ghat and Sarovar Ghat at Varanasi, the Govind Dev Temple at Vrindaban, and temples at Pushkar, Manpur, Puri, etc. He also built forts at Salimpur (Bengal), Manihari (Bihar), Ramgarh (Dhundhar), founded the towns of Akbarnagar (Rajmahal), Manpur (near Gaya), and the small township of Baikunthpur (now called Baikathpur, in Bihar's Patna district), and carried out massive repairs and fresh construction, including of palaces, at the fort of Rohtas. Numerous other palaces, gardens, forts and other buildings were built by him in parts of Kashmir, Punjab, Bihar, Bengal and the Deccan, where he had served over the course of his long and illustrious careers. Man Singh also held the reputation of being a benevolent man, who supported charitable works. Modern Jaipur has communities of 'Afghans' and 'Pathans', who have documents linking their ancestors coming to Jaipur in the 16th century at the invitation and encouragement of Raja Man Singh of Amber. The same Man Singh adapted Bengali architectural features in his later constructions at Amber and elsewhere.

The Short Reign of Bhao Singh

Despite his numerous marriages and a number of children, most of Man Singh's sons had either fallen in battle or died from excesses during the lifetime of their father. Most scholars hold that Man Singh had only one surviving son – Bhao Singh – at the time of his death, though there are some indications that another son, Kalyan Singh, may have been living at the time too. Bhao Singh's (r. 1614–1621) ascension to the Amber *gaddi* was declared by the Emperor Jahangir, over the claims of the late Raja's grandsons.

Jahangir seems to have deliberately overlooked the claims of Man Singh's eldest grandson, Maha Singh, already holding the *mansab* rank of 3,000 *zat* and 2,000 *sawar*. Maha Singh was a grandson of late Raja Man Singh, being the son of Man Singh's eldest and most favourite son, Prince Jagat Singh, who had, unfortunately, predeceased his parents. Maha Singh had previously seen service with the imperial troops. Maha Singh was also, by this time, the brother-in-law of Jahangir, for his sister had married the Emperor in 1608. Evidence also suggests that Maha Singh had been groomed to ascend the Amber *gaddi* by Akbar and Man Singh. He was also close to his imperial brother-in-law. Despite these factors, Jahangir exercised his prerogative as Emperor, placating Maha Singh by granting him the tract of Garha as *inam* (gift), and later raising his *mansab*.

In the course of his short reign, Bhao Singh's *mansab* rank was raised to 4,000 *zat* and 3,000 *sawar*, and eventually to the rank of a *Panch Hazari Mansabdar*, of the rank of 5,000. Sent to campaign against Malik Ambar, Bhao Singh's expedition was not particularly successful against the efficient military tactics of Malik Ambar. This was partially because the formal command had been placed in the hands of the inexperienced Mughal royal prince, Parvez. Bhao Singh died of a brief illness at Burhanpur, then capital of Khandesh, in the winter of 1621.

Mirza Raja Jai Singh I

As Bhao Singh had died without a direct male heir and as Maha Singh too had already died at Berar, the throne of Amber now came to Maha Singh's son, Jai Singh I (r. 1622–1667). The new Raja was later to be more famous as the '*Mirza*' Raja Jai Singh. Jai Singh I was a great grandson of Amber's Man Singh, and the grandson of Prince Jagat Singh. Born on May 29, 1612, the young Jai Singh's formative years had apparently been spent at Dausa, an erstwhile Kachchwaha capital.

(A local tradition holds that while Bhao Singh held the throne of Amber, Maha Singh's wife, a Sisodia princess named Damayanti, remained apprehensive about the safety of her son. It was apparently common knowledge that Bhao Singh viewed the boy as a potential rival to the future claims of his own son, Badri Singh, for the *gaddi* of Amber. Since Maha Singh possessed the *jagir* of Dausa, which his royal grandfather, Raja Man Singh of Amber, had bestowed on him, Maha Singh's wife preferred to live at the fort of Dausa with her young son, Jai Singh, for several years until circumstances altered. While at Dausa, Jai Singh's mother had sought, through the mediation of Empress Noor Jahan and Asaf Khan, imperial favour for her young son. Consequently, Jahangir had granted a *mansab* of 1,000 to Jai Singh.)

The new Raja of Amber was to see service with three Mughal emperors, namely, Jahangir, Shah Jahan and Aurangzeb, and obtain innumerable *jagirs* and other honours. In time his overall brilliance and meritorious services would see his *mansab* increased from a mere 1,000 to the rank of 7,000 – a privilege usually reserved for the royal Mughal princes.

The rebellion of Prince Khurram (the future Emperor Shah Jahan), one of Emperor Jahangir's sons, occurred within a year of Jai Singh succeeding to the *gaddi.* The Amber raja was instructed to guard his territory against Khurram, and raise a force of 9,000 *sawar* to repulse the rebel. In February 1623 Jahangir sent a *Farman* from Ludhiana, en route from Lahore to Agra, commanding Jai Singh to march with his contingents to Delhi. Jai Singh complied, saw his *mansab* rank increased to 3,000 *zat* and 1,500 *sawar,* and in April 1623 marched with the 40,000 strong Imperial Army, under the command of Mahabat Khan and Prince Parvez, to subdue Khurram.

En route to Mandu, where Khurram was encamped following a setback at Bilochpur, Jai Singh received a message asking him to join hands with the Mughal prince. Jai Singh did not respond to this overture. Consequently, Khurram entered Dhundhari territory and looted Amber on April 21, 1623. Jahangir placated Jai Singh, sent him a special *Khillat* (robe of honour) and asked him to continue co-operating with Prince Parvez in overpowering Khurram. When Khurram, having ransacked Bengal, Bihar and Orissa, made a dash to Allahabad, Jai Singh accompanied Mahabat Khan and inflicted a crushing defeat on him in the battle of Hazipur on October 24, 1624. Khurram retreated to the Deccan, sought refuge with Malik Ambar, the Dewan of Bijapur, and subsequently surrendered.

Thereafter, Jahangir deputed Jai Singh to join the imperial expedition, which was sent to subjugate Malik Ambar under the command of Jahangir's highly regarded Afghan commander Peer Khan, on whom the title of *Khan-i-Jahan Lodi* had been bestowed. Later, when *Khan-i-Jahan Lodi* unfurled the banner of rebellion, following the death of Jahangir, Jai Singh refused to join him. He did not respond to Empress Noor Jahan's call for support to Prince Shahriyar and Dawar Baksh. Instead, he slipped away with his retinue from the camp of *Khan-i-Jahan,* and headed for northern India. On his arrival in Ajmer, he obtained an audience on January 14, 1628, with Khurram. In appreciation of the Amber Raja's loyalty, Khurram, on his accession as Emperor Shah Jahan, bestowed *nakkara* kettle-drums on Jai Singh, and raised his *mansab* rank to that of 4,000 *zat* and 3,000 *sawar.*

That April, Jai Singh accompanied Qasim Khan to suppress a rebellion in Mahaban, near Mathura. Returning successful to the Imperial Court on June 25, 1628, he was soon sent to Kabul with

Mahabat Khan to fight Nazr Muhammad. After the enemy had been subdued, Jai Singh was recalled to court in September 1628. A month later, after *Khan-i-Jahan's* flight from Agra, Jai Singh was commanded to join the imperial forces in dealing with the rebel. For his role in the siege of the Ghatpur Fort Jai Singh received congratulations from the Emperor in January 1630. When Shah Jahan marched in person, Jai Singh commanded the vanguard, winning laurels for feats of valour during the course of *Khan-i-Jahan's* surprising attack in Machhili Shahar. Later that year, he served with distinction in the operations against Ahmadnagar.

Mirza Raja Jai Singh of Amber was soon recognized as an able warrior, tactical commander, and diplomat, far superior to many of the Mughal dignitaries at the Imperial Court. During the course of his long life, this Amber ruler apparently took part in every major imperial campaign of his era. The expeditions took him from Qandhar and Balkh in the north-west to Monghyr (Bihar) in the east, as well as to Maharashtra on the western coast of the Indian peninsula, and further south into the Deccan region.

During December 1631, Jai Singh commanded the left wing of the imperial forces against Bijapur. While serving under Prince Shuja and Mahabat Khan, he distinguished himself during the siege of Parenda in February 1634, as well as that of Daulatabad in September 1635. After Aurangzeb had been given command of the Deccan, Jai Singh marched into the Adil Shahi territory with a 12,000 strong contingent, and began the siege of Udai Gir Fort. The siege lasted from June 19,1636 and ended with the fall of the fort on October 19, 1636. In January 1637, Jai Singh captured the fort of Nagpur, and then won laurels at Devgarh Fort in March 1637, forcing Kukia Raja of Devgarh to surrender. In acknowledgement of Jai Singh's services, Emperor Shah Jahan raised his *mansab,* and granted him the *jagir* of Chatsu (present-day Chaksu).

For many years the Amber ruler also served with distinction on the north-western frontier of the Mughal Empire, including at Kabul and Qandhar, under the command of the Mughal princes, Shuja (1638), Murad (1641), Dara Shikoh (1642) and Aurangzeb (1648). In appreciation of Jai Singh's feats of valour and merits as a commander, in 1639 the title of 'Mirza Raja' was granted to him by Emperor Shah Jahan, and his *mansab* raised to 5,000 *zat* and 5,000 *sawar.* (In his writings, the traveller Manucci was to note that by virtue of his merit, Jai Singh had become a man of "great power and riches renowned throughout Hindustan, of whom there was not his like in the kingdom".)

In September 1654, after his recall from Kabul due to differences with Prince Dara Shikoh, Jai Singh served under Sadullah Khan in the imperial operations against Maharana Raj Singh of Mewar who, in contravention with the treaty of February 1615, had begun repair-work at the fort of Chittor. Once hostilities ended, Jai Singh was given charge of the outposts of Mandal, Banera and Phulia.

When the war-of-succession for their father's throne began between the royal Mughal princes, Jai Singh was deputed, along with Prince Sulaiman Shikoh (son of Prince Dara Shikoh), to convince Prince Shuja (then posted as *Subedar* of Bengal), to end his rebellion. Instead, Shuja overran Patna with a force of 14,000. Following the Emperor's instructions, Jai Singh proceeded towards Benares, to rendezvous with a force of imperial reinforcements, which was despatched forth under the command of Qarim Khan and Mahabat Khan. In the ensuing conflict at Bahadurpur, 5 miles north-east of Benares, on February 4, 1658, Shuja was defeated decisively by the imperial side. He fled towards Patna and then on to Monghyr. Shah Jahan charged Jai Singh with pursuing the enemy and conquering Patna. The Amber ruler's *mansab* was raised to 7,000 *zat* and 7,000 *sawar*, including 5,000 *sawar do-aspa sih-aspa*.

Meanwhile, Shuja made overtures for peace to Dara, asking that he be allowed to retain Monghyr. After the battle of Dharmat in mid-April 1658, as the victorious forces of Aurangzeb and Murad made headway towards Agra, Dara Shikoh wrote to Jai Singh, stating that Shuja could be allowed to remain undisturbed in Bengal provided he vacated Monghyr, while Jai Singh himself was to make arrangements for the administration at Monghyr and return soon with Sulaiman Shikoh to the Imperial Court. Shah Jahan too wrote to Jai Singh stating that if Shuja sought imperial pardon, he could be permitted to retain the charge of Bengal and Orissa; and also that Shuja be commanded to attend the Imperial Court.

Aware of the critical situation, Jai Singh sent messages to his heir, Ram Singh, telling him to join Prince Dara Shikoh, for what appeared to be a decisive forthcoming encounter with Aurangzeb. Meanwhile, the Amber raja himself attempted to make haste (as his despatches to Ram Singh record), to reach Agra. However, because of the tardiness of Sulaiman Shikoh, Jai Singh was held up in Allahabad, while the forces of Dara and Aurangzeb clashed at Samugarh late in May 1658. On 8 June 1658 Jai Singh received a letter from the hapless Emperor, detailing the disasters that had befallen him and Prince Dara Shikoh, and exhorting Jai Singh to rush to the rescue. Meanwhile, two days after the decisive battle fought at Samugarh on 29 May, Aurangzeb had informed Jai Singh that the latter's safety and future well-being were dependant on Aurangzeb, and that it would be prudent for Jai Singh to arrest Sulaiman Shikoh and send him to Aurangzeb's camp. (Instead, Jai Singh advised Sulaiman Shikoh to make haste and either join Dara through forced marches via Saharanpur, or, alternately, to seek shelter in the hilly terrain of Garhwal.)

Jai Singh presented himself before Aurangzeb at an imperial audience in Mathura on June 25, 1658. The Mirza Raja was a shrewd politician. The territory of Amber fell within the easy access of Aurangzeb and the imperial forces, and sheer geography was probably a motivating factor that led him to pledge loyalty to the new Emperor. He was well-received, and assigned the *Subedari* of Delhi and the *qasba* of Sambhar in *jagir*.

Later, Aurangzeb used the services of the Mirza Raja to dissuade Jaswant Singh of Marwar from helping Dara Shikoh in the battle of Deorai (March 12–14, 1659). Jai Singh wrote to Jaswant Singh, pointing out that by joining Prince Dara after leaving the field on the eve of the battle fought at Khajua on 5 January 1659, the Marwar ruler had skimmed the brink of disaster. Thus, the letter advised that it would be prudent to return and seek pardon from the Emperor Aurangzeb, if Jaswant Singh wished to maintain his kingdom and status. Once having sworn fealty to the new Emperor, Jai Singh fought against Dara Shikoh in the battle of Deorai. He subsequently pursued Dara Shikoh into the Rann of Kutch area. The capture of Sulaiman Shikoh was facilitated following Jai Singh's advice to Raja Prithvi Singh of Srinagar-Garhwal in December 1660, to yield the fugitive prince to the army under *Kunwar* Ram Singh's command, as the hill-kingdom lacked means to withstand imperial might.

In June 1664, Mirza Raja Jai Singh and the Mughal General Diler Khan were entrusted by Emperor Aurangzeb with commanding the imperial campaign against Shivaji. Possibly taking heed from the calamitous results of the encounters between Shivaji and two important imperial commanders, namely, Afzal Khan (November 2, 1659) and Shaista Khan (April 5, 1663), Jai Singh opted to avoid open combat with Shivaji as much as possible after reaching Poona on March 3, 1665. Instead, he took recourse to the path of diplomacy, albeit against the counsel of Diler Khan. His aim was to procure Shivaji's services against the rulers of Bijapur and Golconda. (Jai Singh had long held that the subjugation of these two kingdoms was a necessary precursor for the conquest of the Deccan.)

Shivaji reportedly responded by sending a letter through a trusted officer named Karmaji. The letter suggested that the Mughal army turn towards dealing with Bijapur, rather than undergo the hardships of campaigning in the hilly region of the Marathas. To this, Jai Singh reiterated that the vast imperial force under his command had been appointed against Shivaji, and suggested that Shivaji accept Mughal supremacy. In the interim, the imperial forces captured the fort of Rudramal, and plundered several tracts under Shivaji's control.

Towards the latter part of May 1665, Pandit Raghunath Rao, Shivaji's guru, attempted to open negotiations with Jai Singh. However, the Mirza Raja held that he was not authorized by the Emperor to negotiate with Shivaji, and insisted that first Shivaji should come before him, unarmed, and then a compromise could be considered. Having received an assurance for his safety, Shivaji, accompanied by a small entourage came to Jai Singh's camp on June 11, 1665, where, following negotiations, Shivaji signed a treaty, known as the Treaty of Purandhar on June 13, 1665. As per the terms of the treaty, Shivaji agreed to yield 23 forts to the imperial forces. He also sent his eight-year-old son, Sambhaji, to the Mughal Court, to enter into Mughal service. The Treaty of Purandhar was a considered a landmark achievement for Jai Singh.

Thereafter, Shivaji assisted the Mirza Raja in his campaigns against Bijapur (January 1666). Jai Singh subsequently emphasized in writing to Emperor Aurangzeb that as Adil Shah and Qutb Shah had united, winning Shivaji's heart and support was necessary, and suggested that the latter be granted an audience by the Emperor. Aurangzeb accepted Jai Singh's suggestion, and commanded Shivaji to present himself at court, promising that he would be permitted to return home in safety afterwards. Following persuasion and a personal assurance for his security and safety by Mirza Raja Jai Singh, Shivaji agreed to attend Aurangzeb's Court. Mirza Raja Jai Singh's role in the treaty of Purandhar, and his persuasion of the famous Maratha leader, Shivaji, to visit Agra enhanced the Amber ruler's reputation. (Jai Singh's military leadership of the Mughal armies in the Deccan between 1627–1665, in Afghanistan from 1629–1653, against the *Khan-i-Jahan,* and at the siege of Parenda of 1634 etc. had already established his reputation as a distinguished general. To this, the crowning achievement, according to Rajasthan's historians, was his successful dealings with Shivaji).[24]

Shivaji's journey north to Agra began in early March 1666. Shivaji and his entourage reached Maluk Chand's Serai on May 11. The next day, Mirza Raja Jai Singh's son, Ram Singh, met Shivaji in the Noorganj garden and escorted him to the Emperor's Audience Hall. However, not only did Shivaji find the Emperor's attitude unpalatable, he felt himself to have been further insulted at being given a place to stand among the *mansabdars* of the rank of *Panj-Hazaari* (or 'Five Thousand'). (One version states that Marwar's ruler Jaswant Singh was among those standing there, on seeing which Shivaji declared that he could not stand behind Jaswant Singh because his soldiers had seen the Marwar raja's back many times!) An angry Shivaji left the Audience hall mid-way, rejecting all attempts and pleas (including by Prince Ram Singh), to make him return to Aurangzeb's presence.

The Emperor wrote to Jai Singh to enquire about any secret assurance given to Shivaji by the Amber ruler. In his turn, Jai Singh requested the Emperor to attempt winning over Shivaji through affection, and suggested that Shivaji be allowed to return to the Deccan and his services used in imperial campaigns against Bijapur and Golconda. Meanwhile, the Emperor was advised by some of his advisors – among them Jafar Khan and Jahanara Begum (and, according to one version, Marwar's Raja Jaswant Singh), that it was dangerous to let Shivaji live. As a security measure, the Emperor commanded that Shivaji be housed in the dwelling of a courtier called Randandaz Khan. However, Mirza Raja Jai Singh's son, Ram Singh, suspecting that the Emperor had taken the step on the advice of Jafar Khan, and fearing for the life of Shivaji, pleaded with Aurangzeb. Ram Singh reminded the Emperor that Shivaji had come to court on the strength of Jai Singh's solemn personal pledge assuring his safety. At this, the Emperor entrusted Ram Singh with the responsibility of looking after Shivaji.

Following a dramatic escape from Agra on August 18, 1665 (which is well-recorded), Shivaji made his way southward to safety. Convinced that Jai Singh's son, Ram Singh, was responsible for Shivaji's escape, Aurangzeb made his annoyance against Jai Singh's son obvious, and Ram Singh temporarily became *persona non grata* at the Imperial

Court. The Emperor ordered a reduction in Ram Singh's rank, and *parganas* assigned to him in *jagir* were taken away, even through Ram Singh's alleged collusion remained unproven.

Unfortunately for Jai Singh I of Amber, in the final years of his eventful life, his loyalty became suspect in the eyes of Emperor Aurangzeb, who believed that the Mirza Raja had a hand in the escape of Shivaji from Mughal captivity within Agra Fort. The Mirza Raja was also held responsible for the failure of the imperial bid to annex the kingdom of Bijapur in the Deccan. Jai Singh's retreat, after more than half a dozen battles fought over a one-month period (December 25 to January 22), earned him the Emperor's censure. Jai Singh's subsequent campaign against Bijapur was equally unsuccessful. Finally, after he retired to Bir in October 1666, the Emperor decided enough was enough. Aurangzeb went so far as to ensure that the Amber ruler was not reimbursed from the Imperial Treasury for expenses incurred against Bijapur – money that had been spent by Mirza Raja Jai Singh I from his personal coffers! On March 23, 1667, the Mirza Raja was superseded and told to return to Agra.

Such treatment seems poor recompense for a man who had ably served the Mughal Empire in good faith for around forty-five years, and the Mirza Raja felt his disgrace most keenly. Already near bankrupt and sorely disappointed because of Aurangzeb's attitude, Jai Singh I was further fated, like many of his predecessors, to die far from his own home territory. He breathed his last while still at Burhanpur in the Deccan in September 1667. (Though another version holds that this occurred on July 22, 1667.)

He seems to have died as a result of injuries from an accidental fall from an elephant, which proved fatal. However, there is some controversy over the cause of Jai Singh's death. Tod notes that Kirat Singh, the Raja's nephew, engineered the poisoning of his uncle at the instigation of Emperor Aurangzeb, who had promised to confer Amber on Kirat in exchange. Kirat employed a servitor called Teja to administer the poison to Jai Singh. Another version holds that Udai Raj, Jai Singh's secretary, administered the poison. On the other hand, the court newsletter (*Akbaar*) of October 30, 1667 records that Jai Singh died of injuries following an accidental fall from an elephant. Aqil Khan's text, *Fatuhati-Alamgiri* records that the Mirza Raja fell from his horse, injured his leg and died on his way to Burhanpur.

Like many of his generation, Mirza Raja Jai Singh I of Amber was more than just a sword-wielding warrior-prince. A statesman, administrator, diplomat and general, Jai Singh I was well-versed in Sanskrit, Turkish, Arabic and Persian too. Keenly interested in scholarship, literature and the arts, he was himself a highly cultured and learned man, and a patron of poets, artists and scholars. Among those who flourished at his Amber Court were eminent writers like the poet Bihari, the author of the *Bihari Satsai*, and Kulpati Misra. Kulpati Misra's compositions include the *Ras-rahasya*, *Durga-bhakti-chandrika*, and *Sangram-Saar*, besides Hindi translations of older classical works like Kalidasa's *Abhigyan-Shakuntalam* and King Harsh Vardhan of Thaneshwar-Kanauj's *Ratnawali*. Other works by Kulpati Misra included the *Nakha Sikha* and the *Rasa-Rahasya*. He was also a notable poet in the 'Braj Bhasha' language.

Meanwhile, the Amber School of Painting had flourished under different successive rulers. The mural tradition too was known, and a well-preserved painted chamber at Amber, commonly referred to as the 'Bhojan-Shala' or dining hall, has elaborately painted murals along all its walls. Some scholars have pointed out that while the famous Mirza Raja Jai Singh I of Dhundhar was a well-known builder, as well as a collector of Persian and Mughal carpets and miniature paintings, his own Amber Court does not seem to have developed any outstanding feature during his reign!

The Interregnum between Mirza Raja Jai Singh and Maharaja Sawai Jai Singh

Ram Singh I (r. 1667–1689), who succeeded Mirza Raja Jai Singh I, continued to serve the Mughal Empire after his accession, just as he had in the years prior to that. He saw considerable service in the north-east too, particularly against the Assamese. Like his forebears, and many a contemporary, the court of this ruler too provided patronage to numerous people of talent. For instance, a text on dance called *Hastak Ratnavali* was penned at Ram Singh I's court in 1673. Himself a writer, with critically acclaimed works like *Roop-Manjari*, *Dhatu-Manjari* and *Chhavi-Tarang* to his credit, Maharaja Ram Singh is responsible for formally putting together the famous *Pothikhana* or 'Great Library', to which later rulers of Dhundhar continued to add.

Ram Singh I was succeeded by Bishan Singh (r. 1689–1700), who campaigned on behalf of the Mughal Emperor against the Jats and on the north-western frontier of the sub-continent. He died at Kohat (or Kabul, according to some) in 1700 and was succeeded by his young son, Jai Singh II, soon to gain fame as Maharaja *Sawai* Jai Singh.

Sawai Jai Singh

In the course of his long reign, which coincided with a tumultuous phase of Indian history, Amber's Jai Singh II (r. 1700–1743 AD) became and remained an important figure in practically all the major contemporary happenings.[25] Born on *Margashirsha Vadi* 6, V.S 1742 (3 November 1688), Jai Singh II formally ascended the *gaddi* of Dhundhar in January 1700. The eleven-year-old Raja went on to earn fame, in the years that followed, not just as a soldier-prince, statesman and diplomat, but also as an astronomer, mathematician and man of science, townplanner and patron of scholars. He is still acknowledged for planning and founding the now internationally famous city of Jaipur (which became the capital of independent India's new state of Rajasthan nearly two centuries later in 1949).

Soon after his accession, the young Jai Singh II was called upon to render military service to the Mughal Empire. This practice was by now customary for most of the ruling families and chiefships that had accepted Mughal dominance over the years. Prior to his inheriting the throne of Amber, Jai Singh had served in the Deccan for about eight months as a ten-year-old. As the ruler of Amber, Jai Singh was once again sent to the Deccan. This time he was posted under Prince Bidar Bakht. During the next few years, the young Raja and his Amber contingent demonstrated their military prowess on many occasions, particularly against the Marathas at Khelna, Khandesh, Malwa and Burhanpur. Emperor Aurangzeb was a witness to Jai Singh's valour at Khelna, and over time his *zat* and *jagir* were gradually increased by the Emperor.

The Deccan experience, interspersed with attending diplomatic parleys and negotiations between the Marathas and Mughal forces, was to serve Jai Singh well in the future. His appointment in 1705, as Deputy Governor *(Naib-Subedar)* of Malwa, similarly helped refine skills relating to administration, law and order, revenue collection and statesmanship. He was also charged with ensuring the safe transit of treasures intended for the Imperial Treasury, and of arms and ammunition to the Deccan. During the Mughal war-of-succession that followed the death of the aged Emperor Aurangzeb in 1707 AD, the eighteen-year-old Jai Singh initially supported Prince Azam's cause. Azarn made Jai Singh the Governor *(Subedar)* of Malwa and increased his *mansab* honours. Later, in the final decisive battle for the crown between the Mughal royal princes Azam and his brother Muazzam (afterwards Emperor Bahadur Shah I) at Jajau, near Agra, on 8 June 1707, Jai Singh opportunely opted to change sides. However, though he eventually did go over to Prince Muazzam's winning side, Muazzam never forgot, nor forgave, Jai Singh's initial opposition.

As such, Muazzam's ascension as Emperor Bahadur Shah I (r. 1707–1712) marked a period of disfavour for the eighteen-year-old Jai Singh of Amber. The Emperor decided to oust Jai Singh, and Amber was sequestrated and handed over to Bijai Singh, Jai Singh's younger brother, who had proved a loyal supporter of Prince Muazzam (Emperor Bahadur Shah) in the war-of-succession. At the same time, an imperial garrison was established at Amber. Jai Singh II now had to resort to all his skills of diplomacy as well as his sword in dealing with the situation. On the one hand, he initiated cautious overtures towards Emperor Bahadur Shah. Simultaneously, he forged a firm working alliance with the ruling houses of Mewar and Marwar. Matters were arranged enabling Jai Singh to wait on the new Emperor at Ajmer for urging the return of his sequestered *watan jagir.* At Bahadur Shah's command, Jai Singh joined the imperial camp – then bound for the south to deal with the Mughal Prince Kambaksh. Despite conciliatory attempts, Jai Singh soon realized that Bahadur Shah was in no hurry to return Amber. Thereupon, he joined Marwar's Ajit Singh in leaving the Emperor's camp surreptitiously on 30 April 1708, and accepting the hospitality of Rana Amar Singh II of Mewar, in early May 1708, at Udaipur.

While planning future actions, the shrewd Jai Singh convinced his allies that the three states ought to strengthen their ties through matrimonial alliances. As a consequence, Jai Singh married Maharana Amar Singh II's daughter, princess Chandra Kanwar. The marriage was accompanied by the condition that any son born to her would succeed to the throne of Amber, regardless of the natural rights of primogeniture favouring any older son of Jai Singh born from a different queen. After the death of Jai Singh, this condition was to lead to serious succession problems between the eldest of Jai Singh's surviving sons, Ishwari Singh, and the younger son, Madho Singh, born to the queen from Mewar. A matrimonial alliance with Marwar was also agreed upon, with the engagement (and almost a decade later, marriage), of Jai Singh with princess Suraj Kanwar, the daughter of Ajit Singh of Marwar.

Thereafter, the forces at the command of Mewar marched alongside the contingents of Ajit Singh and Jai Singh towards Jodhpur. Their joint action saw the retaking of capital from imperial hands. The early part of July 1708 saw Ajit Singh restored on his ancestral throne, before the three armies of Mewar, Marwar and Dhundhar jointly ensured the return of Jai Singh II to the throne of Amber. Almost simultaneously, the 'triple alliance' forces defeated the imperial army near the famous salt-lake town of Sambhar. Sambhar was occupied in October 1708. For several years thereafter, Marwar and Dhundhar jointly ruled Sambhar. Around the same time, widespread resentment and rebellion across many parts of Rajasthan against the Mughal Emperor Bahadur Shah went a long way in forcing him to change his policy towards Jai Singh and Ajit Singh. Individual imperial *farmans* (royal decrees), confirming them as rulers of their lands were issued in the early summer (May-June) of 1710. Later, Emperor Bahadur Shah was prevailed upon to accept Jai Singh back at the court.

Jai Singh's return to power and to imperial grace meant an effective end to the aspirations of his brother, Bijai Singh, upon whom Emperor Bahadur Shah had granted the administration of Amber, after imperial troops had sequestered Jai Singh's lands in 1707. Bijai Singh left the imperial camp for Hindaun, from where he wrote to Jai Singh, seeking reconciliation with his brother, and permission to return to Amber. Jai Singh wrote back, inviting his younger brother back, but when the two met at Sanganer in May 1713, Bijay Singh was arrested and incarcerated at Jaigarh Fort. The unfortunate man was to spend the remaining years of his life in imprisonment. In 1729, when it was reported to Jai Singh II that Bijay Singh was conspiring with Bundi's Rao Raja Budh Singh to wrest the gaddi of Amber, Jai Singh II had Bijai Singh put to death.

Meanwhile, after the death of Emperor Bahadur Shah I in 1712, Jai Singh's standing at the Mughal Court increased. Bahadur Shah I was succeeded by his son, Jahandar Shah (r. 1712–13). His brief reign ended in December 1713 with his defeat, at the hands of Farukhsiyar, in the battle of Agra. During the subsequent reign of Farukhsiyar (r. 1713–19), Amber's Jai Singh continued to hold a high position at court. However, as long as the 'king-makers' – as the Sayyid brothers, the Wazir Sayyid Abdullah Khan and the Bakshi Sayyid Hussain Ali have been called – were powerful at the Imperial Court, Jai Singh's contributions were somewhat marginalized by their influence.[26] Despite this, in October 1713, the Emperor conferred the *Subedari* of Malwa on Jai Singh.

By this time, the Marathas were proving a threat to Mughal supremacy not only in the Deccan, but also in Malwa and Gujarat. As Governor of Malwa, Sawai Jai Singh not only checked the activities of the local Afghans, Ahirs and other groups living in the Malwa area, he also followed a vigorous policy against the Marathas. In May 1715, Jai Singh successfully repulsed the advance of a Maratha contingent, under the command of Kanhoji Bhonsle and Khande Rao Dhabare that was marching towards Malwa. Subsequently, in September 1715, Jai Singh was summoned to the Imperial Court and entrusted with the task of leading an imperial expedition against the Jat chief, Churaman. Over the next two years, Jai Singh, still technically the *Subedar* of Malwa, captured Kaman and besieged Thun Fort. Churaman used the offices of Sayyid Abdullah to negotiate peace terms with the Empire, bypassing Jai Singh – much to the discomfiture of the Amber ruler.

Meanwhile, the prolonged absence from Malwa of the Amber ruler resulted in the Marathas resuming their raids into that province. In October 1717, at the advice of Sayyid Abdullah, the Emperor replaced Jai Singh II as *Subedar* of Malwa. Emperor Farukhsiyar was also coerced by the all-powerful coterie of the 'king-maker' Sayyids into sending Jai Singh away from the Imperial Court. Soon afterwards, Farukhsiyar was deposed in a palace intrigue in February 1719, and later murdered. The imperial Mughal throne briefly went to Rafi-ud-Darajat (r. February-May 1719) and then the latter's elder brother, Rafi-ud-Daulah (r. May-September 1719), before Prince Roshan Akhtar became Emperor, taking the name of Muhammad Shah (r. 1719–1748). The intercession of Marwar's Ajit Singh at this point helped Jai Singh in re-gaining imperial favour, in part, and Jai Singh was posted as the *Faujdar* of Sorath. Fortuitously, for Jai Singh, the downfall and death of the Sayyids towards the close of 1720 saw his own re-ascendance at the Mughal Court.

In fact, Jai Singh's relations with the frequently changing Emperors who occupied the Mughal throne in succession following Bahadur Shah's death are an object lesson in statesmanship, delicate diplomacy, covert and overt negotiations, and stratagems and planning.

The same may be said for the Amber ruler's relations with various Rajput states. Alongside this, Jai Singh further strengthened his position by establishing cordial relations with the Marathas and the Bundelas.

Called upon by Emperor Muhammad Shah to deal with Churaman and the rising Jat power in 1721, Jai Singh had achieved this by 1722 through the use of both the sword and diplomacy. Churaman's nephew, Badan Singh, was won over by Sawai Jai Singh, and in the face of a family feud, Churaman took his own life even as Jai Singh's forces reached Thun and encircled it. The stronghold of Thun was staunchly defended for a couple of months by Churaman's son, Mokham Singh, but was finally wrested by Jai Singh's forces. The fort was systematically torn down and the ruins ploughed over by asses, so that the place would never again be considered worthy of a chiefs abode.

Mokham sought shelter in Marwar with Maharaja Ajit Singh, while Badan Singh granted formal recognition as the chief of the Jats and the title of *Braj-Raj*, acknowledged Mughal suzerainty. In recognition of Jai Singh's role in securing the subordination of the Jats, Emperor Muhammad Shah added the title of *Raj Rajeshwar* to those of *Shri Rajadhiraj Maharaj Maharaja* and *Sawai* already held by Jai Singh.

The grant of the unusual title of *Sawai* has a popular story attached to it. Dhundhar/Jaipur tradition holds that upon Jai Singh's first attendance at the Mughal Court as Raja of Amber, his audacious courage and quick-witted repartee appeased the anger of the Mughal Emperor Aurangzeb, and earned him that appellation. The story runs that Emperor Aurangzeb was annoyed with the Amber family because of the actions of Jai Singh's immediate predecessors, particularly as the Kachchwahas of Amber had long had close and loyal ties with the Empire. On seeing Jai Singh II at his Imperial Court for the first time, Emperor Aurangzeb is said to have taken a tight hold on the hands of the young boy and asked wrathfully, "Your grandfather and father's actions have harmed the Empire. They were traitors to me. What sort of treatment do you expect from me?"

To this Jai Singh replied, apparently unperturbed, "At the time of marriage, among my people, a man takes hold of only one hand of his bride and promises to look after her for the rest of his life. Your Majesty has taken hold of me with both his hands! Why should I worry now about the treatment Your Majesty intends for me?" The bold answer amused the aged Emperor, who promptly conferred the title of *Sawai* – meaning, in the literal sense, "one-and-a-quarter" – upon the young boy-king, thereby implying that Jai Singh II of Amber was [one-and-a-quarter times] a better man than his peers!

Several historians have questioned this belief, suggesting that Aurangzeb had nothing to do with the title of *Sawai.* They hold that it was not until the reign of Emperor Farukhsiyar that the title of *Sawai* was conferred upon Jai Singh II in July 1713. Whatever be the truth, by 1713 the twenty-five-year-old Jai Singh II was being referred to in official Mughal records not just by the title of 'Mirza Raja', which had been conferred by an earlier Mughal Emperor on an earlier ruler of Amber (the 17th century Mirza Raja Jai Singh I), but as 'Mirza Raja *Sawai* Jai Singh'.[27] By the middle of the second decade of the 18th century Jai Singh II was amongst the most influential figures in India. His views carried weight not just at the Mughal Court in Delhi, but also at Hyderabad as well as with the Peshwa and other Maratha chiefs at Poona (Pune) and Satara. His fellow Rajput rulers in Rajasthan similarly valued his opinion and advice.

In October 1729 Jai Singh was appointed *Subedar* of Malwa for the second time, and held the office for about 10 months. In September 1732, he was designated *Subedar* of Malwa for the third and final time in his career. The appointment was important as the incessant Maratha raids into Malwa – a crucial geographical zone – were now of greater danger to the Mughal Empire than had been the case before. Shortly after reaching Ujjain to take up office that December, Jai Singh (who had obtained military help from Mewar), engaged with the attacking forces of Malhar Rao Holker, Ranoji Scindia and other Maratha troops in a battle fought near Mandsaur. The Marathas proved stronger and obtained an indemnity of Rs 6 lakh, along with the promise that 28 *parganas* would be ceded to them in lieu of *Chauth.* The Maratha victory dealt a blow to the prestige of the Mughal Empire and the Rajasthan rulers alike.

It now began to seem that stronger measures were needed to check the Marathas. Following the discomfiture of Mughal authority in Malwa and Gujarat, and Maratha intervention in the internal affairs of the kingdom of Bundi the vulnerability of individual states of the Rajasthan region had already been increasingly realized by the Rajput rulers. Thus, as Jai Singh enjoyed unparalleled influence amongst his fellow-princes of the Rajasthan region, he took a prominent role, along with the Maharana of Mewar, in the convening of a conference of Rajput rulers and chiefs in July 1734. This was to culminate in the signing of the 'Hurda Pact' on 17 July 1734. Though the pact signed at Hurda was eventually not enforced with adequate vigour by all concerned parties, the Hurda Conference and Pact re-confirmed Sawai Jai Singh's position of regional eminence.

The threat from the Marathas remained real, and that November the Mughal *Mir-Bakshi* Khan-e-Daurai was sent into Rajasthan to deal with the Marathas. Sawai Jai Singh II, Marwar's Abhay Singh, and Kota's Durjansal joined him. The Imperial Army clashed with the Marathas at Rampura, but was defeated, and the Marathas moved through the Hadauti area towards Jaipur. In view of the situation, the *Mir-Bakshi* thought it prudent to take the advice of Jai Singh and pay the Marathas Rs 22 lakh as *Chauth* for Malwa. The Emperor was censorious of the action, and made his displeasure known to Jai Singh and the Mir-Bakshi.

In the early part of 1736, Jai Singh met the Maratha Peshwa, Baji Rao, and his entourage very cordially at Bhambhola (near Kishangarh). Jai Singh attempted to secure an agreement between the Mughal Emperor Mohammed Shah and the Maratha Peshwa, Baji Rao. Central to it was the notion of sustaining the Empire with the Mughal Emperor as its nominal head, and adequate scope for the Marathas to take part in administration. This was an idea that had appealed somewhat to the Maratha Peshwa, Baji Rao. It was also an idea that might have changed the entire future history of South Asia – though after the defeat inflicted in 1740 AD on the Mughal Emperor by Nadir Shah of Persia, it became a utopian dream! When peace terms finally remained unresolved as far as the Mughal-Maratha relations were concerned, Jai Singh convinced Baji Rao to return back to the Deccan. En route, the Peshwa occupied most of Malwa.

Not long afterwards, in further testimony of Jai Singh's position as an important 'Grandee' of the Mughal Empire, he was entrusted with the *Subedari* of Agra. Besides having clout at the Imperial Court, and to some extent, influence with the Marathas, by this time Jai Singh's involvement in numerous affairs of neighbours like the kingdoms of Bundi, Bikaner, Marwar, Kota, had made his position unchallengeable. So too had the military defeats he inflicted on many of the above, including Prince Bakhat Singh, holder of Nagaur and brother of the Marwar Maharaja, Abhay Singh, who was beaten in the battle of Gagrana. Mewar too respected his advice.

The powerful ruler of Dhundhar manipulated affairs in the Kota-Bundi area too, and was a prime mover in the ouster of Bundi's ruler, Rao Budh Singh ensuring that Dalel Singh became the next ruler of Bundi in Budh Singh's place. In 1740, Jai Singh played a part in helping Zorawar Singh, ruler of Bikaner, retain his kingdom, following yet another armed attempt to occupy it through force by Abhay Singh of Marwar. This earned him the gratitude of Bikaner. While Bundi was ruled by Jai Singh's protégé-cum son-in-law, Dalel Singh, Kota's Durjansal too fought in several campaigns under Sawai Jai Singh II of Amber. Similarly, Badan Singh, nephew of Churaman and an important Jat leader who became the chief of the Bharatpur area, acknowledged the overlordship of Jai Singh II. He is known to have made regular obligatory attendance at the Kachchwaha ruler's formal *darbar* and other ceremonials of *Teej* and *Dashera* etc., as did Bundi's Dalel Singh.

Jai Singh II was more than just a shrewd statesman and soldier, who could "run with the hares and hunt with the hounds" when necessary. He was also a scholar par excellence, a scientist and planner, and a patron of art, architecture, literature, with the traditionally admired penchant for acts of charity and public welfare. Well acquainted with Indian and Greek mathematics, Jai Singh was aware of contemporary developments in Europe in the field of mathematics. He had various Greek and Arabic works, as well as other European texts dealing with plane and spherical trigonometry, and the use of logarithms etc., translated into Sanskrit. His library included translations and commentaries of the works of astronomers like Aryabhatt, Brahmagupta, Bhaskaracharya, Ptolemy, Mirza Ulugh Beg, Nasir-ul-Din al Tusi, and many others.

Having heard, through Portuguese missionaries about the progress in the field of astronomy in Portugal, Jai Singh sent his own men, accompanied by one of the missionaries, to the court of the Portuguese King Emmanuel in 1727–30. Emmanuel, in turn, sent his envoy, Xavier de Silva, with De la Hire's tables to Jai Singh. When he compared the tables with his own, Jai Singh was able to point out that the Portuguese tables were less exact and had certain errors, which he attributed to the inferior diameters of the instruments used. Jai Singh's own almanac compilation is known as the '*Jiz-i-Muhammad-Shahi*', taking its name from the Mughal Emperor Muhammad Shah.

Jai Singh's keen interest in astronomy and mathematics had already found expression, well before this period, in personal observations of the skies using instruments of brass constructed according to the Persian-Arabic School of Astronomy. When he found that axes of these brass instruments rapidly worn down, displacing the centre and shifting the planes of reference, the Maharaja took to personally designing model-instruments of stone and masonry. Apparently, Jai Singh constructed at least 13 different types of instruments, ranging in height from a few centimetres to 24 metres! These were used for his calculations, particularly at the observatories that were built by him at Delhi, Jaipur, Varanasi (Banaras), Ujjain and Mathura.

These observatories became popularly known over time as 'Jantar Mantars' – a phrase derived from the words *yantra* (instrument or device, i.e., the observation-stations), and *mantra* (formulae). In fact, the structures are gigantic specialized instruments in themselves. Built mainly with stone masonry and lime-and-mortar, with a limited use of brick, parts of the structures in these observatories are lined and overlain with *araish* and marble, not for mere decoration, but to provide a level, smooth surface for accuracy of taking astronomical readings. The choice of brass and other metallic sighting discs, rods and measuring devices etc. was similarly motivated.

The Jantar Mantar at Delhi was the first to be built, coming up during the 1724–27 period. The Jantar Mantar at Sawai Jai Singh's new capital, Jaipur, was constructed next. This came up between 1728 and 1734. It is the largest of the observatories built by Jai Singh, and was intended to serve for regular, daily, observations, even when the Maharaja himself was away from Jaipur. As such, Pandit Jagannath, Kewal Ram and others constantly used it. Jaipur state's records tell us that in 1734, Jai Singh gave regular wages to 20 astronomers at the Jaipur observatory alone! The third of Jai Singh's five observatories was built at Mathura, on top of the old Mathura Fort. Unfortunately, nothing survives of this Jantar Mantar at all. The observatory at Varanasi was the fourth to be built, while that at Ujjain was the fifth and last of Sawai Jai Singh's observatories. The Jaipur Jantar Mantar remains the biggest, most complex and best preserved of the observatories built by Sawai Jai Singh II. A total number of 18 *yantras* were built here. The various instruments served to measure aspects like the sun's declination, the declinations of stars and of planets, the local time, and to determine eclipses etc.

The same thoroughness can be noted in the planning of Jaipur. Sawai Jai Singh not only collected plans of many contemporaneous European cities, he also examined Indian traditions of architecture, and took note of extant cities and towns before the plans of Jaipur were finalized. Known also as Jai Nagar in its earliest years, Jaipur was founded in 1727 by Jai Singh II, and built to plans, under the supervision of Vidyadhar Bhattacharya. Born in the family of Amber-based Bengali Brahmin priests, Vidyadhar was given the title *of Desh Dewan* (State Minister) by Jai Singh.

Jai Singh's dream-city was designed with streets and lanes that intersect each other at right angles, in a latticework of main streets, lanes and by-lanes. Numerous *havelis,* temples, gardens, civic buildings were built at pre-planned places. Certain areas were devoted to specific activities and trades. The city was ringed within a protective wall. Much of the city had taken its visualized form by 1733. In addition to Jaipur, Sawai Jai Singh was also responsible for the building of numerous temples, forts and caravan serais. Among these were the Jaigarh Fort, Raghunathgarh, Ambagarh, and a Sun Temple at the pilgrimage site of Galta near Jaipur. Caravan serais for travellers were built not just in his domains, but also in other provinces, as an act of charity.

Despite his prolonged absences from Amber, and later Jaipur, because of duties connected with the Mughal Empire, Jai Singh consistently patronized scholarship and literary activities at his court. Scholars, artists and experts in various fields thronged to his court. For instance, Sivanand Goswami and his sons were among those acclaimed for their learning relating to the Dharma Shastras, grammar, astronomy, and various related sub-branches. Similarly, Ratnakar Pundarik was well-versed in ritual activities. Litterateurs like Krishna Bhatt and Har Krishna, who wrote in Sanskrit, were among the numerous writers who were attracted to his court. Works in local Dingal and Pingal languages were also written. Qualified and talented people were always valued at his court.[28] Jai Singh himself is known to have composed a commentary on the Sutras, entitled the *Brahma-Bodhini.*

A devout believer of Vishnu, Jai Singh was keenly interested in learning about other belief systems. Vedic practices interested him too.

In this context, it is interesting to note that Jai Singh organized the *Ashvamedha Yagna* – one of the sacrifices performed by a small number of powerful monarchs of the early historical period, which had fallen into disuse over time. In order to conduct this, Jai Singh II carried out consultations with the learned Brahmins of his age, including traditionalists from Kashi (Varanasi). Only after there was agreement regarding Jai Singh's suitability to perform the sacrifice, did the Jaipur ruler perform the *Ashvamedha Yagna*.

Jai Singh was no blind adherent of tradition, though. Without being a professed reformer and harbinger of societal change, he discouraged mutual discrimination between different sub-sections of Brahmins. The prevalent orthodoxy had, over the years, laid down norms about social distance even within sub-groups of the Brahmin caste. For instance, in Jai Singh's time, certain sub-sections of Brahmins did not co-dine. One of the methods the Maharaja adopted to bring mutually exclusive segments together was through organising and hosting group dining festivities across the city of Jaipur on numerous occasions, in which different sub-groups of the same caste ate food together.

What makes Sawai Jai Singh remarkable is that his quest for learning: his interest in mathematics, astronomy and town planning, his construction of astronomical observatories, and the founding of the planned city of Jaipur were carried on in the midst of constant strife, political machinations, court intrigues. The period coincided with the rise of Maratha power, and the slow disintegration of the once-mighty Mughal Empire. Despite heavy odds as far as peace and stability were concerned, imposed by a rather traumatic period of transition after Aurangzeb's death, Jai Singh II persisted with his efforts in that direction. He also made the kingdom of Dhundhar one of the largest tributary states, with an area exceeding 20,000 square miles (some of it was land acquired as *ijara* or Mughal state-granted sub-lease holdings). This was a far cry from the 3,000 square miles that he had inherited when he inherited the Amber throne. (At that time, the three *parganas* of Amber, Dausa and Baswa were all that had comprised the *Watan Jagir* of the Amber ruler.) By and large, the state enjoyed peace and prosperity, and its administration was well-organized and functioned efficiently.

There were flaws too that tempered Jai Singh II's personality. The consummate diplomat, administrator, statesman, man of learning, and patron of the arts, could be thoroughly unscrupulous in his actions, if the need arose. He had a hand in the deposition of Budh Singh of Bundi, as well as the death in 1729 of his own imprisoned brother and erstwhile rival for the Amber *gaddi*, Bijai Singh, as well as a nephew. Historians feel that he had a role in the murder of Ajit Singh of Marwar in June 1724,[29] and certain other intrigues. His role in the death of his son Shiv Singh and one of his queens (Shiv Singh's mother), at Mathura in 1724 too remains suspect! On another plane, Jai Singh was a far better statesman and administrator than a general. Tod holds that "...his courage had none of the fire which is requisite to make a Rajpoot hero; though his talents for civil government and court intrigue, in which he was the Machiavelli of his day, were at that period far more notable auxiliaries".[30] In fact, Tod concedes that when one considers the age in which Jai Singh lived, and how "...amidst revolution, the destruction of the empire, and the meteoric rise of the Mahrattas [sic], he not only steered through the dangers, but elevated Amber above all the principalities around, we must admit that he was an extraordinary man".[31]

Jai Singh II lived through a period that initially saw the final years of Emperor Aurangzeb on the throne. This was followed by the 1707 war-of-succession, and a series of short-reigning and/or weak Mughal Emperors, counter-balanced by ambitious and manipulative courtiers and 'king-makers' at the Mughal Court, on the one hand, and the expansion of Maratha and other regional powers, on the other. Through that turbulent age, Jai Singh held various high offices, including the *Subedari* of Agra once and that of Malwa thrice between 1713 and 1735. Jai Singh II led imperial campaigns against the Marathas, Jats and others, and in an age marked by secret pacts, battles and Mughal-Maratha-Rajput problems, managed to hold his own diplomatically and politically. Although Jai Singh did not aid the Mughal Emperor at the time of Nadir Shah of Iran's invasion, he retained his high position at the Mughal Court, and continued to influence Mughal governance and policies until his death.

Sawai Jai Singh II of Amber/Jaipur died on 21 September 1743, leaving behind a strong state and a reputation not only as a statesman and diplomat, but also as a scholar, builder, and patron of the sciences, arts, and literature.

He was the last Kachchwaha dynasty ruler to use Amber as his capital.

Notes

1. James Tod, *Annals and Antiquities of Rajasthan*, 1832 (1957), Vol. II, p. 280.
2. V.S. Bhargava, *Rise of the Kachhawas in Dhundhar* (Jaipur), Shabd Sanchar, Ajmer & New Delhi, 1979, p.4.
3. Tod's *Annals and Antiquities of Rajasthan*, 1832 (1957), Vol. II, p. 281.
4. Jadunath Sarkar, *A History of Jaipur*, Orient Longman, Hyderabad, 1984.
5. Ibid., p. 22.
6. M.L. Sharma, *History of the Jaipur State*, 1969, p. 21.
7. In *Rajasthan ka Itihas*, 1998, p.105, G.N. Sharma places the establishment of Dulha's kingdom around AD 1137, while Tod as already noted dates the event to AD 967.
8. Tod, op. cit., Vol. II, pp. 281–282.
9. Sarkar, op. cit., 1984, p. 23.
10. M.L. Sharma, op. cit., 1969, p. 23.
11. Sarkar, op. cit., 1984, p. 23.
12. Fateh Singh Champawat, *Brief History of Jeypore State*, 1889, p.10; Tod, op. cit., pp. 141, 303, 347–348.
13. Sarkar, op. cit., 1984, p. 24.
14. Ibid.
15. Dasharatha Sharma, *Rajasthan through the Ages*, Vol. I, Government of Rajasthan, Bikaner, 1966, p. 697.
16. G.N. Sharma, *Rajasthan through the Ages (Vol. II)*, Bikaner, 1990, p. 104.
17. R.N. Prasad, *Raja Man Singh of Amber*, World Press, Calcutta,1966.
18. Birbal was Akbar's minister, counsellor and friend, as well as one of the famed 'Nine Jewels' at his Court.
19. Cited by Prasad, in *Raja Man Singh of Amber*.
20. R.N. Prasad, 'Raja Man Singh of Amber', in Ratnawat and Sharma (eds.), *History and Culture of Rajasthan*, Jaipur, 1999, p. 196.
21. Ibid., p. 197.
22. Ibid., p. 198.
23. By 1715 the *pargana* of Amber consisted of about 700 villages, which had grown to 998 by 1737.
24. G.N. Sharma, 1990, p. 106.
25. See, among others, V.S. Bhatnagar's *Life and Times of Sawai Jai Singh*, Delhi, 1974; G.P. Pilania's *Enlightened Government in Modern India: Heritage of Sawai Jai Singh*, Aalekh Publishers, Jaipur, 2002; A.K. Roy's *History of the Jaipur City*, Manohar, New Delhi, 1978.

26. Jai Singh was prominent in the group loyal to the Emperor. The anti-Farukhsiyar group rallied to the Sayyid brothers. An important member of the latter was Ajit Singh of Marwar, Emperor Farukhsiyar's father-in-law.
27. This title is used in a letter of July 1713 AD sent to Jai Singh II by Jagjiwan Das, the *Vakil* of Amber.
28. Among Sawai Jai Singh II's ministers was Rao Kripa Ram Pandya, who held a Mughal *mansab* rank, and contributed a large sum of money towards the building of the new city of Jaipur.
29. As a fellow-conspirator with Abhay Singh of Marwar, Marwar's minister Raghunath Bhandari, and the Emperor.
30. Tod, op. cit., Vol. II, p. 288.
31. Ibid., p. 291.

III

Maharaja Sawai Jai Singh and Jaipur

A Special Homage on his Third Birth Centenary
Compiled and Edited by Bhupendra Hooja for
Indian Book Chronicle in 1998

17

Humble Tribute to Maharaja Sawai Jai Singh

BHUPENDRA HOOJA

This is a humble effort to pay tribute to a remarkable man, who was born three centuries ago, a warrior prince belonging to the Kachhawaha clan of Rajputs who won acclaim not only as solder or statesman, but also as a scientist and scholar and a patron of arts. Known to history as Maharaja Sawai Jai Singh II (1688–1743), he was a remarkable man indeed, because in his lifetime, he managed to expand the boundaries of his fief and win for himself the title of a *Sawai* (or a quarter above a normal person). He also assumed the title of Maharaja and was recognized as such by the Mughal Durbar and his contemporaries. He was a remarkable man because of his varied interests in mathematics, astronomy, oriental learning as well as in town planning. He is also known for his patronage to scientists, scholars, poets, philosophers, writers and commentators, town planners as well as painters of repute and master craftsmen.

The country paid him tributes, when the 250th anniversary of the founding of the city of Jaipur was celebrated. Now, this year, we pay him homage on the third centenary of his birth. We, in the *IBC* (*Indian Book Chronicle*), join other citizens of Jaipur and our countrymen in paying our tributes by attempting to present a collection of notes and articles, and reviews of books etc., which cover the life and time of Maharaja Sawai Jai Singh II.

We open with an introductory piece by our Associate Editor, Rima Hooja, followed by extracts from an account written by none else but Lt. Col. James Tod (then Political Agent of the East India Company to the western Rajputana states) which he had communicated to the Marquis of Hastings (in 1814–15). Because of his other concerns, he was not able to enlarge upon the note or to develop its historical resources. However imperfect, he did not think it right to suppress this sketch. The extracts have been taken from Chapter 2 of the *Annals of Amber or Dhoondar*, which have been included in Volume 2 of the *Annals and Antiquities of Rajasthan* (Routedge & Kegan Paul Ltd., London, 1957 reprint). Though later-day historians have questioned the historical sources and some facts in Tod's account, it has its value as one of the first compilations or narrations recorded within 75 years of the death of Maharaja Sawai Jai Singh II.

Our second tribute is in the words of Jawaharlal Nehru [XV-Ranjeet Singh and Jai Singh in Chapter Six entitled 'New Problems' in *The Discovery of India* (originally published by Maridian Books Ltd., London)]. In this part of the book, Jawaharlal Nehru had briefly mentioned the personalities and contributions to Indian history of Maharaja Ranjeet Singh of Punjab and Sawai Jai Singh II of Rajputana. (This has been reproduced in Rima Hooja's piece.)

For our third tribute, we turn to the well-known literateur and art lover, Dr Mulk Raj Anand, who paid the handsome personal homage to Maharaja Sawai Jai Singh II in a profusely illustrated special number of *MARG* magazine on the occasion of the 250th celebration of the founding of Jaipur city. We have taken the liberty of quoting some extracts from what Dr Anand had to say on that occasion in his *Dedicatory Epistle* addressed to Jai Singh. In fact, we have borrowed some other ideas or articles from that special number to bring them back to the memory of our contemporary generation.

There have been a variety of books in Hindi and English about the life and times of Maharaja Sawai Jai Singh II or about his contemporary Mughal emperors. Some of these have been introduced and briefly commented upon by two local scholars, Dr R.N. Choudhury and Ms Mohita Kapoor, each representing a distinct age-group.

The first book in the list is a 1939–40 work by Sir Jadunath Sarkar, brought out by Orient Longman in 1983 entitled *A History of Jaipur*. The manuscript was edited by another contemporary scholar, Raghubir Singhji of Sitamau. Most readers must be familiar with the seminal works by Sarkar on Aurangzeb and other later-day Mughals, which also throw light on the happenings in Rajputana of those days. While Dr V.S. Bhatnagar has written a history book (1972) in English and Hindi about the Maharaja and his times, Dr Ashim Kumar Roy has focused his study on the city of Jaipur. Some years ago, the Rajasthan

History Congress also brought out a short volume on the *Cultural Heritage of Jaipur*, edited by Dr J.N. Asopa (1979), which is a compilation of essays covering various aspects of Jai Singh's contributions in various fields of human endeavour and enterprise.

No account of Maharaja Sawai Jai Singh would be complete without a proper detailed mention of his contributions in the fields of mathematics and astronomy. We cover this through a special article by Dr Virendra Narain Sharma, Department of Physics and Astronomy, University of Wisconsin (USA).

We have also managed to collect some other notes and articles of interest. A.K. Roy has offered a brief review of the well-known book by G.R. Kaye, *A Guide to the Old Observatories etc.*, which has been recently reprinted. We are reproducing G.N. Bahura's introduction to the 'Pothikhana' of Jaipur, specially the collections prompted by or in the time of Maharaja Sawai Jai Singh.

There are other contributions by a few local scholars which cover the religious heritage of Jaipur, contributions of Jaipur to Sanskrit literature (specially during the time of Maharaja Sawai Jai Singh), about the Jain community of Amber, Sanganer and Jaipur, contribution of Jaipur towards the development of Persian and Urdu etc. These articles or abstracts have been taken from various compilations and academic journals and brought up-to-date by the concerned writers.

Naturally, there are also some contributions about town planning and the layout as well as the environment of Jaipur city.

We could go on and on, but there is the constraint of time or space, energy and resources. We are quite aware of the gaps – or the topics which have not been touched upon. In a small journal like the IBC, it is not possible to cover all aspects of that colourful personality and the variety of contributions by his contemporaries in Rajputana or elsewhere.

It goes without saying that in the lifetime of Sawai Jai Singh, his favourite city, the new capital of his new-found kingdom, had become an important centre of the search for and study of our ancient cultural roots, old values and traditions. There was a quest for the latest scientific knowledge as well. And, a revival of interest in religious or philosophical and reformist debates and discussions, both oral and in the form of original and translated literature. There was an enrichment of art forms, liberal interaction and exchange of cultures. Perhaps the princely scholar was keen also to assume the mantle of a revivalist 'national' leader among his contemporaries. He tried to assume the mantle of that role in spite of his other human failings. He also brought his princely state close to the portals of modern scientific knowledge, and of town planning.

While remembering him, we should also bear in mind the immense changes which have taken place in the state of Jaipur or in north India or in the sub-continent and the world at large. Since those times, Jaipur and the outside world have changed beyond recognition. Yet there are some human values or personal virtues which we can emulate with profit. At least, we can try and restore the environmental balance and the aesthetic beauty of the layout of Jaipur near to his basic dream and vision. And, we can give due regard or place of importance to the study and research of Vedic, Sanskrit and Oriental learning, as much as to the study of mathematics, astronomy and other fields of modern science. We can also initiate a fresh process of reawakening or cultural renaissance amongst the youth.

18

A Man for Most Seasons

Sawai Jai Singh II of Amber/Jaipur

RIMA HOOJA

Sawai Jai Singh II belonged to the ancient Kachhawaha family of Amber, the origin and early history of which are shrouded in obscurity, despite a number of genealogical tables of considerable antiquity, bardic accounts and few epigraphic records. He was the eldest son of Raja Bishan Singh (Vishnu Singh). Born on *Margashirsha Vadi 6, Samvat 1742* (November 3, 1688 AD), he formally assumed the *gaddi* of Amber on *Phagun Vadi 1, Samvat 1756* (January 1700) upon the premature death of his father. His title then – merely, Raja Jai Singh.

From this modest beginning, the young prince of Amber became "...a statesman, legislator and a man of science", whose character "...is worthy of an ample delineation" to use the words of Lt. Col. James Tod (*Annals and Antiquities of Rajasthan*, Vol. II, pp. 288–89); a man renowned for his learning and for founding and planning the city of Jaipur, and a man invested by the Mughal emperor with the title of *Sawai*, meaning 'one-and-a-quarter', and implying that Jai Singh was slightly better than his peers!

Nehru's Tribute

In his book, *The Discovery of India*, Jawaharlal Nehru wrote the following about Sawai Jai Singh: "He lived during the period of disruption following Aurangzeb's death. He was clever and opportunist enough to survive the many shocks and changes that followed each other in quick succession. He acknowledged the suzerainty of the Delhi Emperor. When he found that the advancing Marathas were too strong to be checked, he came to terms with them on behalf of the Emperor. But it is not his political or military career that interests me. He was a brave warrior and an accomplished diplomat, but he was something more than this. He was a mathematician and an astronomer, a scientist and a town planner and he was interested in the study of history" (p. 260).

Soon after his ascension, the 11-year young *Raja* was given orders to join duty in the Deccan. Posted under Prince Bedar Bakhat, Jai Singh showed his military prowess against the Marathas at Khelna, Khandesh, Malwa, Burhanpur etc., and his *zat* and *jagirs* were gradually raised by the Mughal Emperor Aurangzeb. In 1705, the young *Raja* was appointed Deputy Governor of Malwa. He looked after the defence and law and order situation in the province, assisted the revenue authorities in realizing government dues, arranged for the safe transit of treasures and ammunition to the Deccan, and performed other duties required of a Deputy Governor.

Very soon, however, came the Mughal war-of-succession, following the death of Aurangzeb. Jai Singh supported, and then deserted on the battlefield, what turned out to be the losing side. For this opposition, as Tod noted, "Amber was sequestrated, and an imperial governor sent to take possession; but Jey Sing entered his estates, sword in hand, drove out the King's garrisons, and formed a league with Ajit Sing of Marwar for their mutual preservation" (p. 288).

Thirty Eventful Years

The joint Rajput resistance to Bahadur Shah, cautious overtures to the new and frequently changing emperors at Delhi, and misunderstandings among the Rajput states that occurred during the years that followed, have been amply documented by historians and need not be recounted.

What is relevant is that by 1713, the twenty-five-year-old Jai Singh of Amber had been granted the title of *Sawai* and was referred to in official Mughal records as Mirza Raja Sawai Jai Singh (*Letter from Jagjiwandas Wakil of Amber to Jai Singh of Shravana Vadi 1, Smavat 1770*). He held various high offices such as Governor of Malwa (thrice) and Agra, and led the imperial campaigns against the Marathas, Jats and others. In an age of secret pacts, battles and Mughal-Maratha-Rajput problems, Jai Singh managed to hold his own diplomatically and politically, even securing an agreement between the Mughal emperor and the Maratha Peshwa. Although Jai Singh did not render any aid to the Mughal emperor at the time of Nadir Shah's invasion, he retained his high position at the Delhi court and continued to influence the Mughal government's attitude towards various political problems.

By 1743 AD, the last year of his life, Sawai Jai Singh must have found "...the situation in Rajputana peaceful... Abhai Singh had been subdued; his own relations with Mewar and Kotah were friendly... Bikaner was grateful to him for his recent help;"... (as recounted by V.S. Bhatnagar, pp. 266–67).

A Machiavelli of His Age: An Extraordinary Man

However, it is not for his diplomacy or political and military skills alone that Sawai Jai Singh is primarily remembered; nor even only for the fact that he founded a city (Jaipur). In fact, as Tod recorded, "It would be tedious to pursue this celebrated Rajpoot through his desultory military career during the forty-four years he occupied the *gaddi* of Amber. Although Jey Sing mixed in all the troubles and warfare of this long period of anarchy, when the throne of Timoor was rapidly crumbling into dust, his reputation as a soldier would never have handed down his name with honour to posterity; on the contrary, his courage had none of the fire which is requisite to make a Rajpoot hero; though his talents for civil government and court intrigue, in which he was the Machiavelli of his day, were at that period far more notable auxiliaries" (p. 288).

What makes Sawai Jai Singh remarkable is that his quest for learning, his interest in mathematics, astronomy, town planning, his construction of observatories, and the founding of Jaipur etc. were carried on in "the midst of perpetual wars and court intrigues". In the words of Tod, "When we consider that Jey Sing carried on his favourite pursuits in the midst of perpetual wars and court intrigues, from whose debasing influence he escaped not untainted; when amidst revolution, the destruction of the empire, and the meteoric rise of the Mahrattas, he not only steered through the dangers, but elevated Amber above all the principalities around, we must admit that he was an extraordinary man" (p. 291).

A Remarkable Man...Town Planner... Scientist...

To quote again from Nehru's *Discovery of India*:

- "Jai Singh built big observatories at Jaipur, Delhi, Ujjain, Benares and Mathura. Learning through Portuguese missionaries of the progress of astronomy in Portugal, he sent his own men, with one of the missionaries, to the court of the Portuguese King Emmanuel. Emmanuel sent his envoy, Xavier De Silva, with De la Hire's tables to Jai Singh. On comparing these with his own tables, Jai Singh came to the conclusion that the Portuguese tables were less exact and had several errors. He attributed these to the 'inferior diameters' of the instruments used.

- "Jai Singh was of course fully acquainted with Indian mathematics; he had studied the old Greek treatises and also knew of recent European developments in mathematics. He had some of the Greek books (*Euclid*, etc.) as well as European works on plane and spherical trigonometry and the construction and use of logarithms translated into Sanskrit. He also had Arabic books on astronomy translated.
- "He founded the city of Jaipur. Interested in town planning, he collected the plans of many European cities of the time and then drew up his own plan. Many of these plans of the old European cities of the time are preserved in the Jaipur museum. The city of Jaipur was so well and wisely planned that it is still considered a model of town planning.
- "Jai Singh did all this and much more in the course of a comparatively brief life and in the midst of perpetual wars and court intrigues, in which he was himself often involved. Nadir Shah's invasion took place just four years before Jai Singh's death.
- "Jai Singh would have been a remarkable man anywhere and at any time. The fact that he rose and functioned as a scientist in the typically feudal *milieu* of Rajputana and during one of the darkest periods of Indian history, when disruption and war and tumults filled the scene, is very significant. It shows that the spirit of scientific inquiry was not dead in India and that there was some ferment at work which might have yielded rich results if only an opportunity had been given to it to fructify. Jai Singh was no anachronism of solitary thinker in an unfriendly and uncomprehending environment. He was a product of his age and he collected a number of scientific workers to work with him. Out of these he sent some in the embassy to Portugal, and social custom or taboo did not deter him from doing so. It seems probable that there was plenty of good material for scientific work in the country, both theoretical and technical, if only it was given a chance to function when the troubles and disorders were over,

there was no encouragement of scientific work by those in authority" (pp. 260–61).

A Brilliant Career in Diverse Fields

For a proper estimate of Sawai Jai Singh of Amber/Jaipur, we have to objectively assess both his merits as well as demerits – and he appears to have had both, judging by existing records! Contemporary source material abounds in the form of *Kharitas* or letters to and from other Rajput rulers, the Mughals and the Marathas, along with the *Akhbarat*, *Wakil*, reports, *Parwanahs*, *Azadashts*, *Farmans*, *Iqrarnamas* *Hasb-ul-hukms*, *Mahzarnamas*, *Siaha Hazur*, *Nishans Dastur Komwar*, *Khatut Ahlkaran*, Maratha works and Mughal court records etc.

Later or more recent writings on Sawai Jai Singh II include works by G.H. Ojha, Suryamal Mishran, Kaviraj Shyamaldas and James Tod, as well as by Jadu Nath Sarkar, Irvine, Sardesai and V.S. Bhatnagar though detailed works have remained few in number.

Taken together, all these suggest that Jai Singh enjoyed a brilliant career, excelling in many diverse fields such as mathematics and politics. He was regarded as one of the wisest men of his times. Dr V.S. Bhatnagar is of the opinion (in his book *The Life and Times of Sawai Jai Singh*) that had Sawai Jai Singh survived longer, he might have rightly assessed the extent of danger posed by the growing power of the British (as he did with regard to the Marathas), and would have tried to take suitable measures to counter this new threat. In fact, for about three decades, Jai Singh was directly or indirectly concerned with all the important happenings over much of India.

His Faults

That does not imply, however, that this ruler of Amber/Jaipur was without faults. He was unscrupulous in his actions when the need arose, and was directly responsible for the deposition of Rao Budh Singh of Bundi, and the deaths of his brother and nephew. Some historians believe that he had hand in the murder of Ajit Singh of Jodhpur/Marwar, and many other intrigues. Added to that is the episode of his desertion on the battlefield of Dholpur, his fondness for liquor – when no state business could be discussed, and his temporary acquiescence to the imperial demand for Amber (which the Mughals renamed Mominabad).

His Contributions

Despite his shortcomings, however, the scales tilt in Jai Singh's favour. He made Amber one of the largest states (*albeit* a tributary state) in the country, with an area exceeding 20,000 square miles. His kingdom enjoyed peace, prosperity and security. The administration was well-organized and functioned efficiently. Literature, arts and various kinds of cultural institutions flourished under Sawai Jai Singh's patronage and active encouragement. To him goes the credit for the founding of the city of Jaipur, and for the construction of several *caravan serais* etc. for travellers, both within his domains as well as in other provinces of the Mughal empire. He had imbibed the heroic tales of the Rajputs sufficiently to think in terms of the honour and good of his *watan* Amber, even if it meant going against his paramount power, as he did when he broke away from the Mughal emperor, Bahadur Shah I's camp, and along with Mewar and Marwar, reasserted Rajput strength in Rajputana to free their occupied homelands.

In fact, Jai Singh continued to strive for stability and peace in the traumatic period he was living through, in spite of heavy odds. He had even suggested to the Marathas the idea of sustaining the empire with the Mughal emperor as the nominal head – an idea which apparently appealed to Baji Rao Peshwa towards the end of his career – and an idea which might have changed the entire history of the sub-continent – but an idea which became utopian in the aftermath of Nadir Shah's invasion, and the defeat he inflicted on the dying Mughal empire.

Perhaps if the political and administrative matters of the chaotic times Sawai Jai Singh lived through had been less time-consuming, he could have contributed much more to the fields of science and learning. Nonetheless, what he was able to accomplish in the midst of constant strife, political machinations, and the effects of the dying and disintegrating Mughal empire, entitles him to a place among the remarkable figures of Indian history. In the words of Bhatnagar, Sawai Jai Singh II of Amber/Jaipur "...had in him the rare combination of a scholar and statesman, administrator and legislator, diplomat and soldier". No mean achievements these!

19

Annals of an Extraordinary Man

JAMES TOD

"Jey II, better known by the title of Sowae Jey Sing, in contradistinction to the first prince of this name, entitled the 'Mirza Raja' succeeded in S. 1755 (AD 1699), in the forty-fourth year of Arungzeb's reign, and within six years of that monarch's death. He served with distinction in the Dekhan, and in the war of succession, attached himself to the prince Bedar Bukt, son of Azim Shah, declared successor of Arungzeb; and with these he fought the battle of Dholpur, which ended in their death and the elevation of Shah Alum Bahadoor Shah. For this opposition Amber was sequestrated, and an imperial governor sent to take possession; but Jey Sing entered his estate, sword in hand, drove out the king's garrisons, and formed a league with Ajit Sing of Marwar for their mutual preservation.

"It would be tedious to pursue this celebrated Rajpoot through his desultory military career during the forty-four years he occupied the *gadi* of Amber; enough is already known of it from its combination with the *Annals of Mewar and Boondi*, of which house he was the implacable foe. Although Jey Sing mixed in all the troubles and warfare of this long period of anarchy, when the throne of Timoor was rapidly crumbling into dust, his reputation as a soldier would never have handed down his name with honour to posterity; on the contrary, his courage had none of the fire which is requisite to make a Rajpoot hero; though his talents for civil government and court intrigue, in which he was the Machiavelli of his day, were at that period far more notable auxiliaries".

"As a statesman, legislator, and man of science, the character of Sowae Jey Sing is worthy of an ample delineation, which would correct

These extensive extracts have been 'taken from the *Annals of Amber* in Vol. 2 of the *Annals and Antiquities of Rajasthan* by Lt. Col. James Tod.

our opinion of the genius and capacity of the princes of Rajpootana, of whom we are apt to form too low an estimate..."

(Here, Tod has mentioned in footnotes two works *Calpadrooma* and *Ek she noh goon Jey Sing ca.* – Eds.)

"He was the founder of the new capital, named after his Jeipoor or Jeinuggur, which became the seat of science and art, and eclipsed the more ancient Amber, with which the fortifications of the modern city unite, although the extremity of the one is six miles from the other. Jeipoor is the only city in India built upon a regular plan, with streets bisecting each other at right angles. The merit of the design and execution is assigned to Vedyadhar, a native of Bengal, one of the most eminent coadjutors of the prince in all his scientific pursuits, both astronomical and historical.

"Almost all the Rajpoot princes have a smattering of astronomy, or rather of its spurious relation, astrology; but Jey Sing went deep, not only into the theory, but the practice of the science, and was so esteemed for his knowledge, that he was entrusted by the emperor Mahomed Shah with the reformation of the calendar. He had erected observatories with instruments of his own invention at Dehli, Jeipoor, Oojein, Benaras, and Mathura, upon a scale of Asiatic grandeur; and their results were so correct as to astonish the most learned. He had previously used such instruments as those of Ulug Beg (the royal astronomer of Samarcand), which failed to answer his expectations. From the observations of seven years at the various observatories, he constructed a set of tables.

"While thus engaged, he learned through a Portuguese missionary, Padre Manuel, the progress which his favourite pursuit was making in Portugal, and he sent 'several skilful persons along with him' to the court of Emanuel. (*It would be worth ascertaining whether the archives of Lisbon refer to this circumstance – J.T.*)

"The king of Portugal dispatched Xavier de Silva, who communicated to the Rajpoot prince the tables of De la Hire. (*Second edition, published in AD 1702, Jey Sing finished his in AD 1728. – J.T.*)

"On examining and comparing the calculations of these tables (says the Rajpoot prince) with actual observation, it appeared there was an error in the former, in assigning the moon's place, of half a degree; although the error in the other planets was not so great, yet the times of solar and lunar eclipses he found to come out later or earlier than the truth by the fourth part of a *ghurry, or fifteen puls* (six minutes of time)".

(*Jey Sing always speaks of himself in the third person.*) In like manner, as he found fault with the instruments of brass used by the Toorki astronomer, and which he conjectures must have been such as were used by Hipparchus and Ptolemy, so he attributes the inaccuracies of De la Hire's tables to instruments of 'inferior diameters'.

"The Rajpoot prince might justly boast of his instruments. With that at Delhi, he in AD 1729, determined the obliquity of the ecliptic to be 23E 28'; within 28" of what is was determined to be, the year following by Godin. His general accuracy was further put to the test in AD 1793 by our scientific countryman, Dr W. Hunter who compared a series of observations on the latitude of Oojein with that established by the Rajpoot prince. The difference was 24"; and Dr Hunter does not depend on his own observations within 15". Jey Singh made the latitude 23" 10' N, Dr Hunter, 23" 10' 24" N.

"From the results of his varied observations, Jey Sing drew up a set of tables, which he entitled *Zeij Mahomedshahi*, dedicated to that monarch; by these all astronomical computations are yet made, and almanacks constructed...

"Besides the construction of these objects of science, he erected, at his own expense, *caravan serais* for the free use of travellers in many of the provinces. How far vanity may have mingled with benevolence in this act (by no means uncommon in India), it were uncharitable to inquire: for the Hindu not only prays for all those 'who travel by land or by water', but aids the traveller by *serais* or inns, and wells dug at his own expense, and in most capitals and cities, under the ancient princes, there were public charities for necessitous travellers, at which they had their meals, and then passed on.

"When we consider that Jey Sing carried on his favourite pursuits in the midst of perpetual wars and court intrigues, from whose debasing influence he escaped not untainted; when amidst revolution, the destruction of the empire, and the meteoric rise of the Mahrattas, he not only steered through the dangers, but elevated Amber above all the principalities around, we must admit that he was an extraordinary man. Aware of the approaching downfall of the Mogul empire, and determined to aggrandize Amber from the wreck, he was, nevertheless, not unfaithful to his lord-paramount; for, on the conspiracy which deprived Ferochser of empire and of life, Jey Sing was one of the few princes who retained their fidelity, and would have stood by him to the last, if he had possessed a particle of the valour which belonged to descendants of Timoor.

"Enough has been said of his public life, in that portion of the *Annals of Mewar* with which he was so closely connected, both by political and family ties. The Syeds, who succeeded to power on the murder of their sovereign Ferochser, were too wise to raise enemies unnecessarily; and Jey Sing, when he left the unhappy monarch to his fate, retired to his hereditary dominions, devoting himself to his favourite pursuits, astronomy and history. He appears to have enjoyed three years of uninterrupted quiet, taking no part in the struggles, which terminated, in AD 1721, with Mahomed Shah's defeat of his rivals, and the destruction of the Syeds. At this period, Jey Sing was called from his philosophical pursuits, and appointed the king's lieutenant for the provinces of Agra and Malwa in succession: and it was during this interval of comparative repose, that he erected those monuments which irradiate this dark epoch of the history of India.

[*The Raja says he finished his tables in AD 1728, and that he had occupied himself seven years previously in the necessary observations; in fact, the first quiet years of Mahomed Shah's reign, or indeed that India had known for centuries. – J.T.*]

"Nor was he blind to the interest of his nation or the honour of Amber, and his important office was made subservient to obtaining the repeal of that disgraceful edict, the *jezeya*, and authority to repress the infant power of the Jats, long a thorn in the side of Amber ...in AD 1732, the Raja, once more lieutenant for Malwa, saw that it was in vain to attempt to check the Mahratta invasion, or to prevent the partition of the empire, he deemed himself justified in consulting the welfare of his own house. We know not what terms Jey Sing entered into with the Mahratta leader, Bajirow, who, by his influence was appointed Soobadar of Malwa; we may, however, imagine it was from some more powerful stimulant than the native historian of this period assigns, namely, 'a similarity of religion'. By this conduct, Jey Sing is said emphatically, by his own countrymen, to have given the key of Hindusthan to the Southron. The influence his character obtained, however, with the Mahrattas was even useful to his sovereign, for by it he retarded their excesses, which at length reached the capital. In a few years more (AD 1739), Nadir Shah's invasion took place, and the Rajpoots, wisely alive to their own interests, remained aloof from a cause which neither valour nor wisdom could longer serve. They respected the emperor, but the system of government had long alienated these gallant supporters of the throne. We may exemplify the trials to which Rajpoot fidelity was exposed by one of 'the hundred and nine deeds of Jey Sing', which will at the same time serve further to illustrate the position, that half the political and moral evils which have vexed the royal houses of Rajpootana, take their rise from polygamy...

[Col. Tod then proceeds to give the background and details of the conflict of personalities and interests between Jey Singh and his half-brother Beejay Sing, which ended with the conspiracy and the doubtful manner of the latter's elimination by imprisonment. We need not dwell upon such details. – Ed.]

"The Cuchwaha state, as well as its capital, owes everything to Jey Sing: before his time, it had little political weight beyond that which it acquired from the personal character of its princes, and their estimation at the Mogul court. Yet, notwithstanding the intimate connection which existed between the Amber Rajas and the imperial family, from Baber to Arungzeb, their patrimonial estates had been very little enlarged since Pujoon, the contemporary of the last Rajpoot emperor of Delhi. Nor was it till the troubles which ensued on the demise of Arungzeb, when the empire was eventually partitioned, that Amber was entitled to the name of a *raj*. During those troubles, Jey Sing's power as the king's lieutenant in Agra, which embraced his hereditary domains, gave him ample opportunity to enlarge and consolidate his territory. The manner in which he possessed himself of the independent districts of Deoti and Rajore, affords an additional insight into the national character, and that of this prince.

"At the accession of Jey Sing, the *raj* of Amber consisted only of the three *pergunnas* or districts of Amber, Deosah and Bussao; the western tracts had been sequestrated, and added to the royal domains attached to Ajmer. The Shekhavati confederation was superior to, and independent of the parent state, whose boundaries were as follows: The royal *t'hhana* (garrison) of Chatsoo, to the south; those of Sambhur to the west, and Hastinah to the north-west; while to the east, Deosah and Bussao formed its frontier. The *kotribunds*, as they denominate the twelve great feudalities, possessed but very slender domains, and were held cheap by the great vassals of Mewar, of whom the Saloombra chief was esteemed, even by the first Peshwa, as the equal of the prince of the Chuchwahas.

[Next Col. Tod narrates Jey Sing's campaign against the Birgoojar chief of Deoti. It is a moving account of intrigue and valour which ended with the defeat of the Birgoojar and the merger of Deoti and Rajore to the Maharaja's domain. – Ed.]

[*Rajore is esteemed a place of great antiquity, and the chief seat of the Birgoojur tribe for ages, a tribe mentioned with high respect in the works of the bard Chund, and celebrated in the wars of Prithiraj. I sent a party to Rajore in 1813. – J.T.]*

"...Amongst the foibles of Jey Sing's character was his partiality to 'strong drink'. What this beverage was, whether the juice of the *madhu* (mead), or the essence (*arac*) of rice, the traditional chronicles of Amber do not declare, though they mention frequent appeals from Jey Sing drunk, to Jey Sing sober;...

"In spite of his many defects, Jey Sing's name is destined to descent to posterity as one of the most remarkable men of his age and nation.

"Until Jey Sing's time, the palace of Amber, built by the great Raj Maun, inferior to many private houses in the new city, was the chief royal residence. The Mirza Raja made several additions to it, but Sowae Jey Singh which has made the residence of the Cuchwaha princes as celebrated as those of Boondi or Oodipoor, or, to borrow a more appropriate comparison, the Kremlin at Moscow...

"It was in S. 1784 (AD 1728) that he laid the foundation of Jeipoor. Raja Mull was the *mosaheb*, Kirparam the stationary *vakeel* at Delhi, and Boodh Singh Khombani, with the *oordoo*, or royal camp, in the Dekhan: all eminent men. The position he chose for the new capital enabled him to connect it with the ancient castle of Amber, situated upon a peak at the apex of the re-entering angle of the range called *Khalikho*; a strong circumvallation enclosed the gorge of the mountain, and was carried over the crest of the hills on either side, to unite with the castle, whilst all the adjoining passes were strongly fortified.

"The sumptuary laws which he endeavoured to establish throughout Rajputana for the regulation of marriages, in order to check those lavish expenses that led to infanticide and *satis*, will be again called forth when the time is ripe for the abolition of all such unhallowed acts. For this end, search should be made for the historical legends called the 'hundred and nine acts', in the archives of Jeipoor ...

[*By such researches we should in all probability recover those sketches of ancient history of the various dynasties of Rajpootana, which he is said to have collected with great pains and labour, and the genealogies of the old races, under the titles of* 'Rajavali' *and* 'Raj Taringinl': *besides, the astronomical works, either original or translations, such as were collected by Jey Sing, could be a real gift to science. – J.T.*]

"Like all Hindus, he was tolerant; and a Brahmin, a Mahomedan, or a Jain, were alike certain of patronage. The Jains enjoyed his peculiar estimation, from the superiority of their knowledge, and he is said to have been thoroughly conversant both in their doctrines and their histories. Vidhyadhur, one of his chief coadjutors in his astronomical pursuits, and whose genius planned the city of Jeipoor, was a Jain, and claimed spiritual descent from the celebrated Hemacharya, of Nehrvalla, minister and spiritual guide of his namesake, the great Sidraj Jey Singh". [*He ruled from S.1150 to S.1201, AD 1094–1145. – J.T.*]

"Amongst the vanities of the founder of Amber, it is said that he intended to get up the ceremony of the *aswameda yuga*, or 'sacrifice of the horse,' a rite which his research into the traditions of his nation must have informed him had entailed destruction on all who had attempted it, from the days of Janmeja the Pandu, to Jeichund, the last Rajpoot monarch of Canouj. It was a virtual assumption of universal supremacy; and although, perhaps in virtue of his office, as the satrap of Dehli, the horse dedicated to the sun might have wandered unmolested on the banks of the Ganges, he would most assuredly have found his way into a Rathore stable had he roamed in the direction of the desert; or at the risk both of *jeva* and *gadi* (life and throne), the Hara would have seized him, had he fancied the pastures of the Chumbul. He erected a sacrificial hall of much beauty and splendour, whose columns and ceilings were covered with plates of silver; nor is it improbable that the steed, emblematic of *Surya*, may have been led round the hall, and afterwards sacrificed to the solar divinity. The *Yugsala* of Jey Sing, one of the great ornaments of the city, was, however, stripped of its rich decoration by his profligate descendant, the late Juggut Sing". ...

[*In Vol. 1, p. 63, Tod has given a description of the rite of Aswamedha. – Eds.*]

20

An Epistle of Dedication

MULK RAJ ANAND

In his homage of Jaipur and its builder prince, Sawai Jai Singh II, Dr Mulk Raj Anand, the then Editor of Marg, Bombay, chose to adopt the role of a court poet or chronicler to read out his words of praise in a formal address to the ruler, in what he has called a Dedicatory Epistle. Because of sentiments expressed therein and the fervour of feelings and expressions enriched by the imagination of a mature writer, we are presenting some random selections from the tribute as "the humble devotee" offered it to the Maharaja. – Ed.

"Master-builder" Maharaja Sawai Jai Singh *Wazir-i-Mughal Shahi, Rajinder Rajdhiraj, Sar-Amad-i-Rajgan-i-Hindustan, Raj-Rajeshwar, Shri Rajadhiraj*, commander of one hundred thousand horses, grazer of the stars of their courses and comprehender of cosmos, dreamer-planner of Jaipur, with its kingdom of thousand blandishments, vanquishers of enemies, adventurer into the kingdom of the mind, lover of beautiful women, subtle diplomat trained in the doctrines of Kautilya's *Arthashastra*, Immortal Man – You who carved his own destiny!

"I address this epistle dedicatory to you, who encompassed space and time, bringing prosperity to your kingdom, justice to the folk, you who made a dream city come alive.

"Homage to you that your genius for action made you subdue the earth around you for nearly half a century, in a time of crisis, disruption and despair, when the Mughal King of Kings, Aurangzeb, had left a heritage of bitterness and ruin at Delhi, and when the righteous enemies of fanaticism and misrule had themselves turned into demons of hate, looters of the vast landscape, marauders of the innocents, killers of decency, despoilers of woman's honour, each concerned with his own gain.

"Praise be to you, for discerning the smallest particles of heaven and earth, for making your compass the measure of the heavens, for establishing five *Jantar Mantars* in five different cities for comparison and contrast of observations, so that the most infinitesimal difference in the position of planets be revealed and the science of astronomy be built from the remaining hypotheses left in our heritage by Aryabhata and other ancients.

"O Prince of the village capital of Amber! You who sought to understand the complexity of the universe to dissolve your own ignorance; who loved the least of men and gave them shelter; who answered the question of a native child and filled her eyes with the wonder and the mystery of life; who never caged a bird; who grew flowers in the many gardens of the desert; who built a state which has lasted till our time! O Prince! How is one to sing your praise in our day – more restless and troubled than your own?

"Perhaps, the recounting of the events in your life will by itself be praise enough. They say that you were just thirteen when you were placed on the *gaddi* of Amber. And legend has it that one of the first obligations imposed on you was to go and pay respect to the paramount power, the tyrannical Emperor Aurangzeb.

"I can see you, in the shadow of the Diwan Hall in Amber, constructed by Mirza Raja Jai Singh, the general of the Great Mughal Shah Jahan, with your ministers and your mother, all trying to instruct you on how to offer salutations to the King of Kings.

"One of your nobles tells you how frightening is Emperor's stare. The second one says that the temper of the sword-bearer of Islam is like that of a toothless old lion who cannot masticate but still wants to devour. The third counsellor advises you to bow and salaam with the right hand cupped and answer such questions as the Shahenshah may ask.

"Your own comment on hearing all this advice foreshadows your uncommon common sense. You said: "What am I to say if the Emperor doesn't ask me any questions at all? Or does not even look at me? Or, insults me?" Your wise mother told you: "Speak forth what comes first to your lips, from your heart, freely". Thus prepared you went to Delhi.

"At the Durbar, when everyone was bowing and scraping in the Diwan-i-Khas at the Red Fort, you suddenly heard the *chobdars* announce the arrival of the Emperor. 'The Shadow of God on Earth, the King of Kings, Protector of the Universe, Padshah Aurangzeb, Alamgir – Conqueror of the whole world!' Then, there was not a whisper.

"The Emperor, as he glanced around from the height of his throne, noticed you being held forward for presentation by your attendant. The Grand Vizier whispered to the Emperor: 'Raja Jai Singh of Amber'.

"Aurangzeb jumped down from his high throne, his eyes streaked red, and seizing you with both hands, shook you and said: 'Your father and grandfather have proved to be traitors to me! They have done much harm to the Empire! What do you expect from me?'

"You retained your imperturbable calm and answered in a low voice: 'Protector of the Universe! At marriage, a man takes hold of only one hand of the bride and promises to look after her for life. The Emperor has taken hold of me with both his hands. What more can I ask?'

"Aurangzeb's face relaxed into a cynical smile. The anger vanished. And, beckoning you to a seat near the throne, he said: 'To be sure, you are wiser than your ancestor, Mirza Jai Singh. I give you the title Sawai. You will thus remain superior to all your contemporaries'.

"This confrontation of challenge was only the first of the many of your crowded life. The sycophants, the nobles, the generals and the courtiers did not like the favour shown to you, when the Emperor put you in command, at the young age of fourteen, of a regiment poised to attack the Fort of Vishalgarh, where the Marathas were entrenched. The hillside was similar in contours to Amber, where you had fought many a mock battle as a boy. You pretended to make a direct assault. And then you stole away in the half light of the dawn, by a short cut, far away from the main gateway. The fort lay at your feet. And you were in a position to use the artillery against the defenders. The Marathas submitted.

"This further endeared you to Aurangzeb. But you were brave enough to indicate to His Imperial Majesty, that, while you were a loyal soldier of the Empire, you shared with other Hindus of the realm, the feeling against *jizia*, the poll tax which the Emperor was collecting from every born-Hindu.

"And as it got known that you shared with the Marathas this indignation against injustice, Maharaja Sahu, the chief of the rebels, came to meet you and stayed as your guest, sharing with you his love of learning and his concern for truth. Rumours of these confabulations reached the court. And, the next time you went to the Durbar, there was a frown on the old Emperor's face. So, when Aurangzeb destroyed the shrine of Vishwanath at Varanasi, you remained silently aloof and refused to appear at court.

"Later, the Emperor threatened to the destroy the shrine of Govindji at Mathura. You sped to the holy city, brought the idol away and installed it at Amber. And you let it be known to the oppressor that you would not give up your faith, even though you had been made 'Sawai' of the Mughal Empire.

"You owed to Maharaja Sahu the inspiration to go deep into the books of your inheritance. The first of the classics which Pandit Jagan Nath taught you, when he was sent by Maharaja Sahu to live in Amber as your Guru, was Kautilya's *Arthashastra*. This must have been very useful to you as a guide in the internecine struggle for the throne of Delhi, soon after the death of Aurangzeb in AD 1707. You conducted your relations with the contending princes and sustained yourself on the principle of give and take. Whoever promised to accept your suzerainty over Amber unquestioned, and whoever honoured your faith had your allegiance.

[Here, Dr Anand briefly referred to the contest for Mughal throne between Prince Bedar Bakht, Jai Singh's companion in arms in the Deccan, and the other contender his cousin Bahadur Shah; the latter's incursions into the land of the Rajputs to subdue the Rathore Raja, Ajit Singh of Marwar, and the temporary annexation of Jai Singh's Amber, which was renamed Islamabad and placed under the charge of Jai Singh's younger brother, Bijay Singh.]

But, in the words of the chronicler:

"...it was not long before the confederacy of Rajput Rajas, inspired by you, ejected the imperial forces from the occupied territories. In AD 1710, Bahadur Shah was forced to make peace with the Rajputs. ...(However)...still drunk with power and dissolute, Bahadur Shah died two years later.

"And you witnessed a series of fratricidal wars for the next twenty years... [The atmosphere in and around the Mughal court was one of greed, corruption, power-seeking and intrigues. It took Emperor Muhammad Shah some time to see through the role of the king-maker 'uncles', the Syed brothers, and to appreciate Jai Singh's wits and stratagems to salvage not only his own estates, but also the Mughal Durbar.]

"As soon as the incubus of the Syed brothers was lifted from the court of Delhi, Muhammad Shah called you to the court and presented you robes of honour, and clasped your hand in friendship. You complimented the Emperor by saying: 'In Rajasthan, the adage goes: To have friends you must be one'.

The measure of your influence on Muhammad Shah may be reckoned from the fact that you persuaded the Emperor to listen to you and abolish Aurangzeb's *jizia* or poll tax. And you were appointed Governor of Agra. New titles were showered on you by Emperor Muhammad Shah. You now became: *Sar-Amad-i-Rajgan-i-Hindustan, Raj-Rajeshwar, Maharaj Jai Singh Sawai.*

***

"During the period of mental exile forced on you by the internecine wars, you had put your faith in meditation. You had sought truth in the ancient books. You had gained the necessary detachment to remain calm, refusing to be divided in your mind...

"Strangely enough, it was the innocence of the naïve child in you that had started you on the quest for the secrets of the sphere, which you were to discover and elaborate, in a comprehensive manner, for the first time in our country, after the initiatives of Aryabhat, a thousand years before, had lapsed into insignificance and turned the science of stars into superstition.

"There is a story come down in your family and told in hush-hush whispers to the confidants about how you began your researches in astronomy.

"You had heard the shrieks from a palanquin, as you were emerging from Agra towards Sikri, on the way to Amber. Your retainers had brought the palanquin to your camp. The *purdahnashin* lady hiding behind the curtains of the palanquin had confessed that she, a maid of honour from the house of Syeds, was with child from a young prince and had been turned out by the lover not owning to own any off-spring of her.

"In your magnanimity and understanding of her predicament, you had brushed aside all scandal-mongers and brought the young woman to Amber.

"On that summer night, when you went to see the comforts of the young lady on the terrace of Amber Palace, you were captured by the poetry of the situation. The girl had taken off her veil and revealed a lovely sylph-like form, a solace for your future years to compensate you for the lacerations you had suffered. And then she had said, with the wonder of the child in her eyes: 'Look, Maharaj, the stars are hanging down like lanterns from the sky. I can almost touch them. But I do not know what these bright shining specks are. And how far are they? ...And are there other worlds more happy than our own, Maharaj?'

"And you smiled at her innocence. But you had realized that you did not know very much about the firmament than she did. And you recalled that you had always wondered what other worlds there were besides the planet earth in this vast universe? And, lacking any frame of reference, you had decided that night to find out whatever you could, wherever you could, however you could, the meaning, the significance and the situations of the stars in relation to the earth you stood upon, their relation to each other and to the sun, the moon, the rivers, the seas and the oceans.

"Centuries ago there had been the same naïve speculation about the cosmos and our ancient ancestors had uttered the hymn of creation in the *Rig Veda*: ...

'Non-being then existed not, nor being:

There was no air, nor heaven which is beyond it.

What motion was there? Where? By whom directed?

Was water there and fathomless abyss?...

This world-creation whence it has arisen?

Or whether it has been produced or not?

He who surveys it in the highest heaven,

He only knows it or even he does not know it...'

[Dr Anand then describes how Sawai Jai Singh sought the advice of his Guru, Jagan Nath and tried to read with him everything available in Sanskrit, which language had "profound projections on almost everything in the five thousand years of evolution of consciousness in Bharat." They also studied relevant books in Persian and Arabic. The tables of the 14th century astronomer and grandson of Timur the Lame, Ulugh Beg were also translated, and an emissary sent to Samarkand to study the construction of the observatory there. Dr Anand also referred to the '*Guru-Chela* relationship' between the ruler and Samrat Jagan Nath.]

***

"In your fourteen hour working days, in the Palace of Amber, you devoted the mornings and evenings to study and translate the world classics on astronomy. Thus were rendered Ptolmey's *Almagast*, De La

Hire's *Tabulae Astronomica*, Euclid's *Elements* and Falmsteed's historic treatise on astroboles. Your own prism became a prism of the cosmos...

"...We know that you made Samrat Jagan Nath, the man of knowledge, the first hereditary preceptor of breather of the *Gayatri Mantra* into your ears, until you learnt to sing and dance before the image of Govindji, helping to evolve new rhythms, for penetration into your body-soul.

"There was another Brahmin, a learned Gujarati, Pandit Kewal Ram, the author of the Sanskrit book *Vir Vinod*. You made him compile the logarithmic tables from the Sanskrit *Vibha Sarni*. And then he rendered De La Hire's tables, Ulugh Beg's calculations and other important texts.

"Still another collaborator, whom you sought out from Maharashtra was Pandit Ratanakar, who compiled the *Kalpadruma*, dealing with austerities, fasts, diets, and the appropriate prayers to awaken the *vasanas* or energies ...And while most princes slumbered late into the mornings, you had trained your mind to awaken you before dawn so that you could recite the hymn to the sun after walking down to the edge of the tank, as soon as the first rays of the sun appeared. And, you got the court musicians to play a different mode on the *Shehnai* at dawn from the ones they rendered in the evenings...

"Perhaps you had found in the course of your studies of our Ayurvedic system of medicines, that man's life had been conceived to proceed rhythmically in cycles of twelve years, in which the *Barahmasa*, the twelve months, stimulate sub-rhythms...

"And, though you began at the beginnings, you made sure that what others found out through their observations became a part of your findings. Apart from the Greek books and the Arab researches, embodied in Egyptian and Babylonian inheritances, which you gathered in the translations of your pandits, you sent representatives everywhere, to go and relight your torch in the flame of other people's fire.

"Thus Muhammad Sharif and Muhammad Mehdi were sent to assemble information about the zodiac from the Islamic countries, as far as Tabriz in Iran and Samarkand in Central Asia.

"You asked the Portuguese Viceroy in Goa to send you a scholar who may tell you how Columbus charted his voyage in search of India and lost his way. This brought the learned Padre Manuel de Figueiredo from Goa to Jaipur in AD 1730. He told you of the works of

Copernicus, Galileo, Kepler and Tycho Brahe. Unable to answer all your questions, Padre Manuel offered to go to Europe to procure the necessary books and instruments for your use.

"This Padre came back with another scholar, De Silva Leito, who settled in Jaipur. You also invited two French Jesuits, Father Claude Boudier, who walked from Chandranagar on the Hoogli to Jaipur in 1734. You obtained the maps and globes of the British through the Englishmen living at Surat. The Bavarian Jesuit Father, Andre Stroebel, heard of your deep interest in astronomy and came with his friend, Antoine Gables Perger to stay near you in the precincts of Chandra Mahal.

"In AD 1724, you had constructed, by the permission of the Imperial Court, your first observatory, the Jantar Mantar, at Delhi. The shapes and forms of the various instruments made with masonry exemplify your courage in imaginative construction. You preferred to build in bricks and plaster, instruments which were hitherto available only in brass. This observatory was frowned upon by the nobles. But you spent some months every year, for seven years, in this Jantar Mantar to embody your observations in authentic tables.

"After these years of persistent observation, you felt the need for a laboratory which may be near at hand and you built the Jantar Mantar in Jaipur. And later, for comparative observations you asked for similar Jantar Mantars to be built at Mathura in the Krishna country, in Ujjain of Kalidas's songs of earth and clouds and mountains, in Varanasi where the Ganga takes a bend to go and join the ocean.

"And truly your Samrat Yantra, the Jai Prakash, the Nalri Valaya Yantra, the Digansa Yantra, the Chakra Yantra and other constructions, constitute a world of fantasy which excites wonder in the eyes of even the dullest men, stimulates the half-dead to life, and makes the learned stare breathless before the audacity of your precocious imagination.

"So important did you consider the scientific study of man's place in the cosmos, that you designed the Jantar Mantar, next to your palace in Jaipur, almost as the hub of the little cosmos of the new city.

"Your wise words about this plan of study addressed to the Emperor Muhammad Shah, will ever remain memorable...

"The results of your observations were set out by you in the forms of tables in *Zij-i-Muhammad Shahi*.

"Legend says you told people: 'I know the stars but live with you on the earth, with Govindji in our midst'. And, after you installed the image of the presiding deity in a clearing by the Talkatora lake, you began to actualize the needs of the people to connect themselves to God in their daily life. And, like Kublai Kahan who 'a stately pleasure dome decreed', you ordered a palace for yourself, as *raja*, and habitations for the *praja*.

"Thus was planned the new model village city of Jaipur...In this way, you felt that the human beings around you might be able to discover their own interrelationship with the universe, by living in intimate connection with the stars, and by moving in the active *karma yoga* (union with the cosmos) aspire to the highest consciousness of the 'being-in-situation' in the temporal world, which faces every human being.

"The age of the modern discovery begins, in our country, with your pioneer work. Some of those Indians who say that you had installed temples in Jaipur, have mistaken you to be a mere ritualist. They did not see that you were existing within the framework of an old society, which had accepted, by and large, the world of *Maya* (illusion) as lower than the reality of *Brahman*, in which alone many could attain salvation. In order to remove the delusions of the monist hypothesis you ordered a heaven on earth and you embodied in it the concept of the good life for the body and the mind.

"You had grasped the depth of the Indian theory of music in the *Mahabharata*, put forward again by Raja Bhoja of Dhar, that the seven *swaras*, or strains of music, arise from the seven planets, because sound is the only property of space. You knew that the body-soul lives in imperceptible rhythmic connection with ingrained relationships.

"The practice of yoga had given you the awareness of release. Yet you did not merely want a visual response to the earth and the stars, but participation in rhythm. And, in shifting from the hill fort of Amber to the oasis in the desert seven miles away, you were making a total pattern of life in and through which men may remain human. You wished to uplift the bare stretch of earth, below the Amber hills, into a city state, which might inspire the people to a richer life, along with you and your successors.

"As in your readings in astronomy, so in your study of architecture, you had obviously gained glimpses from the West. It is said that you knew a good deal about Versailles and Luxembourg. Doubtless, you may have observed some features of foreign town plans. But your frequent visits to Sikri and Agra and Shahjahanabad, as well as your stay in Mandu, had inhered you into the Indian tradition.

"The fort wall surrounding the city was obviously derived from the examples of architecture of your feudal ancestors; protection against possible attack and loot was the main consideration. But Pundit Vidhyadhar Bhattacharya, your architect protégé, belonged to a family which had been brought to Amber by Raja Man Singh, your great-grand uncle, the general of Akbar, in his eastern campaigns, and had early shown a talent for building bridges, culverts and fort walls.

"The ancient 'how-to-do-it' book on Hindu architecture, the *Manasra* which you gave the Pandit in his youth, brought confirmation for you of the ancient injunction: 'Live your life well on the earth on which you are a tenant'.

"The ancients had followed a grid pattern. This rigidity was within the framework of the belief that the earth is real, exists, and is a solid substance, from the commonsense point of view, to be built upon by men according to their needs. You agreed with Vidyadher to build solidly in stone and brick and lime. But you told him to study the relation of the sun at various times of the day, in the desert, the airs of the difference seasons to give your people a pleasant 'tenancy' on earth.

"The functional aspect of the town plan of Jaipur is its most significant feature.

"You knew that a city is not only its buildings, but organic whole in which human beings survive, that work is worship, because it procures goods meant for use in the daily life.

"The foresight with which you based yourself on the pragmatic life on earth, has made Jaipur, since it was built, one of the most flourishing *craft-cities* in the East, a living township which was remained a model of construction even for our time.

"The palaces also were extension of the village *havelis*. Of course, as against the big house in Amber, where the Kachhwaha family began its sojourn in the village by the hillside, you planned gardens, open spaces, covered terraces with kiosks and *baradaris*, radiating the very breath of heaven, to enable relaxation in peace and surrender to leisure. You made groves of fruit trees and rose gardens and decorative flowering trees.

"You had learnt all the blandishment of Emperor Shah Jahan and brought in the *pietra durra* inlay work, already carried out in the

Amber palace. You had learnt well the lesson of the Rajasthani craftsmen in making the shiny lime plaster for the outer walls. And Vidhyadhar showed you the beauty of the curved cornice and the pointed *chhajjas* of the Bengali thatched huts, which he placed judiciously amidst the kiosks, to variegate the pattern of the air-houses.

"The ancient Rajasthan balcony, which projected the lattice work into the cantilevered bracket, came to be carved in stone mullions under your direction. And every court of India, invited your craftsmen to lend their hand in the building of their own palaces. In all your affiliations with the stars you did not forget to be of the earth, earthy. You used all the local materials available around you – the soapstone, the pink sandstone, and the Makrana marble.

"The magic of your daring is in the designs of the Jantar Mantar. You had well understood the principle of abstraction from the *Shilpashastras*. You had grasped the emphasis on imaginative reconstruction of materials beyond mere imitation of nature.

"You carried out the total plan of Jaipur within fifteen years and cultivated the soil of your personality in the process, initiating a new architecture.

"You are one of the few feudalists of history in our country, whose philosophy the moderns can emulate.

"There is one cosmos in which man can live if he constantly strives for awareness, to improve his circumstances. Beauty is in the integration of forms, in the imagination of man, and the transformation of nature is in his own hands, through his own eyes, and through the vital energies inside him. The essence of matter is enshrined in solid substance. The quality of life is in the search from the known to the potentially unknown. The only immortality is in the love of life, in the innocence and wide-eyed wonder in the eyes of men and women. The mystery of the spheres is within the search of human beings, if they strive. The end of human existence is the struggle to achieve grace".

Your humble devotee,
MULK RAJ ANAND

21

A Statesman of the 18th Century

Sawai Jai Singh's Contribution to Mughal Imperial Politics

SATISH CHANDRA

Sawai Jai Singh occupied the *gaddi* of Amber for about half a century, during which period he not only raised the prestige of the house of Amber and greatly extended its territories, but also played an important part in the imperial politics of the times. The fortunes of Amber were at a low ebb after the death of Mirza Raja Jai Singh in 1665, following his failure against the Deccan states. The immediate successors were not men of the same caliber, and failed to win the favour of the Emperor. It was Sawai Jai Singh who won back for the Kachhawahas the pre-eminent position they had occupied at the Delhi court since the reign of Akbar and Jahangir.

Views about Jai Singh's Role

Jai Singh's role in the imperial politics of the time is a subject bristling with controversies and difficulties. Many contemporary and almost all subsequent writers have charged him with following a policy of 'treasonable collusion' with the enemies of his master, and having followed a short-sighted policy of cooperation with the Marathas, which not only hastened the downfall of the Mughal Empire, but also led ultimately to the despoilation and enslavement of the Rajput states.

The motives for his policy of cooperation with the Marathas, who were generally recognized as a menace to the freedom and prosperity of all northern Indian powers, are variously described. According to some, he was motivated by considerations of religious sympathy with his co-religionists. [(Thus, Sardesai, *Marathi Riyasat, (Medhya)*, pp. 325–9; Sarkar, *Later Mughals*, pp. 248–9). These views were based largely on certain letters in the Mandloi Daftar which have since been proved spurious (see Dr R. Singh, *Malwa*, pp. 196–8). This may be said to have dealt the final blow to the theory of a Maratha-led Hindu campaign)]. According to some others, he was motivated by a narrow and selfish desire to hold on to Malwa with the aid of the Marathas and thus establish a Kachhawaha hegemony extending from the Salt lake to the Narmada. [(Sarkar, *History of Jaipur* (unpublished manuscript), Dr R. Singh, p. 194. (*Now published by Orient Longman, Ed., 1984.*)] According to still others, it was due to his growing disillusionment with the Delhi court and a deep distrust of the dominant Mughal faction (Dr A.L. Srivastava, *First Two Nawabs*, p. 50).

(In the present paper an attempt has been made to trace the main stages of the development of Jai Singh's policy on the basis of original researches carried by the author. Records have since become available at the Jaipur Court (the *Akhbarat*) and the Marathi material in the Peshwa's *Daftar* is, however; a vast store-house of information in the light of which it is possible to re-examine many issues of Jai Singh's policy and his relations with the Marathas.)

Two Broad Phases

The career of Sawai Jai Singh may be broadly divided into two phases: *the first* from 1698 – the time of his service in the Deccan under Prince Bidar Bakht, to 1721 – the downfall of the Sayyid brothers; and the *second* from 1721 to the time of his death in 1743. During the first period, Jai Singh rose to prominence as a foremost Mughal grandee, defending the Empire against the Marathas and other despoilers, and bidding fair to win back for the Rajputs the old position of being the sword-arm of the Mughals. During the second period, he apparently fulfilled a completely different role, advocating strenuously a policy of peace and friendship with the Marathas and maintaining close and friendly relations with the Peshwa.

The First Phase

Jai Singh began his career in the Deccan with service under Prince Bidar Bakht as the head of a small Rajput contingent sent after repeated Mughal 'reminders'. Soon after he was granted eight months' leave to go home and get married. But the young Kachhwaha prince was resentful of the small favours shown to him, in disregard of his family's services to the Emperors in the past; and so it was not till October 1701, after the death of his father, that he returned to court. His ascension was formally accepted by the Emperor with all the usual ceremonies; but he was accorded only the low *mansab* of 2,000 *zat* and 2,000 *sawar*

(1,000 *do-aspah*). At the siege of Khelna, Jai Singh rendered good service and was recommended by Prince Bidar Bakht for a rise in his *mansab* and the privilege of kettle-drums. Aurangzeb turned down the request on the ground, "No, he is too young and led by others," and twice demoted him for negligence. Again, in 1704, when Bidar Bakht made Jai Singh his deputy in the governorship of Malwa, Aurangzeb vetoed it on the ground that it was "against faith -(*jaiz nest*)" (*Inayat of 68, 72a*). At the time of Aurangzeb's death, Jai Singh still held his original low *mansab* of 2,000+2,000.

Ups and Downs

During his brief reign, Prince Azam, apparently at the instance of his *vazir*, Zhulfiqar Khan, raised Jai Singh to the *mansab* of 7,000 *zat*, 7,000 *sawar*, and the *Subedari* of Malwa. The same rank and the *Subedari* of Gujarat were conferred on Ajit Singh. This might have been the beginning of a new Rajput policy; but after his ascension to the throne, Bahadur Shah I decided to continue with the old policy of Aurangzeb. He sought to expel Ajit Singh from Jodhpur, which he had occupied during the civil war, and to oust Jai Singh from Amber, putting in his place his younger brother Bijay Singh, who had helped Bahadur Shah in the civil war. This provoked a widespread rebellion in Rajputana; and Bahadur Shah was compelled to resile from his policy - especially in view of disturbances elsewhere. Amber and Jodhpur were restored to Jai Singh and Ajit Singh respectively, but no attempt was made to win their confidence and convert them into loyal servants of the crown by a generous policy of concessions such as had been adopted by Azam. What the two Rajas wanted was high *mansabs*, such as had been enjoyed by their ancestors, and the governorship of important *subahs* like Malwa and Gujarat. These demands were not acceded to, and so the two Rajas remained sullen and un-cooperative. [(In November 1711, Jai Singh was given the faujdari of Chitrakut and the mansab of 3500+3000, and Ajit Singh the faujdari of Sorath and the mansab of 4000+4000.) (*Akhbarat* 222, 4 November, December 3, *Parwana d. 17 November*.)]

When Jahandar Shah became king, and Zulfiqar Khan his *vazir*, he once again conferred the *mansabs* of 7,000 *zat*, 7,000 *sawar* and the governorships of Malwa and Gujarat on Jai Singh and Ajit Singh respectively. However, Jahandar was defeated by Farrukh Siyar before the new policy could take effect, but Zulfiqar's policy was continued by the *vazirs*, the Sayyid brothers. Jai Singh took charge of Malwa in 1713, and the same year, he inflicted a severe defeat upon a big Maratha force which had crossed the Narbada. The victory was described as "the biggest since the time of Alamgir". (*Akhbarat* June 6, 17; *Waqia Papers* of the *Maharajah's Army, May 28, 29; Letters May 25,* also see detailed description in Dr. R. Singh's article in *Sardesai Commemoration Volume* pp. 68–2.) Meanwhile, after some initial trouble, Ajit Singh had been appointed to Gujarat – another province increasingly menaced by the Marathas.

Thus, barely six years after the death of Aurangzeb, his policy was completely reversed, and the Rajputs bid fair to resume their position as the sword arm of the Mughal Empire.

Masterful Sayyids

But the development was checked by the developing struggle for power at the court between the Emperor and the masterful Sayyid brothers. Jai Singh was recalled to court in 1715, ostensibly to lead a campaign against the Jats entrenched between Delhi and Agra, but in reality to rescue the Emperor from the domination of his *vazirs*. [(Jai Singh left Malwa in October 1715, and reached court in April 1716. As late as May 1717, the Emperor had promised, "Whatever may be, I shall never take Malwa from you", and promised the support of a high noble with a mighty army to help drive out the Marathas from Malwa (*Letters May, October 5*).] Difficult terrain and under-hand opposition from the *vazir* led to the failure of Jai Singh. In his absence, the position in Malwa had deteriorated. Large bands of Marathas ravaged the province; the deputies of Jai Singh were unable to check them. He petitioned repeatedly to be allowed to return to his province, but party politics reigned supreme at court. Towards the end of 1717, Jai Singh was removed from the governorship of Malwa altogether.

We need not recount here the details of how the Sayyids made a pact with the Marathas in 1718, granting them the *chauth* and *sardeshmukhi* of the Deccan, in return for Martha aid. They set out to depose Farrukh Siyar and set up their own puppet nominee. We, however need to note that Jai Singh took his stand against the Sayyids and their Maratha confederates. [(Duff (*i 393*) asserts that Jai Singh met young Baji Rao in 1719, and established friendly relations with him. This is doubtful, however, for Jai Singh was at Amber at the time.)] He was even prepared for open resistance, but the chicken-hearted

Emperor would have none of it, and suffered disgrace and death. After meditating resistance to the usurpers for some time, Jai Singh finally made his peace with the Sayyids (with the aid of Ajit Singh), and retired to Amber to lead a quiet life.

The Second Phase

With the downfall of the Sayyid brothers in 1721, Jai Singh came into the limelight once again. In 1722, he was given the task of suppressing his old enemies, the Jats, who had established themselves between Delhi and Agra, and were a growing menace to the Kachhawaha territories. The campaign was over within a few months, and Jai Singh could wipe out the disgrace of his previous failure against them.

After this success, Jai Singh might have been expected to take a more conspicuous part in imperial affairs. But, curiously enough, he returned to Amber after the campaign and spent the next six years in constructing his new capital at Jaipur. During this period, the Maratha depredations in Malwa and Gujarat assumed greater proportions. Repeated appeals by the Emperor to Jai Singh to go to the aid of the Governor of Malwa, Raja Girdhar Bahadur, failed to have any effect on him. This has been ascribed to his disgust with court politics or collusion with the Marathas. [(Sarkar, *History of Jaipur*, unpublished manuscript), Dr R. Singh, p. 196, Sardesai, *loc. cit.*)] In reality, since 1725, Jai Singh had been urging upon the Emperor a policy of judicial compromise with the Marathas.

The conditions in 1725 were vastly different from what they had been in 1713, when a strong viceroy like the Nizam-ul-Mulk was in the Deccan, the Marathas were internally divided and lacked a good leader, and were really at the nadir of their power. In 1725, the Nizam-ul-Mulk was in rebellion and his policy towards the Marathas was, at best uncertain. The Marathas had gained considerably in power; Baji Rao had appeared on the scene. But, the Mughal Empire had yet to recover from the series of internal conflicts and wars since the death of Aurangzeb.

Against the Maratha Menace

Accordingly, in 1725, Jai Singh proposed to the Emperor that Shahu Raja and four of his principal men should be taken into imperial service, and Shahu be granted jagirs worth ten lakhs in each of the two provinces of Malwa and Gujarat (*Jaipur Records, Hindi Letters*). Jai

Singh clearly regarded this a profitable basis of peace with the Marathas. As he wrote, "the Marathas want the *chauth* and *sardeshmukhi* of Malwa and Gujarat which comes to 50 lakhs. If a settlement could be reached for 20 lakhs and the Imperialists saved the burden of yearly campaigns, it would be worth it". Jai Singh deemed a settlement in the best interest of the Empire, and advised Sarbuland Khan, the Governor of Gujarat, to agree to the Maratha demand of *chauth*, and thus restore peace to Gujarat.

Even if we disagree with Jai Singh on the wisdom of this policy, there seems no adequate reason to impugn his motives.

In October 1729, Jai Singh was appointed Governor of Malwa once again, and set forth his policy even more, clearly in a remarkable document. He pointed out that the "Marathas had tested Malwa for a long time past. If this year, by reason of heavy concentration of troops, they were unable to enter the *subah* or are chastised (after they have entered), you know what heavy expenditure would be necessary for this object every year in the future. I, therefore, suggest that as Raja Shahu has been ranked as an imperial *mansabdar* since the days of Aurangzeb, Your Majesty should give him a *jagir* worth ten lakh of rupees in the name of his (adopted) son, Khushal Singh, on condition that he prevent any future disturbance in Malwa, and an auxiliary contingent of his troops should attend the subedar of that province. This will give peace to the land and save us from the expense of campaigning (every year)" [*Jagir Records No. 188; in Persian*].

Clearly, Jai Singh aimed at keeping the Marathas out of Malwa. But, after 1725, he considered this possible only by a settlement with the Marathas and not by war. Broadly, he urged a policy of judicious compromise with the Marathas, and going to war with them only as a last resort. Keeping in mind the military, political and economic conditions of the Empire at the time, it was perhaps the most feasible policy. No doubt, Jai Singh hoped that the success of his policy would bring him credit and personal gain.

A faction of Mughal and other nobles at court opposed this policy as "dishonourable" and insinuated that Jai Singh had selfish motives. Accordingly, Jai Singh was saddled with the task of fighting the Marathas in Malwa, i.e., with the task of carrying out a policy he considered impolitic and disastrous. Under the circumstances, it is obvious he had no heart in this fighting. [Jai Singh was appointed Governor of Malwa in October 1729, but was replaced after only a few months by Muhammad Khan Bangash who pursued a policy of all-out resistance. In 1732, Jai Singh was appointed Governor of Malwa for the third time. He was asked to maintain 30,000 horses and foot in equal number and two-third of the revenue was assigned to him; the Diwan was assigned one-third of the income and was to maintain 18,000 horse extra (*Jaipur Records, Hindi Letters No. 28*)].

However, the Mughal had no answer to the Maratha light cavalry tactics, and Jai Singh, with all his resources, fared as badly as the best of Aurangzeb's generals. [(The Mughals made much play of the fact that Jai Singh with all his resources had failed to check the Marathas, and declared, "Jai Singh has ruined the Empire by his secret support to the Marathas" (*S.P.D. XIV–47*)]. The subsequent failure of the Nizam at Bhopal showed that the failure of Jai Singh was not due to an unwillingness to fight, but had deeper military causes. Jai Singh was suspicious of the Mughals and told the Maratha wakil, "I have hitherto guarded the prestige and interests of Baji Rao, because I could not trust the Turks. If the latter triumph over the Deccani forces, they will disregard us (i.e., the Rajputs and Hindustanis" (*S.P.D. XIV–47*).

[Jai Singh's suspicion was not without foundation. Nor is it correct to regard this as an opportunist attempt to hold on to Malwa with the aid of the Marathas (c/f Dr R. Singh, p. 235). In 1736, Jai Singh agreed to give up Malwa to Baji Rao to bring about a Maratha-Mughal accord.)]

The Marathas now threatened to cross into the Doab, the heart of the Empire. The imperialists made their maximum effort, and mustered 75,000 horses, divided into two armies under the command of the *vazir* Qamaruddin and the Mir Bakhsi Khan Dauran respectively. But this huge force was completely immobilized by the Marathas cavalry. Khan Dauran and Jai Singh were cut off and surrounded at Toda Tank by Holkar; and Jaipur lay defenceless before him.

Peace Parleys

This once again convinced Jai Singh of the impossibility of "effectively subduing the Marathas by fighting". Accordingly, in 1735, Jai Singh invited the Peshwa to northern India and offered to bear his expenses. This invitation has been taken mistakenly as an invitation to lead a joint campaign against Delhi (*Sarkar*, pp. 263–4). In his talks with the Maratha envoy, Jai Singh clearly stated that the invitation was for the purpose of securing the *chauth* of Malwa for the Peshwa, and introducing him to the Emperor (after due assurance of safety) for the settlement of his (other) claims. The Wakil was told that, if the visit did not bear fruit, then (and then only) the Peshwa would by free to pursue any other methods he chose (i.e., war) (*S.P.D. XIV–47*).

It was thus meant to be a 'peace' visit for negotiating a settlement, which could not be done effectively by the Peshwa from Poona. To underline the peaceful purpose of the visit, the Peshwa was asked to come with 5,000 men only. [A force under Holkar, Sindhia, Anand Rao Pawar and Baji Bhimrao was sent to Malwa and Bundelkhand, which remained camping till the rains of 1736. The negotiations were long drawn out, and the Peshwa complained that he was being "ruined by the expense of his (idle) armies", but remained in Malwa till June when he was finally convinced that the court would not grant his demands except through war, and left for Poona determined on carrying the war into the heart of the Empire next year (*S.P.D. xxii–333, Hingana Dafter 3–6*)].

It is clear that the Mughal court was apprised of the purpose and nature of the visit. The Peshwa crossed the Narbada in November, and from January onwards, Khan Dauran sent him expense money from the court through Jai Singh. No campaign against the Marathas was undertaken that year by the imperialists. [(Pilaji was sick in Maharashtra, that year, and Irvine's account of skirmishes between him and the wazir Qamaruddin refers to the previous year. Ashub is the only authority for the fight in Rajputa that year between Jai Singh and Holkar (There is no mention of Baji Rao who is described as being busy in the Konkan). From internal and external evidence, I have established that this also refers to the campaign of the previous year (*see my thesis, "Party and Politics at the Mughal Court", Appendix B, lodged in the Allahabad University*) *Thus, Irvine ii 281–84, Sarkar i–277–8, Dr R. Singh, p. 239 are not correct in speaking of fighting this year*)].

It is not necessary to pursue here the course of the negotiations and the cause of their failure. It was due partly to Baji Rao's lack of confidence in the ability of Jai Singh and Khan Dauran to deliver the goods – There was also a strong 'no-compromise' party at court. [(Baji Bhivrao wrote, "In Delhi the Mughals have made common cause. Khan Dauran and Jai Singh are with the Emperor. The spies of the Nizam come and go day and night. At his instance, Qamaruddin, Rashanuddaulah, Saadat Khan and Abhai Singh have invited and divided not to let you succeed. You cannot go to Delhi trusting in them, etc. etc". (*S.P.D. xv, 89, 91*). The Maratha wakil at Delhi warned that the Mughals were "untrustworthy, deceitful, and devoid of faith" (*S.P.D. xiv, 54*)].

The imperialists and Baji Rao also failed to reach agreement. There is strong reason to suspect that the chief differences lay not with regard to Baji Rao's demands on Malwa and Gujarat, which he virtually asked to be ceded to him, but with regard to the Deccan, on which he presented certain far-reaching demands. [(The Peshwa demanded a jagir of fifty lakhs in Khandesh, Bijapur, and Aurangabad, and nomination of the Peshwa as the Deputy Viceroy of the Deccan (under the Crown Prince), all administration being conducted through him, and any additional revenue raised by his efforts being shared half and half (*S.P.D. xv, 94–5*). For further discussions, see my thesis, *loc.cit., pp. 322–5*)].

The Nizam had all along feared a possible deal at his expense and he strengthened the 'no compromise' party by secret promises of support. The terms proposed by Jai Singh through his agent, were a cash indemnity of twenty lakhs, a *jagir* of forty lakhs in Malwa (in lieu of *chauth*) and an assignment on the territory of Dost Md. Khan Rohela (*S.P.D. xiv, 50*).

Marathas at the Door ...

Failure of negotiations made a renewed fight with the Marathas inevitable. Unable to carry his policy at the court, Jai Singh contended himself with securing from the Peshwa a promise not to march the Maratha armies over Amber and Bundi (*S.P.D. xxx, 196*).

The arrival of Nizam-ul-Mulk in Delhi following the dash of Baji Rao to the gates of the imperial capital in 1737, completely altered the political situation. The Mughal "War Party" had played its trump card and everything depended on the success or failure of the Nizam. Jai Singh may have had his doubts about the Nizam's ability to defeat the Marathas, but he did not withhold cooperation and sent a contingent under his son. The Rajputs and Bundelas bore the brunt of the fighting at Bhopal, and left the camp only when the Nizam got himself in a trap and famine began in his camp. [(Dr Y.H. Khan, *Asaf Jah I, p. 213*) ascribes the defeat to the treacherous attitude of the Rajputs and Bundelas who, he says, were secretly sending information to the Maratha camp. But, in his letters, Baji Rao himself makes no mention of this and ascribes the defeat to the Nizam's own pusillanimity (*Brs. Ch. 3*)].

The political situation did not improve. During the invasion of Nadir Shah, Jai Singh did not participate in the fight at Panipat, but sent a contingent under his *wakil* Kripa Ram, who acquitted himself with honour. (Shiv Das, *Rampur State Lib. Ms.*) Subsequently, like the rest of the rulers in northern India, he watched the situation and waited for a move by the Peshwa.

... & Nadir Shah's Knock

All the plans of the Mughal "War Party" since 1724 had thus ended in failure, while the invasion of Nadir Shah heaped defeat and dishonour upon their head. But, like the Bourbons of France, the Mughals had "forgotten nothing and learnt nothing". They resumed the attempt to push the Marathas out of Malwa and Gujarat, instead of concentrating on putting their own house in order first. Baji Rao was dead, but his successor Balaji Rao resumed his policy. It was only the threat of a renewed invasion of the Doab, and the knowledge that the Nizam had once again come to an understanding with the Marathas that compelled the Emperor to heed the advice of Jai Singh and open peace negotiations with the Marathas.

The agreement of 1741, negotiated with the help of Jai Singh, forms a landmark in Mughal-Maratha relations. By it, the Emperor substantially accepted the terms demanded by Baji Rao in 1736. Malwa was ceded for all practical purposes, though the position of Gujarat remained obscure. In return for the Peshwa's demands of a cash subsidy of 50 lakh in Bijapur, Aurangabad and Khandesh and the vice-royalty of the Deccan, the *chauth* of Bengal, Bihar and Orissa was ceded to them (*S.P.D. xv–86*). The last was a device to divert the Marathas from the Doab. But, the Maratha insistence on a cash subsidy to pay off their debts, and their recent accord with the Nizam left the imperialists no alternative. It gave the Doab a fifteen years' respite from the Peshwah hordes, however.

Had the period been well-utilized, it might have enabled the Empire to survive as a north Indian power, if not as an all-India empire. But, the process of internal disintegration was much too deep-seated to be reversed.

The death of Jai Singh in 1743 broke the last safety dyke between the Marathas and Rajputana. Feudal disunity triumphed over imperial unity and the Marathas invited by rival contestants, speedily overran all

Rajputana and even Delhi. But for these subsequent events, Jai Singh cannot really be held responsible.

In spite of his obvious failure to stay the disintegration of the Mughal Empire, or save Rajputana from falling under the domination of the Marathas, Sawai Jai Singh II stands out as a statesman of no mean order, who not only restored the fortunes of the House of Amber, but fought strenuously for the only possible policy that would have given the battle-scarred Empire a breathing space to recoup and reorganize its forces. That he failed was very largely due to causes beyond his control.

(N.B. This paper was first published in the 1948 Indian History Congress Proceedings.)

22

Some Early Glimpses of Jaipur

ASHIM KUMAR ROY

According to Ashim Kumar Roy, "the official name of the city when it was founded was Sawai Jaipur. The name is mentioned in all the documents of the period" (e.g., the 1728 deed of land to Jagannath Samrat, the 1729 invitation letter to Ghasiram Murlidhar to settle here, and the Emperor's letter of 1733 recognizing the city as the new capital). Uptil the end of the 18th century and in the early decades of the 19th century Jaipur was also called Jainagar.

***

The first recorded description of the city is given in Girdhari's *Bhojansara* (1739). Verses 182 to 194 cover the foundation and layout of the city, description of Jainivas and the main streets; the planting and flowering of trees with the sing-song of birds lending it a sylvan backdrop; the founder-ruler's advice and instructions about building and populating the city in the shortest possible time, and its becoming beautiful and important with the blessings of the Brahmins. Verse 195 mentions the various important temples of Govinda-deva, Gopinath, Ganesh and the Sun temple. The poet has also described that the city with thousands of shops had become a place of extensive business for traders from many different places (196). Trade activities are mentioned next. "Many elephants, Arab horses and camels from Kutch come here. Embroidered and plain cloth and jeweled ornaments are brought from different parts of the world (197). The Europeans also live here. They have come after crossing the oceans... (198) ...the merchants of many places have come... Hundis of lacs and crores are current here. They are all happy and do their business peacefully...(200) in ...this city, all the 32 weights are quite correct and precise...(201).

Facts and extracts taken from Ashim Kumar Roy's book *History of Jaipur City*.

The Brahmans engage themselves in Yajnas from early dawn. They study the *Vedas* and teach them to others. Everybody looks to his own religion and all evil deeds are set aside. In every house *Katha* is being performed. They all sing the 18 Puranas...(202)".

(*Hindi rendering by Prof B.D. Verma, published by P.K. Gode in an essay, along with original, in Dr C.K. Raja Presentation Volume, Madras 1946*)

***

In February 1764, the prominent Jains of Jaipur invited the Jainas of Delhi, Agra and other centres for a Jain festival, the *Indradhwaja Puja*. The invitation mentioned the prosperity of Jaipur thus: About this city, it lacks seven things...in this city you would not find wine-sellers, butchers and prostitutes...killing of animals is prohibited... sinful activities are prohibited by the Raja (Madhava Singh) ...there are many Jain residents here...All important courtiers are Jains And, all the merchants are Jains. Six, seven or eight or ten thousand Jain merchants have their residences here. In no other town you would find so many Jains...

In his poetical work, *Buddhi Vilas*, written in mixed Braj and Jaipuri language in 1770, Bakhta Ram Shah of Chaksu mentions among other things (his poem is about the Jain religious beliefs and rituals, and covers a fair account of Jaipur city) that tax concession was one of the main incentives for many artisans and traders who were invited to come to the new city.

There is also a mention of about four thousand Marathas (then camping outside the city) visiting the temples and other sights of the unique new city on 10th January, 1751 and to buy horses, camels and saddlery for which Jaipur was quite famous. This shows the popularity and attraction of the city in less than 25 years of its existence.

As most historians have observed, the disturbed and insecure conditions in north, north-west India, and in the premier cities of Delhi and Agra or Mathura drew many Hindu merchants, traders and artisans to migrate to the comparatively more secure and peaceful capital of the newly strengthened state of Jaipur. New trade routes were also being discovered to avoid the disturbed or desolated territories all round Delhi-Agra, especially towards the north-west and/or south-west as the pincers of the Afghan and Maratha advances closed on the imperial Mughal capitals. Jaipur was touched on some of these routes.

23

... And Many Flowers Bloomed!

V.S. BHATNAGAR

What sets Jai Singh II apart from other powerful and successful figures of his times, like the great Peshwa Baji Rao or the Nizam, is his outstanding contribution in the field of culture, specially in astronomy and town planning, and his remarkable patronage to literature.

Study of Astronomy

He seems to have developed at an early age an aptitude for mathematics and astronomy. To quote the 'Astronomer Prince' Jai Singh himself, who wrote in third person in his preface of *Zeij Muhammad Shahi* (the astronomical tables which he prepared and completed about 1728): "Since...the admiring spectator of the theatre of infinite wisdom and providence Sawai Jai Singh, from the first dawning of reason in his mind and during his progress towards maturity, was entirely devoted to the study of mathematical science, and the bent of his mind was constantly directed to the solution of its most difficult problems, by the aid of the Supreme Artificer, he obtained a thorough knowledge of its principles and rules..."

Jai Singh's natural aptitude for astronomy received abiding inspiration from Pt. Jagannath, a Maratha Brahman, who, it is said, was appointed in 1714 AD to teach Vedas to Jai Singh. Later, Samrat Jagannath translated Ptolemy's *Almagest* and Euclid's *Elements* from the Arabic version of these works.

As his studies progressed, he and the scholars working with him found that the calculation of the places of the stars as obtained from the tables in common use (such as the new tables of Said Gurgani and Khaqani and Tasahilat Mulla Chand Akbar Shahi, and those in the Hindu books and European tables), in very many cases, gave them widely different positions from those determined by observation, especially in the appearance of new moons.

... and Making of Instruments

Jai Singh seems to have noticed this discrepancy some time after 1715 or so, when he had started taking observations on mental instruments such as Zat al Aalqa (a ring instrument of diameter 3 yards), an astrolabe with two rings and Shami'ah etc. But soon he and his growing team of astronomers noted that the metal instruments, such as those earlier to him and used at Samarqand and much earlier by Hipparchus and Ptolemy "did not come up to the ideas which he had formed of accuracy", on account of what they concluded, "smaller divisions, displacement of centres of circles, wearing and shaking of axis, shifting of the planes of instruments..."

Jai Singh, therefore, decided to build masonary instruments of his own invention, such as Jai Prakash, Ram Yantra, etc. "of large dimensions and perfect stability, with attention of the rules of geometry and adjustment to the meridian and to the latitude of the place ..." And to confirm the correctness of the observations, he constructed similar instruments at Sawai Jaipur, Mathura, Banaras and Ujjain. The Delhi observatory was ready by 1921, and it appears from his preface to the *Zeij* that other observatories were also completed before *Zeij* was published in 1728 AD.

Jai Singh even decided to erect similar observatories in other cities also, so that persons devoted to these studies might, by these instruments, observe the phenomenon of the relative position of the stars. Here was Jai Singh's plan to carry the science of astronomy within the reach of the commonest of persons interested in its study. But the multiple problems which he had to face after 1729, and the rapidly changing political scene in the country after 1734, prevented him from carrying out his scheme further.

Contacts with European Science

A couple of years after he had built these instruments and observatories, Jai Singh came to know about the astronomical researches in Europe where the scientists, as he writes, "were constantly labouring to determine with accuracy the subtleties of this science". In 1705, an observatory had been built in Berlin and in 1725, at St. Petersburg.

Earlier observatories had been built at Leined in 1632, at Paris in 1667, and in Greenwich in 1675.

In 1702, la Hire's (1640–1718) and *Tabulae Astronomicae* was published and complete works of Flamsteed (*Historia Celistis Britannica*) had also been published.

Flamsteed had been assigned the task of finding a precise method of determining longitudes. For this he needed stellar catalogues and lunar tables based on more correct observations that hitherto available. Flamsteed took numerous observations for over thirty years, and published these in 1712. He devised a new method for the determination of the co-ordinates of the first point of Aries, a northern constellation. He was the first to make use of an accurate time-peace and optical means for determining stellar co-ordinates. Consequently, his observations were more accurate. His *Celestial History* contained his observations of fixed stars, comets, planets, sun spots, the satellites of Jupiter, catalogues of the fixed stars of Ptolemy, Ulugh Beg, Tycho, Havel and the British catalogue of 2,884 stars. Flamsteed had, for the first time, introduced in common usage, to quote Georgio Abetti (*The History of Astronomy*, 1954, London), "meridian observations of the right ascension of the sun and stars". He improved the lunar tables by introducing annual equation. By acquiring Flamsteed's work, Sawai Jai Singh brought himself in touch with the latest developments in astronomical studies in Europe.

Perhaps it was from Father Manuel de Figueredo, who had been sent by the Goa authorities in response to Jai Singh's request to send a learned scholar and physician, that Jai Singh became fully aware of the recent progress made in some European countries in this field. Shortly after his arrival, Jai Singh sent him to Europe along with several skilful persons, whose names would be of much interest, if we find them some day, to procure books on astronomy and instruments for studying astronomical phenomenons. We find the Padre passing through Udaipur in August 1727, on way to Surat (*Maharana Sangram's letter to Sawai Jai Singh*). He returned in November 1730, along with Father Pedro de Sylva Leitao, who was a scientist as well as physician. Later, some other European mathematicians and scientists, for instance, Claude Bovdier and another French Jesuit, reached Jaipur after taking readings in the Delhi observatory. As Bovdier does not mention his having taken readings at Banaras and Mathura, Kaye (*The Astronomical Laboratories of Jai Singh*, Calcutta, 1918) is inclined to believe that observatories at these places were probably completed after his visit, i.e., after the early months of 1734. But this conclusion does not seem to agree with Jai Singh's own version of his progress in this field.

In 1736, two Bavarian Jesuit scholars also arrived. These European scholars collaborated with the Hindu astronomers, such as Samarat Jagannath and Kewal Ram, and the Muslim astronomers, such as Muhammad Sharif, whom Jai Singh had sent to the place where "the southern pole was overhead", and Muhammad Mehdi who was sent to "further islands", which seem to be either northern Russia or northern Germany.

An Assessment of His Work

What were Jai Singh's findings on receiving the European works on astronomy? In his own words, "On comparing these tables with actual observations, it appeared that there was an error in the former of half a degree in assigning the Moon's place, and there were errors in the other planets, although not so great, yet the times of solar and lunar eclipses, he found to come out later or earlier than the truth by the fourth part of a *ghari* or fifteen *palas* (six minutes). Hence, he (Jai Singh) concluded that since in Europe, astronomical instruments have not been constructed of such size and so large diameters, the motions which have been observed with them may have deviated a little from the truth".

Jai Singh's pride in his own instruments was not unwarranted. Thus, in 1727 AD, he had determined with the instruments at Delhi the obliquity of the ecliptic to be 23E28", which was within 28" of what it was determined by Godin (1704–60) in 1728. Similarly, in 1793 AD, when Dr W. Hunter compared a series of observations on the latitude of Ujjain with that established by Jai Singh, he found a difference of 24" only, while he himself did not rule out an error of 15" in his own observations (as quoted by Tod).

On one ground, however, Jai Singh's decision to discard brass instruments in favour of large immovable instruments of stone and lime "of perfect stability" has been criticized. As Kaye writes, "He stereotyped his designs and hindered further improvements. The larger and more immobile an instrument is, the greater is the difficulty in making alterations and improvements. Jai Singh sacrificed facility for supposed accuracy". But this is the comment of a trained astronomer of the 20th century, who knows about the progress made in the field of astronomy during the past 250 years. Who could have made such a comment even in Europe in 1721?

It is true that Jai Singh's instruments had been designed after the "notions taught by the Muslim astronomers", but he is credited with showing very considerable ingenuity in actual construction.

Prof Soonawala, in *Maharaja Jai Singh II of Jaipur and His Observatories* (Jaipur, 1952), has given a brief and lucid description of the instruments as well as the broad principles on which the instruments are based. (For a more elaborate account, we can turn to A.F. Garret and Chandradhara Guleri's *The Jaipur Observatory and its Builder* and to Kaye's *The Astronomical Observatories of Jai Singh*.)

The Science of Astronomy in Europe

Jai Singh's approach towards the science of astronomy, however, calls for further elucidation. Jai Singh seems to have held the view that "science knows no nationality in the common pursuit of truth". He fully understood the need of collaboration in this difficult field of unlimited dimensions. He, however, did not feel the need to discard his own methods in preference to those followed by the European astronomers. By the time he became fully acquainted with the progress of astronomy in Europe, he had covered a vast ground himself, and considerable work had been done on his tables with the help of the data supplied by the Delhi observatory. Moreover, he found that his own observations were more in conformity with the calculations than those in the European tables.

But how can we understand his failure to adapt telescope, and to make use of the researches of Kepler and Galileo? It is quite possible, as Kaye suggests, that the Catholic Padres did not fully emphasize the importance of the researches of Copernicus, Kepler and Galileo. Galileo (d. 1642) had come in conflict with the *Inquisition* and his books were not removed from the *Index* until 1835 AD

Jai Singh did not have the same advantages as most of his other great contemporaries in Europe had. Among these were Cassini (1625–1712), P. de la Hire (1640–1718), Newton (1643–1727), Flamsteed (1646–1719), Halley (1656–1742), Bradley (1692–1762), Godin (1704–60) and Tobias Mayer (1732–1762), who could share each other's knowledge, and among some of whom there was close collaboration. Thus, for instance, Halley had collaborated with Newton and he also came in contact with Cassini, Kepler and Galileo. Also, the

European astronomers had the advantage of important advancements in astronomy made by Kepler (1571–1630) and Galileo (1564–1642) and of such bodies as the French Academy of Science and the Royal Society.

In India, on the other hand, astronomical research had virtually remained at a standstill since the time *Surya Siddhanta* was written. In the Islamic world also, little progress had been made after the death of Ulugh Beg. In a way, Jai Singh had to fill a long gap in the knowledge of astronomy in India. He tried his best to obtain information about the latest researches in Europe despite the difficulties in the way of transmission of knowledge in those times.

Looking to the fact that Jai Singh could devote only a very small portion of his time to the study of astronomy, unlike his great contemporary figures in this field in Europe, his efforts in this field and the astronomical studies made under his patronage and supervision make his achievements remarkable. His observatories were undoubtedly the best built in India till his time. Moreover, to devote himself so sincerely to science and learning in those chaotic times, when the Maratha tempest was sweeping northern India in all its fury and when the Mughal empire was falling apart dizzily, forms in itself a rare tribute to Jai Singh's love for astronomy.

Architecture and Town Planning

Jai Singh's contribution to the fields of architecture and town planning may also be dealt with, though only briefly. For obvious reasons, there is almost total absence of new architecture works during the period 1700–13 AD For the first seven years, Jai Singh was a minor and remained throughout in the Deccan, striving to make a mark in the imperial service. From 1707–12, he braved the storm which had endangered his own existence as well as that of Amber itself. The period was of constant and serious struggle and considerable uncertainty continued to hover over Amber and its young ruler till 1714. From 1716–20 AD was yet another period of confrontation, precipitating in a crisis in 1719. Hence, all creative activity in the fields of art learning remained in a dormant stage.

During this period, Jai Singh seems to have made only some additions and alterations in the existing palaces at Amber, and at the site where, later on, his dream city took shape to immortalize his name, thrived six villages on a level stretch of land surrounded by wood all round.

Some time after 1720, he started building below the northern edge of the plain a palace which was ready by July 1726. Shortly afterwards, he decided to build a new capital to meet the needs of his rapidly growing state. On November 18, 1727, he laid the foundation of Jainagar. Jai Singh was greatly assisted in his architectural efforts by Vidyadhara Chakravarti whom Jai Singh had picked up young on perceiving his exceptional talents in the field of architecture, and later in 1728 AD made him *Diwan Desh.*

A number of plans preserved in the City Palace Museum throw light on the evolution of the plan of the city (Ref: *MARG*, XXX, No. 4, September 1977). Jaipur was the largest city of this size to be built from the blueprint. Jainagar was nearly complete by 1729 AD, as the records of Jai Singh's frequent visits to the town show.

The City Plan

The town consists of eight wards, if the area occupied by palace is counted, and so the plan is not according to the *Prastara* plan in which town is divided into four, nine, or sixteen wards according to *Manasara*, nor the shape of the town is square or rectangular. From a plan (No. *LS/17*), it seems that originally Jaipur was to have only four rectangular blocks (occupied by the Palace, Purani Basti, Topkhana Desh and the block containing Modikhana and Vishewarji) and the area now occupied by Ghat Darwaza, Topkhana Hazuri and Ramchandraji was left undeveloped, as the map shows that area full of dunes and depressions; and only four *bazaars* (Johri Bazar, Sireh Deorhi, Kishanpole and Gangori) were originally planned. But, we find in the records that Pahadganj, Surajpol, Ramganj and Chandpole were ready and so was Shivpole (Ghat Darwaza).

In 1728, letters were sent to prominent traders inviting them to reside in Jaipur. They were offered trade concessions, and in some cases, free land for their buildings. In a short time, the new city was humming with life, and trade and cultural activity prospered rapidly, as described by Girdhari in *Bhojanasar* (1739 AD)

The uniformity of the town is striking. The view of the city appeared ravishing to Father Jose Tieffethaler, who came to India in 1743. The houses, generally three or four-storeyed high, with decorated doors, windows, and balconies with graceful balustrades or perforated screens, the temples with their cupolas, curvilinear roof pillared kiosks, gently breaking the monotony of the uniformity, these and other architectural features imparted a unique personality to Jai Singh's new capital.

Palace Complex

The palace complex consists of a series of gates or *pols* (from east Sireh Deorhi, Udaipol), spacious squares, pleasing structures like the Diwan-i-am, Diwan-i-Khas, but the most impressive building in the royal sector is the Chandramahal, the seven-storeyed palace. "The main rectangle is in five storeys of different heights, the first three defined by cornices and mouldings, their plain facades being relieved by a pleasing arrangement of the arched windows and a variety of detail. In the fourth and fifth storeys, the terraces, protected by graceful hand-rails, lend an air of openness to the whole structure. The sixth storey of the palace is substantially smaller, while the seventh is an arcaded marble pavilion with curvilinear roof, flanked by two cupolas. The principal façade is on the northern side facing a large ornamental garden with water channels, fountains, partereres, and paved pathways which extend down below the Govinddev's temple up to Badal Mahal" (quoted from V.S. Bhatnagar, *Life and Times of Sawai Jại Singh*, Delhi, 1974). The refined taste of its builder is visible everywhere: in the structural and artistic features of the palace as well as in the picturesque settings.

... and the Temples

The Govinddev's temple built by Jai Singh, though not conceived on the same grand scale as the one built by Raja Man Singh, is, in some respects, of the same architectural character. It is also without a porch and *shikhara*. The idol is installed in a rectangular hall round which runs an arcaded procession – path with a flat decorated ceiling, its heavy but finely proportioned marble pillars supporting the arches being in the characteristic Amber style. The shafts of the pillars, round and bulging at the base, taper upwards, the base and the abacus having broad petals carved in relief.

In this and other temples of the period, one of the noticeable features is an almost total absence of figure carving, which often became the chief cause of inviting the attention of the iconoclasts, and hence of its destruction. Other decorative motifs and structural features, however, were introduced in these temples, which were in harmony with their plain yet dignified appearance.

It is characteristic of the buildings of this period that the use of marble is confined, as in Govinddev's temple and Badal Mahal, to the pillars, the arches and the balustrades only. The outside of these buildings was painted in light yellow colour which, from a distance, looks most pleasing, especially during the rain and in the twilight.

Jai Singh built some other edifices also, such as the Jalmahal in midst of Mansagar, Kalkiji's temple in Sireh Deorhi Bazar and Varadaraj temple on the hillock near the site where he performed the *Asvamedha* in 1741. He also built a palace outside the town which, later on, was converted into the Residency. Jai Singh also built Sudarshangarh and two fortresses – Raghunath Garh and Ambagarh – to the north and south of the Sun temple built by Rao Kripa Ram, Jaipur's representative at Delhi, on the ascent to the Galta.

At Mathura, Sawai Jai Singh is said to have built a temple dedicated to Govardhana. According to Jonathan Scott, who wrote his work in 1780, Jai Singh erected at his own expense "a caravanserai and market in every province of Hindustan for the convenience of the travelers".

It is the volume of Jai Singh's architectural activity and simplicity in outline and decoration, and grace and strength of his buildings, characterized by a few distinguishing structural and artistic features, that put his architectural labours apart from those of his predecessors. Though not of the highest quality, his buildings bear comparison with any other built during the 18th century.

A Patron of Learning

Jai Singh also extended appreciation and honourable patronage to scholars. He invited a number of scholars from all parts of India, including Karnataka and Maharashtra, and was in touch with the scholars and pandits of Bengal, and from time to time, sought their opinion on obtruse points concerning religion, philosophy, or prevailing social customs.

He built a separate colony for them just outside the town, amidst picturesque setting. Even today, Brahmapuri has a quiet charm of its own and a visitor experiences a blissful peace in the hallowed surroundings, which, though now wear a desolate look, used to hum with activity when Jai Singh frequently dropped in to pay his respects to Paundarikaji and Samrat Jagannath, or to meet other scholars, whenever he happened to be in his capital.

In the galaxy of scholars and poets who adorned his court were Shivananda Goswami (*Kulapradipa* – a work of Tantra), Samarat Jagannath, the astronomer, enjoying the title of Rajguru, and who was well versed in music also, Atmaram (son of DhuranDhara and translator of *Raghuamsha* into Bhasha), Ratnakara Paundarika, who died in November 1719 and was the author of *Jaisimha Kalpadruma.*

During 1715–25 or so, a number of works on Vedic rituals were complied, such as *Paundari-kasaptahoraprayoga, Vishnugudhasrauta-karma, Vijapeya hotraprayoga*, etc. Also copies of *Yajuraveda* and *Atharvaveda* were obtained. Dhurandhara Kavi rendered a work on Vedanta into Bhasha. Krishna Deva Bhattacharya wrote a number of works on Bhakti, *Bhaktiphalaviveka Karmavivrati,* and Gokulnath wrote *Bhaktasiddantavivritti.*

Among other scholars and poets were Hari Krishna (*Vedicvaishnavasadachara),* Vishwanath Bhatt (*Ramvilasakavyam),* Harilal Mishra (*Muhurtakalpadruma),* the well-known poet Shri Krishna Bhatta Kavikalanidhi (*Padyamuktavali, Vrittamuktavali, Raghavagitam, Prasasti-mukvali, Alankarakalanidhi Amritdhwani* and *Ishvaravilasamahakavya),* and Nanu Ranu Sagar Kavi (*Kavitakalpataru).* In 1732, Hiralal Kayastha composed *Govindachandrachandrika.*

About this time, Jai Singh acquired a number of works from Europe. Among them were a number of printed books including a Latin Dictionary, Seamen's *Calender*, a treatise on Physics in Latin (1675 AD), an English grammar by Charles Hoole (1663 AD), and *Pathway to Knowledge* (1551 AD)

That Jai Singh had got prepared movable type forms of Hindi alphabet is beyond doubt. [The forms of letters obviously meant for the block maker were seen by the author a number of years ago in the Jaipur Archives but curiously, the paper could never again be traced by him – V.S.B.]

Other scholars at Jai Singh's court were Devaram Paundarika, Jagdish Bhatta, Krishna Kanta (*Vridavanarahasya),* Naraindas (*Bhaktamala)* etc. (G.N. Bahura, *Literary Heritage of the Rulers of Amber and Jaipur*, 1976).

Religious Tolerance

In his religious ideas, Jai Singh, though a devout Vaishnavite, was a liberal in the true catholic spirit of a Hindu and showed reverence for other religions also. He made a number of visits to the shrine of

Khawaja Muin-uddin Chishti at Ajmer, and had acquired a fair insight into Christianity through his acquaintance with the Christian Fathers whom he had invited in connection with his astronomical researches. He did not interfere with the religious affairs of other sects, but he emphasized that the followers of different orders and sects should follow tenets of their sects. Thus, he laid down in case of the *bairagis* and *sanaysis* that they would not keep arms, nor would they try to accumulate wealth, or keep women. He also tried that the various sub-castes among the Brahmans and other *varnas* should come closer. He did his best to improve the facilities for the pilgrims visiting Mathura, Gaya, Prayaga, Govardhana, etc., and purchased plots of lands in these places where subsequently he build *dharmasalas* and *ghats*. He always tried to secure *faujdari* of these places so that he might be able to improve the conditions at these religious centres. He performed nearly all the *srauta yajnas*, including the *Asvamedha*.

The diverse achievements in the fields of politics, religion, science and culture, briefly sketched above, present Sawai Jai Singh as an extraordinarily gifted person. "He had in him the rare combination of a scholar and a statesman, administrator, legislator, diplomat and soldier. He was considered as one of the wisest men of his time, an oracle of the age. Till the very end of his life, he continued to play the role of a great stabilizing force during the period of transition which witnessed the transfer of power from the Mughals to the Marathas. He was essentially a man of peace, and understood better than most of his contemporaries its value and that of progress in science and learning".

"Had the times been less chaotic, had the political and administrative matters not consumed so much of his time and energies, he would have contributed much more in these fields. But even what he could accomplish amidst perpetual wars and the falling debris of the Mughal empire, entitles him to a high rank among the most remarkable men in the long history of this country" (From *Life and Times of Sawai Jai Singh*).

24

Astronomical Efforts of Sawai Jai Singh

VIRENDRA NATH SHARMA

The object of this paper is to review Jai Singh's diversified efforts to rejuvenate astronomy in his country, and to assess him as an astronomer.

Sawai Jai Singh (1688–1743), the statesman astronomer of 18th century India, undertook the "task (of revising planetary tables), which during a long period of time... since Mirza Ulugh Beg, no one had paid attention to" (Ref. *Zij Jadid Muhammad Shahi*). He constructed five observatories in different cities of north India and, after a considerable amount of labour of seven years or more, had a *Zij* prepared. Jai Singh's interests were varied. He collected books, had astronomical texts translated into Sanskrit, and sent a fact-finding scientific mission to Europe.

Masonry Instruments

Jai Singh had been interested in instrumentation long before he decided to erect observatories, and as such, he collected literature on the subject. In 1716, he purchased two books on 'Turiya Yantra' (*File No. 424/1, Jaipur Records, Rajasthan State Archives*). He also initiated his ambitious programme of observing the heavens with instruments of brass constructed according to Persian-Arabic school of astronomy. However, the metal instruments did not measure up to his expectations, and he noted with disappointment that their axes soon wore down, displacing the centre and shifting the planes of reference. A reason for Jai Singh's difficulty could have been the fact that the technology of fabricating large metal instruments had not yet been developed in India. If the surviving specimens at the Jaipur Jantar Mantar are at all indicative of his attempts to construct metal instruments, it is obvious that his early instruments were too heavy, with no attention paid to eliminate the excessive weight. They were simply magnified versions of the small medieval instruments of the East that may still be seen in museums around the globe.

Jai Singh discarded has metal instruments in favour of ones of stone and masonry that he himself designed. De Bois, an eyewitness of his efforts, writes that the Raja prepared the models with his own hands. Altogether, Jai Singh constructed 13 different types of instruments (ranging from a few centimetres to 24 metres in height, for his observations at Delhi, Jaipur, Varanasi, Ujjain and Mathura) (Sharma, 1987; Kaye, 1918).

In 1981–82, the author spent several months studying Jai Singh's instruments at these locations, and noted that the instruments may be classified into three main categories, namely: (1) instruments for laymen, (2) low-precision instruments, and (3) the high-precision instruments. The instruments such as 'Dhruva Pattika' and 'Narivalalya' have been clearly designed with a layman in mind, and are of little value to a researcher. The instruments such as 'Jai Prakasa' and 'Rama Yantra', one the other hand, belong to the medium-precision category.

'Jai Prakasa' is a multi-purpose device and has a varying degree of accuracy. The Jaipur instrument, for instance, measures time with an uncertainty of ± ½ to ±1 min. and the zenith distance and declination both with uncertainty of + 3' of arc. The uncertainty in the measurements of azimuth and right ascension could be anywhere from ± 3' to ± 1 deg.

Despite the fact the Jagannath lauded the 'Jai Prakasa' as the finest of instruments, its utility is rather limited for the kind of precision Jai Singh had in mind (Sharma, 1967). The instrument is a good teaching tool nonetheless, displaying the relationship between the local and equatorial systems of coordinates. Its ability to indicate the approach of a sign of the meridian is quite valuable to a Hindu astrologer.

The 'Rama Yantra', another of his low-precision devices, is most sensitive near the 45° marks around the base line of its vertical walls. The theoretical accuracy of the 'Jaipur Yantra' is ± 1' or arc for the angles of 40°–50°. However, due to the finite width of the penumbra associated with the shadow of the pillar, the accuracies of this order are not possible in practice. And, as such, a precision of ± 6 is the most that one can expect with this instrument. For the zenith angle readings, the accuracies deteriorate at a rapid rate to ± 1° or worse, as the angle approaches zero.

The 'Samrata Yantra' and the 'Sasthamsa' both belong to the third category, that of high-precision instruments, and are two most sensitive instruments indeed. The Samrata of Jaipur is apparently designed to measure time with precision of ± 2 second, right ascension ± 15 of arc and declination ± 1' of arc. With this instrument, an accomplished observer can measure time with at least ± 3 second, and the two angles with ± 1' of arc accuracies, provided the instrument is constructed properly. However, the instruments of Jaipur and Delhi both suffer from a number of constructional defects. As a result, the time measurement accuracy for the Jaipur instrument ranges between ± 10 and ± 90 seconds, depending on the section of the instrument used. Similarly, the uncertainty in declination measurements could by anywhere from ± 1' to ± 15' of arc. With his Samratas, Jai Singh seems to have measured time with a greater accuracy than the instrument of Jaipur is capable of today.

The 'Sasthamsa' of Jaipur is the only sensitive instrument of Jai Singh that still maintains its intended accuracy of ± 1' of arc. (In 1981–82, the author took numerous readings with this instrument, and after becoming familiar with the device, his readings began to fall within the intended uncertainty. On December 23, 1981, for example, he measured the apparent declination of the meridian sun as 23':25' ± 1. This result compares well with the calculated value of 23':26' for the day.)

Jai Singh did not stop after having designed these two high-precision instruments, but continued on with his search for better ones. Accordingly, he sent a delegation to Europe in 1728, one of its goals being to learn about the old and the new instruments for astronomical observations. (*Gazeta 1*). He apparently intended to incorporate these instruments into his Jaipur observatory which, according to De Bois, was still being expanded at the time.

The questions that the Raja addresses to Boudier also reflect his continued interest in instrumentation. "How is the longitude of the moon observed in its off meridian position, and with what instrument?" he wrote to Boudier in 1730–31 (*Letters*, pp. 610–11).

The Telescope

Though Jai Singh's instruments are non-telescopic, he was aware of the telescope and, to some extent, of its potential as well. He had bought one at a cost of Rs 100 for his personal library (*Tozis 3*). In his

Zij-i-Muhammad Shahi, while introducing a chapter, "The Visibility of Moon", he states, "These rules are for naked-eye observations only, although the telescope is now being made in the country. The telescope enables one to see bright stars in broad daylight also – say around the noon hour. It also enables one to see the moon when there is hardly any light in it, or when its face is totally dark and invisible... The planet Saturn (through a telescope) appears oval in shape, an oval whose lower half is larger than the upper. Around the planet Jupiter, there revolve four bright stars. On the face of the Sun there are spots, and the Sun rotates once on its axis within a period of one year". He goes on to add, "Since the telescope is not readily available to an average person, we are going to base our rule of computations for the naked eye only" (*Zij Jadid Muhammad Shahi,* p.189).

Thus, the telescope was indeed available to Jai Singh and his astronomers; and they did use it to some extent at their observatories. In the astronomical endeavours of Jai Singh, it is not the telescope but the "telescopic sight" that is missing. His instruments are not designed to incorporate the telescopic sight. The author believes that the telescopic sight, which had been accepted only decades earlier by the astronomers of Europe, did not reach Jai Singh in time.

Jai Singh's statement regarding the shape of Saturn suggests that the telescope available to him was of an inferior quality. His erroneous statement about the rotational period of the Sun indicates that at his observatories, there was no sustained programme of observing in general with the telescope. His lack of interest in telescopic observation, and that of his astronomers as well, is further indicated by the fact that Jagannath does not include the telescope among the *yantras* for an observatory (Sharma, *Yantradhyaya*).

Hindu, Muslim and European Assistants

Jai Singh's early training as an astronomer had been under Hindu *pundits*, and they remained the mainstay of his programme until the very end. "Brahmins observe day and night at Jaipur", Boudier wrote (*Letters,* pp. 307–308). In 1734, there were 20 Hindu astronomers employed on daily wages at the observatory of Jaipur alone (*Tozis 1*). Keval Ram and Jagannath were his principal Hindu *Jyotisis*.

Jai Singh's interest in Islamic and European astronomy, and his patronizing of Muslim *nujumis* and *firangies* developed somewhat later, i.e., after 1715. An inventory of his library taken in 1715 shows

Sanskrit books only (*File No. 424/1, Jaipur Records, Rajasthan State Archives*). However, soon thereafter, Jai Singh started collecting Persian-Arabic works, and began patronizing the predominantly Muslim astronomers of the Persian-Arabic school. The involvement of Muslim astronomers in his programme peaked around 1725 and then tapered off until the end of his career (*Dastur Kaumvar*). Jai Singh's most decorated *nujumi* was Dayanat Khan (*Dastur Kaumvar*, 19, p. 563). The gifts and honours received by Dayanat Khan from the Raja suggest that he remained associated with him for over two decades. (In 1718, he received his very first gift of Rs 500 from the Raja. The final record of him receiving a gift is in 1739.)

Abdul Khair, *alias* Khair Allah, is said to have been one of his influential consultants (*Brindaban*). (However, the author did not see any record of gifts or honours received by Khair Allah to the Rajasthan State Archives. The Archives mention a dozen or so other *nujumis* however, receiving gifts from the Raja.) It is reasonable to assume that a team of these astronomers wrote the *Zij-i-Muhammad Shahi* under the direction of Jai Singh.

As the involvement of Muslim *nujumis* in his astronomical activities lessened, the involvement of Europeans, primarily of the Catholic faith, increased, reaching a peak around 1733 (*Dastur Kaumvar*, 18, 20; *Tazis 2*). The Europeans played the role of conveyors of European knowledge to the Raja. Accordingly, it was they who led a delegation to Europe, procured texts and instruments, translated de La Hire's tables, and carried out mathematical computations. However, the knowledge the Europeans brought to Jaipur had already become outdated in Europe, for it included neither the theories of Galileo, Kepler or Newton, nor the instruments such as the sextant employed by Flamsteed (Sharma, 1987; Kaye, 1918).

Delegation to Europe

In 1727–28, Jai Singh dispatched a scientific delegation to Europe after learning that the "the business of observatory was being carried on in Europe". The delegation, the very first of its kind, led by Fr. Figuerado, reached Portugal in January of 1729 (*Gazeta 2*). The *Lisbon Gazette* of March 10, 1729, reports that the delegation had come to the country to resolve questions regarding the astronomical tables used in Portugal and India, and to learn about the new and old instruments in astronomy (*Gazeta 1*).

Although the news of the delegation's arrival in Lisbon was duly published in the *Paris Gazette*, there is no mention of its arrival in Paris. The London papers are also silent about the delegation visiting their city. Apparently, the delegation never travelled to those places where the most advanced work on the subject was being carried out at that time. Surprisingly, the records of Coimbra University, the only institution of higher learning in Portugal at the time, say nothing about the delegation reaching their campus either.

The delegation returned in 1730, with some instruments, books on mathematics, and astronomical tables – including the one by de La Hire published in 1702. It is interesting to note that the delegation did not bring back the tables of Flamsteed published in England, which were the most accurate ones by then. In retrospect, the delegation produced very little.

Zij-i-Muhammad Shahi

Jai Singh's stated objective had been to produce a set of improved astronomical tables. The tables, drawn up by a team of observers and *nujumis*, as mentioned earlier, and completed sometime between 1727 and 1735, were dedicated to the reigning emperor Muhammad Shah. The tables are, therefore, called *Zij-i-Muhammad Shahi* (*ZMS*) – the astronomical tables of Muhammad Shah (*Zij-i-Muhammad Shahi*, henceforth abbreviated as *ZMS*, is a 400-page long traditional work on astronomy, of which a dozen copies survive to this day.)

After comparing five different copies of the *ZMS*, the author has concluded that there were at least two editions of this book: [(1) *The British Library, Ref*, (2) *Raja Library Rampur No. 1221*, (3) *Andhra Pradesh State Archives, Hyderabad, Riyazi 300*, (4) *Sawai Man Singh II Museum, Jaipur, and* (5) *Azad Library Aligarh*. The Raza Library copy belongs to the first edition).] The often-reported British Museum copy belongs to the second edition. Further, there were three commentaries said to have been written on the *ZMS* [by (1) *Khairalla* – see G.H. Jaunpur (1835), A.A. Khan Gori (1980)]. To the world of astronomy at large, the ZMS is of little use; it had been superceded by better tables in Europe even before it was published. However, to the traditional scholar of the country, to whom western science was out of reach, it remained a valuable resource for generations. The British Resident of Jaipur, J.P. Straton, writing in 1885, pointed out that the *ZMS* was still being used there at that time (*Purohit Hari Narayan Collection*).

Recently, it has been reported that "all the tables of the *Zij* concerning the sun, moon and planets are taken from de La Hire's work. They, in no way, depend on observations made in India" (Mercier, 1984). [We have not yet completed our analysis of the *ZMS* tables. Nonetheless, on the basis of the work done so far, we have reservations regarding the conclusions drawn in the paper.]

Conclusion

For the sake of rejuvenating astronomy in his country, Jai Singh expended a great deal of energy as well as his personal fortune, and yet he failed to initiate the new age of astronomy in India. However, it would be unfair to conclude that he is solely to blame for his act. The means of communication were still in primitive stages in the early 18th century and played a greater role in keeping the Raja ignorant of the contemporary astronomy of Europe than is generally realized.

Secondly, a complex interaction of intellectual stagnation, religious taboos, theological beliefs, national rivalries, and the simple human failings of his associates also share the blame to certain extent. (For example, Jai Singh's Brahmin pundits would not go to Europe because of a religious taboo against "crossing the ocean". The Europeans (primarily the Jesuits) had rejected Kepler and Newton, because of their theological beliefs. The national rivalries in Europe prompted the Portuguese to keep valuable contacts with a powerful prince of the East all to themselves. Some of these points have been further elaborated by the author in his 1982a, 1928b and 1984.

Jai Singh's primary interest had been lunar phenomena. And, for this, he made the best use of the technology available to him, the technology of building developed in the country. As pointed out earlier, the great 'Samratas' of Jaipur and Delhi are both capable of achieving a precision of ± 1' of arc – the limit for the unaided eye. Further, Jai Singh approached his self-appointed task of updating planetary tables with an open mind and kept this attitude alive throughout his career. If De Bois can be believed, the Raja was ready to set aside all other tables if a better one were available.

Jai Singh's accomplishments were medieval in retrospect, but his outlook was quite modern. For him, the scientific knowledge had no religion or nationality. His efforts were truly secular; astronomers of all faiths participated in it – a fact that alone is no small a compliment to a ruler born in an environment and age of intolerance and bigotry.

References

Brindaban, *Safina-i-Khusgo.f. 123*, Khudabaksha Lib. Patna.

Dastur Kaumvar, 18, 19 & 20, Jaipur State, Rajasthan State Archives, Bikaner.

De Bois, Joseph, *Introduction to de La Hire's Tabuale Astonomicae*, ms, S.M.S. Museum, Jaipur.

Gazeta de Lisboa Occidental (in short *Gazeta*) (1) March 10, 1729, p. 80; (2) January 20, 1729, p. 24.

Jam-I Bahadur Khani by G.H. Jaunpuri, p. 579, Calcutta, 1835; as quoted by S.A. Khan Gori.

Kaye, G.R. (1918), *Astronomical Observatories of Jai Singh*, Calcutta Reprint, 1973, Indological Book House, Delhi.

Khan Gori, S.A. (1980), "Impact of Modern European Astronomy on Jai Singh", *Indian Journal of History of Science*, 15, pp. 50–57.

Letres edifiantes et curieuses (1843), (*in short Lettres tome deuxieme)*, Paris.

Mercier, R. (1984), "Astronomical Table of Raja Sawai Jai Singh", *Indian Journal of History of Sciences*, 19(2), pp. 143–171.

Purohit Hari Narayan Collection, No. 309/10, Rajasthan Oriental Research Institute, Jaipur.

Sharma, R.S. (1967), *Samrata Siddhanta* of *Jagannath Samrata*, Indian Ins. Astro. Sanskrit Research, Reprint 1987, New Delhi.

25

The Maharaja's Observatories

ASHIM KUMAR ROY

G.R. Kaye, *A Guide to the Old Observatories*, at Delhi, Jaipur, Ujjain, Benares.

Originally published by the Superintendent Government Printing, Calcutta, in 1920. Facsimile reprint by the Academic Press, Gurgaon, 1985, p. 108, Rs 80.

G.R. Kaye's book in the *A Guide to the Old Observatories* series of the Archaeological Department is a shortened version of his monograph, *The Astronomical Observatories of Jai Singh* (Calcutta, 1918).

Sawai Jai Singh built five astronomical observatories. Four of these have been described in this book. The fifth one was at Mathura, built on the top of Mathura Fort. Growse, in his *Mathura: A District Memoire* (AD 1882), wrote: "The whole of the Mathura observatory has now disappeared. A little before the Mutiny, the buildings were sold to the great government contractor, Joti Prasad, who destroyed them for the sake of the materials". Growse is silent about the British officer who sold the buildings.

Several Books

Several books have been written on these observatories. A. Garrett and Chandradhar Guleri wrote *Maharaja Sawai Jai Singh of Jaipur and His Observatories* in 1902. Guleri, at that time, was a student in the Maharaja's College, Jaipur. In 1903, he appeared in the B.A. examination of the Allahabad University, and was the only one among the 228 candidates that year to be placed in the first division. Guleri went on to become the Manindra Chandra Nandi, Professor of Indian History and Culture at the Benares Hindu University and the Principal of the Oriental College. But his fame today rests on his contribution to Hindi literature, specially as a short story writer.

Professor M.F. Soonawala of Maharaja's College, Jaipur wrote in 1952 his book, *Maharaja Sawai Jai Singh II of Jaipur and His Observatories*. Soonawala's book was easy to read, well-illustrated and cost only two rupees.

There was also a small booklet in Hindi on Jai Singh's observatory at Varanasi. This work, *Kashi ka Man Mandir*, published by the Nagari Pracharini Sabha in 1943, was authored by Professor Chandi Prasad, who taught Physics for many years at the Queen's College, Varanasi, and was almost an institution by himself.

No Observatory before Jai Singh

About Kaye, the author of the present work, we know very little. Perhaps he was a scholar of history of astronomy and was brought to India by the Archaeological Department to study Jai Singh's observatories. His monograph mentioned above shows the hard and thorough work he was capable of.

Kaye came to believe that most of Hindu astronomy was taken from the Greeks. Whatever might be the truth about Kaye's theory, one thing is certain: the Hindus treated astronomy not as a science to be built upon observations, but as revealed truth, which could be known from authoritative texts.

We have, therefore, no record of any observatory built in India before Jai Singh. Jai Singh's inspiration to build an observatory came from what he had heard of the observatory of Ulugh Beg, built in Samarkand 300 years earlier. His purpose was to record the observed position of the stars, to calculate the eclipses correctly and to improve the calendar.

In actual practice, only two results of his calculations and observations are available. He found that the annual precession of the equinoxes was 51.6"; and the obliquity of the ecliptic was 23°28'. This latter figure was found by actual observation in his Delhi observatory.

Jai Singh firmly believed that the earth stood still, and the universe went round it once a day. His European contacts did not tell him the work done by Kepler and Newton. Perhaps these contacts were pious Catholics.

The present book is competently written. It has been out of print for the last forty years. This reprint would be useful to casual tourists as well as to serious students.

26

A Patron of Architecture

Some Features of the City as Built by Jai Singh II

YADUVENDRA SAHAI

Jaipur, the city of Jai Singh, lacked the advantage of a slow and stately growth that had nursed Amber; but its houses, if not so durable, are at least far more comfortable and convenient, keeping in mind especially the climate of the region. Despite the last four decades' overcrowding and traffic congestions, its wide and open straight streets are distinctly more welcome than the narrow winding tortuous lanes of old Amber.

In Jaipur, we think only of brightness and gaiety, life and valour, while the silent gloom and repose of Amber have been mellowed by the tender hands of time. Jaipur of two hundred and fifty years ago was far ahead of its times. Cities like Amber and Jaipur of the great Sawai are hard to come by.

Theories about Planning

Many theories have been put forward by scholars for the past two and half centuries about how Sawai Jai Singh created his Jayanagar. The theory that he sought inspiration from the blueprints of far away cities with strange sounding names, has recently acquired support. It is presumed on the basis of a chance discovery of the *Book of Atlases* of early 18th century in his 'Pothikhana' collection. He acquired this almost immediately after it was published. Another theory is that it was the brain-child of Vidyadhar, a Bengali Brahman, who first impressed his chief by an 'astronomical architectural' feat while he was still a boy, and for this reason he was given the task of executing it, and was later promoted as Desh-ka-Diwan for his feats, and remained a grandee of the court. But, there is not enough evidence to-date to support such an ambitious claim. A third theory is that one European, Don Xavier, was the brain behind the screen, but the supporters of this theory have not come forward with any evidence. Then, there are hundreds who still believe that Jai Singh took full advantage of the holy text of ancient *Shilpa-shastras,* which long ago, laid specific rules for construction of villages, towns etc. on similar lines. The supporters of this theory say that like Jaipur, Indra's Puri had its nine rivers (sectors), seven gates and straight broad avenues criss-crossed by streets at right angles. If such *Shilpa-shastras* and such cities existed in India or elsewhere, we have not met them yet.

One question which comes to our mind is: Was Sawai Jai Singh incapable of performing such a 'miracle' on his own? Surely, one who was capable of performing the *Aswamedh Yajna* (a feat repeated only after a full millennium), or who corrected an almanac, who constructed five unique stone observatories and recovered a lost kingdom against heavy odds and come out a winner, unscratched, surely he was capable of performing such a simple task as planning a city unlike any other known until then.

It is not as if Sawai Jai Singh performed a complete revolution in town planning. Cities in India always mushroomed round forts, and kings always took residence in a capital rendered difficult of access by natural or artificial barriers, such as deserts, rivers, lakes, mounds of earth, trees and above all by fortresses on mountains. Jaipur possesses all these advantages and more.

Location and Layout

Basically, the city of Jaipur stands on a small plain and the northern part of it on a basin, a bed of a lake, the prolongation of the present Man Sagar. The northern side having the king's palace in it has hills on all the three sides. While building his city, Sawai Jai Singh had the rock faces overlooking the city scraped and dressed to form steep cliffs on top of which he constructed his forts. At the same time, the chipped stone was dressed and used as building material for the houses and city walls. The forts that he constructed were Nahargarh (Sudershanghar) to the immediate north by north-west, Jaigarh deep down north and overlooking the Amber complex, and Amagarh to the east with another fort appendage over that Ghat valley. For protection of the weaker south side, he used existing low hillocks and built the Hathroi fort in the south-west and the Shankergarh (Moti Doongri) in the south-east.

NO MOAT

Sawai Jaipur never had a moat or ditch because Jai Singh was aware that building such a structure would be futile as it would immediately have been filled up by the encroaching sand brought in by the southerly winds. As if to keep the elements of tradition, he built a pit inside, all along the south wall. The river Dhanvantni flowed approximately along the north wall. These served the purpose of moats to some extent.

In the past, there must have been draw-bridges over these, as links between the gates and the main streets. Most of the old residents of Jaipur still recollect the *pukka* bridges that were later on constructed in their place during the times of Sawai Ram Singh II in the mid-19th century. The modern generation cannot visualize these, because in the fifties, the ditches were filled up and the Nehru Bazar, Bapu Bazar, and quite recently the Indra Bazar, have been constructed over those places.

Some Other Features

City Wall

A masonry crenellated wall built of mud, stone, mortar and covered with smooth terracotta plaster, averaging in height about 20 feet and in thickness 9 feet surrounds the whole city, pierced only by the seven gateways. The terracotta colour was chosen because it was the nearest in appearance to the red sandstone, of which ideally the walls should have been constructed. The bondage was not perfect and structurally, it was not a strong wall.

City Wall, Chowkris and Bazars of Jaipur

They were in a real bad shape with even trees growing on many places in the 19th century and almost in ruins. [Sawai Ram Singh II got them repaired by the State Public Works Department in the years 1872–1874 at a cost of Rs 32,749].

Bastions, Towers and Gateways

At some distance from each other, the usual bastions and towers for cannons were erected all along the walls.

The gateways were also constructed in the traditional style, each being well corrected with battlements, parapets, screen walls, surmounted by two kiosks and machicolations over the entrances. The doors were thick, of durable wood reinforced with metal mountings, bosses, and even iron-spiked knobs. Each was provided with a wicket window. The gates were all located at the end of the main roads.

Main Axis and Rectangles

The main road runs east to west forming the central axis, 2 miles and 40 yards, having at its ends, Suraj Pol – facing east, Chand Pol – facing west. Three streets, each over 100 feet wide, cross the central axis at right angles a mile and a quarter long.

South of the main axis, in the original plan of Jaipur, there were four almost equal rectangles. At some later date, the rectangle opposite to the Saharad was further sub-divided into two equal and smaller rectangles by construction of the Chaura Rasta, which still remained a dead end at the wall, where strong cages of wild animals were kept between the ditch and the wall. In 1868, a bridge of 20 feet span, flanked by two marble lions, was constructed joining the Chaura Rasta to this area. There was a gate along the south wall at the end of each of the main roads: Ram Pol, Ghat Darwaza, Shiv Pol (Sanganeri Gate) and Kishan Pol (Ajmeri Gate).

Chowkris

The five rectangles from the east to west were named *chowkris*: Topkhana Hazuri, Ghat Darwaza, Visheshwarji, Modi Khana and Topkhana Desh. On the north of the central axis, there was no *chowkri* opposite Topkhana Hazuri, which was caged by the city wall. Opposite the Ghat Darwaza was Chowkri Ram Chanderji and further north was Chowkri Gangapol. Opposite the two small *chowkris* was the palace enclosure called Chowkri Sarahad, beyond which was the Talktora lake and Raja Mall ka Talab (which was an underdeveloped marshy land). Opposite Chowkri Topkhana Desh was the Purani Basti, which extended right to the foot of the Nahargarh hill. The only gate towards the north was the one leading to Amber called Dhurv Pol (Zorawar Singh Gate). The Ganga Pol faced the east and was situated at the north-east corner of the city.

At the crossing of the main roads were constructed the great squares – *Chaupars*. In the beginning, these squares had deep *baoris*, where the city folks could take their bath and congregate at the times of the *Nahika Nahans* and *Kartik ka Nahans*. (Later on, when in the 19th century, these became the receptacles of the town's refuse, Sawai Ram

Singh converted them into garden squares in 1868 and added the ornamental fountains on marble base and balustrades in 1876, when Rs 2,933.2 and 9 pies were spent). The wide roads criss-crossing at right angles and the big squares gave it the look of a *chaupar* board.

Four Bazars and Hundreds of Shops

Originally, only four bazars were planned for the city: Johri Bazar, Sireh Deorhi Bazar, Kishanpole and Gangori Bazar. According to a map [*LS/14 dated 1725*] in the City Palace Museum collection, which has come to be known as the "progress report map", 162 shops were constructed *by the state*, in each of these bazaars(except only 144 shops on the western side of Kishanpole Bazar). All these shops were uniformed in shape and size; all exterior features were also ordered to be in harmony with each other. Almost immediately afterward, similar bazars were constructed along the Chandpol, Tripolia and Ramganj. They were ready before 1734. All the shops were constructed of stone, covered with plaster, painted a uniform terracotta colour. This was the colour chosen by Sawai Jai Singh, because he wanted to give this impression that they were constructed with red sandstones.

All the shops had a single inner chamber whose door level was raised above the street level. The top of the shop was of uniform height, and a short wall ran along the roof. No building was allowed to be constructed exactly above the shop chambers and the roof tops were left as open terraces for the town folks to sit on and watch the processions etc. from these vantage points. The rim of the roof wall was decorated with uniform *kangooras*. The lintels of the doors were flat in the middle ornamentally arched *todas* in the corners to give them strength and beauty. The doors were made of folding wooden planks of uniform make and green colour.

Works by State

Since many of the shops belonged to the *Raj* and few others to the private *banayas*, all works of construction, repairs and upkeep was done by the *Raj* and the cost was recovered from the owner or tenant. (When in 1868, Sawai Ram Singh II tried an experiment and ordered that each of the principal street in the city be colour-washed with a separate colour for each street, and the shops be furnished with coloured *saibans* to match, the Public Works Department carried out the chief's orders, and all shops and buildings were painted as per orders. The cost of

Rs 6,406–2 as 10 piece was recovered from all, except those who colour-washed and repaired themselves according to the prescribed pattern. But soon afterwards, the Maharaja realized his folly. He at once ordered the restoration of the original uniform colour on all shops and buildings for which the same procedure was adopted.)

Another unique feature about the main roads of the city is that all the old and previously existing temples were allowed to remain *in situ*, even if they came in the middle of the road. These temples exist even to this day in their original locations.

Jalis and Chhajjas

As noted in the poem "Bhojansar" by Girdhari composed in the year 1739, the directive of Sawai Jai Singh – "Jainiwas should come within this city, this is my wish. There should be many cross-roads with shops on them. The backyard of the houses should meet together" – was strictly adhered to.

Havelis and Jharokhas

In fact, all the houses (*havelis*) that hug the bazaars have their entrance in the side lanes, and the back-walls which are towards the main road have only windows and balconies with plaster *jalis* in the *jharokhas*.

The height of the storeys was well defined, and there was a ceiling on the maximum height. The storeys were hardly traceable from the outside, only the windows, *jalis* and balconies gave hints.

Inside the Havelis

The houses are characterized by low storeys, close rooms without free ventilation, with latticed windows, plastered walls with small projections from them called *chhajas*, that is, cornices, broad corridors, lofty terraces and gloomy closets with cantilever like *todas*. Doors and windows (with *jilmils*, Venetian blinds and glass panes introduced in the 19th century) opening vertically from the centre, beautiful balconies and inner galleries on the second and third storeys must have been introduced during the times of Sawai Jai Singh. (Some of the terms used above would need some explanation, especially when used in the present context. We must however skip such details—*Editors.*)

In addition to the usual narrow stairway, the upper floors of many of Jaipur houses (especially the royal apartments and richmen's houses) may be reached by long passages. There are also many subterranean corridors and cellars called *soorangs* and *tai-khanas*, which are built, among other reasons, to provide a cool repose for the hot summers.

Baradaris and Barsatis

By the 'lofty terraces' here is meant the *chandanis* common to all houses, where the people sleep in the summer, and the *chabutras* or real terraces in front of the buildings which are quite often ornamented with fountains, kiosks; and on the terrace, one usually finds a *baradari* (open twelve-pillared structure) or a *barsati* (which could be a simple room with a tin-shed). Here, on the terraces, in the past, guests used to be entertained *mahfils*, *nautch* parties etc., used to be performed. When privacy was desired, *kanats* could be drawn around and curtains could be thrown over the platform for protection from the elements.

Most of the rooms in the houses are small, but it cannot surprise any one, when one counts the number of people actually using the small rooms. There are practically no pieces of furniture, but *gaddas*, *chaddars* and *masnads* provide a good padded covering on the ground to sit or sleep upon. Wherever possible, niches and cupboards are constructed and there is an attempt to use up all possible available space. Shelves (*tands*) are constructed and the window sills are also used when necessary.

Other Features of Domestic Architecture

The balconies are very beautiful as well as prominent features in the architecture of Jaipur. Like an extension or a bastion, they enable the occupier to see the road from end to end, a very necessary arrangement in the days of the *purdah*. The openings were either blocked by fine *chicks* or often by the fine lattice work in plaster. The centre of the lattice work usually had a small square or inverted U-shaped opening which was also windowed up with a wooden plank provided with peep-holes. The roof was curved or domed and there were ample hanging *chhajjas* (or cornice) the ends of which usually hung down at a remarkable angle. The kiosks or domes were surmounted by gold-plated, *kalashs* or *trisuls* (especially during Sawai Ram Singh's reign) or pointing brass flags that fluttered with the wind.

The inner galleries (*rosas*) with ornamental railings (*kataras*) in the private houses ran round the central square on the upper storeys and from these, entrance was gained to the different rooms all around, the staircase being usually at one corner. The chambers facing the sides of the square were open in front and formed common rooms, the private apartments were at the corners and in the rear, one could be reached through these common rooms only.

... and Decorations

The decorations on the walls and ceilings of these rooms were simple. The wall would be either plastered *terracotta* or pale yellow, blue etc.; straight stripes in white or black would be painted to give the semblance of inlay in red sandstone. Quite often, the floor as well as the *dodas* (that is upto 3 feet of side walls) would be decorated with *araish*, or plaster, usually made of powdered crystalline stones like marble and fine lime. A polish was given with agates and *cowries*. The coloured plaster for the other walls was usually made with lime and *surkhi* (or burnt sand) mixed in different proportions, according to the work required; molasses were nearly always introduced to bind the plaster. For the finer work, eggs were sometimes used. This took up the highest of polish.

Another decoration was the painting of subjects like the *Raga-Ragani*, *Baramasa* and animals, birds etc. on the walls or ceiling, in between floral or scroll motifs. The main entrance doorway was often painted with *Dwarpals* flanked with elephants. Ganesh was usually perched in the niche in the *toran* of the *Deorhi* (main gate).

Quite often, talc or really mica was set either in small squares or circles or convexed in all sorts of odd shapes, many times over coloured background. The mirror effect, which could play optical tricks with the onlooker, was often the decoration for the interior rooms of the *Zenana* where wine, women and song played supreme.

Roofs, Doors and Courtyards

The normal roof was constructed with the use of sandstone *patties*, hooks usually being provided for the cloth flap fans. Where the room was large, a semi-circle arch was usually constructed in the middle, and *patties* laid across on either sides. The windows were normally very small openings and usually provided with two-piece wooden planks with small peep holes. The doors were usually low (one had to bend to enter) and provided with stone-frame lintels. The two planks wooden doors were often pasted with cloth over which human figures or floral patterns were painted and covered with shellac. The unpainted doors were usually enforced with brass or metal strips mounting and bosses.

The main entrance to the house was through a tunnel with a decorative frontage provided on either side by domed *gookhas* with flat, raised platforms and the bloated half balcony-type facade. Rooms on either sides of the tunnel were for the guards. The usual practice was for the tunnel to lead through a winding passage into the first courtyard, surrounded on all sides with cloisters and rooms. This also had passages that led into the second, third or a fourth courtyard, each surrounded likewise with cloisters and rooms. In case the courtyard was very large, it could be provided with a centrally constructed *baradari* (pillared open hall) or even a garden of sort. It was not rare to find a large *Peepal* or *Neem* tree growing in the middle of these courtyards which soared high above the two or three storeys.

Havelis: Miniature Palaces

Following the layout of the chief's palace, the citizens and the nobles aimed at building a miniature palace of their own. They had all the various sections, if they could help it, like the *Deorhi*, *Diwan Khana*, *Sahen ki Kothri* (sleeping chambers), *Zenana* (female chambers), *Pothikhana*, *Rasora* (kitchen), *Kothiars* (store houses for provisions), *Athithi Ghar* (guest house), *Kapatdwara* (strong room), *Saparni-ki-Kothri* (bathing house), *Sandas-ki-Kothri* (latrine), *Feel-khana* (elephant stable), *Shutar-khana* (camel house), *Atish* (horse stable), *Rathkhana* (chariot house) *Buggie-khana* (carriage house), *Farash Khana* (furniture store-house), *Sawan-badho* (open pavilion for the hot months, usually having a creeper-vine roof) and others. However, simple or small the house may be, a room or quite often just a corner, area or place was set aside, and assigned the above-mentioned high sounding names.

Little wonder then that even soldiers like Sir David Ochterlony who passed by in 1817 (when the glory of the Jaipur city was really at its lowest ebb) was impressed by the "spacious and magnificent – a common verdict on a nearer acquaintance". (Recently, the SMS Museum authorities have discovered many photographs of Jaipur taken around 1850s.)

Overall View

The wide streets lined with houses of tolerably regular form, the cupolas, the mathematical plan, the overhanging hills and forts, the gaily dressed people, and above all, the clear sky combine to form a most pleasing impression. But taken apart, very few buildings are grand or even artistic in construction, although they may be fantastic, bizarre and striking from their very singularity and often startling naïve disregard of artistic principle. Shops run along both sides of the more important streets, each being a single cell in a continuous arcade. Everyone has an inner room in the rear above which is a second, third and sometimes even a fourth storey, which usually belongs to houses unconnected with the shops. On most of the roads, second floor was not even reached, but the line was preserved by a perforated screen wall. The upper and lower parapets are crenallated and sometimes perforated, and each storey is marked by the overhanging (*chhajja*) sunshades and cornices, by these the walls are protected and direction is given to the weave cloth which was projected over the pavements on occasions of feasts or to get protection from the elements.

The grand feature of the whole is the unsparing use of the foiled horizontal arch, in shops or private houses everywhere, in niches and in the many kiosks which project above the general outline and change all along from flat through round to pointed. The roofs also take many forms, from the ruined one of thatch, to the peculiar segmental boatshaped vault, crowned with gilted pinnacles. The walls are all exceptionally thin. There is an endless variety of tracery, the fantastic mouldings and the occasional 'barbarity' of a temple spire in juxtaposition with ugly, unkept coloured washed domes – all give the most fascinating skyline encountered anywhere in the world. It is not rare to come across Indian, Mughal, Persian, Grecian, Italian, Saracenic, Edwardian, even Victorian tinsheds.

Temple Architecture

A word now about the temple architecture. Not considering the very old temples that existed from before the foundation of the city and which were allowed to remain *in situ* without any disturbance, the first temple to be built in the new city was that of Shri Govind Devji. There is a legend that, at first, Sawai Jai Singh built his residential quarters at the site of the present temple and the deity was housed elsewhere in the complex. The deity appeared to him in his dreams and ordered him to move elsewhere, and house the deity in its present locale. Perhaps this legend was circulated by way of a humble excuse for the residential, non-temple like structure of the temple. The flat roof, small dark dingy chambers and in fact all the architectural features indicate that this temple was built in a hurry, possibly it was at first used as a residence. The trend is a repetition of other such contemporary structures like the Nathadwara and Mathura temples. The Mughal lamp was already flickering and there definitely was no threat of temple destruction from that side. There was no reason to build ordinary looking temples that would not attract attention from afar. Besides, most of the other temples built by Sawai Jai Singh in his city were of the traditional pyramid shape, tapering domes or cupolas, all with gilted *kalashs* on top, and arches on the outside called *kabanava* made of two long brackets, the masonry being in horizontal courses, the soffit of the arch being foiled, although sometimes rounded, thus exposing the flat architrave. This was the true Hindu arch, as met earlier in Mount Abu, Sanganer, Amber and elsewhere, as against the true arch with its radiating voussoirs. In all these traditional temples, we still do not meet the European arch. Even, the Hindu arch is modified here by the waving ribs within.

The temples are in the Rajput or Chalukya style, and generally of a mixed form, unlike those met in Amber and Sanganer, which were chaste. Most of Jaipur's temples also lack the usual profuse carvings. The spine is like the Bengali truncated paraboloid construction, crowned with a lotus, and gilt or stone *kalashs* as pinnacle with a flag staff and *trisul-damru* in case of Shiv temples. These last type made their appearance in the 19th century under Maharaja Ram Singh II. The *Mandap* is usually a domed building, rather Jain in form, with a curious dentated moulding repeated all over the roof which often remains an octagonal pyramid. There may or may not be a covered gate, with the saracenic top (as found in the secular buildings). The high steps leading to the platform on which the temple stands, and the minuteness of the decorations and carvings round the building tend to give a grandeur and apparent size to the comparatively small edifices. The want of light in the interior and the height of the roof produce quite a solemnizing and appropriately gloomy effect. The *Naubat Khanna* is kept out of sight, unlike the visible counterparts in the past. Most of the temples have a series of courts surrounded by arcades and calls for promenade, residence of officials, *pathshalas*, libraries, *rasoaras*, *kothiyars* etc. as in the secular buildings of the city. Only, unlike there, we find the profuse use of exclusive building materials like marble and silver, gold mountings in the constructions of doors. The staircase and floor are usually constructed by the locally available Raiwala marble which was inlayed with black marble from nearby Baislana mine in Kotputli. The better Makrana marble is reserved for the carvings and important areas. The sandstone used was obtained locally from near Karauli, the more exclusive Jodhpur stone being reserved for exclusive use.

The Main Palace

And finally now a few more words about the palaces of Sawai Jaipur. Whatever architectural features that have been mentioned above about the secular buildings are naturally to be found in the buildings of the palaces, only of course, on a far more grander scale. The main palace can be reached by traversing seven tunnel gates and several courtyards along a circuitious route. The main palace called Chandra Mahal is seven floors high and is the tallest structure in the city. Sawai Jai Singh had utilized the *sarhad* of the hunting grounds *baghichas* (pleasure gardens) of his forefathers, as the locale of his residential quarters. Hence, the location of the buildings and gardens had to follow a pre-defined pattern. It was the greatness of Sawai Jai Singh that he was able to create such a well-planned, comfortable palace under the circumstances. The palace complex was so large that it was possible for him to establish all the minor industries connected with it in the most comfortable manner. He was also able to make exceptionally large structures within, which were completely hidden from the onlooker's eye from without the palace walls. One of the earliest descriptions of the palace made by an outsider was by Bishop Heber in 1825: "...an extremely high front of seven or eight storeys, diminishing in the centre to something like a pediment, and flanked by two towers of equal height toped with open cupola".

This is a fairly accurate description of the Mukat Mahal and proves that it already was complete and in its present shape in 1825, much before the times of Sawai Ram Singh II who, according to popular lore, is attributed to have constructed this top floor. Sawai Jai Singh constructed the Jai Niwas Garden and Nichla Bagh in the tradition of the Mughal gardens. His *Diwan-i-Aam* and *Diwan-i-Khas* were like their Mughal counterparts, only he named them *Sabha Niwas* and *Sarvotbhadra* to provide the Hindu element.

27

Historical Literature on Sawai Jai Singh II

R.N. CHOWDHURI

A historical review of the available literature on Sawai Jai Singh II, on the occasion of his third birth centenary (3 November, 1988) would reveal that his remarkable contributions to our cultural heritage are as relevant today as they were during his time. For forty-four years (from 1699 to 1743 AD) he was the most dominant personality in one of the dark periods of Indian history. Jai Singh, the son of Vishnu Singh and Indra Kumari, succeeded his father at the age of eleven. It is said that Aurangzeb called him 'Sawai', that is one and a quarter more intelligent than his illustrious ancestors. A consummate diplomat, he is remembered even today for (1) extending his kingdom and establishing dominance over other states of Rajputana; (2) the foundation of the new capital city of Jaipur, now called the Pink City; (3) construction of five astronomical observatories and promotion of the study of astronomy; (4) revival of Vaishnavism; (5) patronage of Sanskrit scholars; and (6) remoulding the local customs and traditions on secular basis.

Sources: Primary and Secondary

The *primary* sources on Jai Singh II are archival records, the most important being the *Kapaddwara* records of the royal household available in Rajasthan State Archives, Bikaner. The Devasthan records, the *Nuskhya Punya*, deal with the religious history of Jaipur. Poet Girdhari of Jai Singh's court wrote *Bhojanasara* (dietics) in 1739, which describes the city of Jaipur and its Bengali architect, Vidhyadhar Bhattacharya, and is now preserved in the Bhandarkar Oriental Research Institute, Poona.

Perhaps the most well-known and widely read is Shri Krishna Bhatta's *Ishvaravilasa Mahakavya*, a work in Sanskrit by the court poet Ishvari Singh (1743–1750), written in 1749, which give a detailed description of the *Asvamedha Yagya* performed by Jai Singh.

Surajmal Mishra of Bundi wrote *Vamsha Bhaskar* in 1841, which is critical about Jai Singh's intervention in the succession disputes of Bundi.

A modern historiographer, Kaviraj Shyamaldas, wrote *Vir Vinod* in 1875, printed by the Mewar state in four volumes, tracing the history of Jai Singh with other states of Rajasthan on the basis of a few original letters.

The *secondary* sources of Jai Singh II may be classified into three categories: (1) monographs and special studies on his astronomical contributions; (2) history of Jaipur State, and (3) general history of Rajasthan.

About Astronomy: Books, Observatories and Instruments

***Recent Books*:** The first special study about Jaipur observatory was made by A.H. Garret, assisted by Pandit Chandra Sekhar Guleri, entitled *The Jaipur Observatory and its Builder* in 1902 (Allahabad), which is a useful and informative pioneering effort.

Sixteen years later, in 1918, G.R. Kaye published his well-known work *The Astronomical Observatories of Jai Singh* (Calcutta), which is a scholarly analysis of the astronomical contributions of Jai Singh with special reference to the Samarkand (1393–1449 AD) Scientific School of Ulug Begh whom he calls a 'martyr prince'.

Thanks to the initiative of Dr G.S. Mahajani, the first Vice-Chancellor of Rajasthan University and a distinguished mathematician of Cambridge, the Jaipur Astronomical Society, founded by him in 1946, published a very important and indispensable booklet in 1952. This booklet entitled *Maharaja Sawai Jai Singh II of Jaipur and his Observatories* was written by M.F. Soonawala, Professor of Physics, Maharaja's College, Jaipur (Bani Mandir, Jaipur). Explaining the historical background and the broad theoretical principles of Jai Singh's astronomical studies, the author tells us that Jai Singh took 16 years from 1718 to 1734 to construct his principal observatories at Jaipur and Delhi.

We may cover this book in some detail, as summed up below:

Soonawala's Book

***Jai Singh's Own Studies*:** Jai Singh first studied *Euclid* through the translations of Nasir-ul-Din al Tusi, a Persian astronomer, who had built an observatory at Maragha in 1259 AD and had published his tables as the *Ithkanic Tables*. Ptolemy's great work *Syntaxis*, known in Arabic translation as *Almagista*, the main source of Arab astronomy for centuries, appeared in Europe as *The Almagest*.

Jai Singh adopted the tables of Ulugh Beg with the help of Jagannath, a Maratha Brahmin. He is reported to have translated into Sanskrit, Ptolemy's *Syntaxis*, called *Siddhanta* and *Rekha Ganit*, which are available in City Palace (*Pothikhana*) Library. Renowned Sanskrit scholars, Pandit Kewal Ram and Pundarik Ratnakar, assisted him in the translation work. Kewal Ram wrote *Jin Vinod*, *Vibhag Sarni* (logarithmic tables), *Tura Sarni* (Ulugh Beg's tables) and *Drig Prakash Sarni* (la Hire's tables).

Jai Singh dispatched learned scholars like Muhammed Mahadi to the Middle East and Padre Manuel de Figueirvado to Portugal to procure books and astronomical instruments. Jai Singh had invited the French Jesuit Father Claude Boudier and Pons in 1734, followed by Father Andre Stroble, a Bavarian Jesuit, in 1740.

***Observatories*:** He first built his first observatory at Delhi and then at Jaipur, Mathura, Varanasi and Ujjain. He had invented his own instruments of stone and lime in place of brass, such as *Jai Prakash*, *Ram Yantra* and *Samrat Yantra*.

In chapter III, the author gives details of Jai Singh's astronomical studies covering 15 pages. Perhaps the most important chapter (IV) is the description of his astronomical instruments. *Jai Prakash* is the most versatile instrument with a diameter of 27' in Delhi and 18' in Jaipur. Other instruments are *Samrat Yantra*, *Nari Valaya Yantra*, *Kapali Yantra*, *Misra Yantra*, *Chakra Yantra*, *Kranti Vritti Yantra* and the most ambitious *Yantra Raj* of 7' diameter in brass, which are unique examples of his love for science. Jai Singh wrote *Yantra Raj Karika* dealing with the many novel features of these instruments.

Prof Soonawala has thus made Jai Singh's astronomical calculations easily accessible to everyone interested in this field.

A Recent Book on Political Achievements

Dr V.S. Bhatnagar, in his well-known monograph on *Life and Times of Sawai Jai Singh (1688–1743)*, which is a doctoral dissertation of

Rajasthan University, published in 1974, has consulted, for the first time, unpublished primary sources of the period. Although the work deals mainly with Jai Singh's political achievements focusing on his role in Mughal court, the intensive wars among the Rajput states, relations with the Marathas and Jats, and his cultural contributions have also been studied briefly. Development of trade and commerce during his times could have been covered as well. This book has also been published in Hindi by the Rajasthan Granth Academy.

On a School of Science and the Renaissance

Prof A. Rahman, in his monograph on *Maharaja Sawai Jai Singh II and Indian Renaissance* (Navrang, New Delhi, 1987), has attempted to answer the question: Why, in those unsettled times, did Jai Singh decide to invest in observatories?

This illuminating study includes interesting and revealing material in chapters on "Motives of Jai Singh"; "Methodology followed by Jai Singh"; "School of Scientists under the Patronage of Jai Singh"; "Development of Arts and Craft"; and "Development of Agriculture".

The author has taken pains to study the contribution on Jai Singh by the Soviet scholars, particularly Sobirov. The book is profusely illustrated.

Prof Rahman has observed: "His purposes were also political to secularize the calendar; social and cultural – to bring to the people the importance of science and demonstrate its utility and inculcate in them the habit of making observations" (p. 30). He quotes from the account of the Soviet scholar, Sobirov:

> The study of the works of Sawai Jai Singh shows that his scientific school gave not only a new direction in the growth of mathematics and astronomy in general, but also made a number of fundamental discoveries (p. 30).

Jai Singh reviewed the ecliptical movement of the planets, and discussed the elements of the orbits.

Dr Rahman analyses in detail the scientific activities of Jai Singh given by Maulana Hazoor Allahi in his famous book *Zij Jadid Muhammad Shahi*. Praising Jai Singh's technological advancement, the author gives examples of *araish*, the technique of lime-plastering, a big and small furnace called *kharat* and *turfan* for manufacturing guns, a mint, storage of water in tanks and dyeing and printing.

Referring to the geometrical design in the planning of Jaipur, which followed the pattern of a square with broad roads lined by *bazars* and *chaupars* at the cross-section of the main roads, Prof Rahman observes:

"He (Jai Singh) was trying to show to his people that through the use of science and technology and the culture, new aesthetics and artifacts could be developed" (p. 30).

In conclusion, the learned scholar, who is a distinguished scientist and Director of the National Institute of Science, Technology and Development Studies at New Delhi, states that Jai Singh collected scientists of different schools of thought and religions together "to synthesize knowledge and give it a secular base, and to use that as a basis of further development of Indian science and society" (p. 74) "A critical study of his work would promote understanding of the three major traditions of science – Indian, Central and West Asian, and European. The vision of a new future India is perhaps central to his scientific activities" (p. 77).

A Hindi Biography

For readers interested in Hindi, Rajendra Shankar Bhatt, a former Director of Information and Public Relations of Rajasthan, has written a balanced and comprehensive account of Sawai Jai Singh II (since translated into English by National Book Trust. Eds.). His penetrating and in-depth study has been appreciated by the students of history.

About the City

Dr Ashim Kumar Roy, in his PhD thesis entitled *History of the Jaipur City* (Manohar, 1978) has devoted three out of seven chapters to Jai Singh: Ch. I: Jai Singh, the Founder of the City, Ch. II: Planning of the Jaipur City, and Chapter VII: Religious Life. We are told that Jai Singh stored water for the city of Jaipur from a nearby stream called *Darbhavati*, which is not traceable now. "He had altogether 27 wives and perhaps four concubines, the largest number ever had by the rulers of Amber and Jaipur" (p. 9). Jaipur *Pothikhana* has 18 Arabic and Persian manuscripts on astronomy including *Lavaheul-Qamar*, an Arabic translation of the *Chanda Sidhanta* acquired by Jai Singh in 1725 (p. 17).

Roy has summed up Jai Singh's achievements in astronomy as follows:

1. He accurately found out the declination of the ecliptic with his *Samart Yantra*.
2. By observation, he determined the figure of the annual precession of the equinoxes.
3. He revised the star catalogue of Ulugh Beg.
4. He got the tables prepared by indicating the position of the planets for the almanac makers.

Dr Roy is the first scholar to state that the almanac makers did not follow the correct position of planets in their almanacs. "He failed to create an interest in his countrymen in observational astronomy" (p. 18).

To a devout Hindu, Jai Singh was a defender of Hindu faith, for he installed the idol of *Govindadeva* in his palace in Jaipur in 1735. He also brought four Vaishnava images to Jaipur from Vrindaban, e.g., Gopinath, Radha Damodar, Gokulnanda, and Radha Vinode (pp. 26–28).

Quoting Tod, who has given credit to Vidhyadhar for the design and execution of the city of Jaipur, the learned scholar, without any supporting evidence, states: "The original plan of the city of Jaipur was *probably prepared by Jai Singh himself* (p. 41). According to Dr Roy, the width of the road in Johari Bazar was 101 ft and the smallest lane (Sonthiliwalon ka Rasta) was only 15 ft wide".

The book deals with the decay (1800–1835 AD) and growth of Jaipur (1835–1892) and its modernization (1922–1940).

Heritage

One of the recent publications on Jaipur is the *Cultural Heritage of Jaipur*, a collection of articles edited by J.N. Asopa and published by the Rajasthan History Congress in 1979. In this book, Ch. 3 deals with "Jaipur and its Environs: A Study in Architecture" by Dr Satya Prakash, former Director of Archeology, Rajasthan (pp. 12–29), Ch. 4 "Sawai Jai Singh, Patron of Architecture" by Yadvendra Sahai (pp. 30–42), Ch. 5 "Town Planning in Jaipur" by Dr A.K. Roy (pp. 43–47), Ch. 8 "Sawai Jai Singh's Contribution to Culture" by Dr V.S. Bhargava (pp. 63–75) and Ch. 13, "Contributions of Jaipur to Sanskrit Literature" by Dr Prabhakar Shastri (pp. 201–236).

Dr Shastri has mentioned that 17 Sanskrit scholars had composed 72 works relating to ethics, law, grammar, astrology, literature, history and incantation. Of these works, Goswami Shiv Nath Bhatt wrote 40 books; Kavi Kalanidhi Shri Khrishna Bhatt composed seven works; Kevalram Jyotishry wrote five books; and Jagannath Samrat three works, including *Ishwar Vilas*. All these works are very important (pp. 209–10).

Some Popular Books

We have a number of popular books on the history of Jaipur by reputed historians like Sir Jadunath Sarkar, Mathura Lal Sharma and Thakur Fateh Singh Champawat, which are stimulating and useful.

Jaipur Gazetteer, compiled by Major C.A. Baylay, Political Agent, in 1876, is a rapid survey of the development of Jaipur.

The well-known German work of Breitzler entitled *Jaipur Studien Zur Stadt Und Sozial-Geographic Einer Indischan Gross Stadt*, published by Ruhr University, Bochum, in 1970, is available in the Rajasthan University Library.

Among the books on general history of Rajasthan, the first work was published in 1829, by James Tod entitled *Annals and Antiquities of Rajasthan*. A number of textbooks on Rajasthan history are also available in Hindi written by Dr G.N. Sharma, Dr V.S. Bhargava, Dr Kalu Ram Sharma and Prof Divakar, which only provide glimpses of Jai Singh's political achievements.

28

Some Books About Jai Singh II and His City

MOHITA KAPUR

Jadunath Sarkar: A HISTORY OF JAIPUR, *Orient Longman, New Delhi, 1984, p. 416, Rs 175.*

The manuscript of this book was originally written in 1939–40, but it was published in 1984. The fact that Jadunath Sarkar agreed that, if so desired, some omissions might be made from the manuscript reflects that it was desired to be a favourable comment by the sponsor, Maharaja Man Singh II, who commissioned Sarkar to write this book. However, it was published without deletions. The manuscript has been edited by Raghubir Singh of Sitamau.

Generally speaking, Sarkar is obsessed with the typically "medieval" Indian backwardness – conservatism, feudalism, inferiority, the tradition of anti-modernism – and holds it responsible for all Indian failures against enemies who obtained foreign help (e.g., the Rajput... "humiliation by Marathas and their French-led battalions").

A better title of the book would have been "A History of Kachchawahas", for it concentrates more on dynastic achievements and less on the state as a whole with its masses and their pre-occupations.

Care has been taken to prove Col James Tod (who wrote *Annals and Antiquities of Rajasthan*), and the local tales and bardic sources of history wrong, wherever possible. Their inauthenticity has been emphasized upon and argued out.

Sarkar has painstakingly disproved the prevalent notions, to thwart the grip of tradition and gossip over historical facts: ... "an authentic account must henceforth replace the ignorant or prejudiced outpourings of bardic traditionalists and the short perfunctory and unfair narrative which Lt Col Tod has vouchsafed to the annals of the most illustrious dynasty of Rajasthan ......" Sarkar has apparently tried to do justice to whatever he portrayed; but he did leave some ground uncovered and, therefore, his analysis remains one of a limited perspective. It ends up by being an uncritical eulogy.

The Kachchawaha dynasty has been praised at every turn for its bravery and military exploits. Jai Singh's achievements are considered extremely praiseworthy: "the family fortunes and prestige had sunk very low and the future looked hardly more promising ... But, the glory of the Kachchawaha royalty was retrieved by the genius and opportunism of Sawai Jai Singh II and raised to an even loftier pitch than under the great Man Singh or Mirza Raja Jai Singh".

Jai Singh has been defended in his policy towards the Mughal Emperor: ... "if the life work of Jai Singh did not benefit the empire as Man Singh's did or the first Jai Singh's had done, it was not his fault".

Details of events have been given, for which a lot of hitherto (1940) unused source material from the Jaipur State Archives has been used.

Jai Singh's efforts (during his first subedari of Malwa made routes safe for traders (1714–17). His subduing the Jats led by Churaman was indicative of a 'statesmanly policy'. His Maratha policy (second subedari of Malwa) is considered practical – as that of a "true statesman and experienced man of action". It was the policy of coming to terms with the Marathas by mutual concessions and living amicably by their side. Diplomatic appeasement and war had to be used only as the last resort. Indeed, the best word used by Sarkar for Jai Singh is 'opportunistic'.

An interesting description of Peshwa Baji Rao's meeting with Jai Singh in 1736, at Jaipur is given: he (Baji Rao) had the 'manners of a mosstrooper' blowing smoke into the face of his host, while Jai Singh played the 'perfect host', as a "first class grandee of the polished court of Delhi".

Opportunistic as he was, Jai Singh apparently realized the futility of backing a spent force, the Mughal Empire – and moulded his Rajputana and Maratha policies accordingly. He also aimed at acquiring the 'local hegemony'. Sarkar feels he sought to give political unity to the *Dhundhar* country by acquiring *parganas* through formal imperial rescripts – it was to be a legitimate hold, a rational and systematic policy.

Though Sarkar refrains from commenting directly on Jai Singh with regard to his policy towards Raja Budh Singh and his State of Bundi, a subtle remark points at him:... "this injustice to the legitimate heir (Budh Singh's son Umed Singh) of Bundi began a course fraught with the greatest evil to Rajputana". As history stands witness, almost all principal states of Rajputana were involved in the subsequent war of succession.

The Hurda Conference of 1734, which had been called to unite Rajput rulers and to chalk out their programme against Maratha incursions, does not find any mention with reference to Rajput-Maratha relations and Jai Singh. In the chair was Maharana Jagat Singh of Udaipur. Being deprived of its leadership, Jai Singh ceased to take any interest in its efforts.

Though Jai Singh's plans of establishing a regional hegemony met with failure, especially because of his weak successors, Sarkar has made an important observation: "Absolute local autonomy was the life-breath of every Rajput State and sub-clan, however small" – and rightly, this feature was to dominate Rajputana politics till the acknowledgement of British paramountcy. Sarkar minces no words: "The noblest Hindu martial race" could not forget "their petty feuds and merge their local independence......for the sake of mutual defence and progress......" Rajputana, therefore, became a mere "geographical expression", a bundle of warring atoms, as Prof M.S. Jain says in his book *Adhunik Rajasthan Ka Itihas* (Panchsheel Prakashan, Jaipur, 1988, p. 428, Rs 60).

A full chapter has been devoted to the city of Jaipur (out of five on Jai Singh II). Sarkar has quoted from accounts by European travellers to emphasize the impressive character of the city, its neatness, methodical layout, and attention to details of beauty and planning. Sarkar is less overt in his praise of Jai Singh's achievements in astronomy. No new discoveries are attributed to him (even those of the instruments are accompanied with doubt).

Contrasting with what A.K. Roy quoted from Bundi court-poet Surya Mal Mishran, Sarkar has quoted an extremely flattering paragraph from *Vamsha Bhaskar (IV) 3089–3102* (p. 233). This raises a question about his motives.

Quoting forms of address from letters, Sarkar has projected Jai Singh as possessing unmatched power and military leadership in Rajputana. He has been portrayed as a 'Hindu ruler', paying heed to his co-religionists – he got the *jaziya* tax as well as the practice of attaching the property of deceased religious men abolished.

Jai Singh's works of public charity and social reform too have been touched upon. For the failures of the latter, Sarkar blames the "backward self-willed society" and rightly so, for social change needs the preparation of the mental attitudes and a social climate of receptibility.

Determined to shower praise on Jai Singh, Sarkar completely overlooks Jai Singh's pledge to the Mewar Maharana, which was to bring havoc on Jaipur State after his death. (Jai Singh had promised to make his son by the Princess of Mewar his successor, even if he was not his eldest son). Roy, similarly, refrains from expressing an opinion on it. M.S. Jain, however, has mentioned this as one of the two principal wrongs done by Jai Singh to Rajputana by his selfishness and short-sightedness. The other was not letting the Hurda Conference meet with success in its endeavours.

* * *

V.S. Bhatnagar: LIFE AND TIMES OF SAWAI JAI SINGH, *Hindi Granth Academy, Jaipur, 1972, p. 227, Rs 19.*

The year 1712 has been identified as a turning-point of sorts – with the death of the Mughal Emperor Bahadur Shah, a number of changes came about. The principal one was a change in the Rajput perspective of Mughals; they realized the limitations of loyalty to the decadent empire. This is the opinion expressed by Prof Bhatnagar, but not well argued with post-1712 occurrences. It was primarily Jai Singh who exhibited this realization, and that too, almost two decades later.

It was also after 1712, that Jai Singh's sphere of influence was to enlarge, and more so after 1720. Subjugation of Jats in 1722 is highlighted for the commercial prosperity that followed in its wake.

Prof Bhatnagar has also tried to shed new light on Jaipur-Kota relations by arguing that Jai Singh and Durjan Shal of Kota were not antagonistic to each other, as is commonly believed.

With regard to his pledge to the Mewar Maharana (mentioned above), Jai Singh has been defended by illustrating his attempts to prevent a future war of succession between Ishwari Singh (the eldest son) and Madho Singh (son by Mewar princess) by giving the latter a *jagir* equal to a small state. But obviously enough, the harm could not be prevented.

As regards Jai Singh's Maratha policy, Prof Bhatnagar is of the opinion that he wished to make the Marathas a pillar to support the crippled Mughal Empire, having realized that a martial solution was neither possible nor desirable. What is more convincing, however, is that Jai Singh also desired to maintain his influence in central Malwa by acknowledging Maratha dominance in southern Malwa. Also, Jai Singh is said to have felt that it was in Maratha interest to have him as mediator between them and the Mughal Emperor; but again, this is not convincingly argued.

With regard to relations with Bundi, Budh Singh has been held guilty of irresponsible conduct, and Jai Singh has been defended by the argument that he did not desire to unseat Budh Singh during the latter's life-time, but was forced to.

Incompatible relations between Udaipur Maharana and Jai Singh have been held responsible for the failure of the Hurda Conference.

Unqualified praise has been showered on Jai Singh for his diplomacy, intelligence, social reform attempts, martial abilities, administration, etc., as his "extraordinary achievements".

However, this kind of evaluation appears rather one-sided. On a more critical assessment, Jai Singh's life and achievements seem centred more around his selfish ambitions and aspirations, and less motivated by far-sightedness regarding interests of Rajputana as a whole. His desertion of Prince Azam, his Maratha policy, his attitude towards Budh Singh of Bundi, his pledge to the Mewar Maharana, and his attitude towards the Hurda Conference adequately reflect this. His dominance over other Rajput rulers was as much a result of the absence of challenge from a person of equal calibre in Rajputana, as of his own capabilities – it was luck, as much as his strength.

The chapter on Jai Singh's administration has been done extremely well – some details of political, financial, judicial, and land revenue administration have been stated with well-documented source material. The chapters on political history are replete with factual information which gets dull, at times, going into irrelevant details (e.g., the meeting of Peshwa Baji Rao and Jai Singh... "they sat under a mango tree on a carpet ......").

Undoubtedly, Jai Singh's achievements in the field of his 'extra-curricular' activities were great, especially in the context of his times and circumstances. A whole chapter has been justifiably devoted to his "service" to science, art and literature. His open-minded synthesis of Indian astronomical methods with those of Greece, Central Asia and Europe was indeed commendable.

The monuments he added to Amber are fine specimens of strong architecture (Nahargarh, Jal Mahal, Jaigarh). The city of Jaipur was not merely built to cater to necessities of royalty; seven of nine blocks were reserved for the residence of masses and their markets. Anything about the layout of the city would only be needless reiteration – its excellence is a well-known fact.

Literacy writings of Jai Singh's times have also been listed carefully as is his patronage of learned men. Most writings were based on *Dharma Shastras*. The principal scholars were Janardan Bhatt. Goswami, Chakrapani, Niketan Goswami, Ratnakar Bhatt Pundarik, Brajnath Bhatt and Shri Krishna Bhatt, among many others. His attempts at social reform, though failures, were indicative of his progressive ideas. His last days have not been written about at all.

On the whole, the book is a well researched and documented work, which initially drags owing to its emphasis on minute details.

* * *

Rajendra Shankar Bhatt: SAWAI JAI SINGH, *National Book Trust, New Delhi, 1972, p. 204, Rs 3.50* (in Hindi).

The book is interesting because of its lucid diction and journalistic approach to historical writing, which otherwise often gets dull because of the emphasis on factual detail.

Eight of the thirteen chapters are devoted to Jai Singh's political activities, and among the rest, one each to astronomy, the city of Jaipur, the *Ashwamedha Yajna* and his patronage of literature.

The one on *Yajna* is particularly interesting for the additional information it offers about various *yajnas* in general, and the *Ashwamedha* in particular. The *Yajna-sthal* was near the Man Sarovar (today's Jal Mahal). A vivid description of other memorials and sites is also incorporated.

The chapter on Jaipur city and its layout also furnishes information of basic interest for a layman; for example, the Nahargarh Fort was earlier called Sudarshangarh. The road from Tripolia divides the perpendicular roads so that nine equal *chokris* have been created. These were kept nine in number as symbols of Kuber's (the lord of wealth) nine treasures. The *chaupars* also served as water tanks. Water also flowed in the centre lane dividing the main roads in two in the 'once-upon-a-time' Jaipur.

The concluding chapter discusses the controversial descriptions of the last days of Jai Singh given by Surya Mal Mishran (*Vansha Bhaskar*) and Shyamal Das (*Vir Vinod*); and though the author sees no reason why Mishran should have deviated from fact, he refrains from reaching a conclusion.

Writing in 1971–72, the author lamented the lack of historical writings on Jai Singh (quite a few have appeared since this work) and concludes that it was possibly due to the "exceptional qualities and outstanding merit" of Jai Singh which posed a great challenge to the historians undertaking an evaluation of the ruler. To his own euology of Jai Singh, the author has finally added excerpts from the writings and speeches of personalities like Jawaharlal Nehru, V.V. Giri and Zakir Hussain.

It makes good reading, but is once again reiterative of the tradition of praise that has been showered upon Jai Singh for his merits and achievements as a statesman, a builder – and all else.

* * *

Ashim Kumar Roy: HISTORY OF THE JAIPUR CITY, *Manohar Publications, New Delhi, 1978, p. 260.*

Ashim Kumar Roy has concentrated more on Jai Singh's achievements as a builder and town planner: "The planning of the new capital and the implementation of the plan showed not only his vision but also his administrative ability. No other king before him, however powerful, had been able to construct a planned city in India. As builder and town planner, he was perhaps second to none in the history of this country".

He is careful enough to restrain himself from giving an opinion on controversial matters, e.g., Jai Singh's last days, about which two poets have written entirely different accounts. According to the *Ishwar Vilas Mahakavya* of Shri Krishna Bhatt (the court poet of Jaipur), composed in 1749, Jai Singh devoted himself to the study and practice of Vaishnavism and other religious matters. But, according to *Vansha Bhaskar* (1840, Surya Mal Mishran, the court poet of Bundi) Jai Singh's last years were spent in drunkenness and debauchery. Roy merely gives the explanation as Bundi's bitter memories of Jai Singh's intervention in the state as the cause of the "unnecessarily harsh judgement".

Roy has identified the periods 1723–29 and 1740–43 as the "most fruitful" years of Jai Singh's life. The activities he undertook in these two blocks of time are those "for which he is remembered". These are divided into four categories: (i) planning and construction of his capital, (ii) enlargement of the state of Amber and establishing its leadership over the other states of Rajputana, (iii) building of five astronomical observatories and the study of astronomy, and (iv) reform and revival of Hinduism, particularly of Vaishnavism, in northern India.

In his opinion, Jai Singh was a clever politician and statesman, a learned man whose academic interests "were mainly religion and astronomy".

Jai Singh's political achievements have been dealt with only briefly, as Roy's main focus is on the city of Jaipur and its development. Jai Singh's interests in economy, town planning and religion have 'deserved' close attention as they have left "a lasting effect on the character and the look of the city".

In Roy's opinion, Jai Singh's contribution to astronomy was the correction of certain astronomical constants. Some new instruments were also devised for this purpose. His contribution, apart from building the observatories, is considered 'negligible', because he deviated from the mainstream of Hindu astronomy in his method of calculations. Jai Singh's technical achievements (despite being labelled 'negligible'), were: (a) finding out the declination of the ecliptic, (b) the designing of the Samrat Yantra, (c) finding out the accurate figure of the annual procession of the equinoxes, and (d) revising the star catalogue of Ulugh Beg.

In the religious sphere, in spite of the heavy religious atmosphere, Jai Singh kept aloof from the people's religion of his times (*Nath Panth* or *Dadu Panth*). He tried to revive many *yajnas* of the Vedic times and became famous as a performer of the *Ashwamedha*. All praise for Jai Singh, Roy also writes about his attempts at reforming monastic orders. In his opinion, Jai Singh tried to make Jaipur an important Hindu centre – it has more temples today than all north Indian cities, except Varanasi.

One out of seven chapters has been devoted to Jai Singh, and largely the traditional sources as Tod, Kaviraj Shymaldas, Surya Mal Mishran have been used, apart from others like Kaye and Garret and

Guleri (on observatories). Other chapters are on subsequent developments in the life of the city. The book makes a good general reading.

* * *

After going through the above books, one still feels the inadequacy of historical interpretation in terms of Jai Singh's motives and goals in a long-term perspective. It is difficult to accept an absolutely uncritical, in fact extremely praiseworthy, analysis, for no human has been perfect so far – and one can safely say, no one will ever be.

Besides, some comparative analysis of the science of town planning, architecture and astronomical beliefs and methods of the India of Jai Singh's time and the West can also be looked into profitably to fill a blank in history.

Another notable fact is that all prominent scholars of Jai Singh's court were Bengalees.

One wonders about the state of religion in the context of masses during his reign.

Also, a systematic enquiry into the condition of masses, their means of livelihood, their handicrafts and cottage industry products and the nature of trade would be fruitful to understand Jai Singh's policies in these respects and only then would his real contribution be assessed, for his political, astronomical and architectural achievements reflect but one face or facet of his personality.

29

Manuscripts in the Pothikhana of Jaipur

Glimpses of Historical Information

GOPAL NARAYAN BAHURA

The Pothikhana of Jaipur has been a repository of important and valuable manuscripts in Sanskrit, Hindi, Rajasthani, Arabic, Persian and Urdu, written during the last seven centuries. Dealing with a variety of subjects and containing excellent specimens of calligraphy and illustration of high class paintings, these collections had their beginning long before Sawai Jai Singh founded the city of Jaipur.

Though the manuscripts collected by his ancestors were also quite important, care to sort out (with seals) and to preserve them appears to have been taken during the time of Mirza Raja Jai Singh and his son, Ram Singh. However, Sawai Jai Singh established a regular department for this end in his new capital, Jainagar. His keenness to collect rare and important manuscripts is evident from the efforts made to acquire a copy of *Bhushundi Ramayana* through Kalyandass, pupil of Swami Valmik [*Arzi No. 565, Descriptive List of Documents in the Kapad-dwara Collection, Jaipur, Part I* published by National Archives of India, 1971] and the purchase made through Chaturbhuj Kashmiri, Abdullah Najumi and Hakim Misi Jaman Khan of Jusi etc. between 1785 V.S. (1728 AD) and 1795 V.S. (1738 AD) [*Catalogue of Manuscripts in Maharaja of Jaipur Museum, 1971 AD, pp. 10, 11, 14, 15, 74, 75 etc.* It is known from the *bahis* (account books) and other archival papers [*exiting in the Kapad-dwara (Department of the Personal Store etc. of the Maharajas). Some Lekhakas, who wrote books for Sawai Jai Singh, have also made a mention of his 'Pustakagrha' in their colophonic remarks*] dating 1794 V.S. (1737 AD) to 1811 V.S. (1754 AD) that the *Karkhanas* (departments) established by Sawai Jai Singh were named as *grhas* (houses of stores), *Pustakagrh* and *Chitragrhas* were two of them, which afterwards came to be known as *Khasa-Pothikhana* (the Royal Library) and *Suratkhana* (Paintings Department) from the time of Sawai Madho

Singh I. A number of skilled calligraphists, painters, poets and scholars were attached to the usual staff for the upkeep of the stores, who added to the stock with their accomplishment. The employees were mostly hereditary. Whenever a talented person came to a ruler, he was given employment on a vacant post or by creating a new one for him.

Amvali, Khasa Muhar and Pothikhana Collections

The collections continued to increase with new purchases and additions by the employed and attached poets, scholars and artists, and occasional presents received by the rulers. The queen-mothers, Maharanis and other inmates of the seraglio also maintained their own collections. Some of them also wrote books in their leisure time. Their belongings were called *amavali* and after their deaths, the same were taken over by the respective departments and *Karkhanas*. That is why, a note *amavali se aaee* (received from the *amavali*) is noticed for such articles in the record or on the upper and the last leaf of manuscripts.

The most valuable and important assets were kept under *Khasa Muhar* or the personal seal of the ruler, which was opened and put back only under his orders by the *Khasa Muhar Officer*. A proper record of the articles taken out and/or placed back was kept by the store-keeper. A counter-entry was made by the *Khasa-Muhar Officer* also. The *muhar* (seal) remained in the custody of the Maharaja himself and was issued to the officer whenever needed. Thus, such manuscripts were issued to the usual staff of the *Pothikhana* only to be copied or mended, and the same were placed back after the needful was done. Copies of very important manuscripts, under *Khasa Muhar*, are found to have been prepared by the later *Lekhaks* or scribes. Consequently, two collections came into existence: (1) *Khasa Muhar Collection*, and (2) *Pothikhana Collection*, which remained in the charge of Pothikhana officials. A third collection was added in 1962 V.S. (1905 AD) when the manuscripts of Ratnakar Pudarik, guru of Sawai Jai Singh, and his descendents, were acquired and preserved in the Pothikhana.

The manuscripts of *Khasa Muhar Collection* number above 7,800, and these may be put into three categories according to their period of collection and creation: (1) manuscripts belonging to pre-Sawai Jai Singh period; (2) those collected, composed and written for Sawai Jai Singh; and (3) others related to post-Sawai Jai Singh period, more appropriately, to Sawai Pratap Singh period.

In the first category, a single manuscript bears the date of Raja Bharmal's time, a few are contemporary of Raja Man Singh (1589 to 1614 AD) and the largest number is of those collected, composed and written for Mirza Raja Jai Singh and his scholar son, Ram Singh I (1667 to 1689 AD). Only a few, but important ones, bear the dates of Kanwar Kishan Singh and his son, Raja Vishnu Singh, grandson and successor of Ram Singh.

Sawai Jai Singh's Collection

Collection made by Sawai Jai Singh may be roughly classified as under:

(a) Published books, maps, charts and manuscripts (mostly astronomical) acquired from abroad.
(b) Manuscripts of astronomical works written by scholars under his patronage.
(c) Works on religion and devotional philosophy composed by scholars of different *sampradayas* for him, some of them finally amended by himself.
(d) Manuscripts of important works of general interest, related to various branches of learning, acquired by him or copied out by his *Lekhaks* in his *Pustakgrha*.

The third period begins with the sons of Sawai Jai Singh, Sawai Ishwari Singh and Sawai Madho Singh I. His own compositions are also available in the collections.

Since Pratap Singh's Time

But, the most conspicuous figure in the post-Jai Singh age was Sawai Pratap Singh, an eminent poet of Hindi. There are about three dozen works written by him. Manuscripts of his own compositions, as well as those of the members of his poetic circle, form the largest group in this section of collection. The Pandits and Lekhaks remained busy in editing, copying and arranging his writings, according to their subjects, descriptions and tunes etc.

Though the compositions of Sawai Pratap Singh and other poets of his court centred round their devotion to the theme of Krishna and Radha, they also represent the social and domestic conditions of the time. The allied arts of music and painting also developed during this period, and Jaipur became a centre of these noble pursuits.

The tradition was maintained during the reigns of Jagat Singh and Jai Singh III also, and many good poems were written by the court poets and others. Padmakar, the famous Hindi poet, flourished in the court of Jagat Singh.

Then came Sawai Ram Singh and this was a period of all-round progress in Jaipur. The collection of Pothikhana became richer with the edition of new writings and important printed books.

(A catalogue of the *Khasa Mohar* collection has been prepared and author-wise index to the registers has been published. The manuscripts of the other collections are above 5,000 in number, while they have still to be fully catalogued.)

A cursory survey of these manuscripts will show that though mostly eulogical (especially *Bhasha* manuscripts), they cover a wide range of subjects and provide much useful data for study in various branches of learning. A few points, noted below, may be of interests of scholars:

- The earliest dated manuscript in these collections is a copy of *Bhuvanadipak-Virthi* by Sinhatilaka Suri, written at Bijapur in 1326 V.S. (1269 AD). The next oldest copy is that of *Vidyananda-Vyakarana* dated 1441 V.S. (1384 AD).
- There are copies of the *Samhitas* of all the four Vedas and Sayana's commentary dated the last quarter of the 17th century. The collections are rich in respect of manuscripts dealing with Vedic rituals. Copies of the latter ones primarily belong to the time of Sawai Jai Singh (1699–1743 AD).
- There are numerous works on Dharmashastra. Some of them were complied for Sawai Jai Singh, and the earlier works seem to have been collected for reference. Almost all the Smritis and works by distinguished authors are available.
- Similarly, there are copies of Puranas and Upapuranas written in a fine hand-writing. The *Vishnavakuta-Chandrika,* commentary on *Vishnu Purana* by Ratnagarha Battacharya, scribed in 1702 V.S. (1645 AD) in the reign of Jai Singh I at Aurangabad, is very important and rare. Commentaries on *Bhagavatam* by all the eminent authors are found in the collections. An index to various Puranas, prepared by the court pandits, is very useful.
- Besides the Upanishads, and general philosophy (Vedanta, Nyaya, Sankhya and Yoga), devotional philosophy was a subject of great

interest to Sawai Jai Singh. He collected all the principal works of the founder exponents of the different Vaishnava sects, including their commentaries of *Vyasa-Sutras* the *Bhagavata* and *Gita*. These manuscripts are unique sources for the study of the subject.

Some idea of the works written under the patronage of some of the rulers may be had from the following:

About Raja Man Singh

Daman Manjari, a drama (in Sanskrit) composed by Mohan Kavi, contains an internal evidence that it was staged in the court of Raja Man Singh I, and *Karnata* artists adored his court. It also provides information about some social customs and court etiquette.

In *Mansinhapratapa Kallola* (Sanskrit), a poem of Trimalla Kavi, a description of the royal insignia of Raja Man Singh is given, e.g., *chhatra*, *chanwar*, horses, elephants etc.

Two most important poems, *Manacharitas* (in Bhasha) by Amritrai and Narottam Kavi, deal with the life and achievements of Raja Man Singh. The accounts described in them can be taken as contemporary evidence for many historical events. They also contain important references to the socio-economic conditions of the time. Amritrai gave the date of his composition as 1642 V.S. (1585 AD), the twenty-ninth year of Akbar's reign, and the manuscript bears the date of script as 1670 V.S. (1613 AD) just one year before the death of Raja Man Singh. Narottam's work is more detailed and it was scribed by Manohar Mahatma, a favourite Lekhak of Mirza Raja Jai Singh in 1697 V.S. (1640 AD). (In both of these contemporary poems, there is no mention of the feast episode, said to have taken place at the time of Kunwar Man Singh's visit to Udaipur, while many other historical events are described therein.)

In *Manvamshavarnana*, by an unknown author, there is an evidence of the acquisition of Shilamayi (idol of goddess Durga) from Banga-desha and the construction by Raja Man Singh of a temple of the goddess near the palace. Also, there is a reference to the five coloured flags and the location of the palace and the temple on the bank of the Mahavata lake.

Mirza Raja Jai Singh

Gopal Bhatt, son of Damodar Tailang, has given a vivid account of the court of Mirza Raja Jai Singh. He asserts that he was an eye-witness to the account rendered by him – it is not based on hearsay. The manuscript is dated 1718 V.S. (1661 AD) and bears a seal of Mirza Raja's time.

The famous Hindi poets Behari and Kulapati flourished in his court; and the latter continued till the time of Vishnu Singh (Jai Singh's great grandson) for whose pleasure he wrote *Durgabhakti Chandrika*. Perhaps it was Mirza Raja Jai Singh at whose instance the drama *Abhijnan Shakuntla* of Kalidas and *Ratnavali* of Shri Harsha were first translated into Hindi. The latter translation was by Padmapani, while the name of former translator is not known.

Mirza Raja's taste in other branches of learning is evident from other manuscripts collected by him, e.g., copies of the four Vedic *Samhitas*, all standard Sanskrit *Kavyas*, *Vaishnava-Kutchandrika*, *Parasiprakash* – a grammer of Persian rendered into Sanskrit and containing Sanskrit equivalents of Persian words and *Chhandogopalam* – a rare prosodical work by Kashinath.

Two of his Ranis were also interested in having good books in their collections. Several manuscripts are marked to have been written for Maharani Chandrawatiji and were consequently received from the Sarkar in the Pothikhana, as for a example, copy of *Rasikpriya* of Keshavdas (ms 1847, where the scribe has noted this fact).

This manuscript has got a few decorative figures of Krishna with cows, and others representing the early art of painting at Amber.

Similarly, Rani Anand Kunwari of the Chuhan family (daughter of Shyamdas of Karauli) has been praised as particularly interested in acquiring knowledge, giving alms and devoting herself to the meditation of Hari.

[A couplet to this effect is noticed on the extra leaf of a copy of *Behari Satsai*.]

Ram Singh

Mirza Raja's son and successor, Ram Singh can be regarded as the original builder of the Pothikhana collection. We come across his seal dated 1718 V.S. bearing the letters 'रामस्य' and an effigy of a lion put on more than 1,000 select manuscripts, though an earlier seal of his father's time dated 1069 A.H. and accession note dated 1075 A.H. are also visible on a lesser number of books.

Ram Singh himself was an author of *Rupamanjari*, *Dhatumanjari* (both in Sanskrit) and *Chhavitarang* (in Hindi). The authorship of

Rajopayoginipaddhati and a drama *Janaki Raghavam* is also ascribed to him.

Harijivan Mishra was one of his teachers, as evidenced by a note written on a fragmentary copy of *Pingal-Hamir*, saying that fourteen leaves were issued to Harijivan Mishra for teaching. The manuscript bears the seal of Ram Singh.

In a drama, *Shringarvapika*, it is indicated in the Sutradhar's speech that the author, Vishwanath Bhatt, taught and dedicated his work to Ram Singh.

Most of the manuscripts copied for Ram Singh are by Ramkrishna and Ramnath Pandits, whom he took with him to Assam and Afghanistan during his postings there. Frequent reference to Rangamati and Jomrud are found in the colophonic remarks. Ram Nath continued to be active in the time of Vishnu Singh also.

From a small piece of poetry *Kridavinod* by Mohanrai Patur, a maidservant of Ram Singh, it becomes evident that the ladies of the harem were also educated and trained in the art of poetry.

Kunwar Kishan Singh

The promising career of Kunwar Kishan Singh, son of Ram Singh, was cut short in the prime of youth. He has left manuscripts in evidence of his interest in the fine arts of music, poetry and painting. He acquired a valuable manuscript of *Rasapradipatika* on *Sangitaranakar* Marathi by Nurkhan. The copy is decorated with four very fine illustrations representing the Deccan School of Painting and was written at Jaisinghpura (Aurangabad) for Maharajkumar Kishan Singh in 1737 V.S. (1680 AD). Janardan Bhatt composed a work *Kishenvilas* comprising 710 *dohas* on moral conduct. A 456 feet long horoscope of this Maharajkumar is embellished with very fine illustrations, which stand as specimens of painting in Amber in the later 17th century.

Vishnu Singh

Manuscripts belonging to the time of Vishnu Singh, grandson and successor of Ram Singh, represent his interest in Agamic works and drama. There are stray verses about his bravery in operations against the Jats of Mathura and Agra districts. A reference to his founding Vishnupura is also noticed in *Sawai Jai Singh Charit* by Atmaram Kavi, who has given a detailed account of Jai Singh's life and achievements. The copy is contemporary, but unfortunately it remained incomplete.

With his guru, Ratankar Dikshit, Sawai Jai Singh performed the daily rituals, observed *vratas*, distributed the sixteen gifts (*Sodasa Mahadan)* and organized performance of the big *yajanas*, e.g., *Vajapeya, Agnistoma Pundarika* and *Ashvamedha*. In *Ramavilas Kavya*, the author Vishwanath Bhatt gives an eye-witness account of the *Vajapeyayajna* performed by Ratankar Dikshit in 1765 V.S. The manuscript is dated V.S. 1766. Ratanakar compiled a voluminous Dharmshastric book *Jaisimhakalpadruma* for Jai Singh.

Sawai Jai Singh: Books on Astronomy

Much ink has already been spilt by the scholars in the country and abroad in describing the interest, works and achievements of Sawai Jai Singh in the field of astronomy. Books written by foreign authors also were collected by him for study and the same now constitute a valuable section of the *Pothikhana*. Some of the most important works are mentioned here [for other works the reader is requested to go through the introductory portion of *The Literary Heritage of the Rulers of Amber & Jaipur*, pp. 54–59]‡

(a) European Books

1. *Astrological Tables* by Philip of Hire K.M. 7832 presented to Sawai Jai Singh by Joreph Du Boio on 10th September, 1732 AD.
2. Grosser, *Atlas uber die Ganze Welt* (A Large Atlas of the Whole World), published by Johann Paptist, Homanne in 1725 from Nuremburg, acquired by Sawai Jai Singh in 1730 AD. (Mr Frederick Liest, a scholar from Princeton University, who visited the City Palace Museum in April 1978, pointed out that he had not come across anywhere any copy of this *Atlas* except the one in the University of Princeton. He further pointed out that this copy maintained its original binding.)
3. *Pathway to Knowledge* by Robert Recorde on the principles of Geometry in two parts (printed by Paules Churchyard in London in 1551 AD) (the earliest printed book in the collection).
4. *Ad Astrorum Indicia Facili* by Dr Chardi Dario (printed in Italy in 1557 AD).
5. *Historiae Coelestics Britannica* in three volumes by Flamsteedious (printed in London in 1725 AD).
6. *The Seaman's Kalandar* (16th century).

7. *Description and Use of Sector & Other Instruments* (printed in London in 1636 AD).
8. *Observations Chinoise* by F.R. Gaubil of the campagnic of Jesus (printed in 1732).

(b) Persian and Arabic Books

9. *Zich Ulughbegi* translated into Sanskrit in 18th century, (acquired for Sawai Jai Singh from Surat through Nanearam Joshi).
10. *Sarah Shamsia Hisab*, by Moulana Ali Barjandi (Arabic) 924 A.H. (acquired in 1725 AD).
11. *Tahrir-ul-Majisty*, by Hakim Batati Musa Unani Aristotles 16th century (acquired in 1725 AD).
12. *Saraha Tazkirah Mulla Nizami*, by Mulla Nizami Hasan bin Mohammed Neshapuri alias Nizam Naimullah (Arabic) (acquired in 1725 AD).
13. *Sarah-e-Chighmani*, by Md.-bin-Umar Chighmani (Arabic) 16th century (acquired in 1725 AD).
14. *Zich Barjandi*, by Mulla Chand-bin-Bahauddin. Bears seal of 1628 AD (acquired in 1725 AD).
15. *Zich Khagani (Ailkhani)*, by Jamshed-bin-Masud-bin-Mohammed alias Chayas-at Sadulla Sabib Kashmiri. Composed in 816 A.H. (1499 AD) (acquired in 1728 AD).
16. *Tahfim-al-Avval*, by Abu Rehan Mohammad-bin-Ahmed, son of Alberuni in 900 A.H. (acquired in 1725 AD through Hakim Misi Jaman Khan of Jagir).
17. *Lavahe-ul-Qamar*, an Arabic work on Astronomy, 1667 AD (acquired in 1725 AD).
18. *Mannzar-e-bin-e-Hasim*–composed 1007 Hijri; copied 1070 A.H. (acquired in 1725).
19. *Zich Mahammad Shahi*, written for Sawai Jai Singh by Jagaman under orders of Emperor Muhammad Shah (1723/4 AD).
20. *Zich Shahjahani*, by Ibrahim Dehlavi. Composed in 1627 AD (acquired in 1725 AD).
21. *Zich Nityanandi*, Sanskrit rendering of Shajahan period work of Nityananda, son of Devadatta (acquired in 1727 AD).

Among the Vaishnavas

Along with his studies in science and ritualistic activities, Sawai Jai Singh had also developed an interest in devotional philosophy of the

Vaishnavas. He collected all the principal works of the founder exponents of the different sects. Having critically studied these works, he made out that there was no material difference in these schools of devotion. He, therefore, composed a commentary *Brahmabodhini* on the *Sutras* and tried to reconcile the views of the different *acharyas*. He also got some coordinating works written by his associate scholars. Appreciating his attempts, Venkatacharya of the Ramanuja Sampradaya has complimented him thus: "As in the past, Nrsimha (fourth incarnation of Vishnu) suppressed the antimony between manhood and animality of a lion (by joining the head of a lion with the neck of a man) so does the wise and learned King Jai Singh make the representatives of different sects speak firmly with one voice rectifying their outward difference" (English translation of the original in Sanskrit).

In order to introduce some uniformity in the method of worship in various Vaishnava sects, he got a book *Prabhoor Vaidiki Puja Padhati* written by Vrajnath Bhatt. Similarly, a work *Vaidika Vaishnava Sadachar Vidhi* was compiled by Hari Krishna Mishra at his instance, which laid down the common code of conduct for all the Vaishnavas. Earlier compositions on Dharmashastra were also collected for reference, and thus the collection became rich with the best works on the subject.

During his last years, Sawai Jai Singh became more and more inclined towards the *Gaudiya Sampradaya* and became a perfect devotee of Govinddevaji. This was due to his association with the Goswamis of Vrindavana and the influence of Krishnadev Bhattacharya and Beladeva Vidyabhushan who were sent to him by Vishwanath Chakravarti, the famous commentator on Bhagavat. The works composed by most of the eminent exponents of Chaitanya Sampradaya are available in the manuscript collection of Sawai Jai Singh.

This aspect of his career has, however, been dealt with the least by the writers of political and dynastic history of the period.

Enthusiastic Successors

Sawai Jai Singh's sons, Sawai Ishwari Singh and Sawai Madho Singh I, who succeeded him one after the other, were also enthusiastic lovers and patrons of arts and literature. They were authors in their own right. *Bhaktmala* (Sanskrit) by Ishwari Singh and *Madhavnandini Padyavali* and *Shabdakaumudi* by Madho Singh preserved in the collection speak of their authorship. Unfortunately, no copy of the historical poem, *Ishvaravilasa Kavya* composed under orders of Ishwari Singh by Shri Krishna Bhatta, *Kavi-kalanidhi*, is available in the Pothikhana. But there are some very important Sanskrit and Hindi works composed and, scribed during the short reign of this prince. *Agamika* works by Kishormani Bhatt, selected portions compiled from the *Yamalas*, a compendium of useful medicinal prescriptions etc. bear testimony to his varied of taste in spite of his life of unrest after accession to the gaddi.

Many scholars, poets and artists came to Jaipur from Udaipur with Madho Singh. They added to the galaxy of courtiers gathered from his father's time. Creative activities multiplied during his reign and many good poems and dramas were composed for his pleasure, e.g., *Madhav-vijavakavyam* by Dwarkanath Bhatt, the *Padya Tarangini* by Vrajnath Bhatt, *Madhav Vilas* or *Arvashatak* by Shyam Sunder Lattu, which provides a vivid description of Jaipur city of his days, and *Rukmini-Madhavanatakam* by Krishnadatta (all in Sanskrit) and *Premsar* in Hindi by Shri Lalji or Aruna Kavi.

A very interesting and important work *Rajaritinirupana Shatak* was compiled by Dalpatirai in Sanskrit under orders of Sawai Madho Singh and his guru Vrajbhushanlalji Goswami of Kankroli. It describes names and functions of the different officers and departments required to run government according to the Mughal system of administration.

The art of good penmanship continued to receive encouragement by successive rulers. Most manuscripts are written in clear and neat handwriting by the Lekhaks of Pothikhana in Devanagari script. Many pieces are collected as specimens of calligraphy in Persian scripts, but the two manuscripts *Gitapancharatna* written with gold and silver inks by Ghasiram Mahatma during the time of Sawai Prithvi Singh are unique.

Sawai Pratap Singh

Sawai Pratap Singh was himself an eminent poet of Hindi and an ardent admirer of poetry and art. His court was like a beehive of poets, scholars and artists who shared his munificence. Manuscripts containing his own works and those of his court poets and associates form the bulk of the collection. It was during his time that a re-organization of the Pothikhana took place, and efforts to preserve and arrange the manuscripts according to their subjects were made. Important works were got bound in *parcha, misru, velvet* and *chhint.*

About twenty of his works have since been published in *Varjnidhigranthavali*; rest more than a dozen works have remained unknown and unpublished. A manuscript of *Rajniti-gadya* in Hindi prose is very interesting. It lays down a code of conduct for a ruler. *Hayanamavali* is another work in which the breeds, qualities and the names of his favourite horses are compiled. His other works, published and unpublished, deal with the love of Krishna and Radha.

One of his court poets, Krishnadatta by name, has described the daily routine of life and bravery shown against the Marathas, in the form of a dialogue between the poet and the Peshwa.

Besides composing stray verses and minor works on poetry, some of his court poets have translated several *Parvas* of the *Mahabharata* in Hindi verses. It was under orders of Sawai Pratap Singh that Gumaniram Kayastha rendered a Hindi translation of *Ain-e-Akbari*, the famous compendium of Emperor Akbar's institution of administration and accounts. This work, if published with annotations by competent editors, may prove very useful to scholars. *Dharmajahai* by Shri Kishna Mishra, *Amrit Sagar* (in Hindi), *Pratapsagar* in Sanskrit and *Radhagovind Sangitsar* are works on Dharmshastr, Ayurveda and music, compiled for him and they reflect his versatile interest in learning.

Pratap Singh enriched his collections by acquiring valuable objects from many sources. The *Razmnama* (Arabic translation of the *Mahabharata*) by Faizi and the *Royal Ramayan*, both profusely illustrated with finest paintings, are said to have been acquired at a fabulous price. Though the exact time and circumstances of the coming of these immortal works of art and literature to Jaipur are not definitely known, it is certain that the former bears seal of the *Mir Kutubs* (Keepers of the Royal Library) from the time of Emperor Akbar to Shah Alam (1759–1806 AD). These manuscripts, therefore, might have come here during the time of Shah Alam or his successor. In the latter case, the credit goes to Jagat Singh.

Traditions Continued

Another interesting account of Sawai Pratap Singh's liberality and desire to spread Indian knowledge abroad is found in a Bengali book *Vaidik Gaveshana* (Pt. I) by Umakant Hasra. According to it, he gave a complete copy of the four Vedas with an index in Persian script to a Frenchman, Lt. Col Antonio Louis Henri Polier in 1778 AD Polier sent his collection to the British Museum in London through Joseph Bank in 1789 AD Rosen prepared a resension of *Rigveda* from the above set. Raja Ram Mohan Roy was very much pleased to see the copy during his visit to the west.

Ganapati Bharati, guru of Sawai Pratap Singh in poetics, compiled two *Hazaras* (anthologies containing 1,000 or more verses each) for his (king's) pleasure. One is *Shringar Hazara* and the other *Veer Hazara*. There are many historical references to the valour of Pratap and his ancestors in the latter.

Sawai Jagat Singh, son and successor of Sawai Pratap Singh, had also received good education and took interest in Hindi poetry. The famous Hindi poet, Padmakar flourished in his court and composed *Jayadvinod* and *Ramrasayan* under his orders. Earlier, Padmakar had written *Pratap-Prashasti* in praise of Pratap Singh.

An important historical poem, *Jayavansha Mahakavyam* was composed by Sitaram Parvaniker during the time of Sawai Jai Singh III (1818–1835 AD). It is a complete history of Amber-Jaipur rulers in Sanskrit verses. Sawai Ram Singh (1835–80 AD) also followed his ancestor's traditions.

30

Town Planning in Jaipur

ASHIM KUMAR ROY

When Jai Singh built his new capital in Jaipur, he made it a planned town. This would not be surprising if he was building in the 20th century, but in the 18th century northern India, the idea was quite novel. Jai Singh had practically no model to copy.

New towns were built in northern India in plenty: Fatehpur Sikri, Muradabad, Udaipur, to name a few. Even Delhi had been built a number of times from Tughlakabad to Shahjahanabad. But, none of these was a planned town. Shahjahanbad no doubt had two planned streets, but that was all. This we know from Bernier. But otherwise, as Bernier says, it was a haphazardly built town with a few palaces and a large number of hovels all mixed up.

It is thus apparent that, as in many other things, Jai Singh was a pioneer also in the matter of town planning in northern India.

Jai Singh perhaps did not get much aid from the Shilpashastras. The Shilpashastras are actually compendiums of many arts: iconography, architecture, town planning etc. In building the temples and the numerous sculptures which adorn them, the Shilpashastras have always been used in our country, but nobody, at least in northern India, seems to have thought very much of their town planning chapters. Another point of interest is that two of the most important among them, viz., *Manasara* and *Kamikagama*, are both south Indian works. They together give a list of more than a dozen types of town plans. Jai Singh evidently did not adopt any of them. One reason for this might be that he had not seen these works. (The only work on Shilpashastras that G.N. Bahura, the Librarian of the City Palace, has been able to locate in Jai Singh's collection is by one Mandana *Sutradhara*, an architect of Maharana Kumbha of Mewar, who flourished in the first half of the 15th century).

Some Parameters: Natural or Otherwise

How did Jai Singh go about planning the town then? It appears that he first selected the site and tried to fit in his idea with it, keeping in view the topographical constraints of the site. There were hills to the east, north, and to the north-west of the site. The new city had to be built in such a manner that not only were the hills avoided, but also the rain water flowing down the hills did not damage the town wall. Another important physical constraint was a low ridge running approximately west to east through the proposed site. The main road, which practically was the axis of the town, had to be built along this ridge. This is the Chandpole-Surajpole road; and it is, because of the directions of the ridge, not due west-east, but turned 15 degrees in the clockwise direction.

One of the constraints was artificial. Jai Singh had already constructed a garden, the Jai Nivas, on the site, and he wanted the new city to be built round about this garden. This we know from *Bhojanasara*. This work on dietetics was written by Girdhari, one of the court poets of Jai Singh, in 1739. In the first about 60 lines of this work, Girdhari describes how the city was built. Jai Singh, according to him, gave the following instructions to Vidyadhar: "Jai Nivas should come within the city, that is my wish. There should be many cross-roads with shops on them. The backyards of the houses should meet together".

The last instruction is not clear, Girdhari's exact words are, *ghari pichhware sari*. However, the point does not appear to be important.

Vidyadhar's Brief Contribution

Vidyadhar's official position at that time was that of a senior clerk in the Accounts Department, but in practice he was a factotum of Jai Singh. He had in 1726 built the Jaigarh in Amber, and had been duly rewarded for the same. He, it appears, was the engineer-in-charge also of building the new capital. (Numerous documents of the *Sigha Imarati* (Works Department), now in the Bikaner Archives, show that materials brought in for building the city were being delivered to Vidyadhar and another senior official).

Apart from these, Vidyadhar was also the person who approved the building plans of the people who wanted to build their residential houses in the new city. Late Saroop Narain Purohit of

Purohitji-ka-Katla had the original *pattas* which his ancestor, Ghasiram Murlidhar, received from Jai Singh. Ghasiram was told in this document to come and settle down in Jaipur and to start his business. He was given tax concessions for this purpose and told that Vidhyadhar had been instructed to look after him, and he should act according to Vidhyadhar's instructions. (This last point is interesting. Vidhyadhar could not obviously have given any instructions on the matter of Ghasiram's trade and business. It may perhaps be surmised that the instructions were to be regarding the building that Ghasiram would build for his residence). There is a map (*LS/17*) in the City Palace museum, showing the allotment of plots to various people for building houses. The exact specification of each house to be built on the plots is also given. These relate to the height of the plinth, the height of the first floor, the thickness of the walls etc. Vidhyadhar was thus keeping a watch that flimsy buildings were not built in the new city.

So far as the planning of the town was concerned, we have practically no written documents (except the one *doha* of Girdhari mentioned earlier) to show how Jai Singh proceeded. What Jai Singh probably did was to get some sketch maps prepared showing the various possibilities, so that he could choose among them. Some of these maps are still available in the museum (City Palace). Unfortunately, the maps are too few in number to make out how Jai Singh's ideas gradually developed and took shape.

A Progress Report

One map (*LS/14*) in the museum is interesting. It gives the progress report of the construction of shops on the main roads. The map has been drawn on a piece of cloth. On the back of this map, the date given is 1725. It is thus quite possible that the construction of the town had started some years earlier than the generally accepted date, 29th November, 1727, when probably the religious rites connected with the building of the town were performed.

It appears that the building of the shops in the Ramganj Bazar and Ghat Darwaza had not been taken up by that time. (However, we know from other records that these two areas had been completed by 1734.)

An interesting thing is the progress report written on the map. It mentions that, on the roads, which are now known as Johari Bazar, Sireh Deodhi and the Gangori Bazar, 162 shops had been constructed on each side of the road. On the eastern side of the Kishanpole Bazar, the number of shops constructed was 162, but on the western side the number of shops was 144. A bazar was contemplated on the corner of Kishanpole and Chandpole Bazars, the place where the Kotwali is now situated, but evidently it was not built.

A State Enterprise

The most important thing that we learn from this map is the method adopted by Jai Singh to ensure a planned and uniform look for the city. By constructing shops on both sides of the main roads, he ensured the width of these roads. Secondly, since all the shops had been constructed by the state at the same time and on the same plan, the roads had a uniform look.

The shops were later sold to the members of the public. (Late Saroop Narain Purohit once told the present writer that he had heard from the older residents that the shops had been sold at a price of Rs 200 to Rs 300 each.)

Some maps in the museum show that the plots for temples and residential buildings were earmarked for certain people. This meant that the prominent people of the state were expected to build their residential houses in the newly founded city. This ensured that there would be a good proportion of rich people in the population, who would add to the good look of grand buildings for themselves. Hanuman Sharma tells us that he had seen a circular order dated *Chaitra Vadi V.S. 1785* (AD 1728) sent to the important jagirdars of the state informing them that residential houses would be built for them by the state, and they should pay for these buildings in instalments by sending 10 percent of their annual revenue to Vidhyadhar regularly (Hanuman Sharma, *Nathawaton Ka Itihasa*, Jaipur, p. 164).

Thus, Jai Singh ensured in all possible manner that his newly built capital would have a planned, prosperous and uniform look.

31

The City of Jai (Victory) and Joy

MULK RAJ ANAND

"On the silken darkness of a desert dawn emerged the dream of Jaipur city in the eyes of Sawai Jai Singh..."

[...That is how Dr Mulk Raj Anand gave a poetic opening to his Homage to Jaipur in the commemorative number of the *Marg* magazine in September 1977. He went on to recall ...]

"Legend has it that he first brought the image of his presiding deity, Govindji, to the 'Palace of Clouds'. He had worshipped this idol morning and evening, since he fetched it from Mathura to Amber, when it had been threatened with demolition by Emperor Aurangzeb...

And as he believed that the enlightened will is the beginning of all operations, he also brought with him his Brahmin Guru, Samrat Jagan Nath, who daily conducted the recitation of the Rig-Vedic hymn to the Sun, the Gayatri, and set to work on translations of various world texts on Astronomy into Sanskrit.

"... a frequent member of his itinerant court was Vidhyadhar Bhattacharya, a Bengali architect, whom he had got trained, to advise him on all constructions. Born in 1693, Vidyadhar had early shown signs of prodigious talent in the art of building. There is a document which shows that Vidyadhar was put in charge of the total planning, building and decoration of the projected city".

How did Sawai Jai Singh come to build his city. In the words of Dr Mulk Raj Anand: "The inspiration for the creation of the complex clearly came from the many-splendoured genius of Sawai Jai Singh himself. Although the village capital of Amber had a formidable fort wall on the triangle of mountains, protecting it on all sides, it had twice fallen to hostile armies in Sawai Jai Singh's youth. The population had also grown, because of the large establishment necessary for functioning of Sawai Jai Singh as one of the principal military and civil advisers of the Mughal dynasty, thrice appointed Governor of Malwa. Also, he was in charge of a huge cavalry and several regiments of foot soldiers. The philosopher in him had come to believe, in his maturity, that, he too, like Akbar before him, must build structures for the living, working and releasing the sense of wonder in himself and his people.

"Sawai Jai Singh had a vision of a heaven on earth, from the midst of the miseries of feudal disruption, and saw to the realization of his vision in one of the few planned cities of the world – Jaipur. That this city has lasted out almost intact for two and a half centuries, shows that the city was not a mere experiment in architecture, but evolved from a comprehensive outlook about the needs and interests of men and women. The way he advised Vidyadhar, to establish each lane and street and sector, as the venue of a craft and for the buying and selling of goods and services, shows Jai Singh's grasp of the need for change from the feudal rent-collecting set-up to the state as collector of taxes from the sale of merchandise.

"In paying homage of Jaipur, therefore, we pay homage to the genius of a prince who often adventured from the precincts of his palace to pursue knowledge, to mingle with the people in their festivals and whose abounding love for the men and women is obvious from the fact that he found an abode for the least of them in the miniature cosmos of Jaipur – the city of victory, which immortalizes his name."

(Extracts from pp. 2–4 of Vol. XXX, Number 4, September 1977 of *MARG* – A Magazine of Arts, Bombay).

32
Amber-Jaipur Paintings

ASHOK KUMAR DAS

We know very little about the artistic heritage of the Amber-Jaipur region, as we have no extent material from this area prior to the first quarter of the 17th century. The relationship of the Kachchwaha rulers of Amber with the imperial Mughals was close and cordial: Raja Bhar Mal (1547–73) and Bhagwant Das (1573–89) held important positions in the Mughal court, and spent most of their time with the court. Raja Man Singh (1590–1614) was also a close friend of Akbar the Great (1556–1605). Growing up in the highly cultured atmosphere of Akbar's court, he must have imbibed the finer traits of Mughal art and culture to a large extent. We have extensive literary references in two contemporary Hindi works entitled *Manacharitra*, written by Amrita Rai and Narottem Kavi, corroborating the existence of wall paintings in Amber (G.N. Bahura in an essay in Hindi. *The Researchers*, Jaipur, XII–XIII, 1972–73, pp. 63–70).

Mughal Influence

Raja Man Singh: From Amrita Rai's works we learn that there was 'beautiful pictures' painted on the walls of the palace built by Raja Man Singh at Amber. Amongst these were paintings of many birds, animals, flowers and flowering plants. Narottam Kavi's description of the wall paintings is more specific, as he identifies their subjects as detailed from the *Ragamala*, *Krishna Lila*, *Amaru-Sataka*, *Nayaka-Nayika-Bheda* and the well-known text of erotics, *Koka-Sastra.* He mentions paintings of cranes, peacocks, *Suka Sari* and other birds and animals, flowers and floral plants in bright hues of red, yellow, green etc.

A few panels of wall paintings have also been found in Man Singh's palace at Amber. These show Krishna playing at his flute under the *Kadamba* tree or grazing the cows, and flanked by two milk-maids.

The milk-maids are tall, slender and well-proportioned, and wear striped and designed *lehnga* (full skirt) and short *choli* (short blouse). Such female figures are fairly common in the so-called 'popular Mughal' works.

Raja Man Singh's interest in paintings is further evidenced from traces of paintings found in Makhdum Shah's *maqbara* (tomb) in Amber, the ruined tower at Mauzzambad (Mozumabad) and in the Gaurishankar Mahadev temple at Baikatpur (Baikunthpur) in the Barh sub-division of Patna district in Bihar – all places associated with the life of Raja Man Singh.

Mirza Raja Jai Singh of Amber (1621–1667) played an equally important role in the Mughal court under Emperors Shah Jahan and Aurangzeb. We know of his impeccable taste in art, architecture and literature but we were not fortunate so far in finding illustrated manuscripts or miniatures prepared during his long reign, with the exception of two rather ordinary copies of *Rasikapriya* and *Krishna Rukminiveli* prepared in 1639 AD for one of his queens, Chadrawati. These manuscripts contain several frontpiece designs and a couple of illustrations of Krishna with milk-maids in a folkish style. A few highly damaged folios of an unidentified manuscript written in *Nagari* script are preserved in the Maharaja Sawai Man Singh II Museum, in which there is one example containing the likeness of Mirza Raja Jai Singh. The style of this damaged miniature is well-developed and resembles Mughal works of late 17th century with their mellow colour scheme, fine linework and intimate character studies.

A different type of material, a 34-feet-long scroll, illustrating numerous drawings and designs depicting the scenes based on poems of Surdas entitled *Sapta-Loka-Ajara-Amara-ka-Kharda*, has recently come to our notice. Here, the painter has adopted a style more akin to folkish style of the *Rasikapriya* and the wall paintings at Amber. He has used flat colours against various kinds of background, simple architecture, pools and fountains, trees and shrubs etc.

The scroll is not dated, but on stylistic ground, the illustrations have been ascribed a date in the third quarter of the 17th century. The paintings have a simplicity and story telling quality encountered in the scrollparts (*jarano pata*) of Bengal.

The only dated material from the time of *Raja* Ram Singh I (1667–1689) is an unusual horoscope (*janampatra*) of Kanwar Kishan Singh, who predeceased his father in 1682 at Parenda in the Deccan.

This 456-feet-long horoscope contains numerous illustrations of the stars, planets, deities, portents, *dikpalas* (lords of the ten quarters), etc., painted in the Mughalized court style. This unique horoscope appears to have been prepared by painters, well-versed in the Mughal-inspired Amber style.

A number of lively portraits of Mirza Raja Jai Singh, Ram Singh I, Kishan Singh and Bishan Singh were prepared by the court painters in a style which was not far from the contemporary Mughal court style. A painting showing Bishan Singh (1689–1699) hunting with a hawk, in a marshy countryside, however, is painted in a simple, spontaneous and naturalistic style, which is very different in character from the minute studies of Kishan Singh holding a falcon or Ram Singh I standing in his regal splendour.

Kishan Singh, in spite of his untimely death, got a copy of *Rasapradipa Tika*, a Marathi commentary of Sarangadeva's *Sangita-Ratnakara*, written by Nur Khan at Jaisinghpura (modern Aurangabad) in 1679 AD This manuscript contains four miniatures in a style similar to early Golconda paintings.

Raja Bishan Singh's name is associated with a fragmentary manuscript on 'massage' prepared in 1692 AD As the illustrations merely show a fair-complexioned prince resembling the young Raja and his dark masseur wearing loins-cloth and do not show any landscape or architecture or subsidiary figures, it does not help us to determine the exact course of Amber-Jaipur painting during his short rule.

New Phase

Maharaja Sawai Jai Singh (1699–1743) started a new and significant phase in the development of Amber-Jaipur paintings.

Painters were at work from the early part of his long reign as evidenced by the discovery of a dated *Ragamala* set prepared in Amber in 1709 AD (Sridhar Andhare has published this incomplete *Ragamala* set preserved in the collection of Kankroli Maharaj. S.K. Andhare, 'A dated Amber Ragmala and the Problem of Provenance of the 18th century Jaipuri Paintings', *Lalit Kala*, 15, 1972, pp. 47–51). Similar sets of *Barahmasa*, *Ragamala* and *Sadritu-Varnan* have also been found in recent years. A beautiful painting of the Barari Ragini, which is more refined than the Kankroli example, is preserved in the Maharaja Sawai Man Singh II Museum. (These paintings show Shah Jahan period columns, arches, painted or decorated dado, *dilhedar* doors and deep pinkish brown *chajjas*, which were fairly common in Amber and Jaigarh fort being constructed at this time. The typical tree with its highly conventionalized foliage painted in lighter tones is fairly common in all these paintings.)

The male figures of these paintings have a faint likeness with the young Maharaja Sawai Jai Singh, whose formal portrait painted approximately at the same time is preserved in the Maharaja Sawai Man Singh II Museum. This striking portrait is much more sensitive and lively than the formal study of the Maharaja made at a later date by the chief court painter, Sahib Ram. From contemporary court records preserved in the Rajasthan State Archives, Bikaner, we come to know that two Mughal painters, Fazil Muhammad and Sadeq Muhammad, were brought by the Maharaja from Delhi. These painters must have worked in the painting atelier, known as the *Suratkhana*, which was substantially reorganized by Sawai Jai Singh in 1725.

The ancestral collection of Mughal, Deccanese and Rajasthani paintings were regrouped and mounted in large *Mathru* bound albums at this time. (Ashok Kumar Das, *Treasures of Indian Paintings*, Jaipur 1976, Introduction.) When the building of his newly-planned capital city of Jaipur was completed around 1728–29, the whole palace complex along with all state departments like Pothikhana and Suratkahana were transferred to the Chandra Mahal complex. Besides Fazil Muhammad, the name of another Muslim painter, Muhammad Shah, is also known to us as an illustrator of manuscripts.

One of the most significant productions of this period is a lavishly produced manuscript of *Sarasarasa-grantha*, a Brajbhasha work on poetics by Sivdas Rai, one of Sawai Jai Singh's favourite court poets, who normally resided in Agra. The manuscript is unique in every respect. It is written in two scripts: within the normal margined area, in elegent *Nastaliq*, and on the outer margins, in Nagari. The space between the lines of the text in either script is embellished with an overlay of gold. There are 39 full-page illustrations of superb quality painted in 1737 AD As the manuscript was written in Agra in Arabic script, with the original Brajbhasha text written on the margins, it seems that it was meant for some patron who was not conversant with Nagari, and Emperor Muhammad Shah looks like a probable candidate. The paintings are superbly drawn by a group of at least four different painters. Almost all the 39 illustrations deal with the Krishna theme. A variety of rich and fresh colours – green, yellow, violet, mauve, blue, red and gold – have been used to make a rich pallette. One of the finest examples in the manuscript deals with Krishna's Holi play with the Gopis.

A Portrait Painter

The celebrated Jaipuri portraitist, Sahib Ram started to paint from the later part of Sawai Jai Singh's reign. He was active for more than sixty years, during which he painted the portraits of Sawai Jai Singh, his son and successor Sawai Ishvari Singh and his brother, Sawai Madho Singh I, as also those of Sawai Prithvi Singh, Sawai Pratap Singh and Sawai Jagat Singh. His portraits are painted in a stereotyped style with special attention devoted to dress, ornaments and physical features. The portraits of Sawai Jai Singh and Sawai Pratap Singh, wearing a white dress, are, however, exceptions where Sahib Ram has captured the spirit and personality of the 'sitters'.

Post-Jai Singh Phase: Hunting Scenes

After Sawai Jai Singh's death, his sons Ishvari Singh and Madho Singh I, who successively occupied the Jaipur throne, extended similar patronage to painting, and a number of beautiful and remarkable paintings were prepared at the Jaipur atelier. Besides Sahib Ram, Lal, Ramji Das, Govinda, Hiranand and Trailokya made their names as good painters.

Lal specialized in painting large hunting pictures and scenes of animal fights. Sawai Ishvari Singh took particular delight in watching animal fights and had a new watching pavilion, known at the 'Moti Burji' constructed near the Chaugan solely for this purpose. Lal was commissioned to paint a series of large pictures showing Ishvari Singh enjoying the fights of elephants, camels, dogs, buffaloes, as also pig-sticking and tiger-killing specially staged for him in the Jaipur Chaugan. These paintings are executed in a lively and straight-forward manner in which the fully developed Mughal technique of perspective, foreshortening, overseeing etc. has been discarded and traditional Indian concept of a bird's eye-view distorted perspective has been adopted. The gory scenes have been presented in graphic manner with the horrid details.

Lal's study of Sawai Madho Singh's pig-sticking expedition in the bushy countryside outside a well-laid garden to the east of Sanganer river is a typical example of similar large hunting scenes painted during this time. It has a savage fury and pristine vigour not generally found in insipid court pictures of this period. The Jaipuri painters excelled in portraying genre scenes envisaging numerous persons and details of fauna, landscape and vegetation.

Suratkhana: Additions

Sawai Ishwari Singh and Sawai Madho Singh I were responsible for re-arranging the large collection of paintings accumulated by Sawai Jai Singh and his predecessors, and painting beautiful frescoes on palaces and monuments. From an entry of the Pothikhana records, we come to know that in 1745, it had nearly 2,500 miniatures, and two newly acquired albums of 75 and 64 miniatures, costing Rs 350 and Rs 225 respectively, were entered in the *Suratkhana*, which included pictures of kings and emperors, European subjects, calligraphic panels etc. The long list of 2,498 paintings in the Suratkhana included pictures of deities of Mughal emperors from Babar to Muhammad Shah, all the Kachchawaha rulers, past and present rulers of Udaipur, Jodhpur, Bikaner, Bundi and leading nobles, generals and feudatories. It also included pictures of Europeans, saints and holy men, ordinary men and women, birds and animals, scenes of hunting, processions, wars and even ships. There is an entry of 13 *Barahmasa* paintings, 59 paintings of the *Mahabharata* and 81 erotic paintings also. From this list, it is clear that the Kachchwaha rulers were keen collectors of portraits of kings and emperors, though pictures of women were even more numerous. European pictures and pictures of birds and animals were collected in large numbers. Most of these paintings are still preserved in the City Palace collections. The list of paintings does not include illustrated manuscripts which were included in the *Pothikhana* list of more than 3,600 titles.

The reorganized Suratkhana supplied the painters with costly papers known as *Mansinghi*, *Sialkoti*, *Dumoharya*, *Daulatabadi*, *Gujarati* and *Sawai Jaipur*, and gold foils, dyes, prepared colours, cloth for lining, striped *mashru* for binding, and even gemstones, pearls, crystals etc. extensively used for decorating the large portraits. A portrait of Maharaja Sawai Madho Singh I standing full-face with formal regal attire cost seventy six rupees and eight annas in 1751 AD.

Madho Singh I, in spite of his heavily-built frame and not very attractive look, was interested in having himself painted in various postures wearing different types of costumes – *puja* dress, wrestler's outfit, full regal costumes, hunting dress etc. Albums full of his portraits were prepared by his painters Sahib Ram, Sitaram, Khusala, Udai, Hiranand etc. and presented to him as *nazar* at frequent intervals. He is shown in *puja*, in sports, in hunting expeditions, *darbars*, *zenana majlis* or watching elephant fights and religious festivities. Though these paintings are of little artistic merit, they have a socio-cultural and documentary value not frequently met within contemporary art studies.

As a result of Madho Singh's interest in wall paintings, the newly built Madho Niwas in the Chandra Mahal was richly decorated with panels of frescoes showing the Maharaja in company of female dancers, musicians and courtesans.

APPENDIX

Constructing Rajasthan

LLOYD I. RUDOLPH AND SUSANNE H. RUDOLPH

(In conversation with Rima Hooja at
Jaipur Literary Festival, January 23, 2008)

Our topic is "Constructing Rajasthan". What we have in mind in using the term "constructing" is the way perception and interpretation shape what is seen and believed.

The contemporary construction of Rajasthan was largely the result of the pursuit of Rajasthan Studies whose history is touched on below. Rajasthan Studies articulated a sense of place and launched the contemporary study of Rajasthan's regional identity.

Our role in the contemporary story of the construction of Rajasthan's regional identity began in 1956 when, as fresh Ph.Ds with grants from the Ford Foundation to study post-colonial politics in India, we drove in a Land Rover from London to Jaipur. Our first book, *The Modernity of Tradition: Political Development in India*, published in 1967, *inter alia*, examined the onset of democratic politics in Rajasthan. *Essays on Rajputana* was published in 1984. It brought together essays written between 1966 and 1983 that reflect the historical and ideological transformations that have shaped Rajasthan, such as the integration of the princely states into independent India, the formation of the state of Rajasthan from princely states, the demise of the 'old regime' including the end of princely rule and land reform that 'resumed' *jagirs*.

In the mid-1960s* we launched a newsletter from the University of Chicago that listed scholars working on Rajasthan, their coordinates, publications, and current research on Rajasthan.

The *Idea of Rajasthan*, the first of six volumes published on Rajasthan Studies, was conceived in November 1981 when Karine Schomer, then an Assistant Professor of Hindi and Rajasthani *bhasha* at the University of California, Berkeley, convened a meeting of 17 scholars of Rajasthan who were attending a West Coast meeting of the Association of Asian Studies. They decided to revive the network created in the 1960s by the Rudolphs and to call themselves the Rajasthan Studies Group (RSG).

The RSG gradually expanded to include an international membership and in 1983-84 began to work with a parallel group in India founded and led by Dr Rajendra Joshi of the University of Rajasthan and Professor Satish Chandra of Jawaharlal Nehru University. By 1991, the group had registered itself as the Institute for Rajasthan Studies or IRS.

In December 1987, the RSG and leading scholars of Rajasthan in India took the lead in organizing the first of five international seminars on Rajasthan. The *Idea of Rajasthan* is based on papers presented there and papers written earlier for annual meetings of the Association of Asian Studies. From 1981 when The *Idea of Rajasthan* was conceived until it went to press ten years later, its four editors led by Karine Schomer applied themselves to the task of producing a persuasive, well-organized volume of clearly written scholarly papers.

Four more international seminars followed and resulted in the publication of additional transdisciplinary volumes dealing with Rajasthan: *Folk, Faith & Feudalism*, edited by N.K. Singhi and Rajendra Joshi (1995); *Religion, Ritual and Royalty*, edited by N.K. Singhi and Rajendra Joshi (1999); *Desert, Drought & Development: Studies in Resource Management and Sustainability*, edited by Rakesh Hooja and Rajendra Joshi (1999); *Multiple Histories: Culture and Society in the Study of Rajasthan*, edited by Lawrence A. Babb, Varsha Joshi and Michael W. Meister (2002); and *Institutions and Social Change*, edited by Surjit Singh and Varsha Joshi (2003).

The contemporary construction of Rajasthan calls for the mention of several recent books. Three involve Giles Tillotson. The

* With the help of Suzanne Renneau, our secretary at the time.

first is by Giles and his wife, Vibhuti Sachdev. It is a remarkable analytic and theoretical account of *The Building of Jaipur: The Making of an Indian City* (New Delhi, Oxford University Press, 2002). The second is Giles Tillotson's evocative rendering of travellers' and visitors' impressions of Jaipur through the centuries, *Jaipur Nama: Tales from the Pink City*, Penguin Books, 2006. And, the third is his recently published edited volume, the visually and analytically compelling, *Tod's Rajasthan* (Mumbai, Marg Publications, 2006).

Finally, the construction of Rajasthan has been comprehensively and authoritatively realized in todays chairperson, Rima Hooja's learned yet thoroughly engaging *A History of Rajasthan* (New Delhi, Rupa, 2007).

Contributors

Late Bhupendra Hooja had worked for All India Radio and BBC London (UK) before joining the Indian Administrative Service and being allotted its Rajasthan cadre. For 21 years he was Chief Editor of *Indian Book Chronicle.* His writings on various disparate themes included many on both modern-day Rajasthan and its history.

Susanne H. Rudolph is William Benton Distinguished Service Professor Emeritus, University of Chicago (USA) and former President of the American Political Science Association and of the Association of Asian Studies. Author or editor of a number of books, she has, along with husband Lloyd, authored *Essays on Rajputana,* and *Reversing the Gaze: Amar Singh's Diary.* She has worked extensively on Rajasthan and on India. Both Susanne and Lloyd Rudolph have jointly been conferred the Colonel James Tod award of the Maharana Mewar Foundation, Udaipur.

Lloyd I. Rudolph is Professor Emeritus of Political Science, University of Chicago (USA). Along with wife Susanne he has spent more than 12 research years in Rajasthan starting with their first visit in 1956. He is one of the editors of the two-volume *The Idea of Rajasthan*, besides having authored a number of books. With wife Susanne he has been a major force behind the Rajasthan Studies Group of the Association of Asian Studies in USA and the Institution of Rajasthan Studies, Jaipur.

Dilip K. Chakrabarti teaches archeology at University of Cambridge (UK) and is the author and editor of a number of books on Indian archaeology.

Michael W. Meister is W. Norman Brown Professor of South Asian Studies at the University of Pennsylvania (USA). He has authored numerous works on architecture and iconography and has been the editor of *Encyclopaedia of Indian Temple Architecture.*

Lawrence A. Babb is Professor of Anthropology and Asian Studies at Amherst College, Massachusetts (USA). He has done field research in central, northern and western India on both Hindu and Jain communities and on the trade in western India.

John E. Cort is Professor of Asian and Comparative Religions at Denison University in Granville, Ohio (USA). He has written extensively on the Jains in India.

K.K. Maheshwari is the founder of the Indian Numismatics Historical and Cultural Research Foundation and its Indian Institute of Research in Numismatics at Nasik, which is a prime research centre on Indian numismatics. Besides working on numismatics, he is a businessman.

G.S.L. Devra is former Vice Chancellor, Kota Open University and Emeritus Professor of Indian History and Culture at Jamia Millia University, New Delhi.

Ranbir Sinh author of *A History of the Shekhawats* has had a long association with the IPTA theatre movement, including the writing of plays.

Ram Pande is Editor of *Shodhak: A Journal of Historical Research* and has organized many seminars mostly on Rajasthan history on behalf of *Shodhak*. He is a retired Government of Rajasthan officer.

Late Colonel James Tod came out to India in 1799. He was Political Agent Resident at Udaipur from 1818 to 1822 when he returned to London and became honorary librarian of the Royal Asiatic Society from 1823 to 1831. He is well known for his two books, viz., *Annals and Antiquities of Rajasthan* and *Travels in Western India.*

Late Mulk Raj Anand, well-known litterateur and art lover, is universally acknowledged to be amongst the major writers of Indian literature in English. He edited *MARG* for many years.

Satish Chandra is well-known as an expert in medieval Indian history. A former Chairman of the University Grants Commission, he has taught history at Aligarh Muslim University, University of Rajasthan and Jawaharlal Nehru University, New Delhi. He is Chairman, Institute of Rajasthan Studies, Jaipur.

Late Ashim Kumar Roy, a former IAS officer is the author of a well-known book on the history of Jaipur published in 1978.

V.S. Bhatnagar has been Professor and Head of Department of History, University of Rajasthan. Amongst his many writings on the history of Rajasthan is a book on the life and times of Maharaja Sawai Jai Singh II.

Virendra Nath Sharma worked at the Department of Physics and Astronomy, University of Wisconsin (USA). He has written about Jai Singh's and other contemporaries work on astronomy in a number of Science History journals.

Late Yaduvendra Sahai worked in the City Palace Museum at Jaipur as its Director.

Late R.N. Chowdhuri was a history teacher who later became Director of College Education in the Government of Rajasthan.

Mohita Kapur taught history at Kanodia College, Jaipur.

Late Gopal Narayana Bahura was a scholar who had a long association with the Jaipur Pothikhana.

Late Ashok Kumar Das is a former Director of Sawai Man Singh II Museum at City Palace, Jaipur.

EDITORS

Rakesh Hooja is a writer and senor civil servant serving in the Indian Administrative Service which he joined after teaching at University of Rajasthan. He is presently Additional Chief Secretary (Development), Government of Rajasthan and Director, HCM Rajasthan State Institute of Public Administration, Jaipur, having worked on important positions in the Governments of India and of Rajasthan. Author or editor of 28 books (two of which have won Government of Rajasthan cash awards and merit certificates), about three dozen monographs, and over 390 articles, reviews, comments, he is also associated with the editing of some journals. He holds a PhD in Social Sciences in addition to Masters Degrees from University of East Anglia (UK) and University of Rajasthan and a Post Graduate Diploma from University of Mysore. His Rajasthan centric books include *Greening the Desert; and Democratic Decentralization and Planning* (co-authored); and two co-edited volumes *Desert, Drought and Development* (edited for Institute of Rajasthan Studies) and *Administration of Desert and Drought Prone Arid Areas*, as well as *Jaipur: Profile of a Changing City* (co-authored). He is recipient of T.N. Chaturvedi award of IIPA for his writings on public administration.

Rima Hooja possesses a Doctorate on Indian Archaeology from University of Cambridge (UK) and has been Associate Professor of Indian History and Culture at Kota Open University. Her books include *A History of Rajasthan* (winner of Publishers Excellence Award)*; Prince, Patriot and Parliamentarian: A Biography of Karni Singh of Bikaner; Crusader for Self-Rule: Tej Bahadur Sapru and the Indian National Movement; The Ahar Culture and Beyond;* and *Devata Murti Prakaranam* (translated). She has been Visiting Fellow at Royal Asiatic Society London (UK), Institute of Rajasthan Studies, Jaipur and Institute of Development Studies, Jaipur respectively and is Director MSID Jaipur.

Rakshat Hooja has done an M.Phil. from the School of Social Sciences, Jawaharlal Nehru University, Delhi. A strong proponent of the spread of Open Source Software, he has also been writing frequently including on land-water management issues and watershed development. He is presently Associate Director, Minnesota Studies in International Development Programme in India at Jaipur and Associate Editor *Indian Book Chronicle*, as well as Director IDA Systems Private Ltd.